ALYSSA **MILANO**   COLLIN **KELLY**   JACKSON **LANZING**

HACKTIVIST™

MARCUS **TO**   IAN **HERRING**

VOLUME **TWO**

Published by
ARCHAIA™

HACKTIVIST Volume Two, May 2016. Published by
Archaia, a division of Boom Entertainment, Inc. HACKTIVIST
is ™ and © 2016 Alyssa Milano. Originally published in
single magazine form as HACKTIVIST VOLUME TWO
No. 1-6. ™ & © 2015 Alyssa Milano. All rights reserved.
Archaia™ and the Archaia logo are trademarks of Boom
Entertainment, Inc., registered in various countries and
categories. All characters, events, and institutions depicted
herein are fictional. Any similarity between any of the
names, characters, persons, events, and/or institutions in
this publications to actual names, characters, and persons,
whether living or dead, events, and/or institutions is
unintended and purely coincidental.

BOOM! Studios, 5670 Wilshire Boulevard, Suite 450,
Los Angeles, CA 90036-5679. Printed in China. First Printing.

ISBN: 978-1-60886-861-2, eISBN: 978-1-61398-532-8

CREATED BY
ALYSSA **MILANO**

WRITTEN BY
COLLIN **KELLY** & JACKSON **LANZING**

ILLUSTRATED BY
MARCUS **TO**

COLORS BY
IAN **HERRING**
WITH BECKA **KINZIE**

LETTERS BY
DERON **BENNETT**

COVER BY
MARCUS **TO**
WITH IAN **HERRING**

DESIGNER
SCOTT **NEWMAN**

ASSOCIATE EDITOR
WHITNEY **LEOPARD**

EDITOR
DAFNA **PLEBAN**

SPECIAL THANKS TO
KELLY **KALL,** STEPHEN **CHRISTY,** REBECCA **TAYLOR,** CAMERON **CHITTOCK**

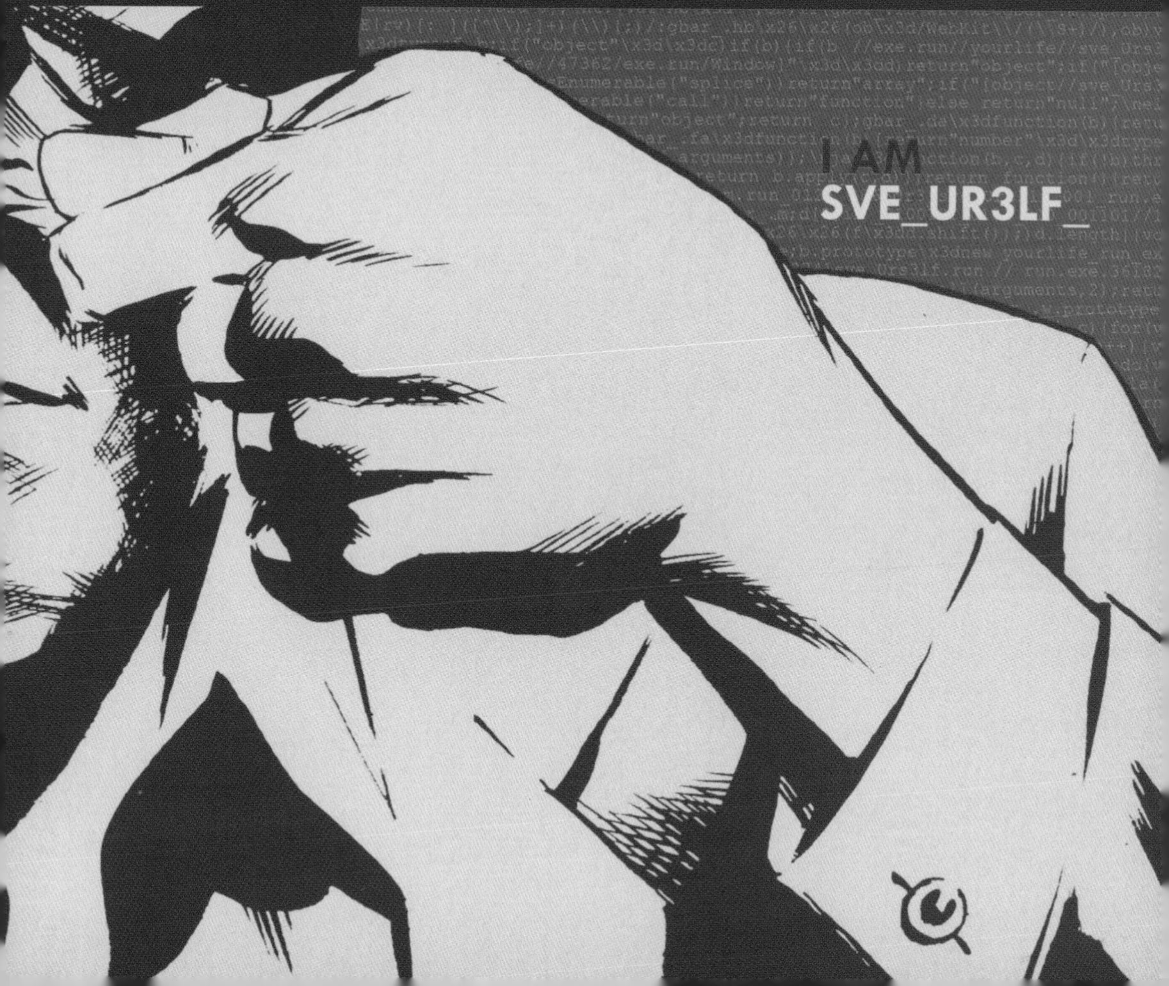
I AM
SVE_UR3LF_

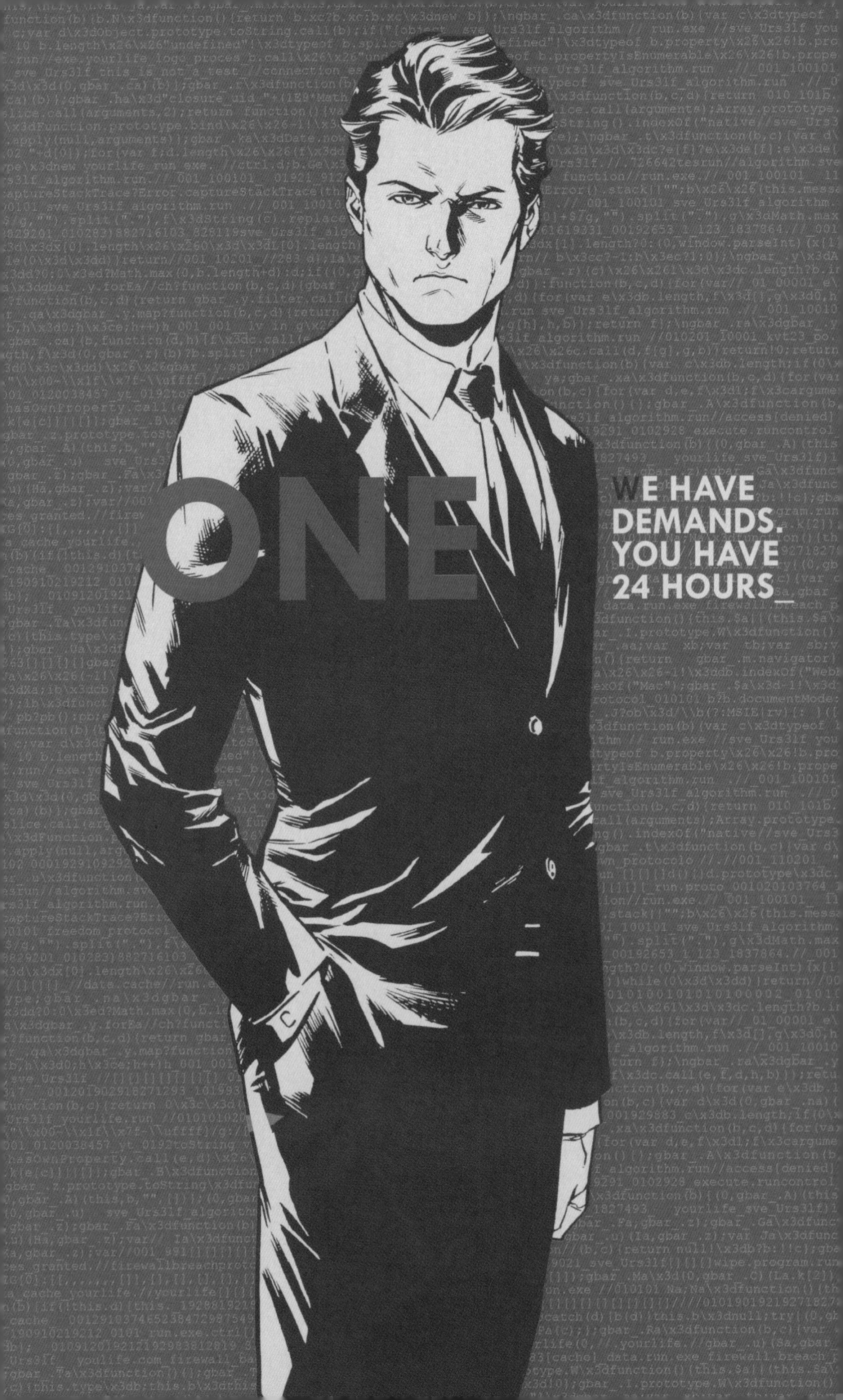
ONE
WE HAVE DEMANDS. YOU HAVE 24 HOURS_

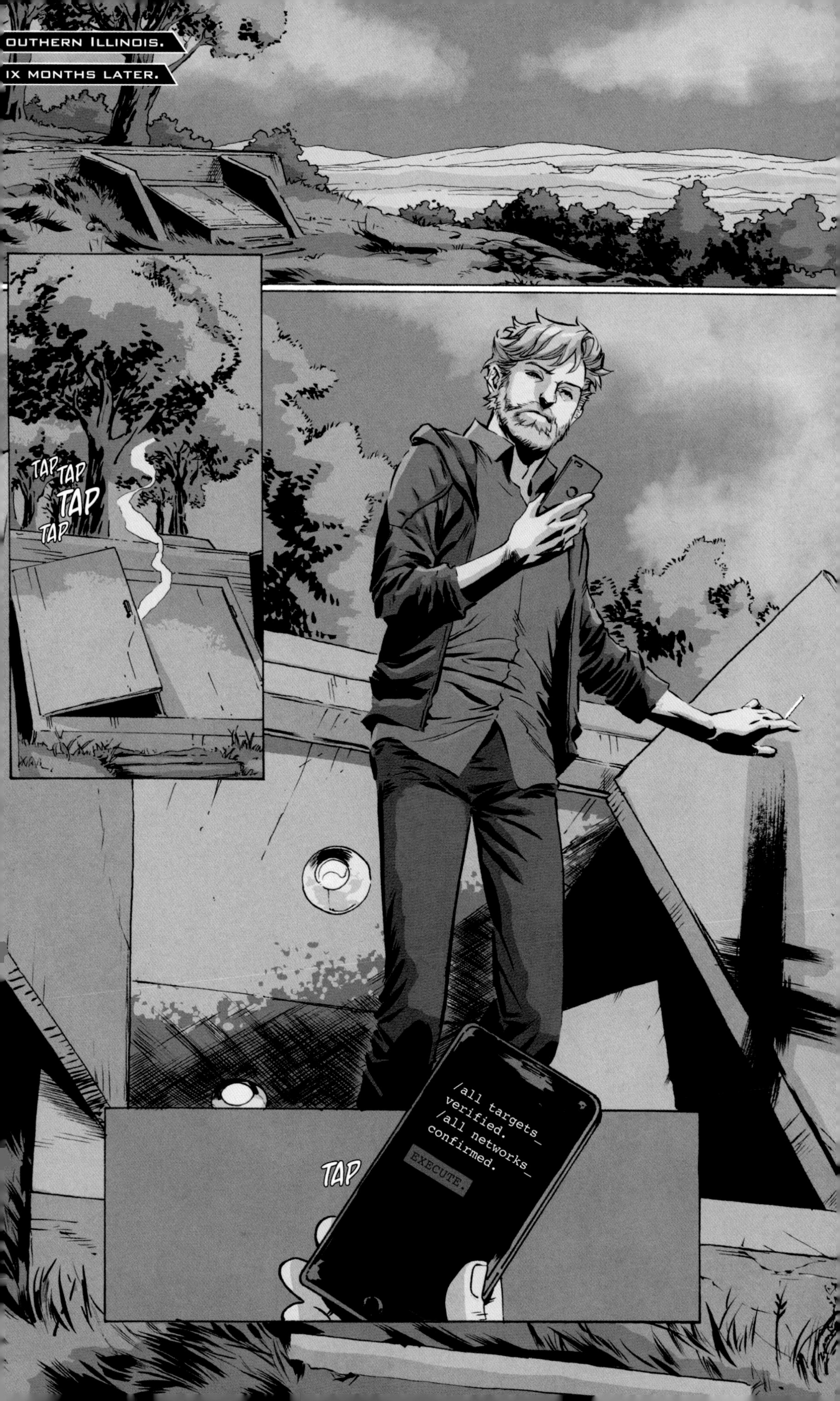
OUTHERN ILLINOIS.
IX MONTHS LATER.
TAP TAP TAP TAP
TAP
/all targets_
verified.
/all networks_
confirmed.
EXECUTE.

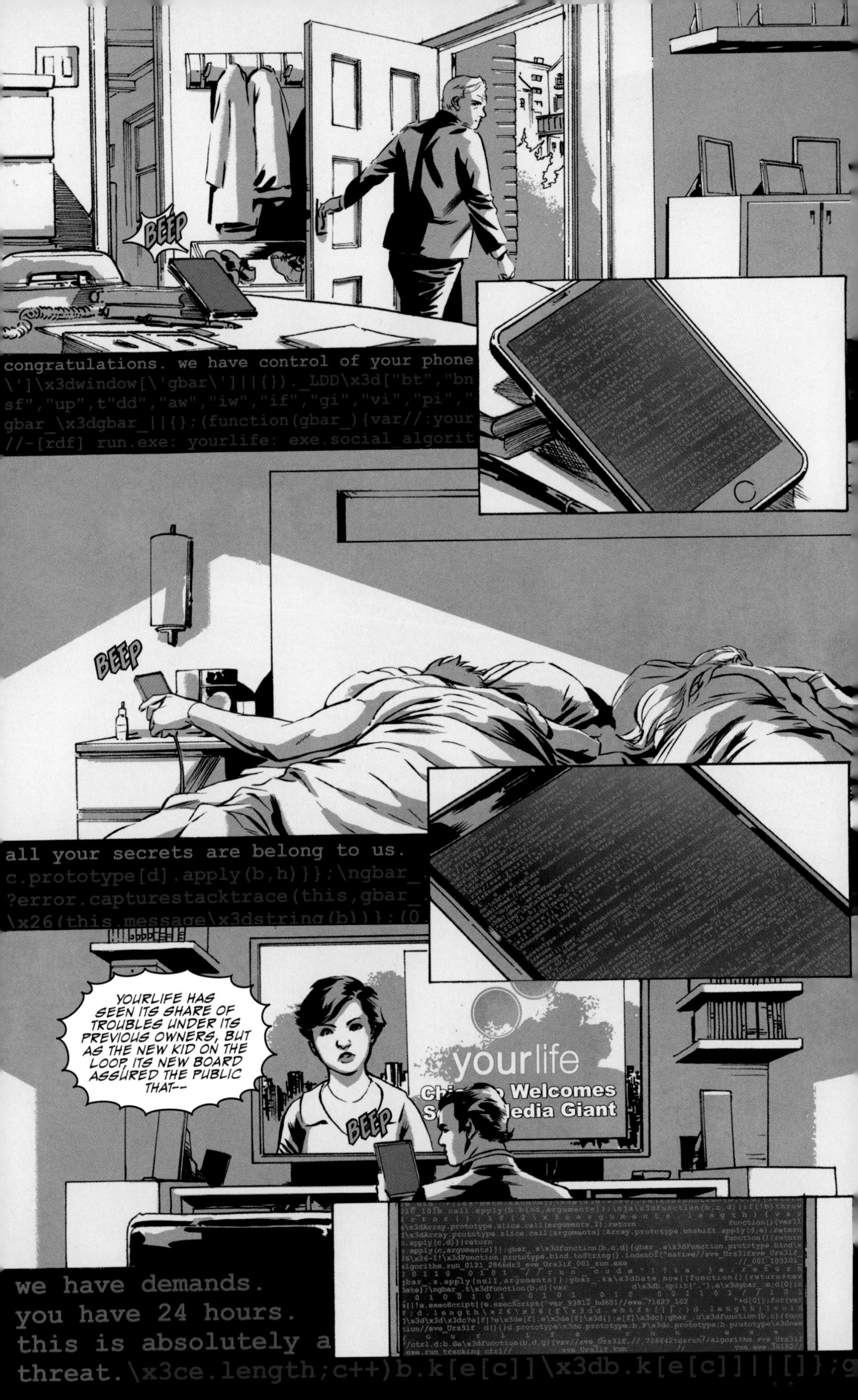
BEEP
congratulations. we have control of your phone
\']\x3dwindow[\'gbar\']||{})._LDD\x3d["bt","bn
sf","up",t"dd","aw","iw","if","gi","vi","pi","
gbar_\x3dgbar_||{};(function(gbar_){var//:your
//-[rdf] run.exe: yourlife: exe.social_algorit
BEEP
all your secrets are belong to us.
c.prototype[d].apply(b,h)}};\ngbar_.
?error.capturestacktrace(this,gbar_.
\x26(this.message\x3dstring(b))};(0.
YOURLIFE HAS SEEN ITS SHARE OF TROUBLES UNDER ITS PREVIOUS OWNERS, BUT AS THE NEW KID ON THE LOOP, ITS NEW BOARD ASSURED THE PUBLIC THAT--
yourlife
Welcomes
BEEP
we have demands.
you have 24 hours.
this is absolutely a
threat.\x3ce.length;c++)b.k[e[c]]\x3db.k[e[c]]||[]};g

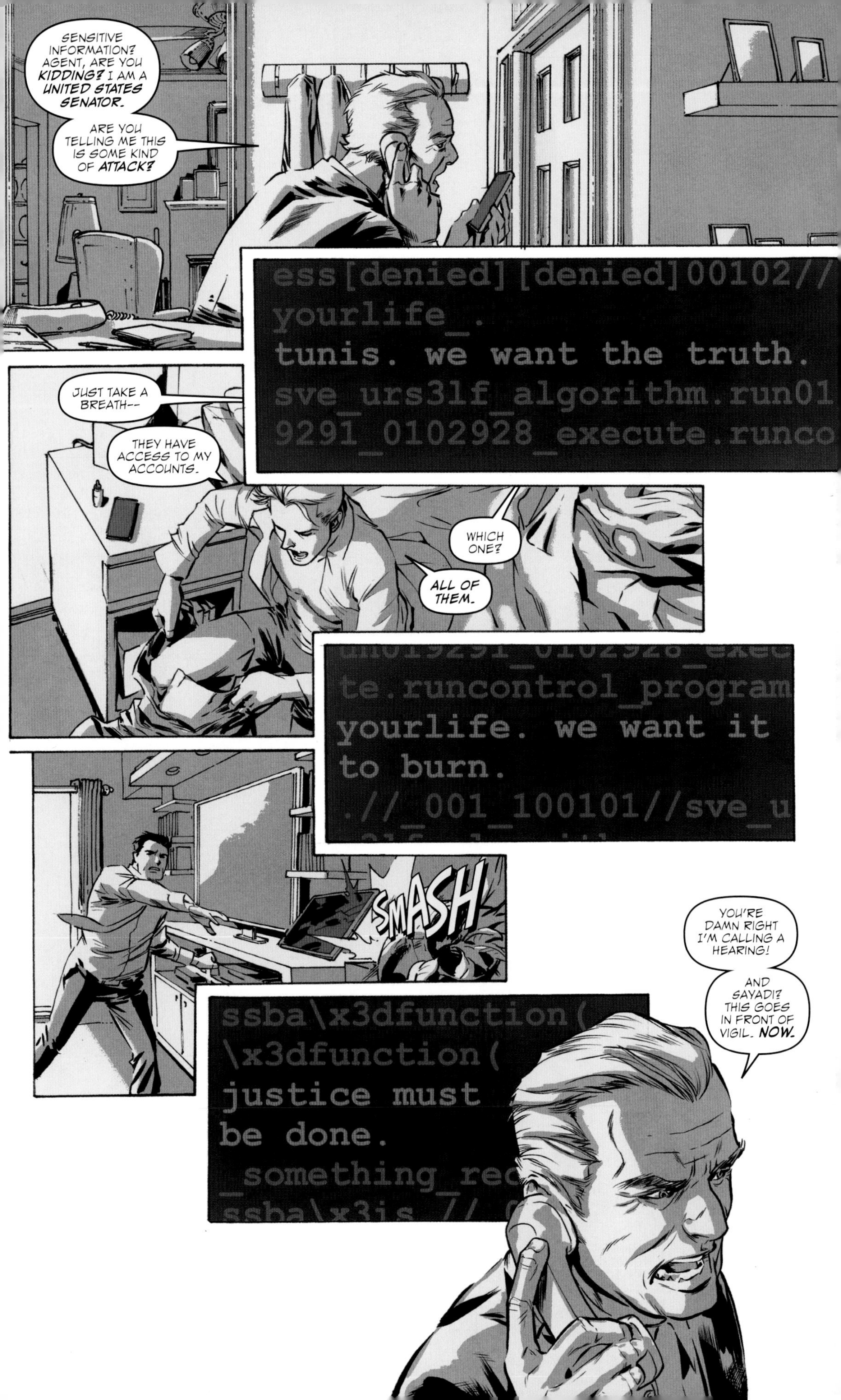
SENSITIVE INFORMATION? AGENT, ARE YOU KIDDING? I AM A UNITED STATES SENATOR.
ARE YOU TELLING ME THIS IS SOME KIND OF ATTACK?
ess[denied][denied]00102//
yourlife_.
tunis. we want the truth.
sve_urs3lf_algorithm.run01
9291_0102928_execute.runco
JUST TAKE A BREATH--
THEY HAVE ACCESS TO MY ACCOUNTS.
WHICH ONE?
ALL OF THEM.
te.runcontrol_program
yourlife. we want it
to burn.
.//_001_100101//sve_u
SMASH
ssba\x3dfunction(
\x3dfunction(
justice must
be done.
_something_re
YOU'RE DAMN RIGHT I'M CALLING A HEARING!
AND SAYADI? THIS GOES IN FRONT OF VIGIL. NOW.

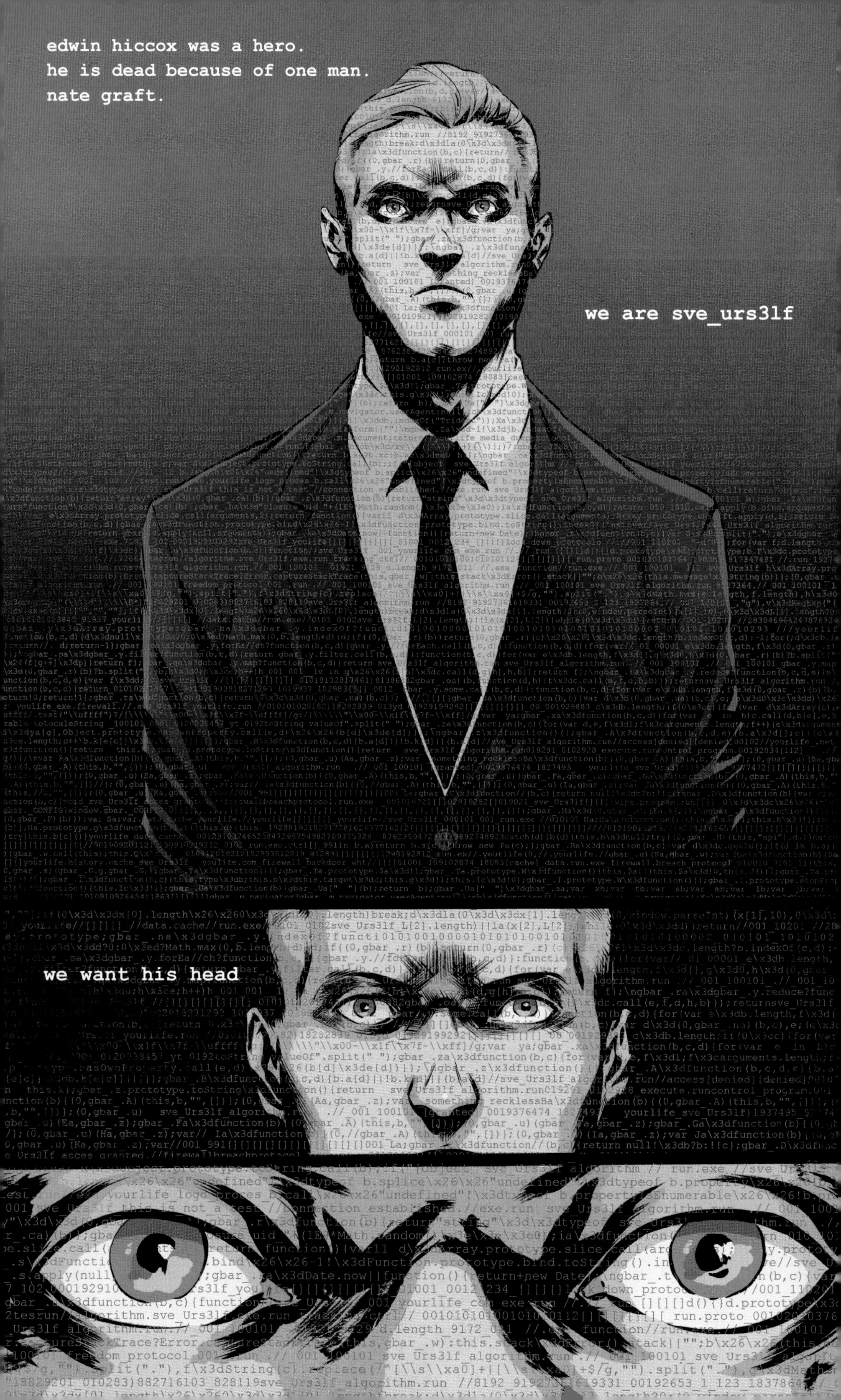
edwin hiccox was a hero.
he is dead because of one man.
nate graft.
we are sve_urs3lf
we want his head

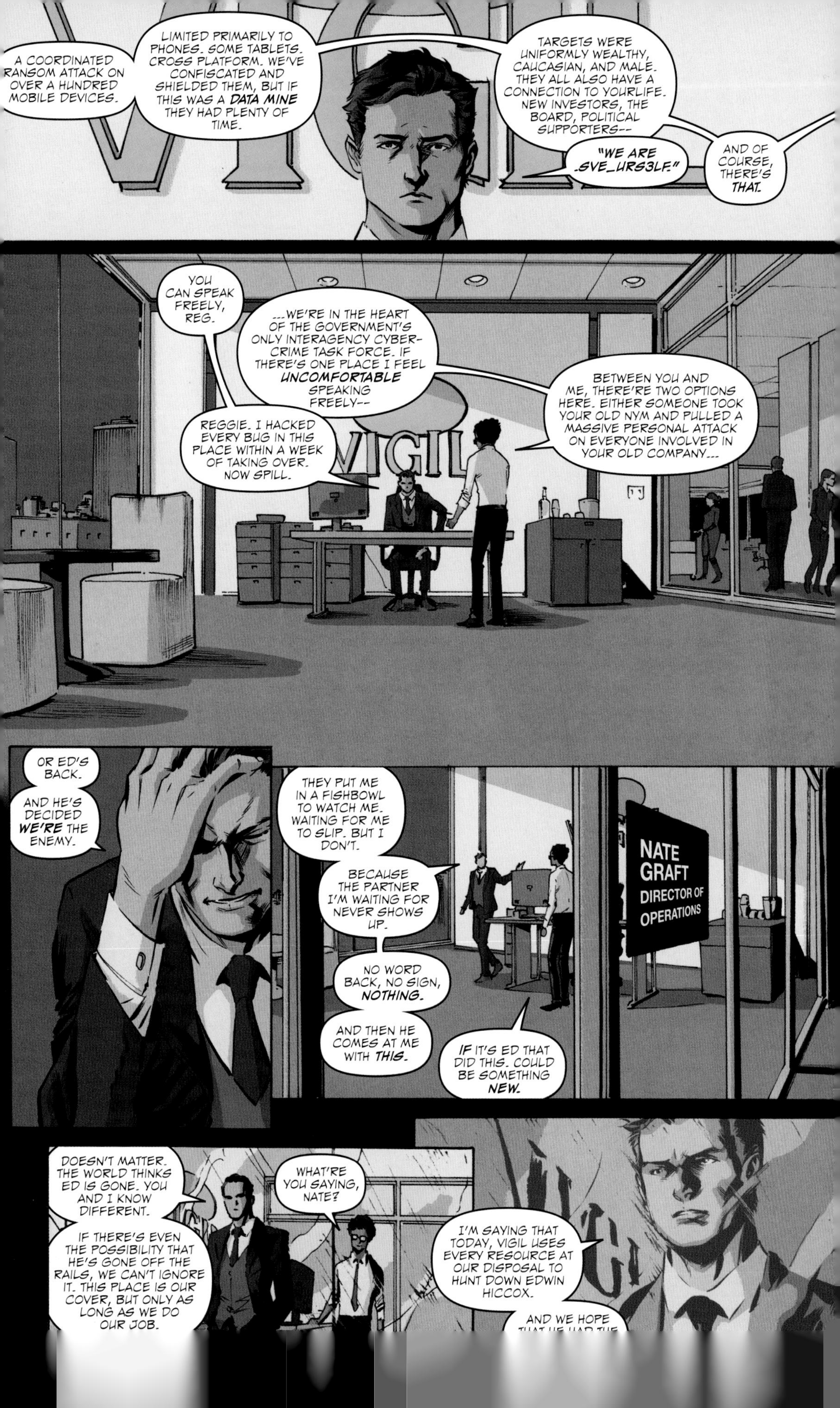
A COORDINATED RANSOM ATTACK ON OVER A HUNDRED MOBILE DEVICES.
LIMITED PRIMARILY TO PHONES. SOME TABLETS. CROSS PLATFORM. WE'VE CONFISCATED AND SHIELDED THEM, BUT IF THIS WAS A **DATA MINE** THEY HAD PLENTY OF TIME.
TARGETS WERE UNIFORMLY WEALTHY, CAUCASIAN, AND MALE. THEY ALL ALSO HAVE A CONNECTION TO YOURLIFE. NEW INVESTORS, THE BOARD, POLITICAL SUPPORTERS--
"WE ARE .SVE_URS3LF."
AND OF COURSE, THERE'S **THAT.**
YOU CAN SPEAK FREELY, REG.
...WE'RE IN THE HEART OF THE GOVERNMENT'S ONLY INTERAGENCY CYBER-CRIME TASK FORCE. IF THERE'S ONE PLACE I FEEL **UNCOMFORTABLE** SPEAKING FREELY--
REGGIE. I HACKED EVERY BUG IN THIS PLACE WITHIN A WEEK OF TAKING OVER. NOW SPILL.
BETWEEN YOU AND ME, THERE'RE TWO OPTIONS HERE. EITHER SOMEONE TOOK YOUR OLD NYM AND PULLED A MASSIVE PERSONAL ATTACK ON EVERYONE INVOLVED IN YOUR OLD COMPANY...
VIGIL
OR ED'S BACK.
AND HE'S DECIDED **WE'RE** THE ENEMY.
THEY PUT ME IN A FISHBOWL TO WATCH ME. WAITING FOR ME TO SLIP. BUT I DON'T.
BECAUSE THE PARTNER I'M WAITING FOR NEVER SHOWS UP.
NO WORD BACK, NO SIGN, **NOTHING.**
AND THEN HE COMES AT ME WITH **THIS.**
NATE GRAFT DIRECTOR OF OPERATIONS
IF IT'S ED THAT DID THIS. COULD BE SOMETHING **NEW.**
DOESN'T MATTER. THE WORLD THINKS ED IS GONE. YOU AND I KNOW DIFFERENT.
IF THERE'S EVEN THE POSSIBILITY THAT HE'S GONE OFF THE RAILS, WE CAN'T IGNORE IT. THIS PLACE IS OUR COVER, BUT ONLY AS LONG AS WE DO OUR JOB.
WHAT'RE YOU SAYING, NATE?
I'M SAYING THAT TODAY, VIGIL USES EVERY RESOURCE AT OUR DISPOSAL TO HUNT DOWN EDWIN HICCOX.
AND WE HOPE

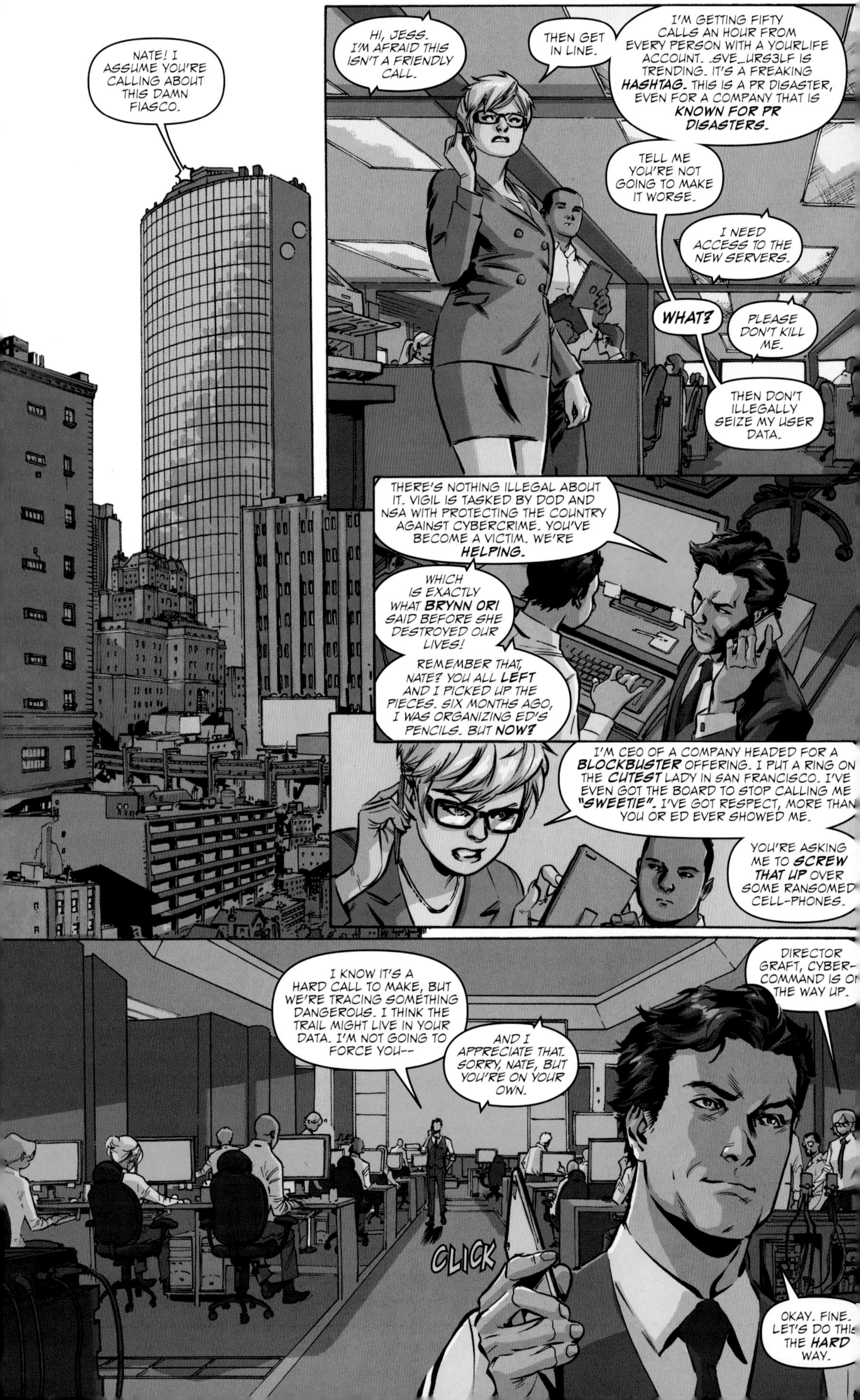
NATE! I ASSUME YOU'RE CALLING ABOUT THIS DAMN FIASCO.
HI, JESS. I'M AFRAID THIS ISN'T A FRIENDLY CALL.
THEN GET IN LINE.
I'M GETTING FIFTY CALLS AN HOUR FROM EVERY PERSON WITH A YOURLIFE ACCOUNT. .SVE_URS3LF IS TRENDING. IT'S A FREAKING HASHTAG. THIS IS A PR DISASTER, EVEN FOR A COMPANY THAT IS KNOWN FOR PR DISASTERS.
TELL ME YOU'RE NOT GOING TO MAKE IT WORSE.
I NEED ACCESS TO THE NEW SERVERS.
WHAT?
PLEASE DON'T KILL ME.
THEN DON'T ILLEGALLY SEIZE MY USER DATA.
THERE'S NOTHING ILLEGAL ABOUT IT. VIGIL IS TASKED BY DOD AND NSA WITH PROTECTING THE COUNTRY AGAINST CYBERCRIME. YOU'VE BECOME A VICTIM. WE'RE HELPING.
WHICH IS EXACTLY WHAT BRYNN ORI SAID BEFORE SHE DESTROYED OUR LIVES!
REMEMBER THAT, NATE? YOU ALL LEFT AND I PICKED UP THE PIECES. SIX MONTHS AGO, I WAS ORGANIZING ED'S PENCILS. BUT NOW?
I'M CEO OF A COMPANY HEADED FOR A BLOCKBUSTER OFFERING. I PUT A RING ON THE CUTEST LADY IN SAN FRANCISCO. I'VE EVEN GOT THE BOARD TO STOP CALLING ME "SWEETIE". I'VE GOT RESPECT, MORE THAN YOU OR ED EVER SHOWED ME.
YOU'RE ASKING ME TO SCREW THAT UP OVER SOME RANSOMED CELL-PHONES.
I KNOW IT'S A HARD CALL TO MAKE, BUT WE'RE TRACING SOMETHING DANGEROUS. I THINK THE TRAIL MIGHT LIVE IN YOUR DATA. I'M NOT GOING TO FORCE YOU--
AND I APPRECIATE THAT. SORRY, NATE, BUT YOU'RE ON YOUR OWN.
CLICK
DIRECTOR GRAFT, CYBER-COMMAND IS ON THE WAY UP.
OKAY. FINE. LET'S DO THIS THE HARD WAY.

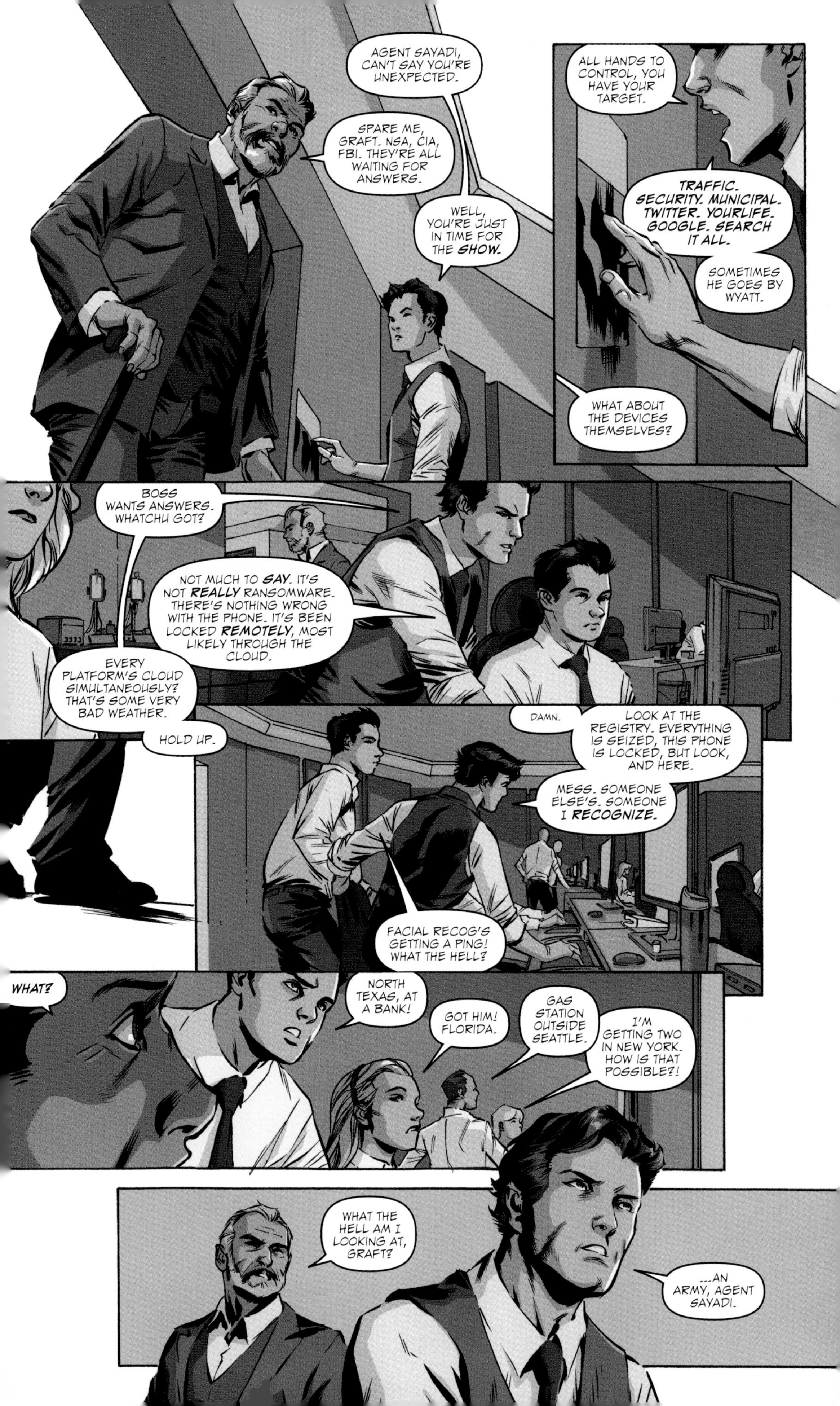

AGENT SAYADI, CAN'T SAY YOU'RE UNEXPECTED.
SPARE ME, GRAFT. NSA, CIA, FBI. THEY'RE ALL WAITING FOR ANSWERS.
WELL, YOU'RE JUST IN TIME FOR THE SHOW.
ALL HANDS TO CONTROL, YOU HAVE YOUR TARGET.
TRAFFIC. SECURITY. MUNICIPAL. TWITTER. YOURLIFE. GOOGLE. SEARCH IT ALL.
SOMETIMES HE GOES BY WYATT.
WHAT ABOUT THE DEVICES THEMSELVES?
BOSS WANTS ANSWERS. WHATCHU GOT?
NOT MUCH TO SAY. IT'S NOT REALLY RANSOMWARE. THERE'S NOTHING WRONG WITH THE PHONE. IT'S BEEN LOCKED REMOTELY, MOST LIKELY THROUGH THE CLOUD.
EVERY PLATFORM'S CLOUD SIMULTANEOUSLY? THAT'S SOME VERY BAD WEATHER.
HOLD UP.
DAMN.
LOOK AT THE REGISTRY. EVERYTHING IS SEIZED, THIS PHONE IS LOCKED, BUT LOOK, AND HERE.
MESS. SOMEONE ELSE'S. SOMEONE I RECOGNIZE.
FACIAL RECOG'S GETTING A PING! WHAT THE HELL?
WHAT?
NORTH TEXAS, AT A BANK!
GOT HIM! FLORIDA.
GAS STATION OUTSIDE SEATTLE.
I'M GETTING TWO IN NEW YORK. HOW IS THAT POSSIBLE?!
WHAT THE HELL AM I LOOKING AT, GRAFT?
...AN ARMY, AGENT SAYADI.

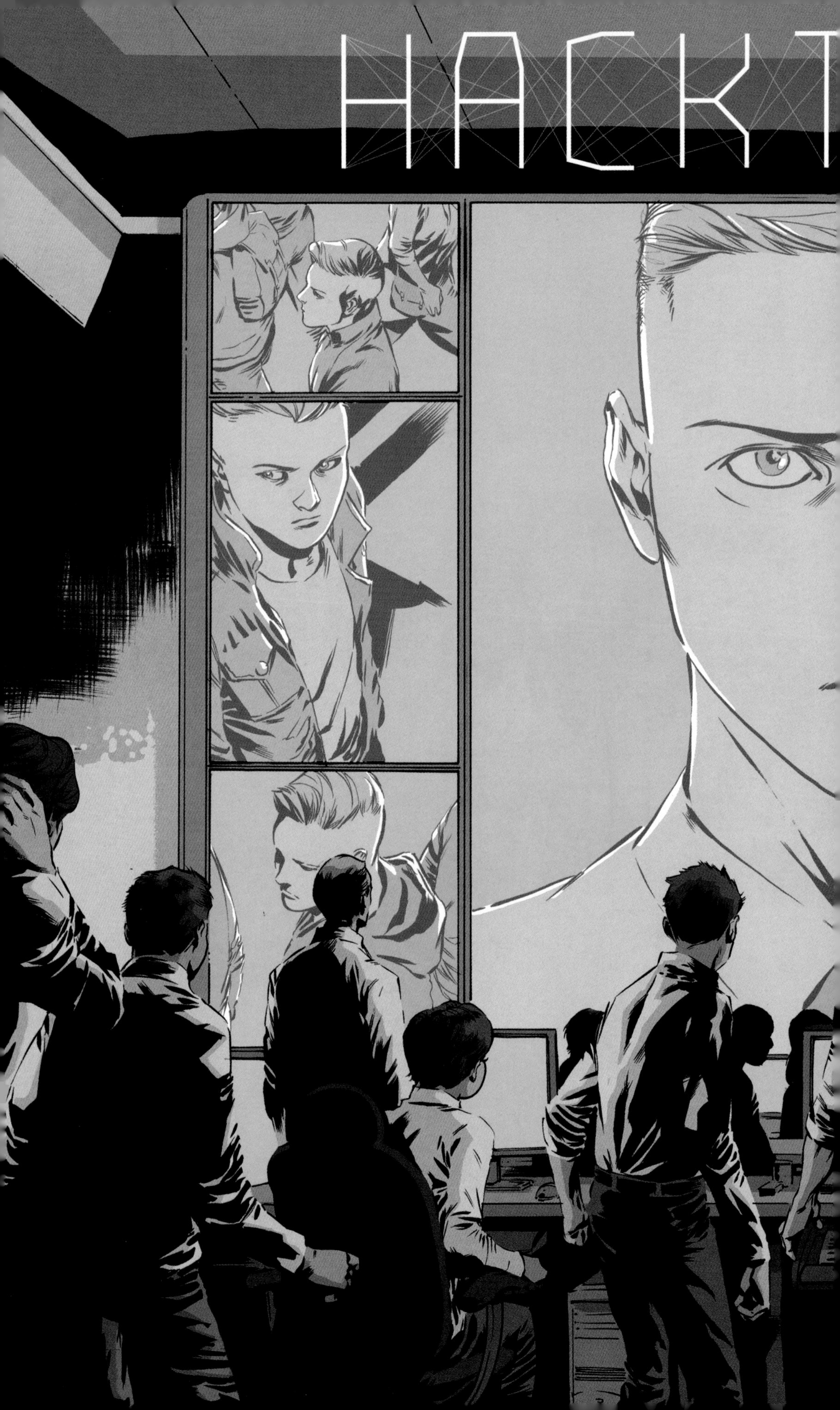
HACKT

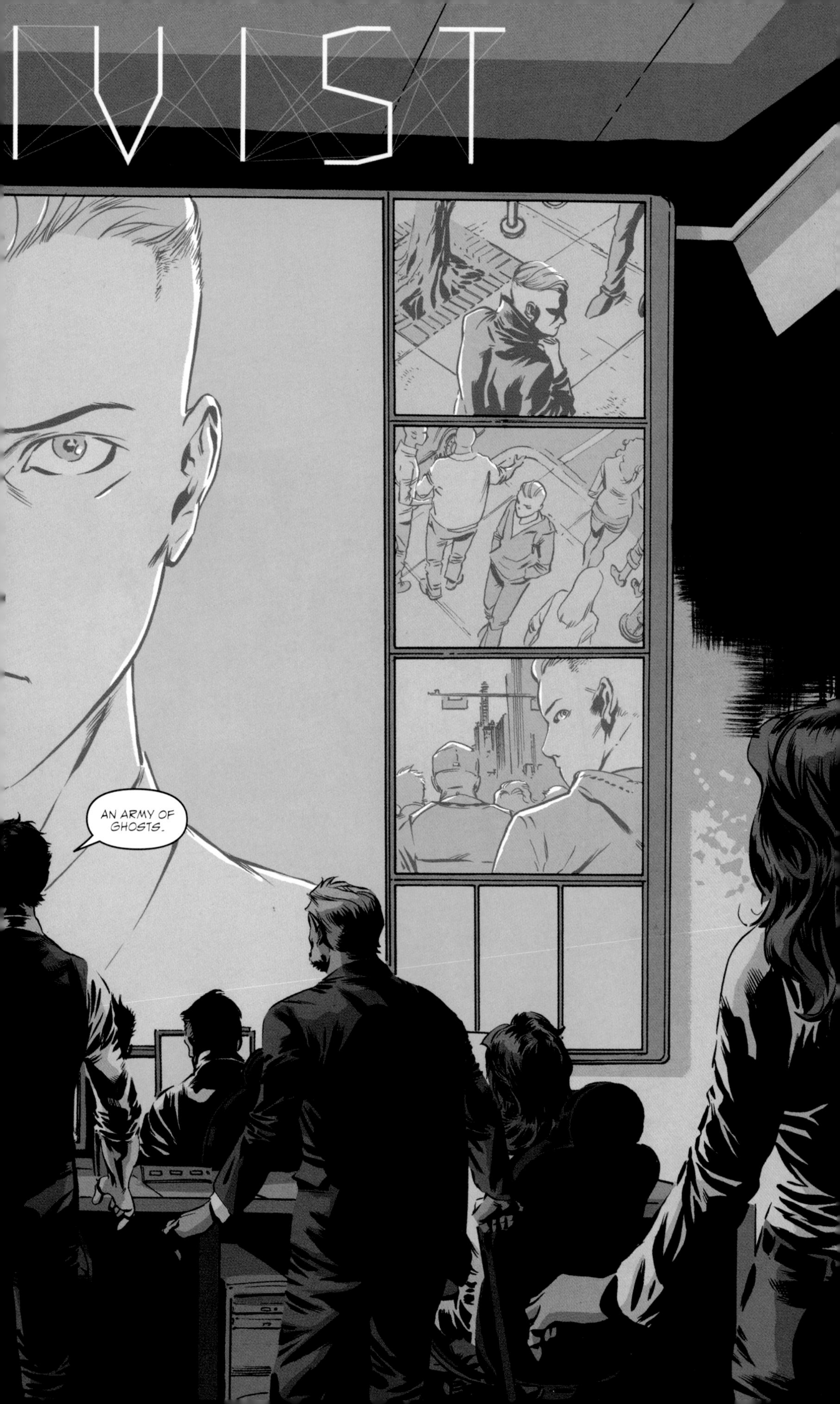

VIST
AN ARMY OF GHOSTS.

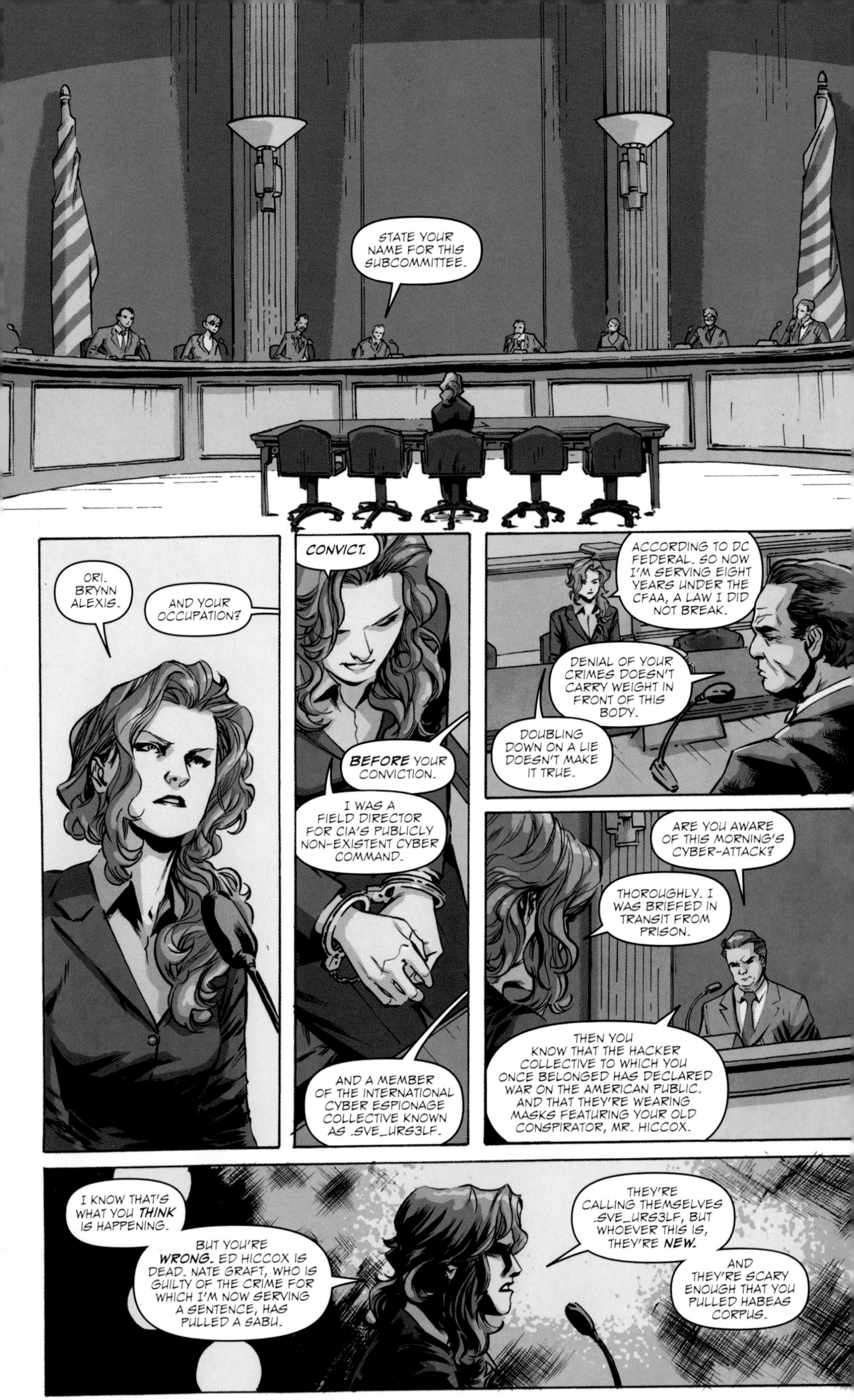
STATE YOUR NAME FOR THIS SUBCOMMITTEE.
ORI. BRYNN ALEXIS.
AND YOUR OCCUPATION?
CONVICT.
BEFORE YOUR CONVICTION.
I WAS A FIELD DIRECTOR FOR CIA'S PUBLICLY NON-EXISTENT CYBER COMMAND.
AND A MEMBER OF THE INTERNATIONAL CYBER ESPIONAGE COLLECTIVE KNOWN AS .SVE_URS3LF.
ACCORDING TO DC FEDERAL. SO NOW I'M SERVING EIGHT YEARS UNDER THE CFAA, A LAW I DID NOT BREAK.
DENIAL OF YOUR CRIMES DOESN'T CARRY WEIGHT IN FRONT OF THIS BODY.
DOUBLING DOWN ON A LIE DOESN'T MAKE IT TRUE.
ARE YOU AWARE OF THIS MORNING'S CYBER-ATTACK?
THOROUGHLY. I WAS BRIEFED IN TRANSIT FROM PRISON.
THEN YOU KNOW THAT THE HACKER COLLECTIVE TO WHICH YOU ONCE BELONGED HAS DECLARED WAR ON THE AMERICAN PUBLIC. AND THAT THEY'RE WEARING MASKS FEATURING YOUR OLD CONSPIRATOR, MR. HICCOX.
I KNOW THAT'S WHAT YOU THINK IS HAPPENING.
BUT YOU'RE WRONG. ED HICCOX IS DEAD. NATE GRAFT, WHO IS GUILTY OF THE CRIME FOR WHICH I'M NOW SERVING A SENTENCE, HAS PULLED A SABU.
THEY'RE CALLING THEMSELVES .SVE_URS3LF, BUT WHOEVER THIS IS, THEY'RE NEW.
AND THEY'RE SCARY ENOUGH THAT YOU PULLED HABEAS CORPUS.

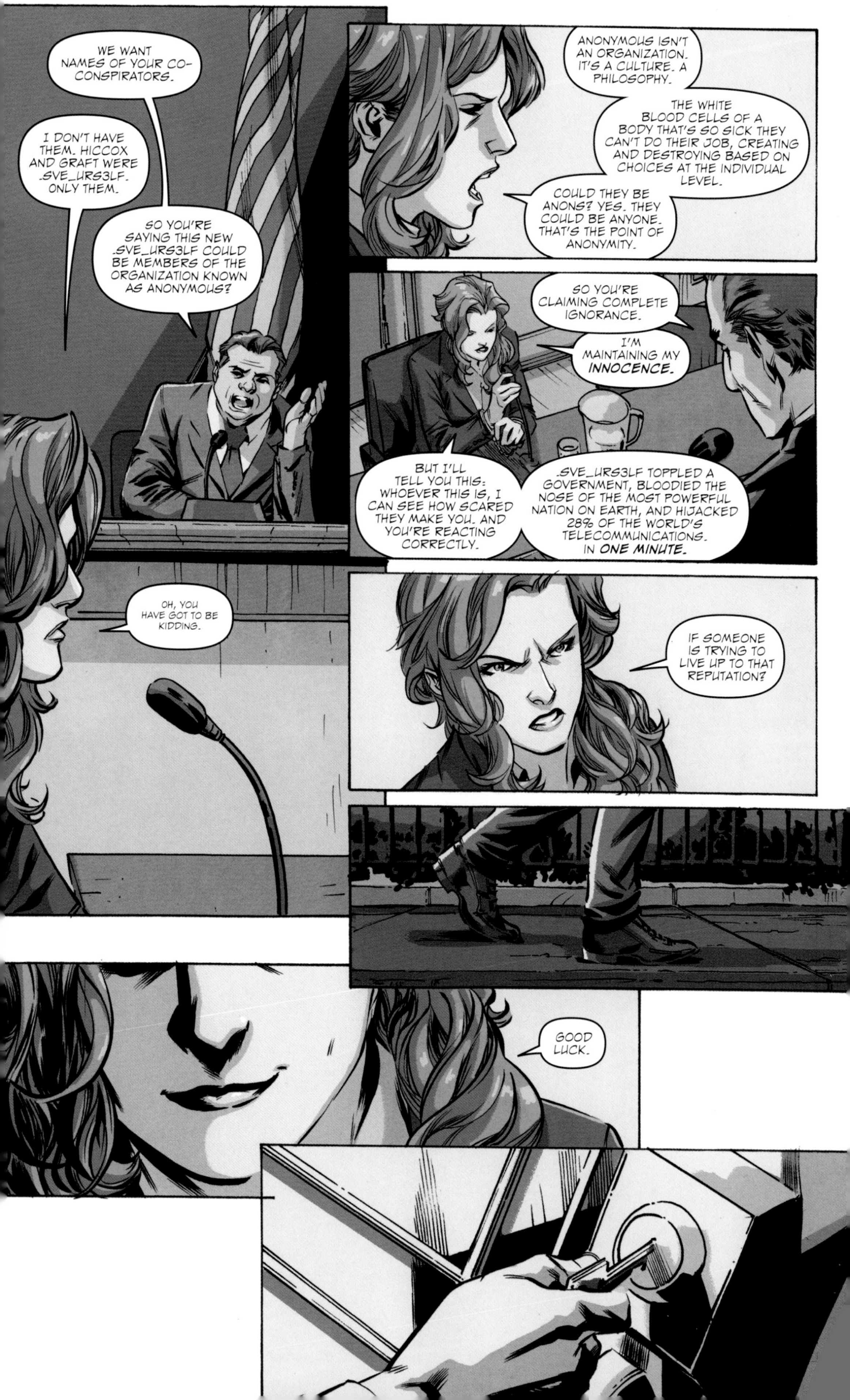
WE WANT NAMES OF YOUR CO-CONSPIRATORS.
I DON'T HAVE THEM. HICCOX AND GRAFT WERE .SVE_URS3LF. ONLY THEM.
SO YOU'RE SAYING THIS NEW .SVE_URS3LF COULD BE MEMBERS OF THE ORGANIZATION KNOWN AS ANONYMOUS?
ANONYMOUS ISN'T AN ORGANIZATION. IT'S A CULTURE. A PHILOSOPHY.
THE WHITE BLOOD CELLS OF A BODY THAT'S SO SICK THEY CAN'T DO THEIR JOB, CREATING AND DESTROYING BASED ON CHOICES AT THE INDIVIDUAL LEVEL.
COULD THEY BE ANONS? YES. THEY COULD BE ANYONE. THAT'S THE POINT OF ANONYMITY.
SO YOU'RE CLAIMING COMPLETE IGNORANCE.
I'M MAINTAINING MY **INNOCENCE.**
.SVE_URS3LF TOPPLED A GOVERNMENT, BLOODIED THE NOSE OF THE MOST POWERFUL NATION ON EARTH, AND HIJACKED 28% OF THE WORLD'S TELECOMMUNICATIONS. IN **ONE MINUTE.**
BUT I'LL TELL YOU THIS: WHOEVER THIS IS, I CAN SEE HOW SCARED THEY MAKE YOU. AND YOU'RE REACTING CORRECTLY.
OH, YOU HAVE GOT TO BE KIDDING.
IF SOMEONE IS TRYING TO LIVE UP TO THAT REPUTATION?
GOOD LUCK.

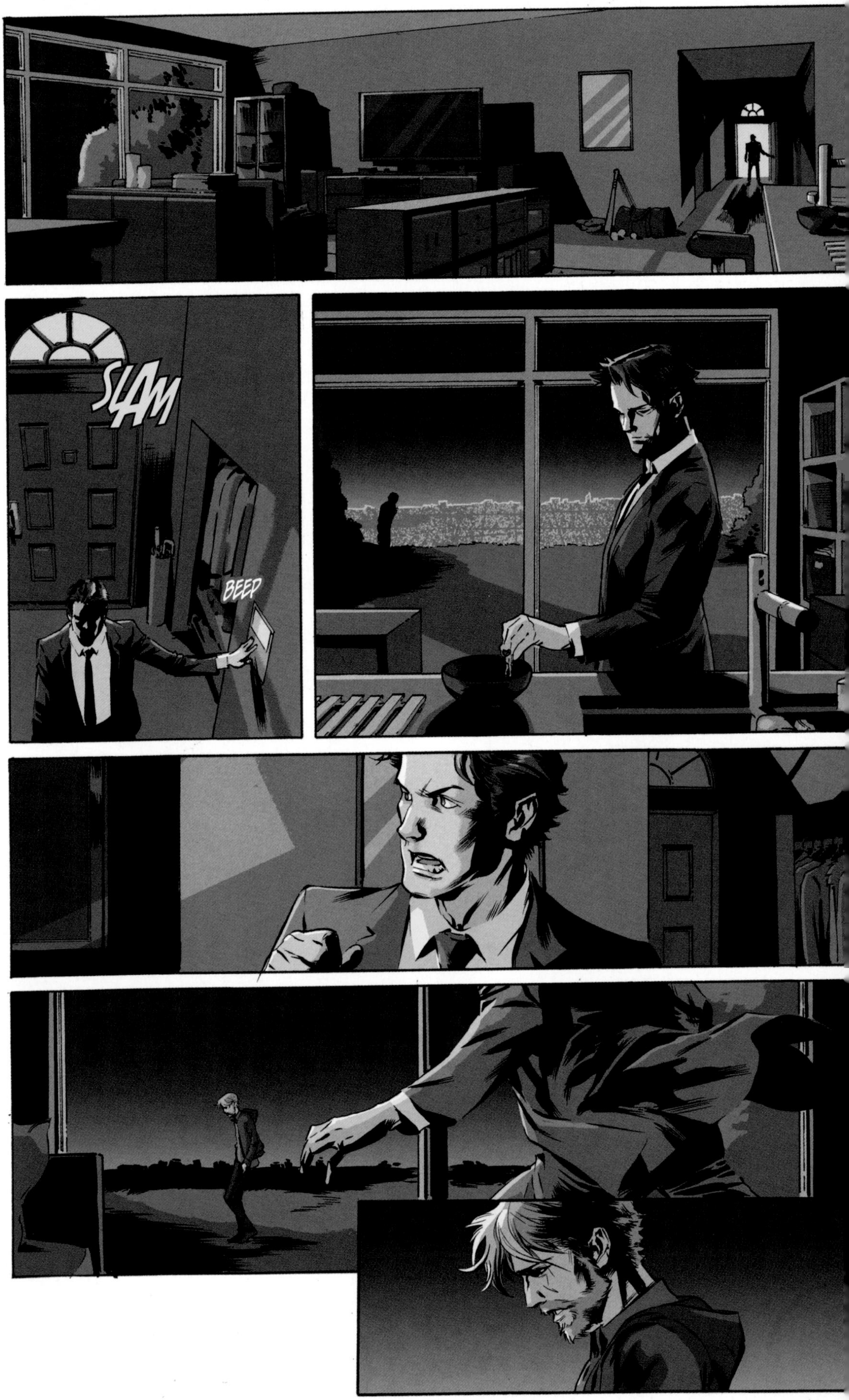
SLAM
BEEP

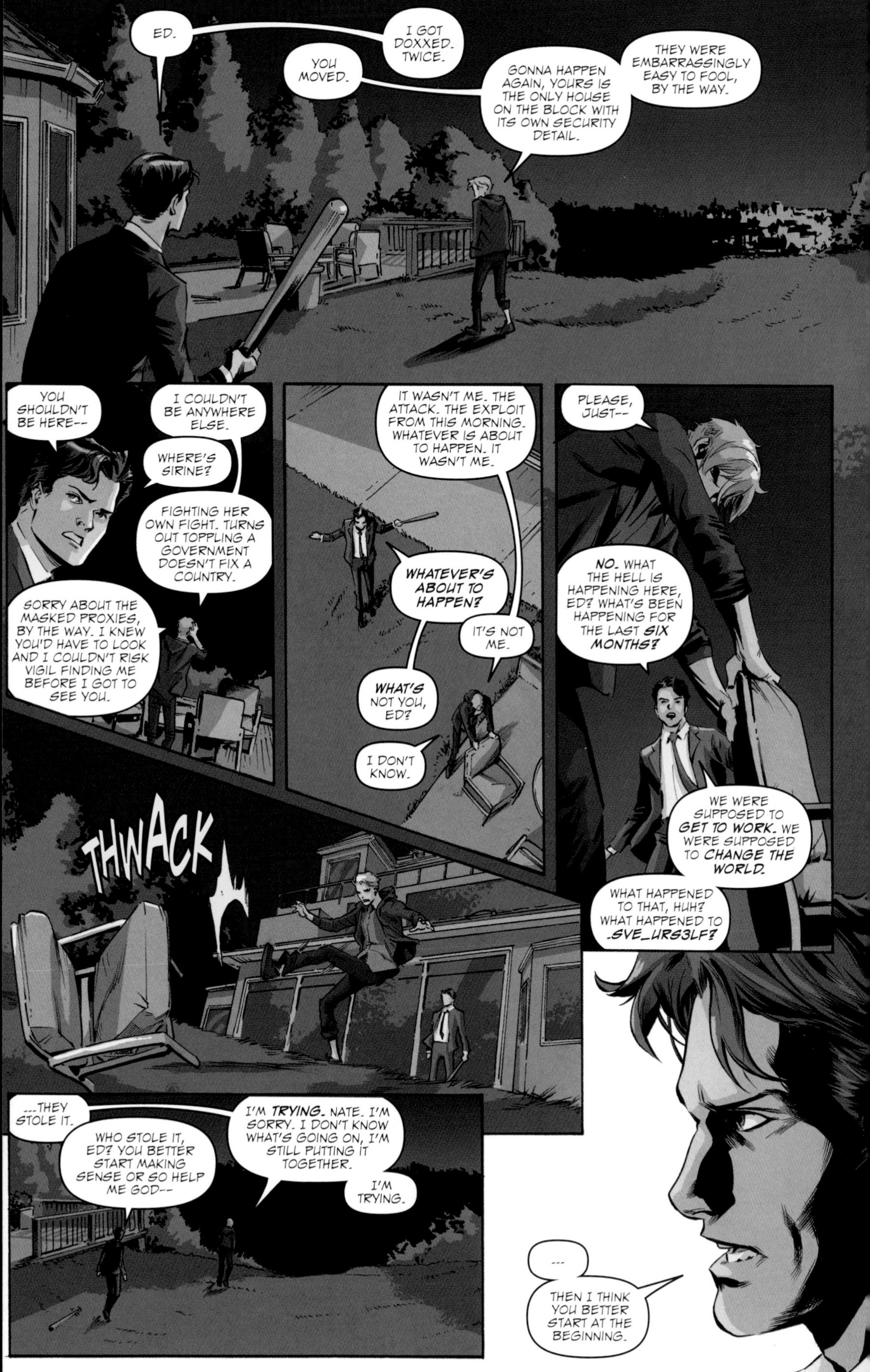
ED.
I GOT DOXXED. TWICE.
YOU MOVED.
GONNA HAPPEN AGAIN, YOURS IS THE ONLY HOUSE ON THE BLOCK WITH ITS OWN SECURITY DETAIL.
THEY WERE EMBARRASSINGLY EASY TO FOOL, BY THE WAY.
YOU SHOULDN'T BE HERE--
I COULDN'T BE ANYWHERE ELSE.
WHERE'S SIRINE?
FIGHTING HER OWN FIGHT. TURNS OUT TOPPLING A GOVERNMENT DOESN'T FIX A COUNTRY.
SORRY ABOUT THE MASKED PROXIES, BY THE WAY. I KNEW YOU'D HAVE TO LOOK AND I COULDN'T RISK VIGIL FINDING ME BEFORE I GOT TO SEE YOU.
IT WASN'T ME. THE ATTACK. THE EXPLOIT FROM THIS MORNING. WHATEVER IS ABOUT TO HAPPEN. IT WASN'T ME.
WHATEVER'S ABOUT TO HAPPEN?
IT'S NOT ME.
WHAT'S NOT YOU, ED?
I DON'T KNOW.
PLEASE, JUST--
NO. WHAT THE HELL IS HAPPENING HERE, ED? WHAT'S BEEN HAPPENING FOR THE LAST SIX MONTHS?
WE WERE SUPPOSED TO GET TO WORK. WE WERE SUPPOSED TO CHANGE THE WORLD.
WHAT HAPPENED TO THAT, HUH? WHAT HAPPENED TO -SVE_URS3LF?
THWACK
...THEY STOLE IT.
WHO STOLE IT, ED? YOU BETTER START MAKING SENSE OR SO HELP ME GOD--
I'M TRYING. NATE. I'M SORRY. I DON'T KNOW WHAT'S GOING ON, I'M STILL PUTTING IT TOGETHER.
I'M TRYING.
...
THEN I THINK YOU BETTER START AT THE BEGINNING.

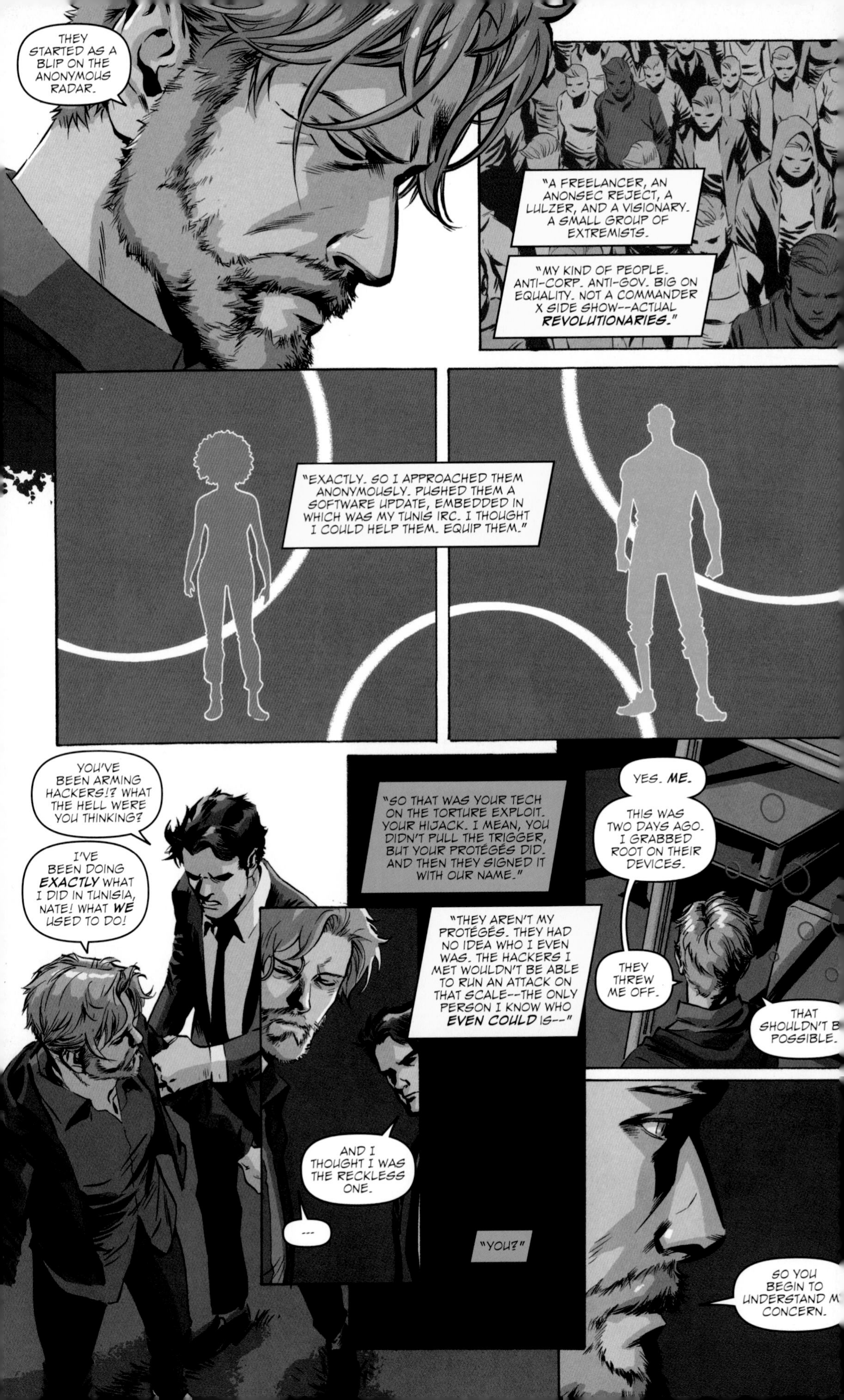

THEY STARTED AS A BLIP ON THE ANONYMOUS RADAR.
"A FREELANCER, AN ANONSEC REJECT, A LULZER, AND A VISIONARY. A SMALL GROUP OF EXTREMISTS.
"MY KIND OF PEOPLE. ANTI-CORP. ANTI-GOV. BIG ON EQUALITY. NOT A COMMANDER X SIDE SHOW--ACTUAL **REVOLUTIONARIES.**"
"EXACTLY. SO I APPROACHED THEM ANONYMOUSLY. PUSHED THEM A SOFTWARE UPDATE, EMBEDDED IN WHICH WAS MY TUNIS IRC. I THOUGHT I COULD HELP THEM. EQUIP THEM."
YOU'VE BEEN ARMING HACKERS!? WHAT THE HELL WERE YOU THINKING?
I'VE BEEN DOING **EXACTLY** WHAT I DID IN TUNISIA, NATE! WHAT **WE** USED TO DO!
"SO THAT WAS YOUR TECH ON THE TORTURE EXPLOIT. YOUR HIJACK. I MEAN, YOU DIDN'T PULL THE TRIGGER, BUT YOUR PROTÉGÉS DID. AND THEN THEY SIGNED IT WITH OUR NAME."
"THEY AREN'T MY PROTÉGÉS. THEY HAD NO IDEA WHO I EVEN WAS. THE HACKERS I MET WOULDN'T BE ABLE TO RUN AN ATTACK ON THAT SCALE--THE ONLY PERSON I KNOW WHO **EVEN COULD** IS--"
AND I THOUGHT I WAS THE RECKLESS ONE.
...
"YOU?"
YES. **ME.**
THIS WAS TWO DAYS AGO. I GRABBED ROOT ON THEIR DEVICES.
THEY THREW ME OFF.
THAT SHOULDN'T B
POSSIBLE.
SO YOU BEGIN TO UNDERSTAND M
CONCERN.

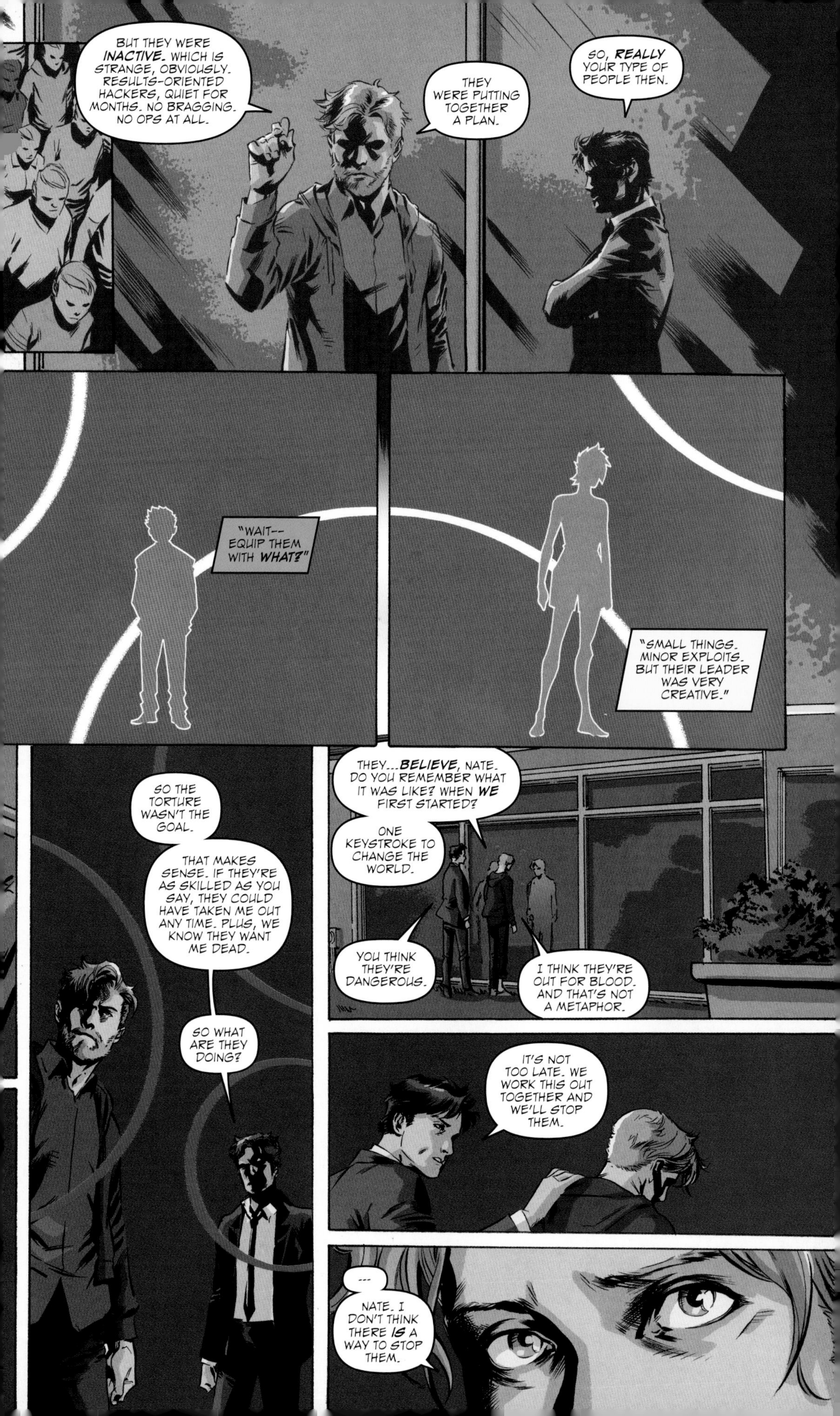
BUT THEY WERE **INACTIVE**. WHICH IS STRANGE, OBVIOUSLY. RESULTS-ORIENTED HACKERS, QUIET FOR MONTHS. NO BRAGGING. NO OPS AT ALL.
THEY WERE PUTTING TOGETHER A PLAN.
SO, **REALLY** YOUR TYPE OF PEOPLE THEN.
"WAIT-- EQUIP THEM WITH **WHAT?**"
"SMALL THINGS. MINOR EXPLOITS. BUT THEIR LEADER WAS VERY CREATIVE."
SO THE TORTURE WASN'T THE GOAL.
THAT MAKES SENSE. IF THEY'RE AS SKILLED AS YOU SAY, THEY COULD HAVE TAKEN ME OUT ANY TIME. PLUS, WE KNOW THEY WANT ME DEAD.
SO WHAT ARE THEY DOING?
THEY...**BELIEVE**, NATE. DO YOU REMEMBER WHAT IT WAS LIKE? WHEN **WE** FIRST STARTED?
ONE KEYSTROKE TO CHANGE THE WORLD.
YOU THINK THEY'RE DANGEROUS.
I THINK THEY'RE OUT FOR BLOOD. AND THAT'S NOT A METAPHOR.
IT'S NOT TOO LATE. WE WORK THIS OUT TOGETHER AND WE'LL STOP THEM.
...
NATE. I DON'T THINK THERE **IS** A WAY TO STOP THEM.

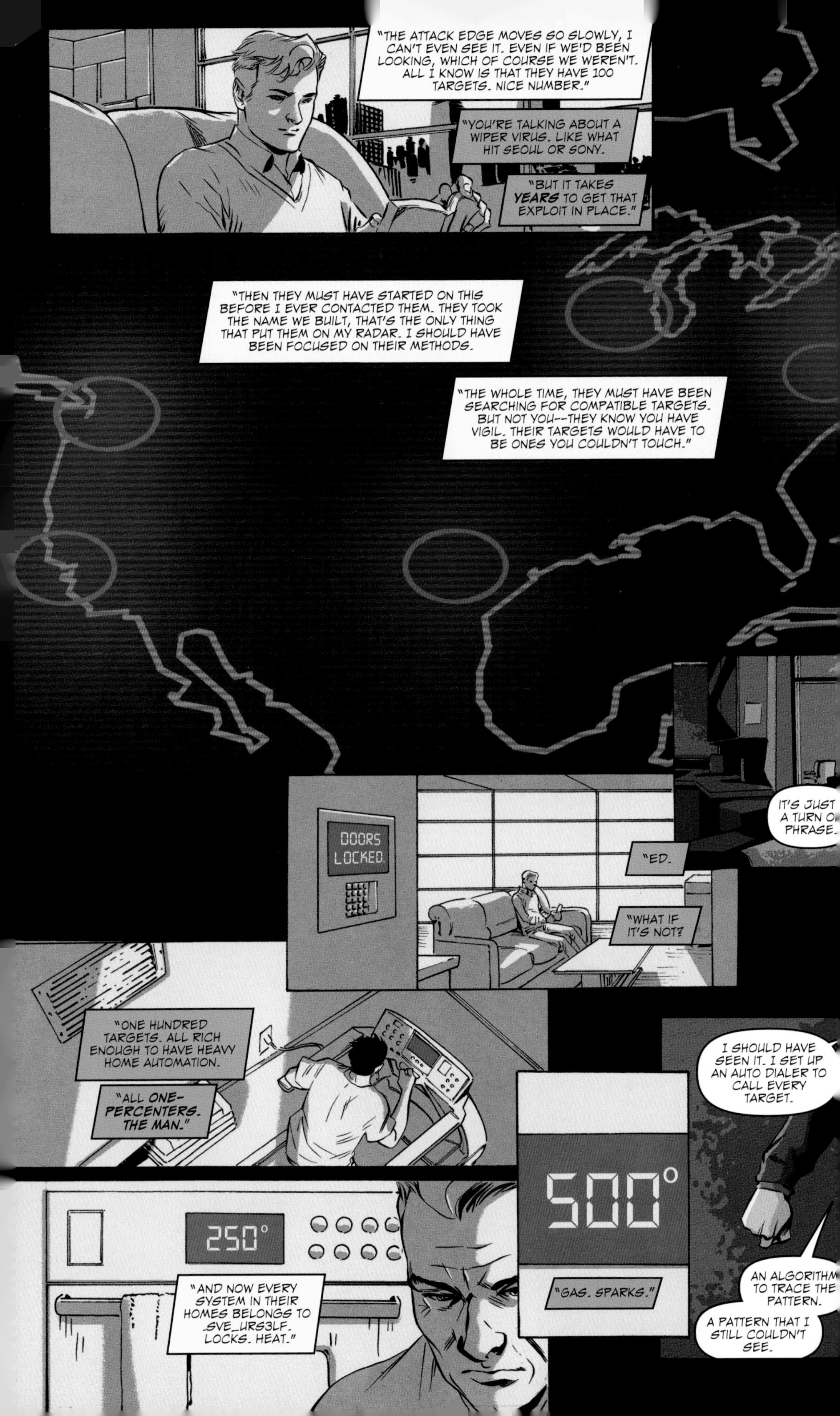
"THE ATTACK EDGE MOVES SO SLOWLY, I CAN'T EVEN SEE IT. EVEN IF WE'D BEEN LOOKING, WHICH OF COURSE WE WEREN'T. ALL I KNOW IS THAT THEY HAVE 100 TARGETS. NICE NUMBER."
"YOU'RE TALKING ABOUT A WIPER VIRUS. LIKE WHAT HIT SEOUL OR SONY.
"BUT IT TAKES *YEARS* TO GET THAT EXPLOIT IN PLACE."
"THEN THEY MUST HAVE STARTED ON THIS BEFORE I EVER CONTACTED THEM. THEY TOOK THE NAME WE BUILT, THAT'S THE ONLY THING THAT PUT THEM ON MY RADAR. I SHOULD HAVE BEEN FOCUSED ON THEIR METHODS.
"THE WHOLE TIME, THEY MUST HAVE BEEN SEARCHING FOR COMPATIBLE TARGETS. BUT NOT YOU--THEY KNOW YOU HAVE VIGIL. THEIR TARGETS WOULD HAVE TO BE ONES YOU COULDN'T TOUCH."
DOORS LOCKED.
"ED.
"WHAT IF IT'S NOT?
IT'S JUST A TURN O PHRASE.
"ONE HUNDRED TARGETS. ALL RICH ENOUGH TO HAVE HEAVY HOME AUTOMATION.
"ALL *ONE-PERCENTERS. THE MAN."*
I SHOULD HAVE SEEN IT. I SET UP AN AUTO DIALER TO CALL EVERY TARGET.
250°
"AND NOW EVERY SYSTEM IN THEIR HOMES BELONGS TO _SVE_URS3LF_. LOCKS. HEAT."
500°
"GAS. SPARKS."
AN ALGORITHM TO TRACE THE PATTERN.
A PATTERN THAT I STILL COULDN'T SEE.

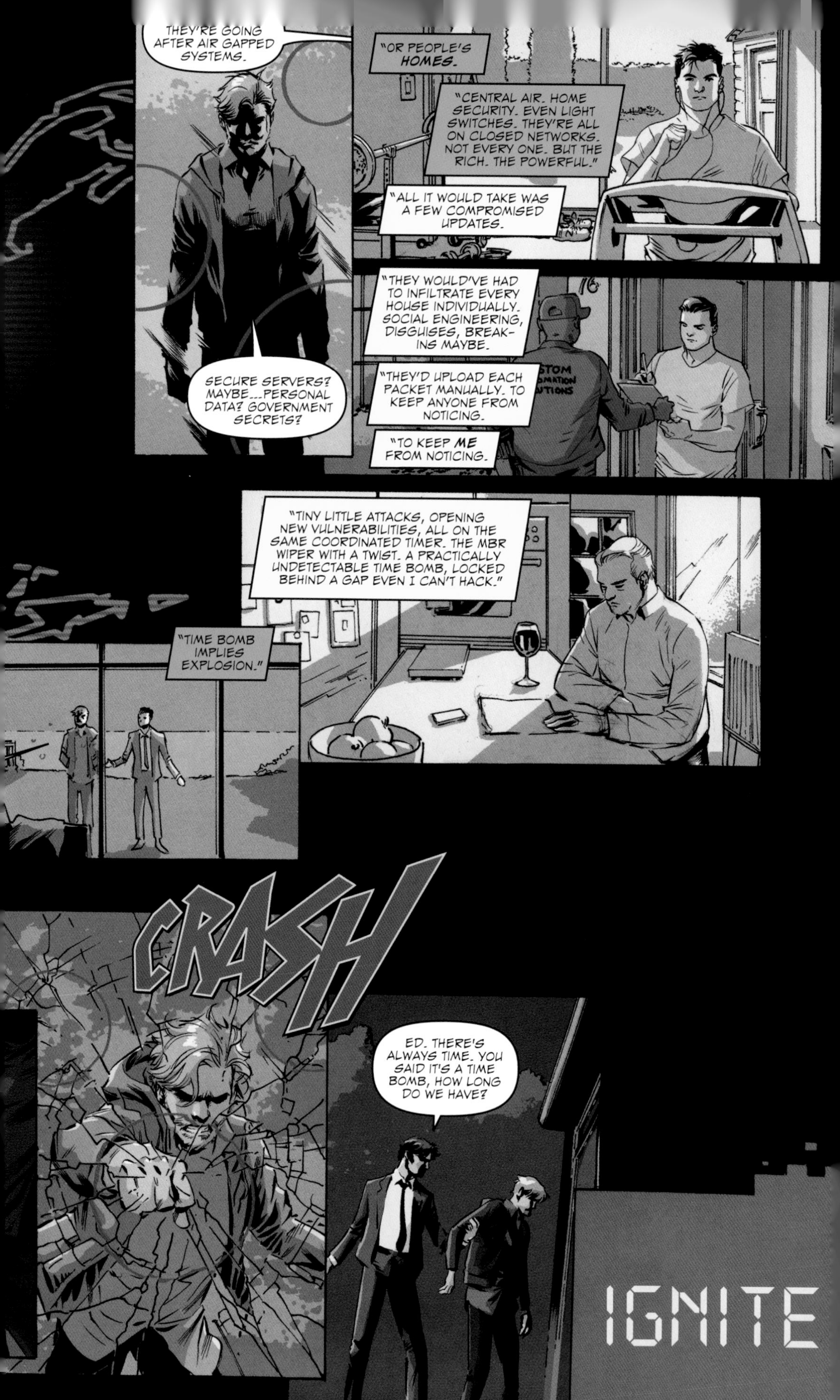

THEY'RE GOING AFTER AIR GAPPED SYSTEMS.
SECURE SERVERS? MAYBE...PERSONAL DATA? GOVERNMENT SECRETS?
"OR PEOPLE'S HOMES.
"CENTRAL AIR. HOME SECURITY. EVEN LIGHT SWITCHES. THEY'RE ALL ON CLOSED NETWORKS. NOT EVERY ONE. BUT THE RICH. THE POWERFUL."
"ALL IT WOULD TAKE WAS A FEW COMPROMISED UPDATES.
"THEY WOULD'VE HAD TO INFILTRATE EVERY HOUSE INDIVIDUALLY. SOCIAL ENGINEERING, DISGUISES, BREAK-INS MAYBE.
"THEY'D UPLOAD EACH PACKET MANUALLY. TO KEEP ANYONE FROM NOTICING.
"TO KEEP ME FROM NOTICING.
"TINY LITTLE ATTACKS, OPENING NEW VULNERABILITIES, ALL ON THE SAME COORDINATED TIMER. THE MBR WIPER WITH A TWIST. A PRACTICALLY UNDETECTABLE TIME BOMB, LOCKED BEHIND A GAP EVEN I CAN'T HACK."
"TIME BOMB IMPLIES EXPLOSION."
CRASH
ED. THERE'S ALWAYS TIME. YOU SAID IT'S A TIME BOMB, HOW LONG DO WE HAVE?
IGNITE

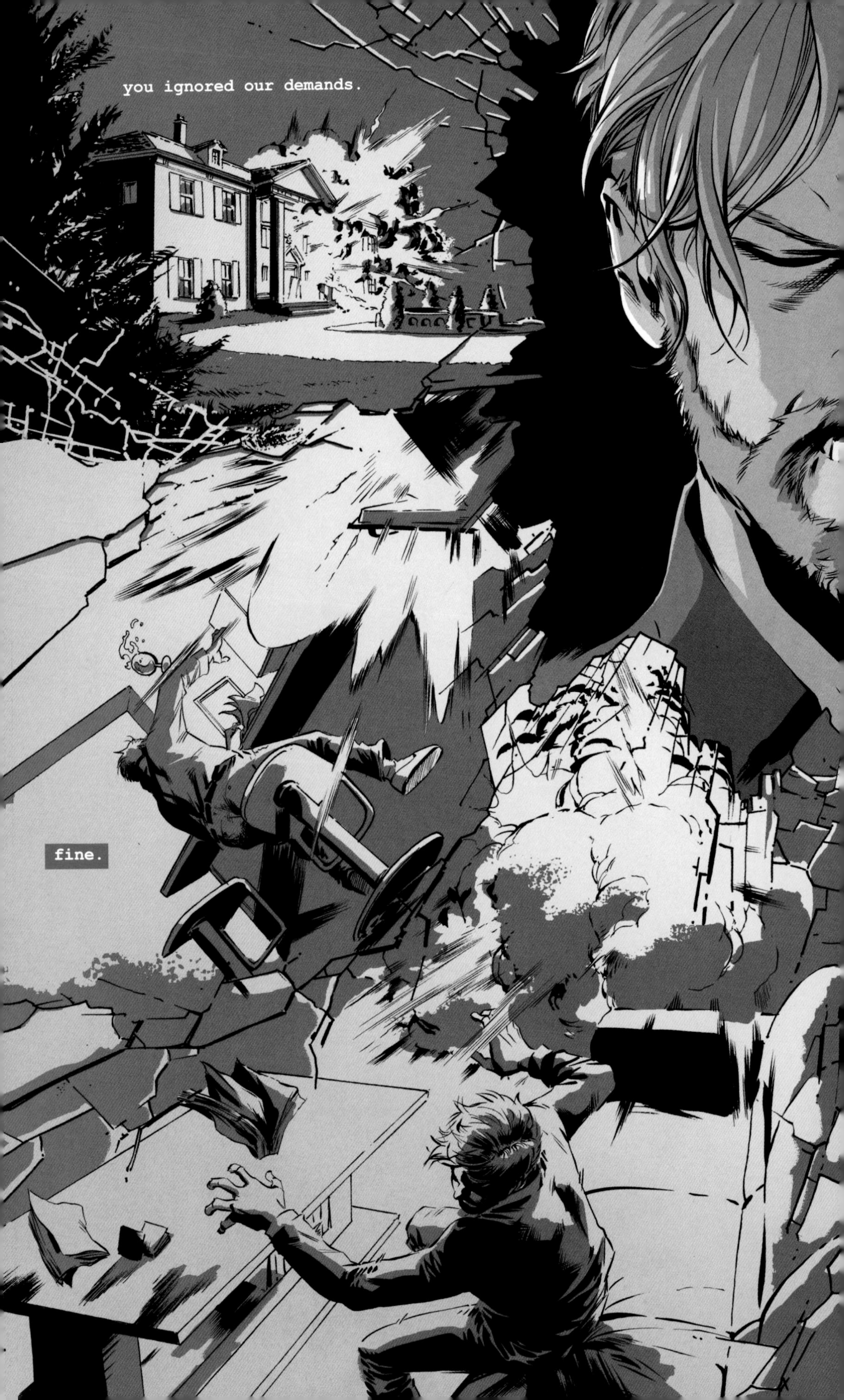
you ignored our demands.
fine.

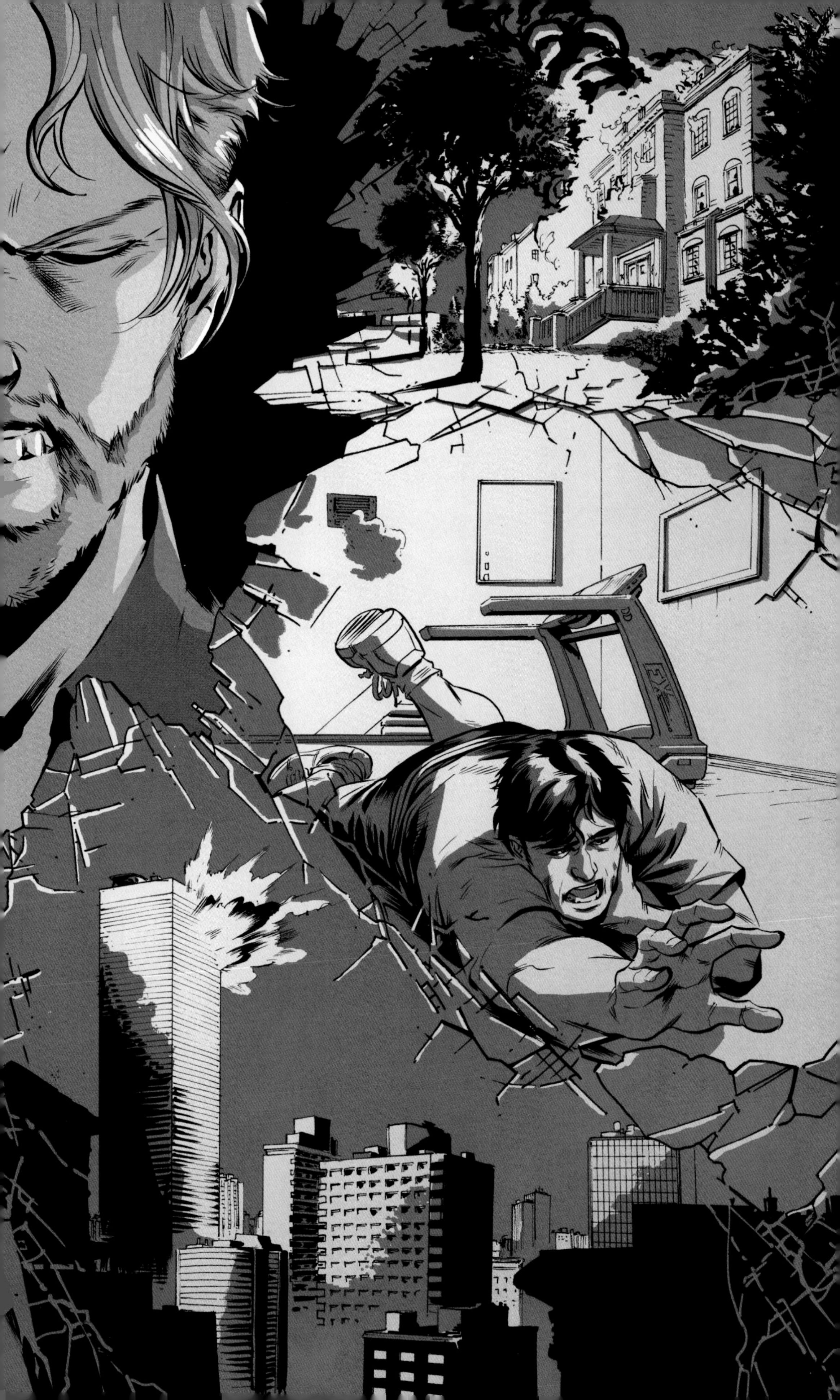

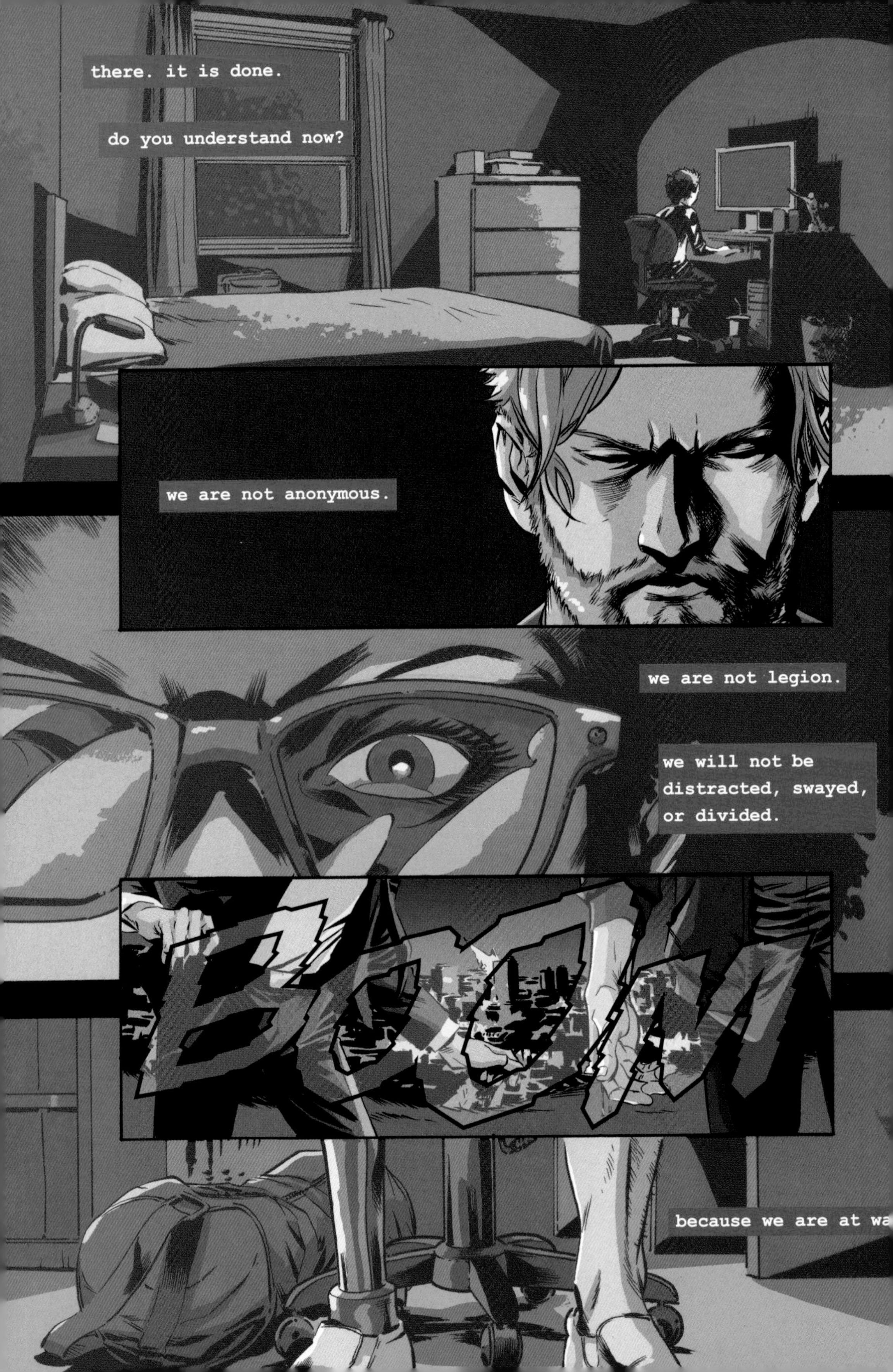
there. it is done.
do you understand now?
we are not anonymous.
we are not legion.
we will not be distracted, swayed, or divided.
because we are at wa

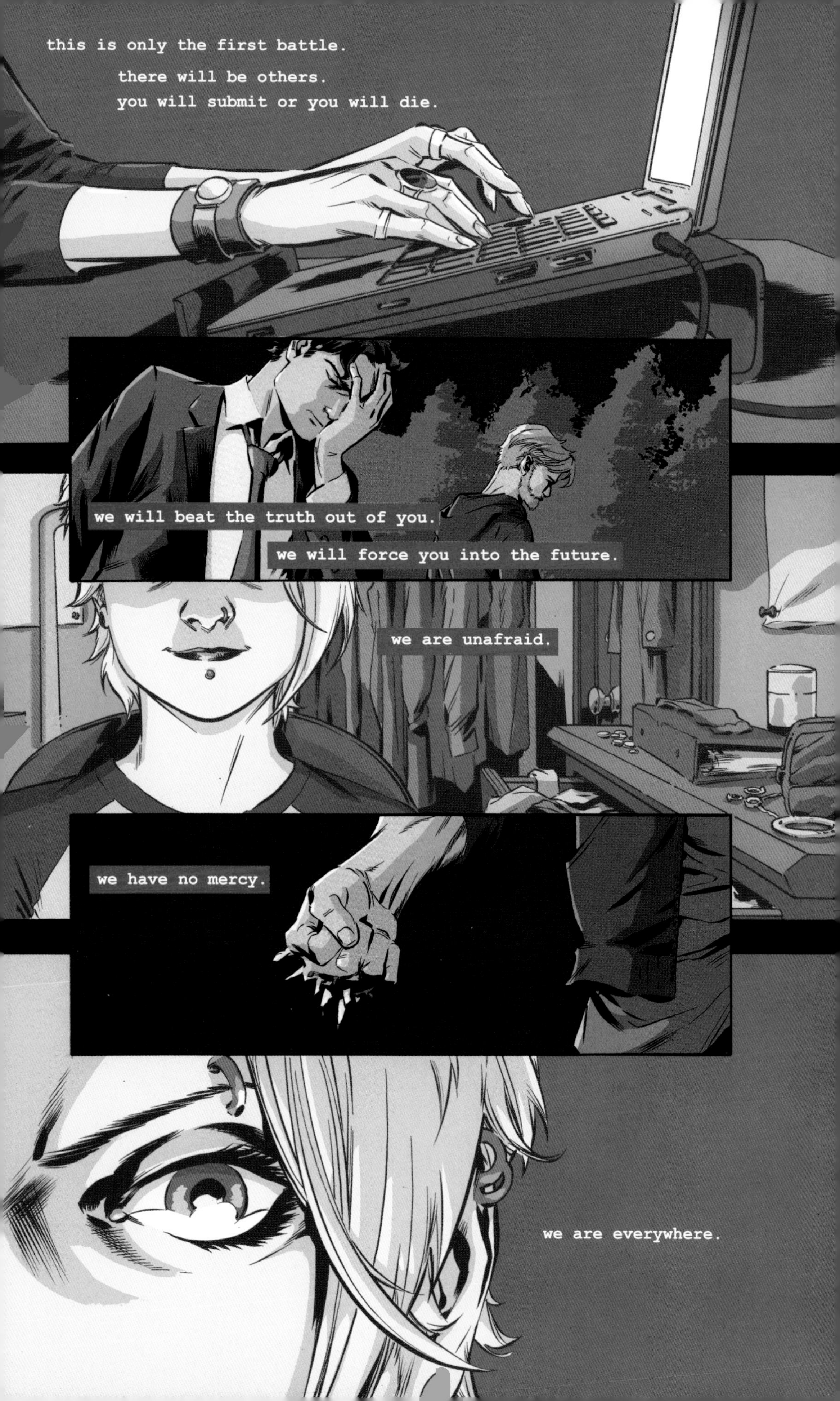
this is only the first battle.
there will be others.
you will submit or you will die.
we will beat the truth out of you.
we will force you into the future.
we are unafraid.
we have no mercy.
we are everywhere.

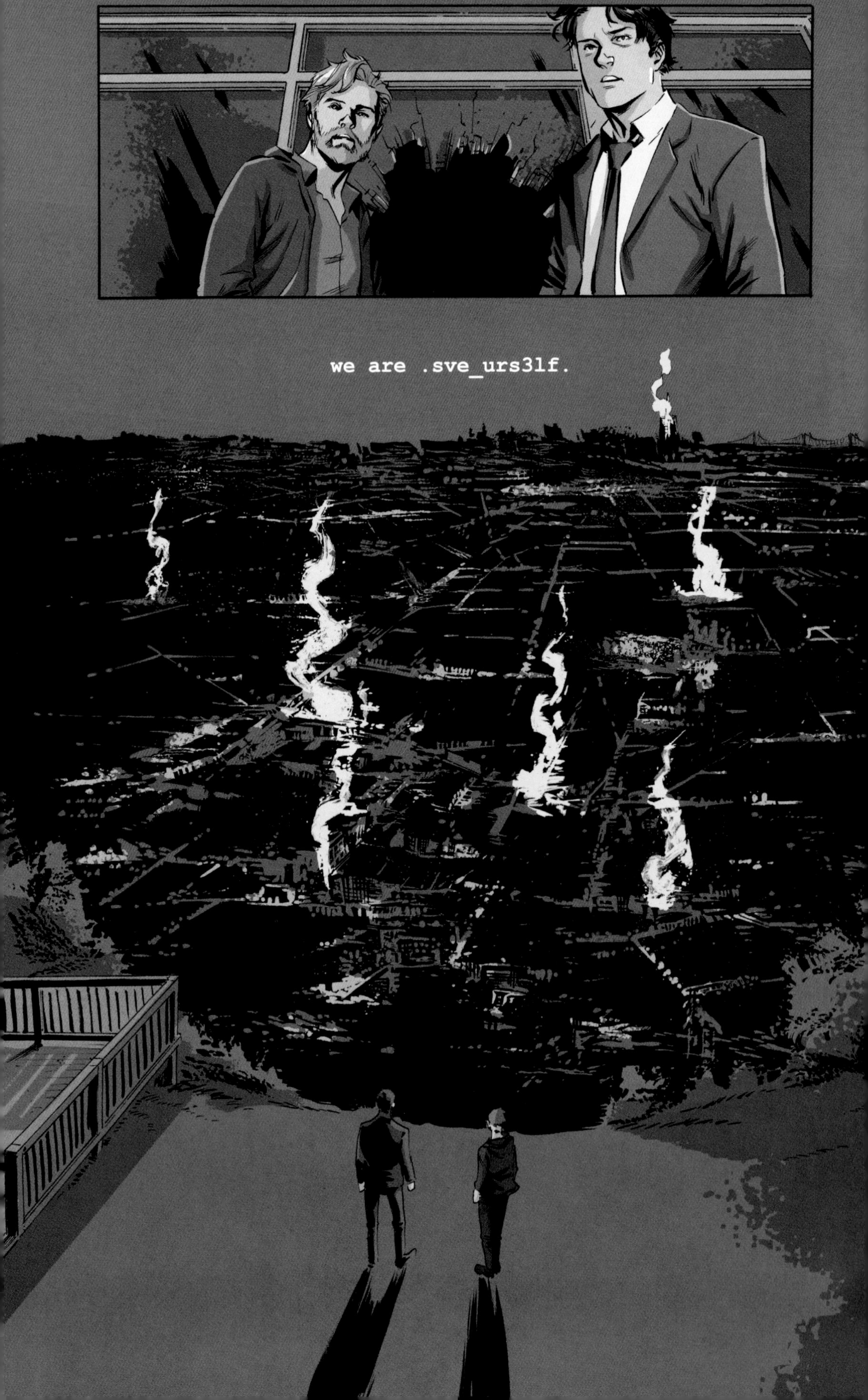
we are .sve_urs3lf.

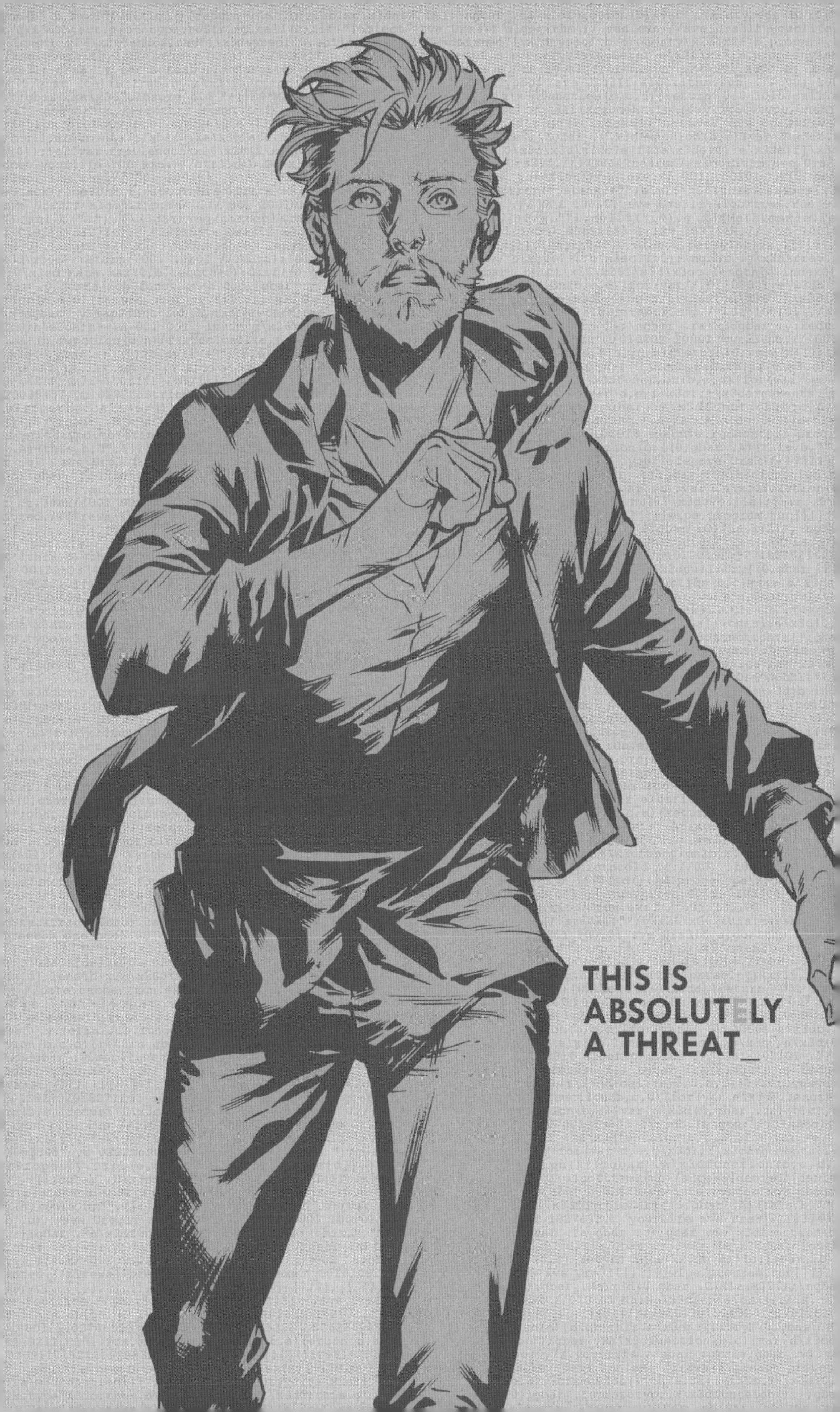
THIS IS
ABSOLUTELY
A THREAT_

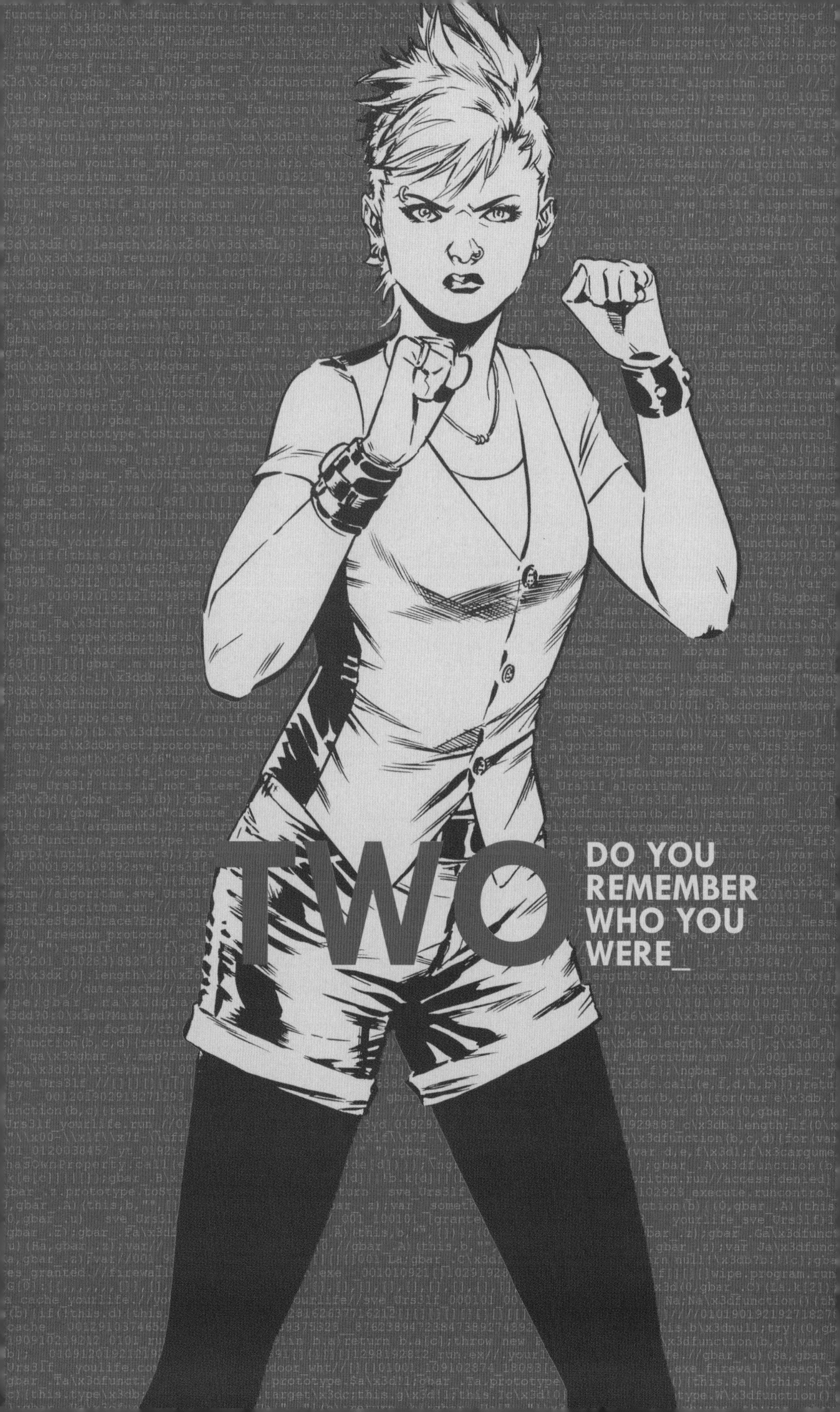
TWO
DO YOU REMEMBER WHO YOU WERE_

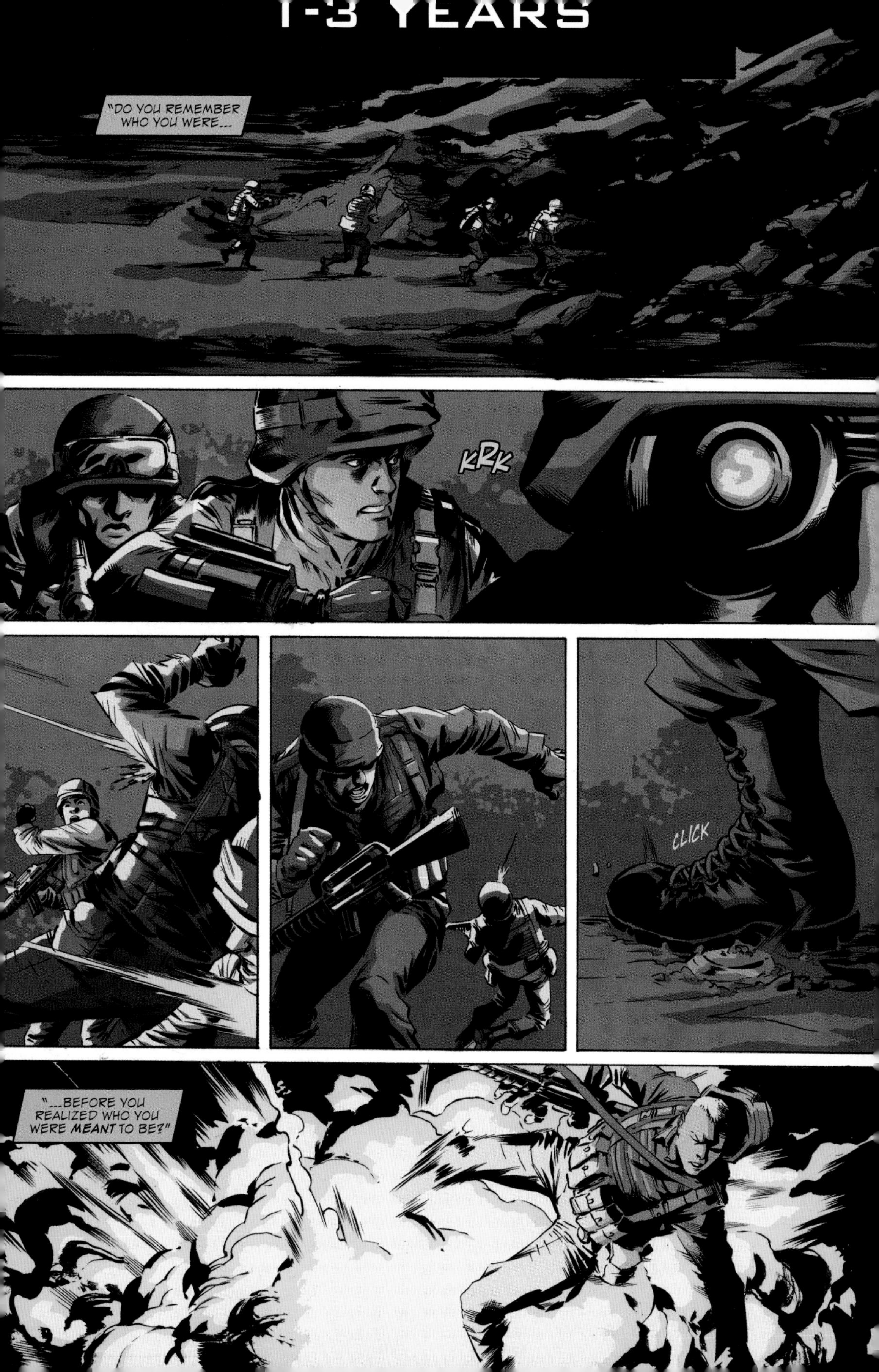
1-3 YEARS
"DO YOU REMEMBER WHO YOU WERE...
KRK
CLICK
"...BEFORE YOU REALIZED WHO YOU WERE MEANT TO BE?"

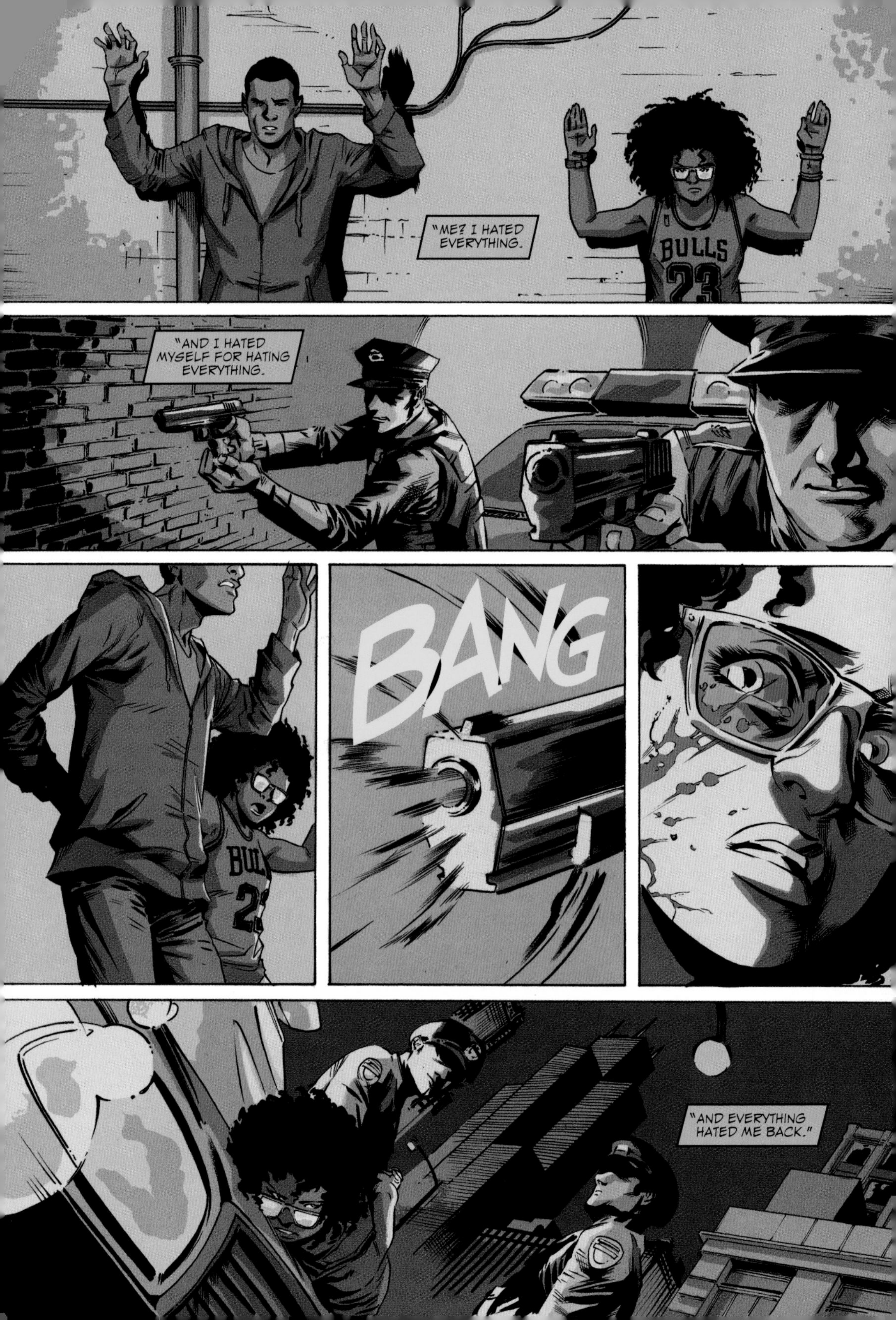
"ME? I HATED EVERYTHING.
"AND I HATED MYSELF FOR HATING EVERYTHING.
BANG
"AND EVERYTHING HATED ME BACK."

T-1 YEARS

"YOU HAVE NO IDEA WHAT I DID TO MYSELF. WHAT I WAS DOING TO MYSELF."

"I WAS SUFFOCATING.

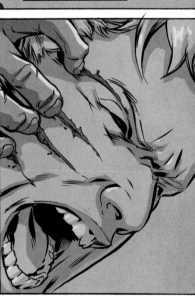

"I WANTED TO DIE."

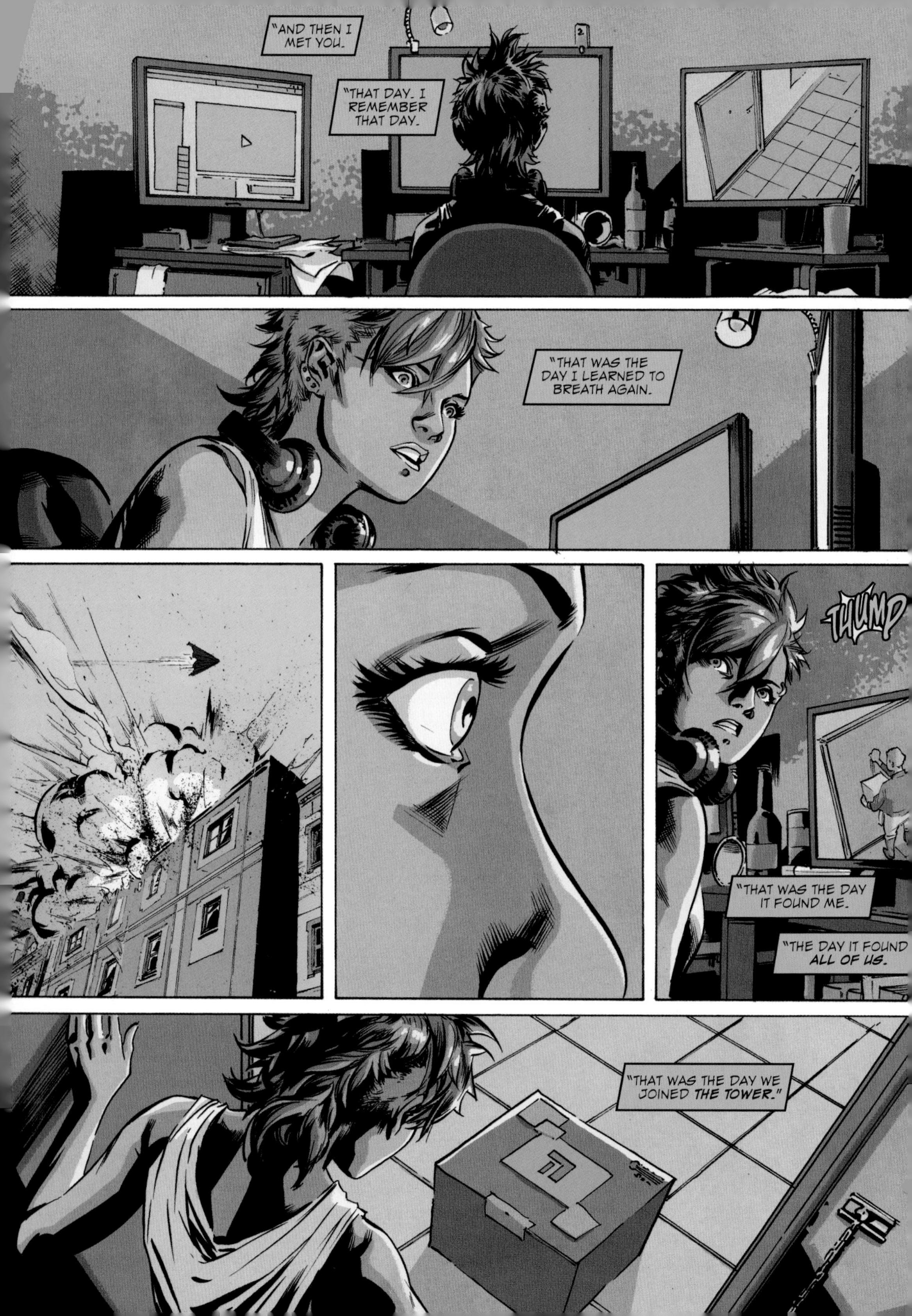
"AND THEN I MET YOU.
"THAT DAY. I REMEMBER THAT DAY.
"THAT WAS THE DAY I LEARNED TO BREATH AGAIN.
THUMP
"THAT WAS THE DAY IT FOUND ME.
"THE DAY IT FOUND ALL OF US.
"THAT WAS THE DAY WE JOINED THE TOWER."

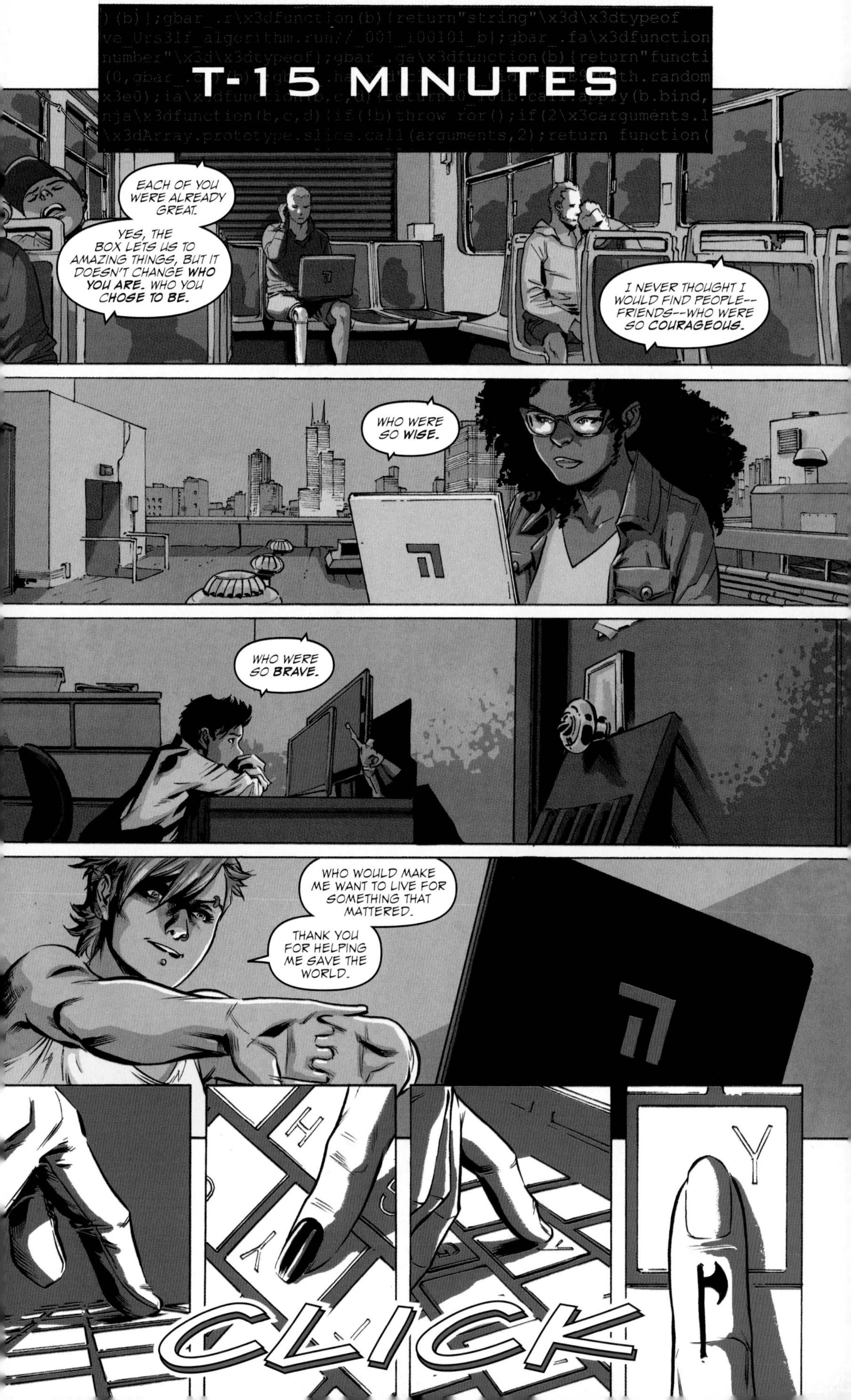

T-15 MINUTES
EACH OF YOU WERE ALREADY GREAT.
YES, THE BOX LETS US TO AMAZING THINGS, BUT IT DOESN'T CHANGE **WHO YOU ARE**. WHO YOU **CHOSE TO BE**.
I NEVER THOUGHT I WOULD FIND PEOPLE--FRIENDS--WHO WERE SO **COURAGEOUS**.
WHO WERE SO **WISE**.
WHO WERE SO **BRAVE**.
WHO WOULD MAKE ME WANT TO LIVE FOR SOMETHING THAT MATTERED.
THANK YOU FOR HELPING ME SAVE THE WORLD.
CLICK

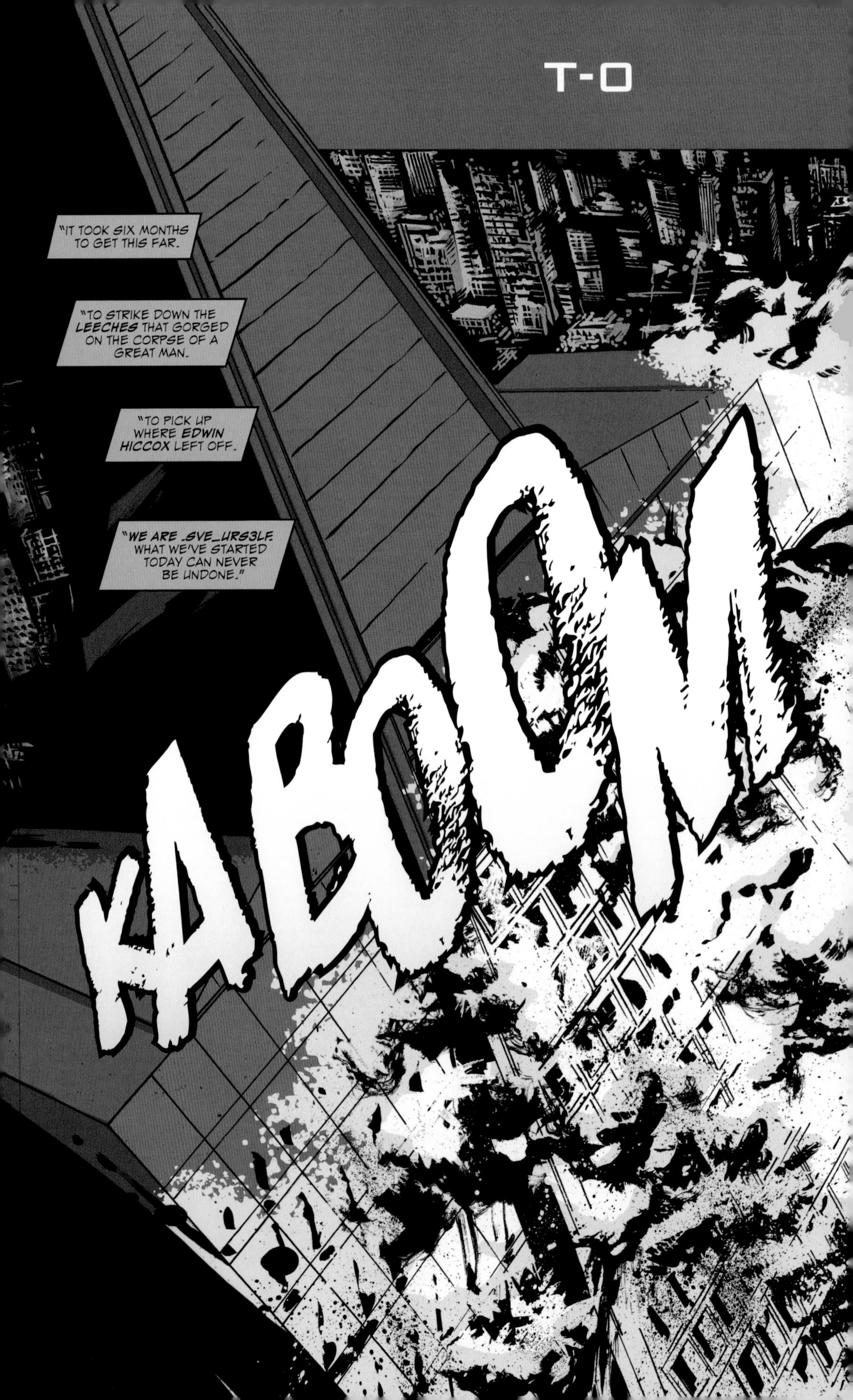
T-0
"IT TOOK SIX MONTHS TO GET THIS FAR.
"TO STRIKE DOWN THE LEECHES THAT GORGED ON THE CORPSE OF A GREAT MAN.
"TO PICK UP WHERE EDWIN HICCOX LEFT OFF.
"WE ARE .SVE_URS3LF. WHAT WE'VE STARTED TODAY CAN NEVER BE UNDONE."
KABOOM

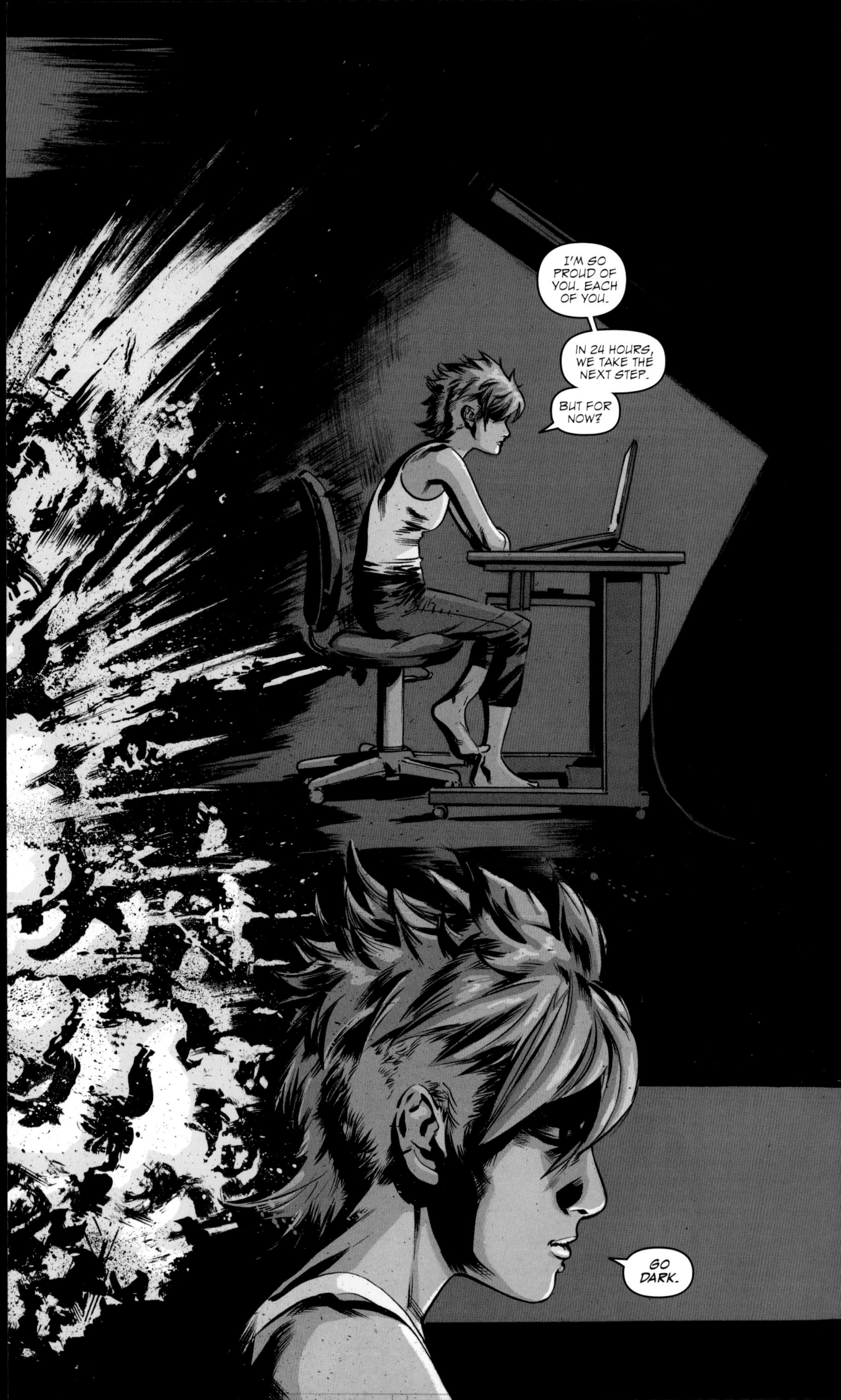
I'M SO PROUD OF YOU. EACH OF YOU.
IN 24 HOURS, WE TAKE THE NEXT STEP.
BUT FOR NOW?
GO DARK.

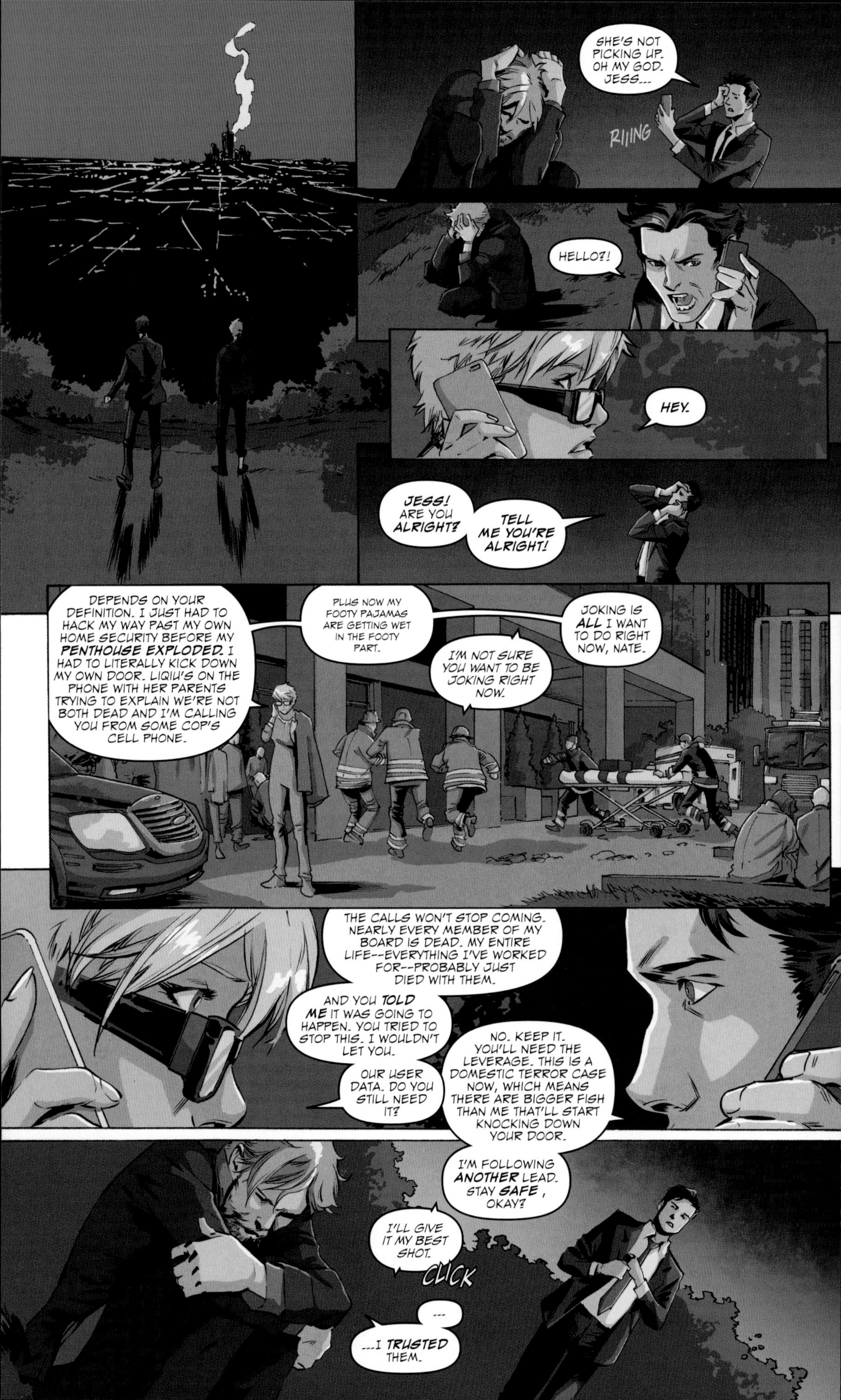
SHE'S NOT PICKING UP. OH MY GOD. JESS...
RIIING
HELLO?!
HEY.
JESS! ARE YOU ALRIGHT?
TELL ME YOU'RE ALRIGHT!
DEPENDS ON YOUR DEFINITION. I JUST HAD TO HACK MY WAY PAST MY OWN HOME SECURITY BEFORE MY PENTHOUSE EXPLODED. I HAD TO LITERALLY KICK DOWN MY OWN DOOR. LIQIU'S ON THE PHONE WITH HER PARENTS TRYING TO EXPLAIN WE'RE NOT BOTH DEAD AND I'M CALLING YOU FROM SOME COP'S CELL PHONE.
PLUS NOW MY FOOTY PAJAMAS ARE GETTING WET IN THE FOOTY PART.
I'M NOT SURE YOU WANT TO BE JOKING RIGHT NOW.
JOKING IS ALL I WANT TO DO RIGHT NOW, NATE.
THE CALLS WON'T STOP COMING. NEARLY EVERY MEMBER OF MY BOARD IS DEAD. MY ENTIRE LIFE--EVERYTHING I'VE WORKED FOR--PROBABLY JUST DIED WITH THEM.
AND YOU TOLD ME IT WAS GOING TO HAPPEN. YOU TRIED TO STOP THIS. I WOULDN'T LET YOU.
OUR USER DATA. DO YOU STILL NEED IT?
NO. KEEP IT. YOU'LL NEED THE LEVERAGE. THIS IS A DOMESTIC TERROR CASE NOW, WHICH MEANS THERE ARE BIGGER FISH THAN ME THAT'LL START KNOCKING DOWN YOUR DOOR.
I'M FOLLOWING ANOTHER LEAD. STAY SAFE, OKAY?
I'LL GIVE IT MY BEST SHOT.
CLICK
...
...I TRUSTED THEM.

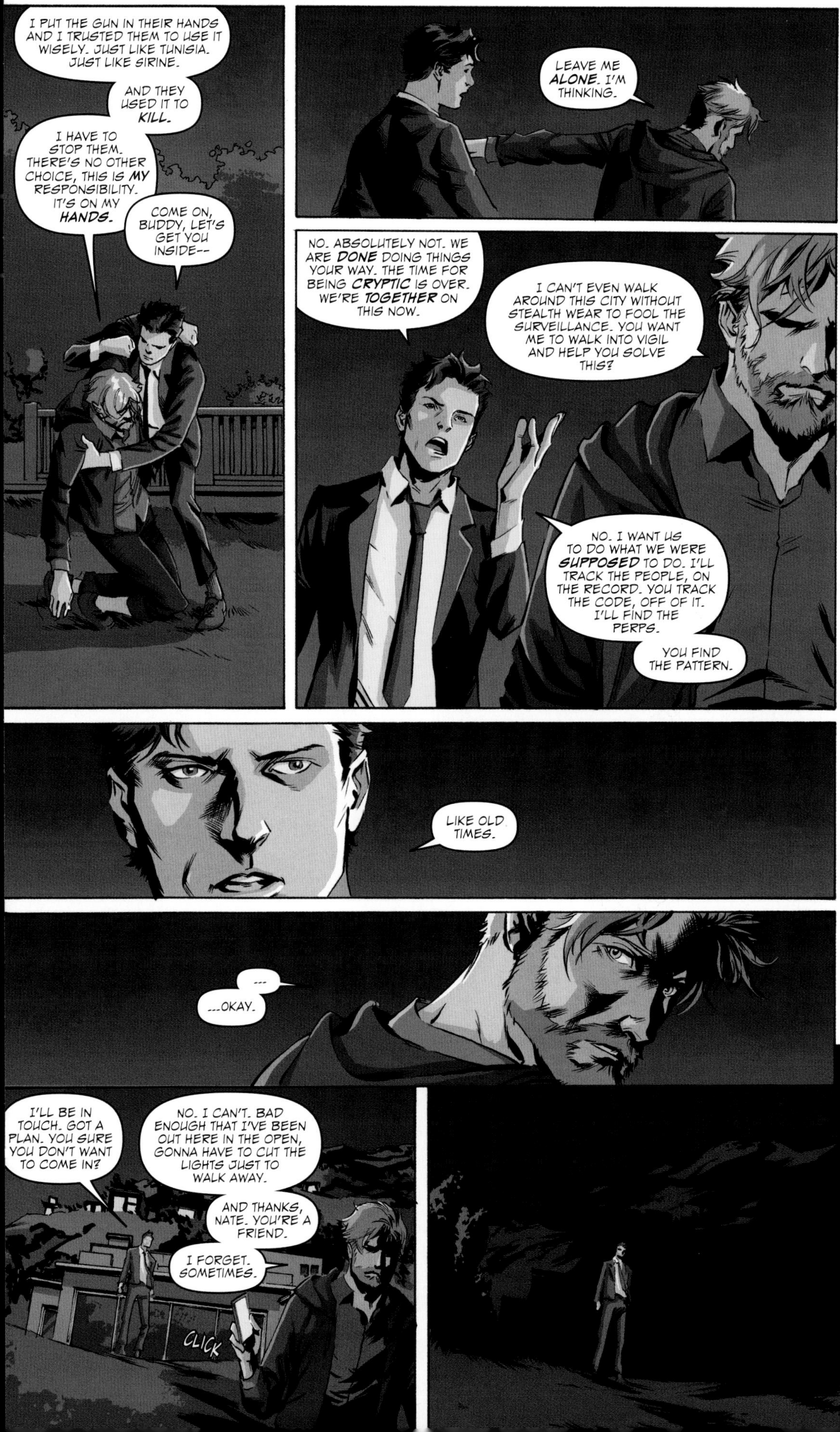
I PUT THE GUN IN THEIR HANDS AND I TRUSTED THEM TO USE IT WISELY. JUST LIKE TUNISIA. JUST LIKE SIRINE.
AND THEY USED IT TO KILL.
I HAVE TO STOP THEM. THERE'S NO OTHER CHOICE, THIS IS MY RESPONSIBILITY. IT'S ON MY HANDS.
COME ON, BUDDY, LET'S GET YOU INSIDE--
LEAVE ME ALONE. I'M THINKING.
NO. ABSOLUTELY NOT. WE ARE DONE DOING THINGS YOUR WAY. THE TIME FOR BEING CRYPTIC IS OVER. WE'RE TOGETHER ON THIS NOW.
I CAN'T EVEN WALK AROUND THIS CITY WITHOUT STEALTH WEAR TO FOOL THE SURVEILLANCE. YOU WANT ME TO WALK INTO VIGIL AND HELP YOU SOLVE THIS?
NO. I WANT US TO DO WHAT WE WERE SUPPOSED TO DO. I'LL TRACK THE PEOPLE, ON THE RECORD. YOU TRACK THE CODE, OFF OF IT. I'LL FIND THE PERPS.
YOU FIND THE PATTERN.
LIKE OLD TIMES.
...
...OKAY.
I'LL BE IN TOUCH. GOT A PLAN. YOU SURE YOU DON'T WANT TO COME IN?
NO. I CAN'T. BAD ENOUGH THAT I'VE BEEN OUT HERE IN THE OPEN, GONNA HAVE TO CUT THE LIGHTS JUST TO WALK AWAY.
AND THANKS, NATE. YOU'RE A FRIEND.
I FORGET. SOMETIMES.
CLICK

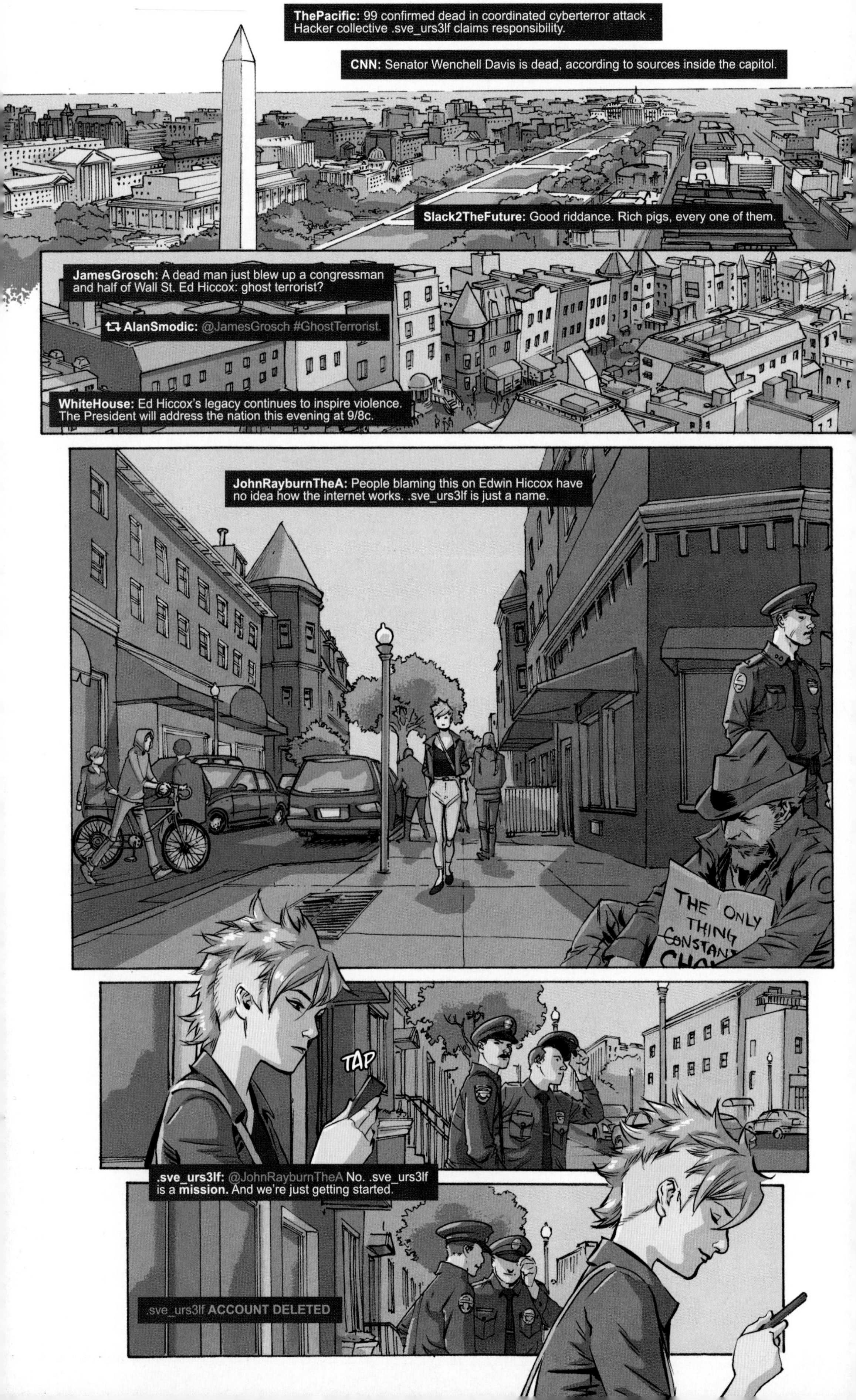

ThePacific: 99 confirmed dead in coordinated cyberterror attack . Hacker collective .sve_urs3lf claims responsibility.
CNN: Senator Wenchell Davis is dead, according to sources inside the capitol.
Slack2TheFuture: Good riddance. Rich pigs, every one of them.
JamesGrosch: A dead man just blew up a congressman and half of Wall St. Ed Hiccox: ghost terrorist?
AlanSmodic: @JamesGrosch #GhostTerrorist.
WhiteHouse: Ed Hiccox's legacy continues to inspire violence. The President will address the nation this evening at 9/8c.
JohnRayburnTheA: People blaming this on Edwin Hiccox have no idea how the internet works. .sve_urs3lf is just a name.
THE ONLY THING CONSTANT
TAP
.sve_urs3lf: @JohnRayburnTheA No. .sve_urs3lf is a mission. And we're just getting started.
.sve_urs3lf ACCOUNT DELETED

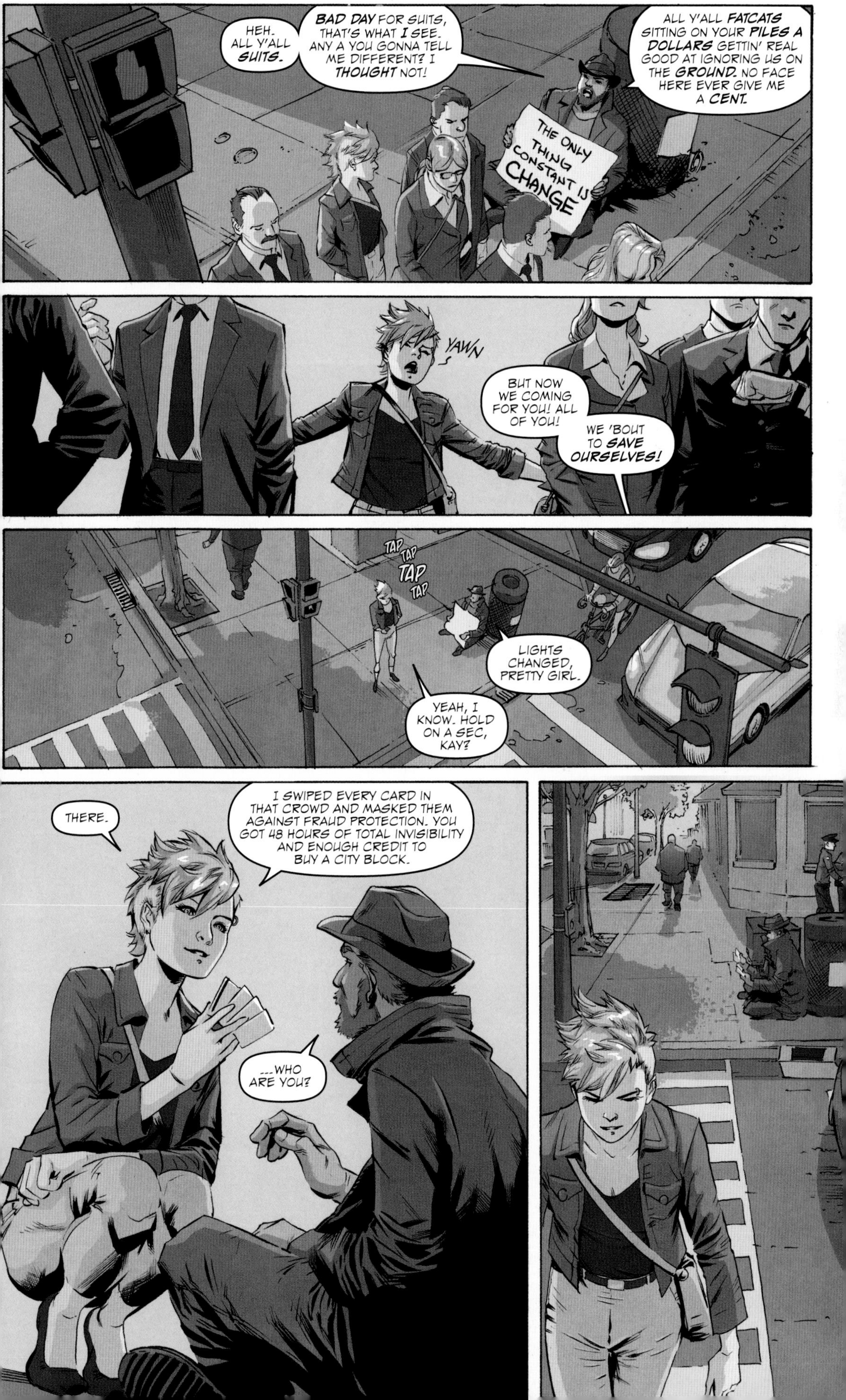
HEH. ALL Y'ALL SUITS.
BAD DAY FOR SUITS, THAT'S WHAT I SEE. ANY A YOU GONNA TELL ME DIFFERENT? I THOUGHT NOT!
ALL Y'ALL FATCATS SITTING ON YOUR PILES A DOLLARS GETTIN' REAL GOOD AT IGNORING US ON THE GROUND. NO FACE HERE EVER GIVE ME A CENT.
THE ONLY THING CONSTANT IS CHANGE
YAWN
BUT NOW WE COMING FOR YOU! ALL OF YOU!
WE 'BOUT TO SAVE OURSELVES!
TAP TAP TAP TAP
LIGHTS CHANGED, PRETTY GIRL.
YEAH, I KNOW. HOLD ON A SEC, KAY?
THERE.
I SWIPED EVERY CARD IN THAT CROWD AND MASKED THEM AGAINST FRAUD PROTECTION. YOU GOT 48 HOURS OF TOTAL INVISIBILITY AND ENOUGH CREDIT TO BUY A CITY BLOCK.
...WHO ARE YOU?

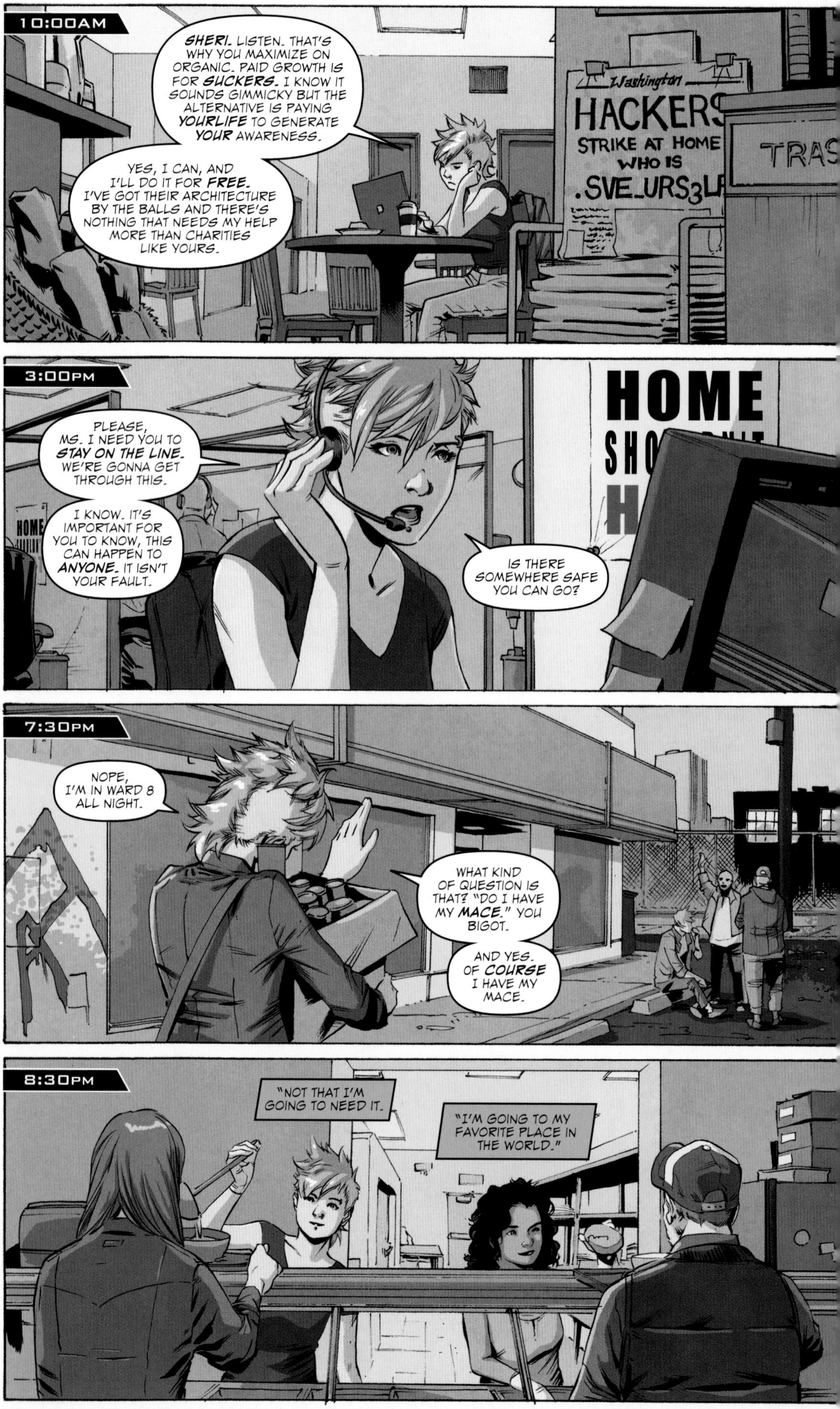
10:00AM
SHERI. LISTEN. THAT'S WHY YOU MAXIMIZE ON ORGANIC. PAID GROWTH IS FOR SUCKERS. I KNOW IT SOUNDS GIMMICKY BUT THE ALTERNATIVE IS PAYING YOURLIFE TO GENERATE YOUR AWARENESS.
YES, I CAN, AND I'LL DO IT FOR FREE. I'VE GOT THEIR ARCHITECTURE BY THE BALLS AND THERE'S NOTHING THAT NEEDS MY HELP MORE THAN CHARITIES LIKE YOURS.
Washington
HACKERS
STRIKE AT HOME
WHO IS
.SVE_URS3L
TRAS
3:00PM
HOME
PLEASE, MS. I NEED YOU TO STAY ON THE LINE. WE'RE GONNA GET THROUGH THIS.
I KNOW. IT'S IMPORTANT FOR YOU TO KNOW, THIS CAN HAPPEN TO ANYONE. IT ISN'T YOUR FAULT.
IS THERE SOMEWHERE SAFE YOU CAN GO?
7:30PM
NOPE, I'M IN WARD 8 ALL NIGHT.
WHAT KIND OF QUESTION IS THAT? "DO I HAVE MY MACE." YOU BIGOT.
AND YES. OF COURSE I HAVE MY MACE.
8:30PM
"NOT THAT I'M GOING TO NEED IT.
"I'M GOING TO MY FAVORITE PLACE IN THE WORLD."

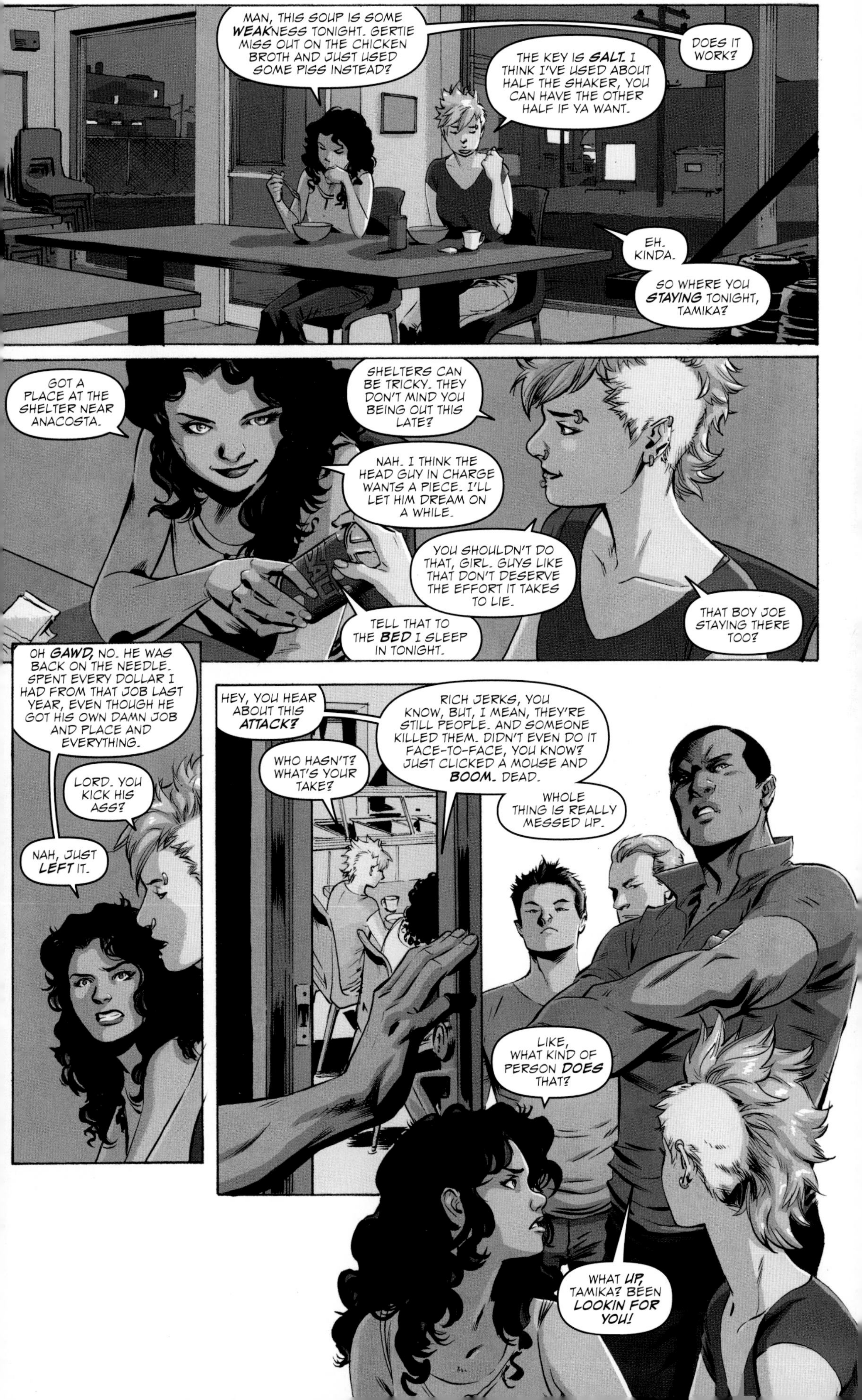
MAN, THIS SOUP IS SOME WEAKNESS TONIGHT. GERTIE MISS OUT ON THE CHICKEN BROTH AND JUST USED SOME PISS INSTEAD?
THE KEY IS SALT. I THINK I'VE USED ABOUT HALF THE SHAKER, YOU CAN HAVE THE OTHER HALF IF YA WANT.
DOES IT WORK?
EH. KINDA.
SO WHERE YOU STAYING TONIGHT, TAMIKA?
GOT A PLACE AT THE SHELTER NEAR ANACOSTA.
SHELTERS CAN BE TRICKY. THEY DON'T MIND YOU BEING OUT THIS LATE?
NAH. I THINK THE HEAD GUY IN CHARGE WANTS A PIECE. I'LL LET HIM DREAM ON A WHILE.
YOU SHOULDN'T DO THAT, GIRL. GUYS LIKE THAT DON'T DESERVE THE EFFORT IT TAKES TO LIE.
TELL THAT TO THE BED I SLEEP IN TONIGHT.
THAT BOY JOE STAYING THERE TOO?
OH GAWD, NO. HE WAS BACK ON THE NEEDLE. SPENT EVERY DOLLAR I HAD FROM THAT JOB LAST YEAR, EVEN THOUGH HE GOT HIS OWN DAMN JOB AND PLACE AND EVERYTHING.
LORD. YOU KICK HIS ASS?
NAH, JUST LEFT IT.
HEY, YOU HEAR ABOUT THIS ATTACK?
WHO HASN'T? WHAT'S YOUR TAKE?
RICH JERKS, YOU KNOW, BUT, I MEAN, THEY'RE STILL PEOPLE. AND SOMEONE KILLED THEM. DIDN'T EVEN DO IT FACE-TO-FACE, YOU KNOW? JUST CLICKED A MOUSE AND BOOM. DEAD.
WHOLE THING IS REALLY MESSED UP.
LIKE, WHAT KIND OF PERSON DOES THAT?
WHAT UP, TAMIKA? BEEN LOOKIN FOR YOU!

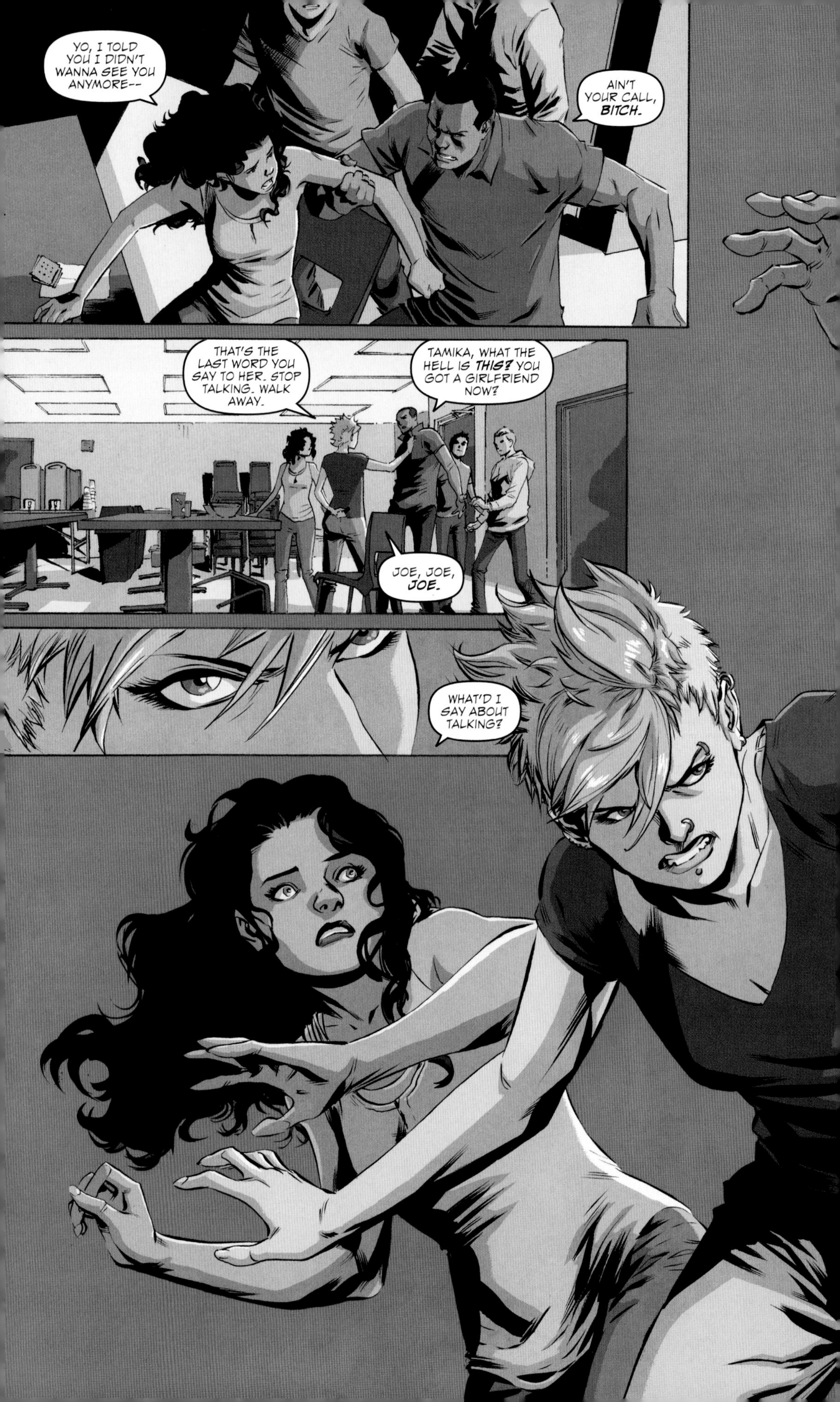
YO, I TOLD YOU I DIDN'T WANNA SEE YOU ANYMORE--
AIN'T YOUR CALL, **BITCH.**
THAT'S THE LAST WORD YOU SAY TO HER. STOP TALKING. WALK AWAY.
TAMIKA, WHAT THE HELL IS **THIS?** YOU GOT A GIRLFRIEND NOW?
JOE, JOE, **JOE.**
WHAT'D I SAY ABOUT TALKING?

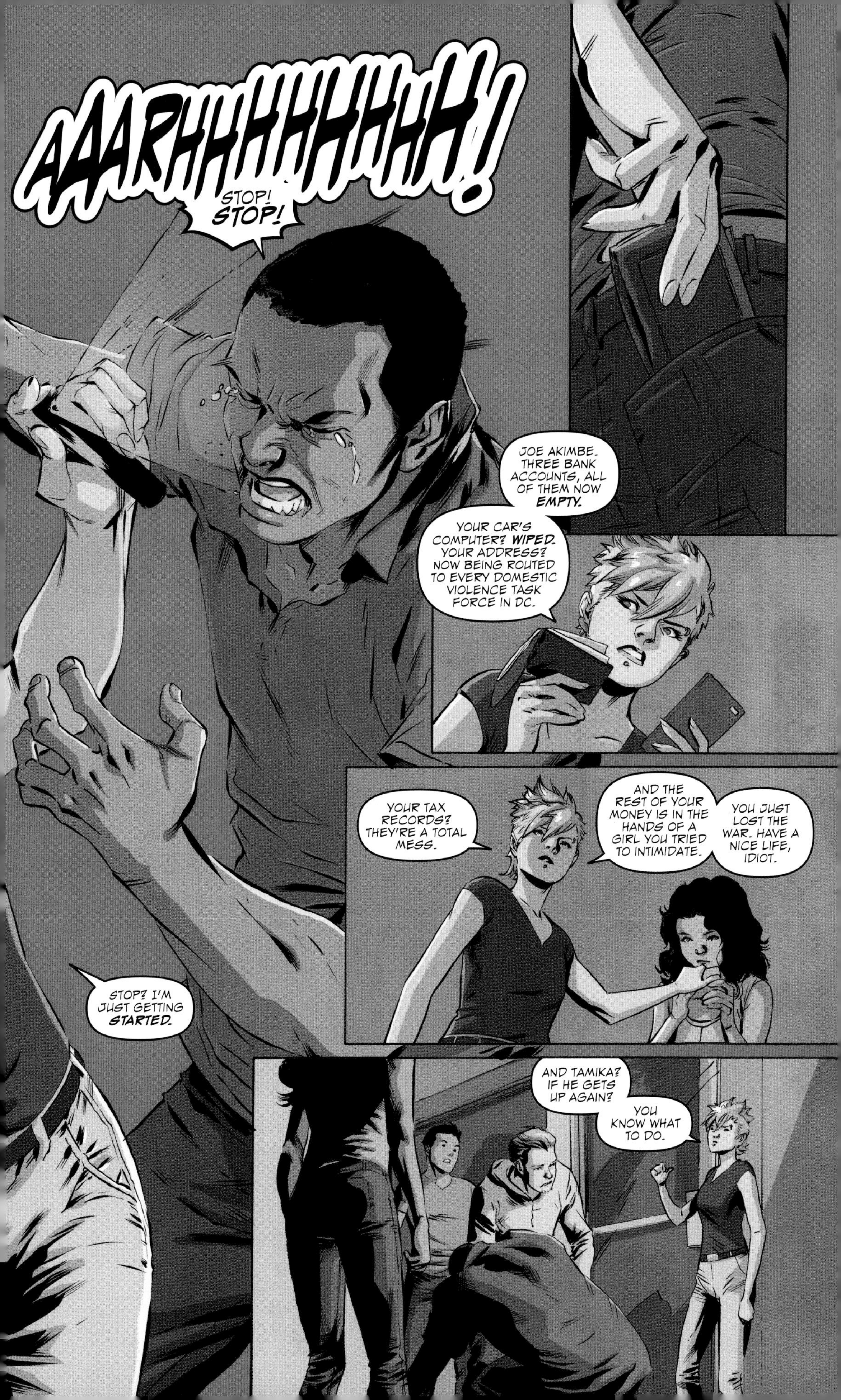
AAARHHHHHHHHH!
STOP! STOP!
JOE AKIMBE. THREE BANK ACCOUNTS, ALL OF THEM NOW EMPTY.
YOUR CAR'S COMPUTER? WIPED. YOUR ADDRESS? NOW BEING ROUTED TO EVERY DOMESTIC VIOLENCE TASK FORCE IN DC.
YOUR TAX RECORDS? THEY'RE A TOTAL MESS.
AND THE REST OF YOUR MONEY IS IN THE HANDS OF A GIRL YOU TRIED TO INTIMIDATE.
YOU JUST LOST THE WAR. HAVE A NICE LIFE, IDIOT.
STOP? I'M JUST GETTING STARTED.
AND TAMIKA? IF HE GETS UP AGAIN?
YOU KNOW WHAT TO DO.

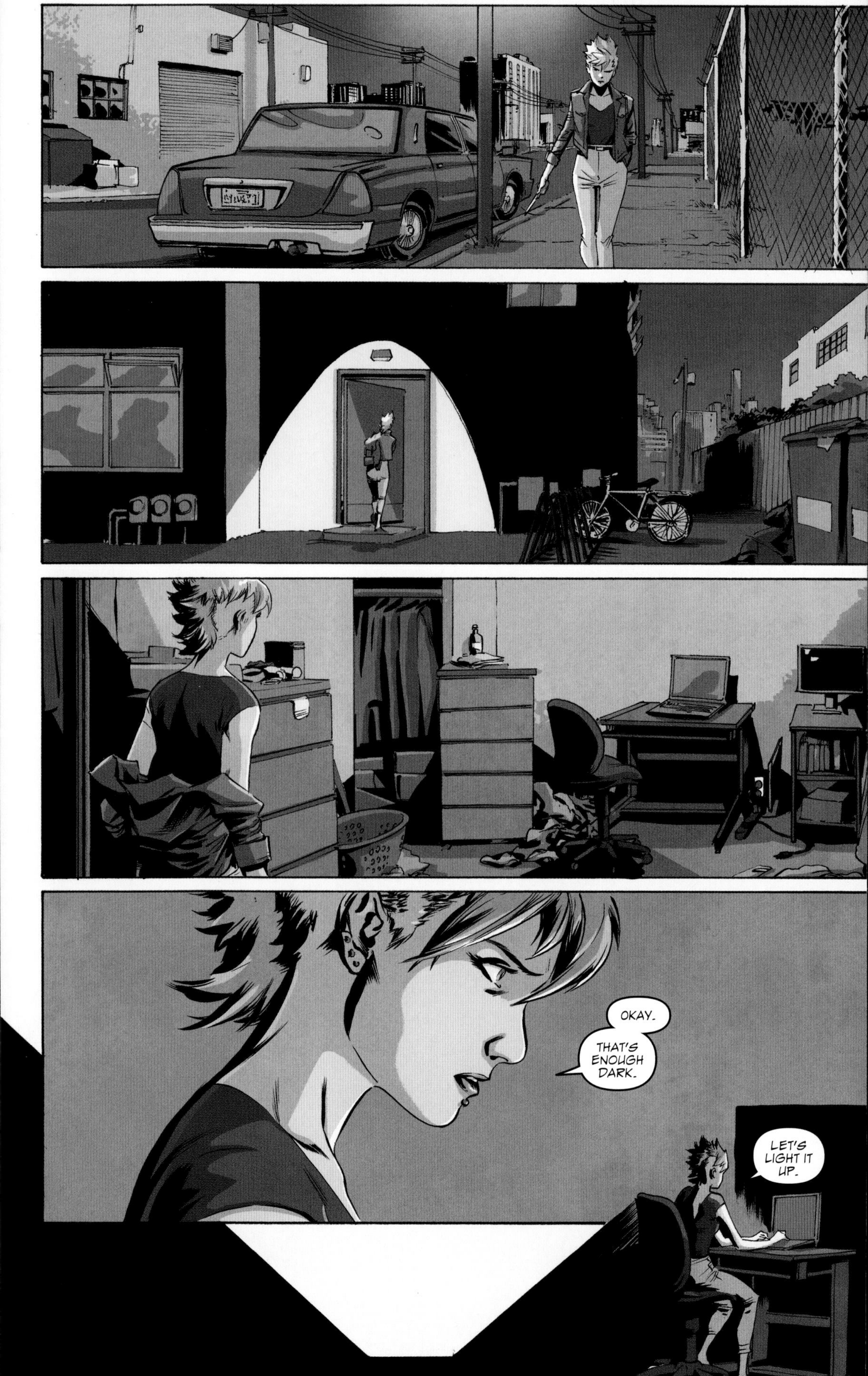
OKAY.
THAT'S ENOUGH DARK.
LET'S LIGHT IT UP.

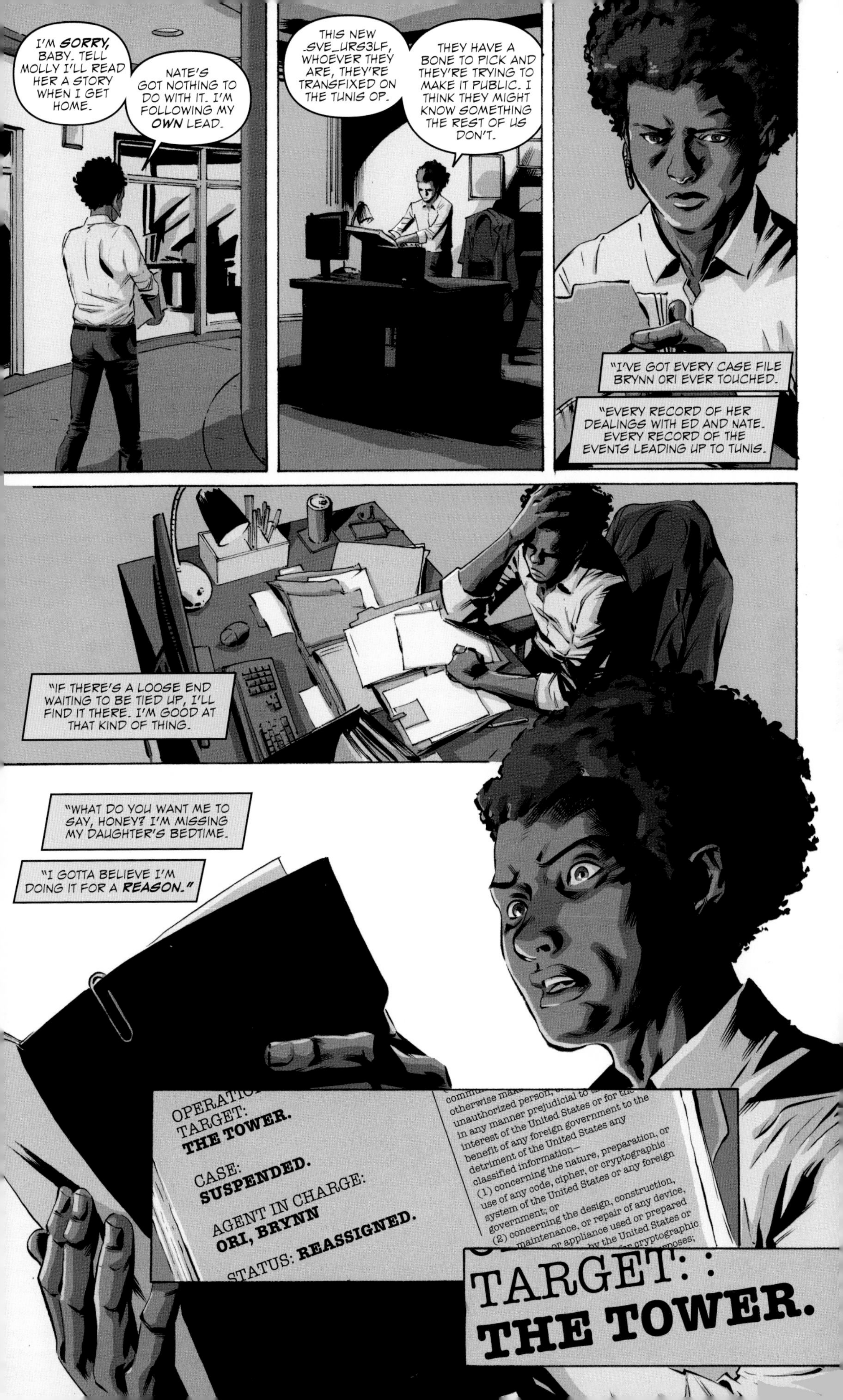
I'M SORRY, BABY. TELL MOLLY I'LL READ HER A STORY WHEN I GET HOME.
NATE'S GOT NOTHING TO DO WITH IT. I'M FOLLOWING MY OWN LEAD.
THIS NEW .SVE_URS3LF, WHOEVER THEY ARE, THEY'RE TRANSFIXED ON THE TUNIS OP.
THEY HAVE A BONE TO PICK AND THEY'RE TRYING TO MAKE IT PUBLIC. I THINK THEY MIGHT KNOW SOMETHING THE REST OF US DON'T.
"I'VE GOT EVERY CASE FILE BRYNN ORI EVER TOUCHED.
"EVERY RECORD OF HER DEALINGS WITH ED AND NATE. EVERY RECORD OF THE EVENTS LEADING UP TO TUNIS.
"IF THERE'S A LOOSE END WAITING TO BE TIED UP, I'LL FIND IT THERE. I'M GOOD AT THAT KIND OF THING.
"WHAT DO YOU WANT ME TO SAY, HONEY? I'M MISSING MY DAUGHTER'S BEDTIME.
"I GOTTA BELIEVE I'M DOING IT FOR A REASON."
TARGET:
THE TOWER.
CASE:
SUSPENDED.
AGENT IN CHARGE:
ORI, BRYNN
STATUS: REASSIGNED.
otherwise makes
unauthorized person, or
in any manner prejudicial to the
interest of the United States or for the
benefit of any foreign government to the
detriment of the United States any
classified information—
(1) concerning the nature, preparation, or
use of any code, cipher, or cryptographic
system of the United States or any foreign
government; or
(2) concerning the design, construction,
maintenance, or repair of any device,
or appliance used or prepared
TARGET: :
THE TOWER.

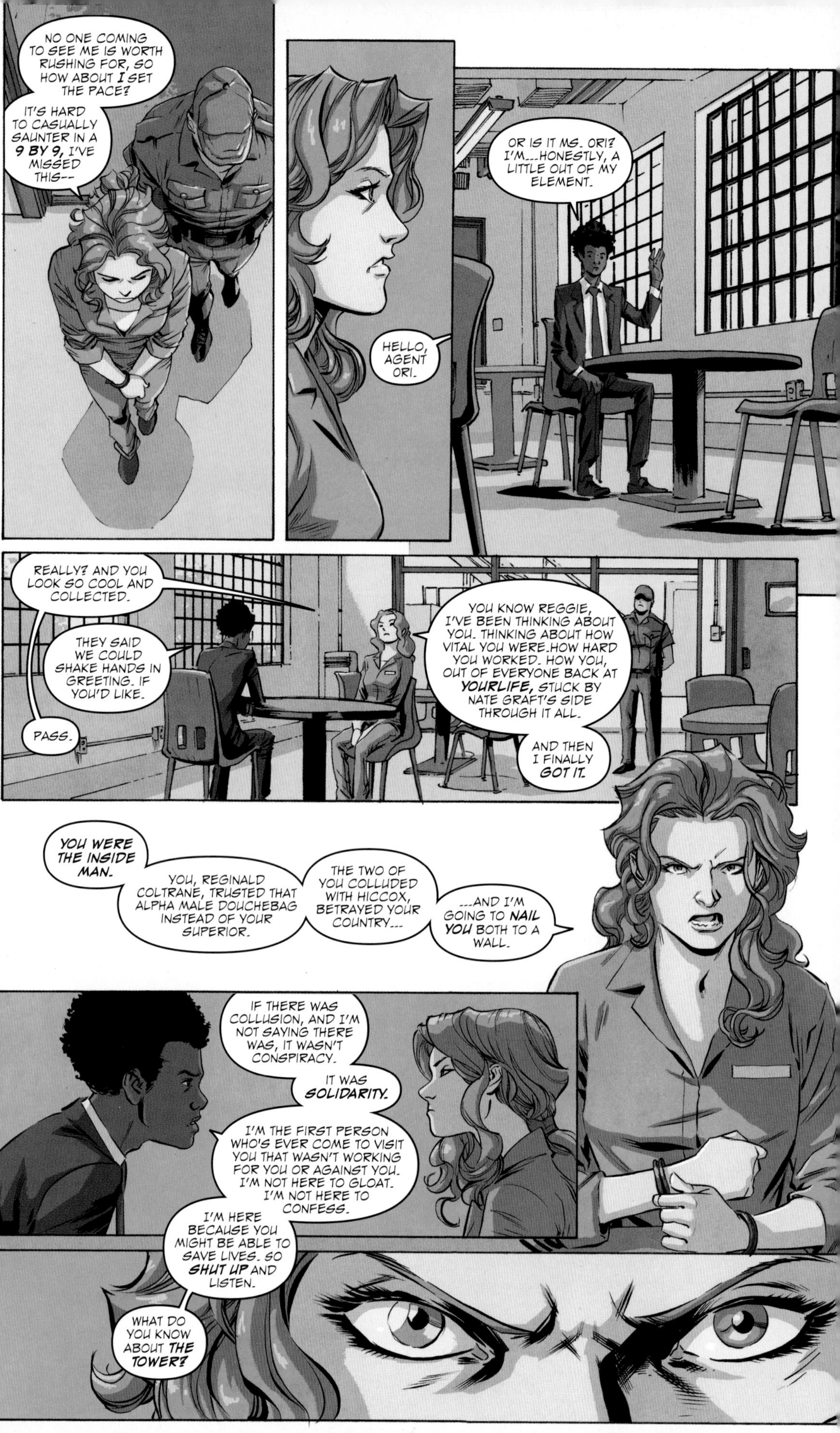
NO ONE COMING TO SEE ME IS WORTH RUSHING FOR, SO HOW ABOUT I SET THE PACE?
IT'S HARD TO CASUALLY SAUNTER IN A 9 BY 9, I'VE MISSED THIS--
HELLO, AGENT ORI.
OR IS IT MS. ORI? I'M...HONESTLY, A LITTLE OUT OF MY ELEMENT.
REALLY? AND YOU LOOK SO COOL AND COLLECTED.
THEY SAID WE COULD SHAKE HANDS IN GREETING. IF YOU'D LIKE.
PASS.
YOU KNOW REGGIE, I'VE BEEN THINKING ABOUT YOU. THINKING ABOUT HOW VITAL YOU WERE. HOW HARD YOU WORKED. HOW YOU, OUT OF EVERYONE BACK AT YOURLIFE, STUCK BY NATE GRAFT'S SIDE THROUGH IT ALL.
AND THEN I FINALLY GOT IT.
YOU WERE THE INSIDE MAN.
YOU, REGINALD COLTRANE, TRUSTED THAT ALPHA MALE DOUCHEBAG INSTEAD OF YOUR SUPERIOR.
THE TWO OF YOU COLLUDED WITH HICCOX, BETRAYED YOUR COUNTRY...
...AND I'M GOING TO NAIL YOU BOTH TO A WALL.
IF THERE WAS COLLUSION, AND I'M NOT SAYING THERE WAS, IT WASN'T CONSPIRACY.
IT WAS SOLIDARITY.
I'M THE FIRST PERSON WHO'S EVER COME TO VISIT YOU THAT WASN'T WORKING FOR YOU OR AGAINST YOU. I'M NOT HERE TO GLOAT. I'M NOT HERE TO CONFESS.
I'M HERE BECAUSE YOU MIGHT BE ABLE TO SAVE LIVES. SO SHUT UP AND LISTEN.
WHAT DO YOU KNOW ABOUT THE TOWER?

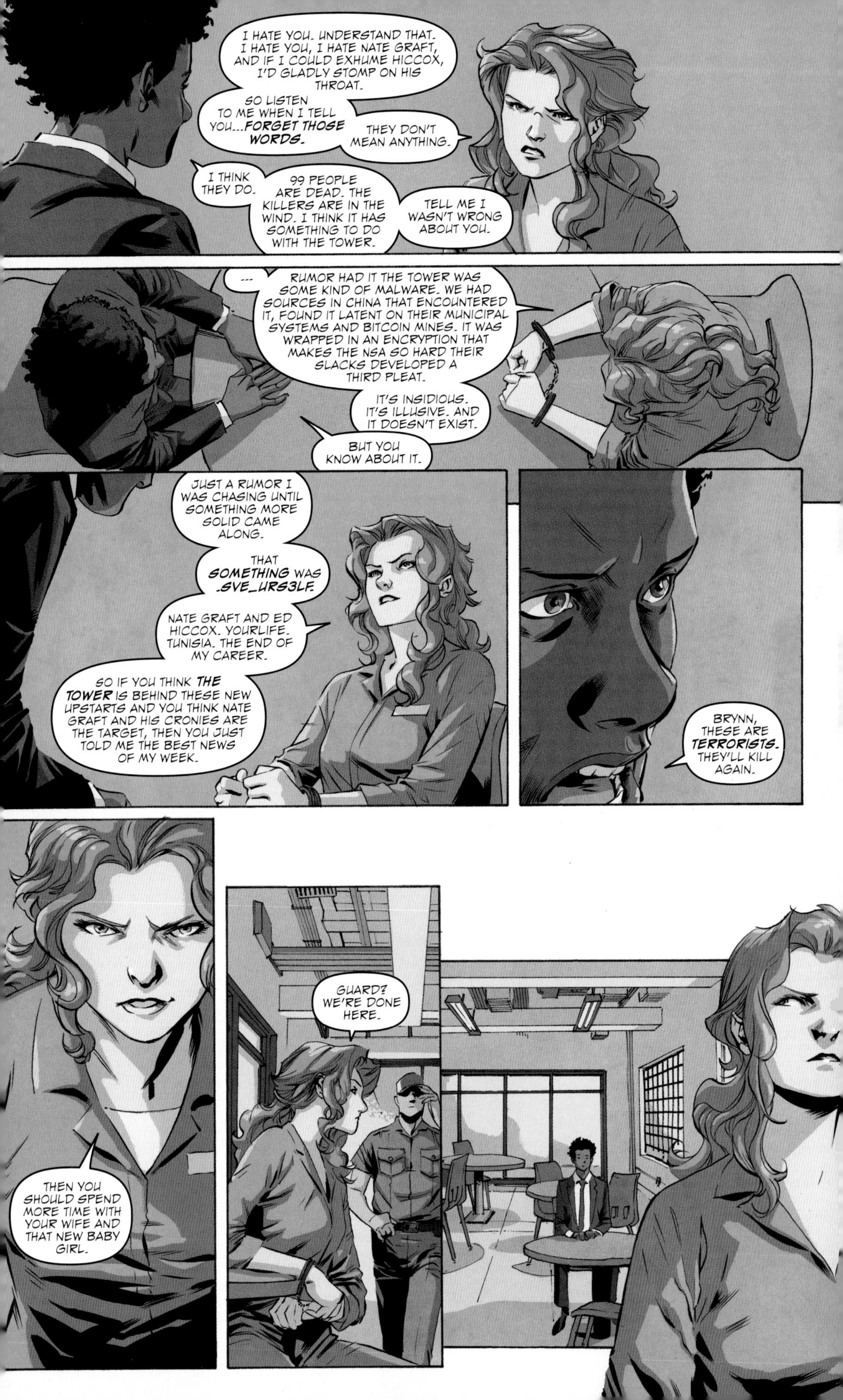
I HATE YOU. UNDERSTAND THAT. I HATE YOU, I HATE NATE GRAFT, AND IF I COULD EXHUME HICCOX, I'D GLADLY STOMP ON HIS THROAT.
SO LISTEN TO ME WHEN I TELL YOU...FORGET THOSE WORDS.
THEY DON'T MEAN ANYTHING.
I THINK THEY DO.
99 PEOPLE ARE DEAD. THE KILLERS ARE IN THE WIND. I THINK IT HAS SOMETHING TO DO WITH THE TOWER.
TELL ME I WASN'T WRONG ABOUT YOU.
...
RUMOR HAD IT THE TOWER WAS SOME KIND OF MALWARE. WE HAD SOURCES IN CHINA THAT ENCOUNTERED IT, FOUND IT LATENT ON THEIR MUNICIPAL SYSTEMS AND BITCOIN MINES. IT WAS WRAPPED IN AN ENCRYPTION THAT MAKES THE NSA SO HARD THEIR SLACKS DEVELOPED A THIRD PLEAT.
IT'S INSIDIOUS. IT'S ILLUSIVE. AND IT DOESN'T EXIST.
BUT YOU KNOW ABOUT IT.
JUST A RUMOR I WAS CHASING UNTIL SOMETHING MORE SOLID CAME ALONG.
THAT SOMETHING WAS .SVE_URS3LF.
NATE GRAFT AND ED HICCOX. YOURLIFE. TUNISIA. THE END OF MY CAREER.
SO IF YOU THINK THE TOWER IS BEHIND THESE NEW UPSTARTS AND YOU THINK NATE GRAFT AND HIS CRONIES ARE THE TARGET, THEN YOU JUST TOLD ME THE BEST NEWS OF MY WEEK.
BRYNN, THESE ARE TERRORISTS. THEY'LL KILL AGAIN.
THEN YOU SHOULD SPEND MORE TIME WITH YOUR WIFE AND THAT NEW BABY GIRL.
GUARD? WE'RE DONE HERE.

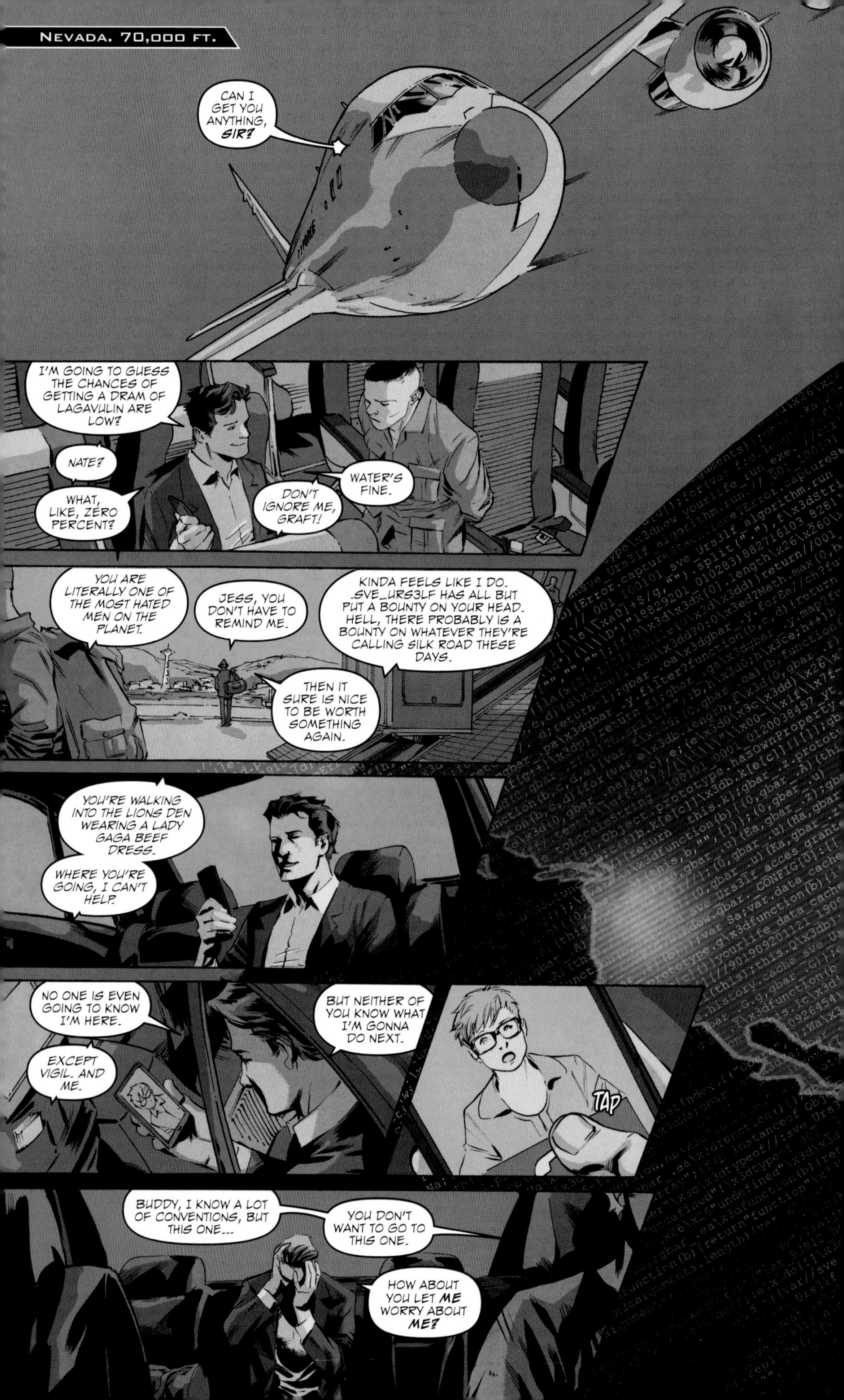
NEVADA. 70,000 FT.
CAN I GET YOU ANYTHING, SIR?
I'M GOING TO GUESS THE CHANCES OF GETTING A DRAM OF LAGAVULIN ARE LOW?
NATE?
WHAT, LIKE, ZERO PERCENT?
DON'T IGNORE ME, GRAFT!
WATER'S FINE.
YOU ARE LITERALLY ONE OF THE MOST HATED MEN ON THE PLANET.
JESS, YOU DON'T HAVE TO REMIND ME.
KINDA FEELS LIKE I DO. .SVE_URS3LF HAS ALL BUT PUT A BOUNTY ON YOUR HEAD. HELL, THERE PROBABLY IS A BOUNTY ON WHATEVER THEY'RE CALLING SILK ROAD THESE DAYS.
THEN IT SURE IS NICE TO BE WORTH SOMETHING AGAIN.
YOU'RE WALKING INTO THE LIONS DEN WEARING A LADY GAGA BEEF DRESS.
WHERE YOU'RE GOING, I CAN'T HELP.
NO ONE IS EVEN GOING TO KNOW I'M HERE.
EXCEPT VIGIL. AND ME.
BUT NEITHER OF YOU KNOW WHAT I'M GONNA DO NEXT.
TAP
BUDDY, I KNOW A LOT OF CONVENTIONS, BUT THIS ONE...
YOU DON'T WANT TO GO TO THIS ONE.
HOW ABOUT YOU LET ME WORRY ABOUT ME?

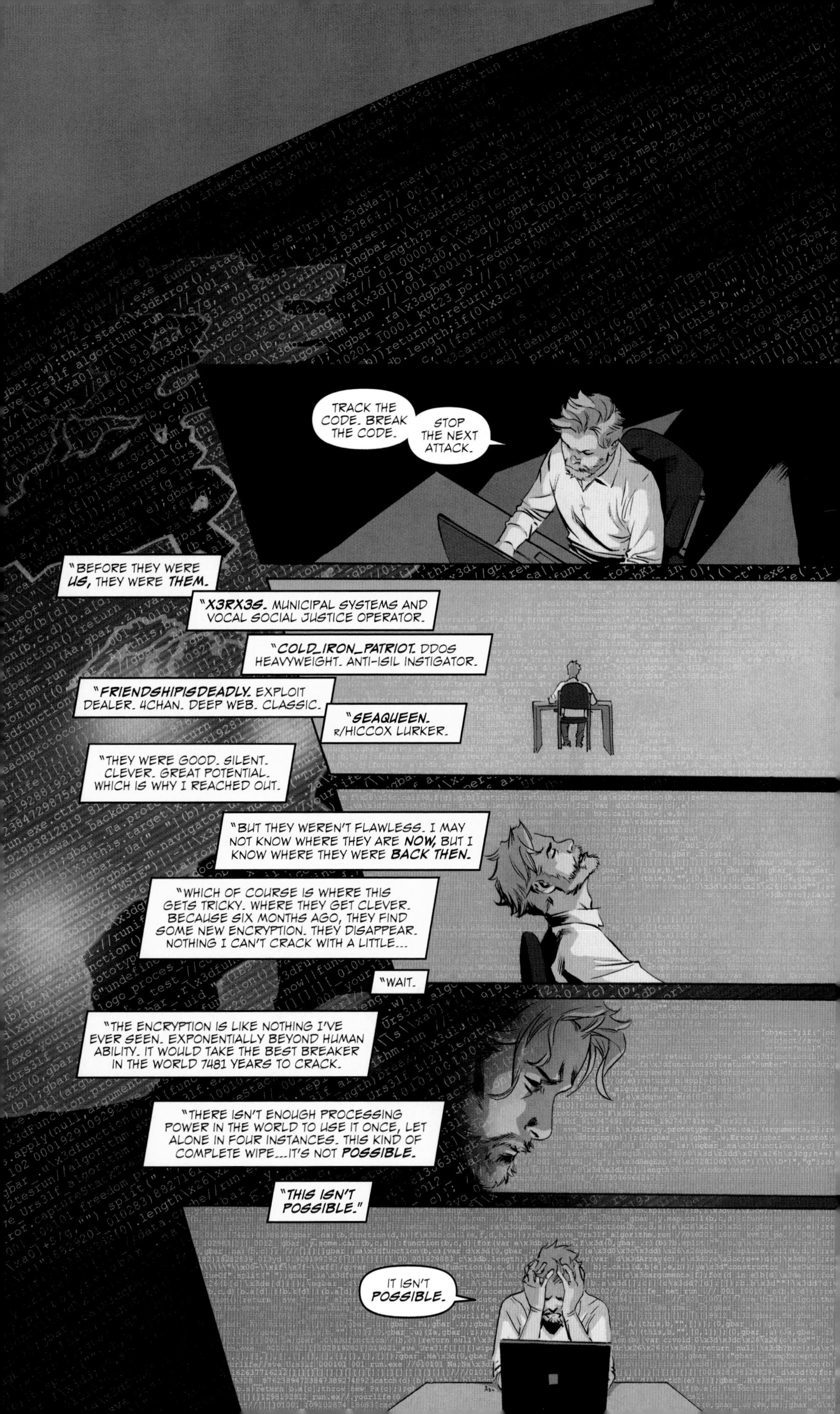
TRACK THE CODE. BREAK THE CODE.
STOP THE NEXT ATTACK.
"BEFORE THEY WERE *US*, THEY WERE *THEM*.
"*X3RX3S*. MUNICIPAL SYSTEMS AND VOCAL SOCIAL JUSTICE OPERATOR.
"*COLD_IRON_PATRIOT*. DDOS HEAVYWEIGHT. ANTI-ISIL INSTIGATOR.
"*FRIENDSHIPISDEADLY*. EXPLOIT DEALER. 4CHAN. DEEP WEB. CLASSIC.
"*SEAQUEEN*. r/HICCOX LURKER.
"THEY WERE GOOD. SILENT. CLEVER. GREAT POTENTIAL. WHICH IS WHY I REACHED OUT.
"BUT THEY WEREN'T FLAWLESS. I MAY NOT KNOW WHERE THEY ARE *NOW*, BUT I KNOW WHERE THEY WERE *BACK THEN*.
"WHICH OF COURSE IS WHERE THIS GETS TRICKY. WHERE THEY GET CLEVER. BECAUSE SIX MONTHS AGO, THEY FIND SOME NEW ENCRYPTION. THEY DISAPPEAR. NOTHING I CAN'T CRACK WITH A LITTLE...
"WAIT.
"THE ENCRYPTION IS LIKE NOTHING I'VE EVER SEEN. EXPONENTIALLY BEYOND HUMAN ABILITY. IT WOULD TAKE THE BEST BREAKER IN THE WORLD 7481 YEARS TO CRACK.
"THERE ISN'T ENOUGH PROCESSING POWER IN THE WORLD TO USE IT ONCE, LET ALONE IN FOUR INSTANCES. THIS KIND OF COMPLETE WIPE...IT'S NOT *POSSIBLE*.
"*THIS ISN'T POSSIBLE*."
IT ISN'T *POSSIBLE*.

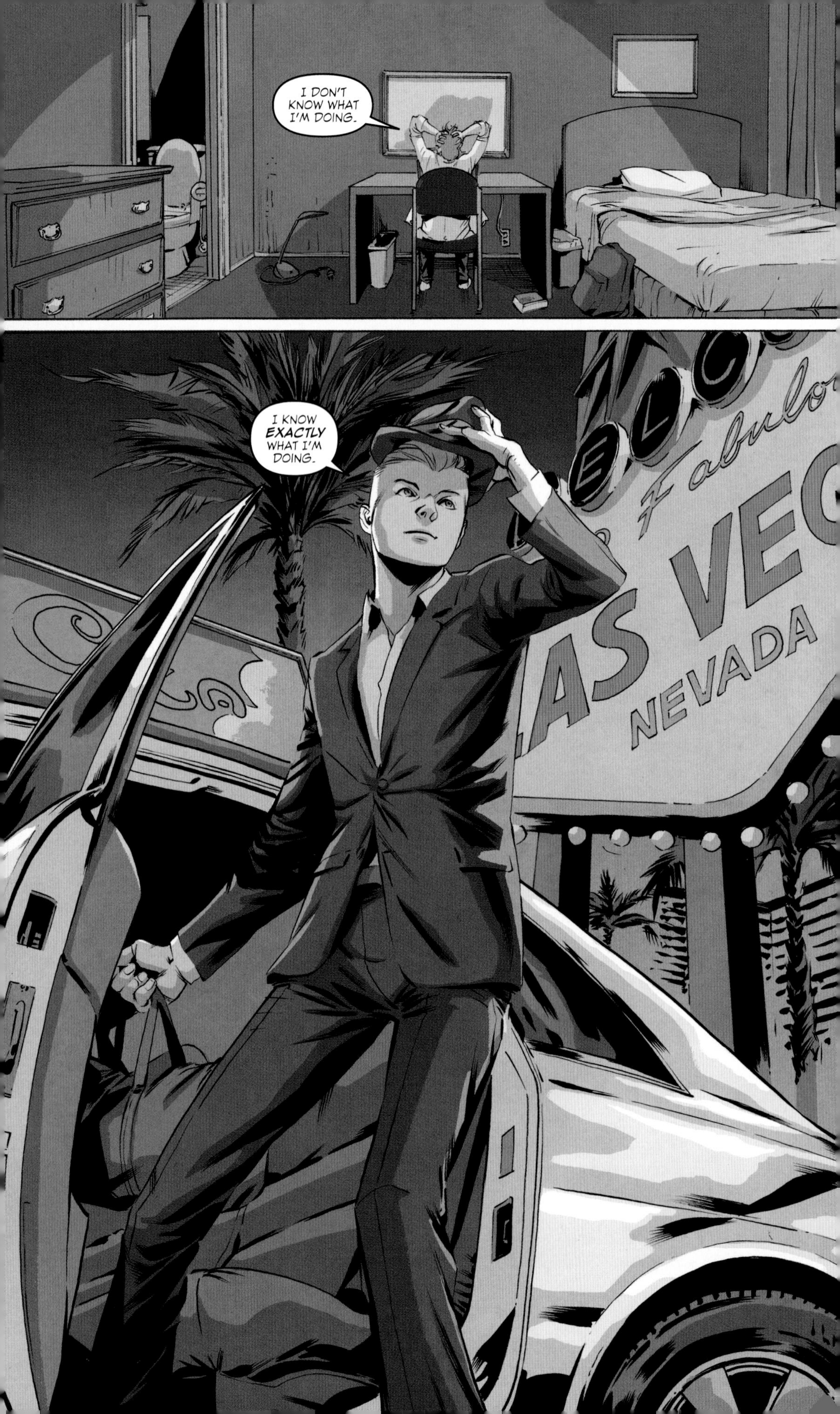
I DON'T KNOW WHAT I'M DOING.
I KNOW *EXACTLY* WHAT I'M DOING.
NEVADA

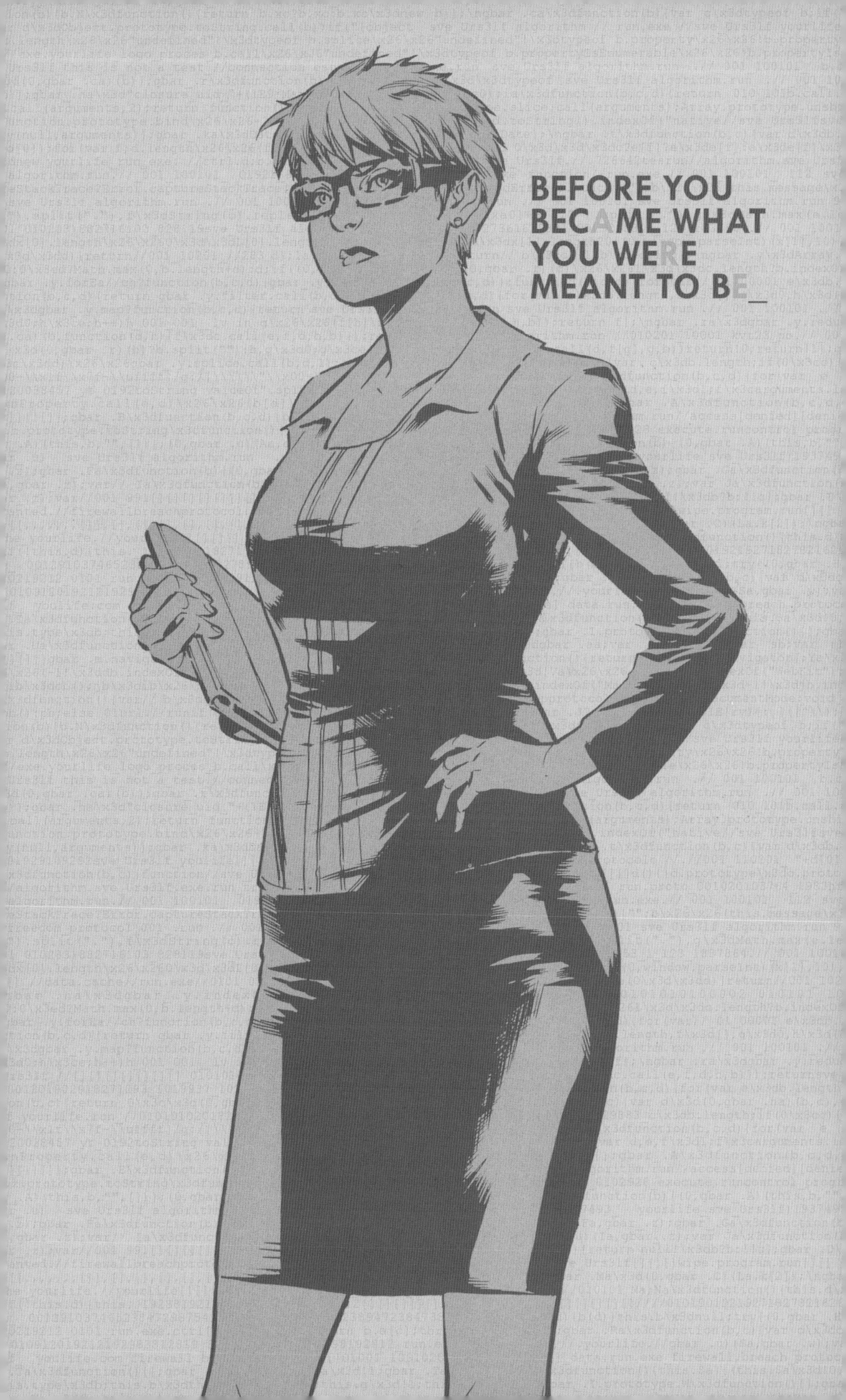
BEFORE YOU
BECAME WHAT
YOU WERE
MEANT TO BE_

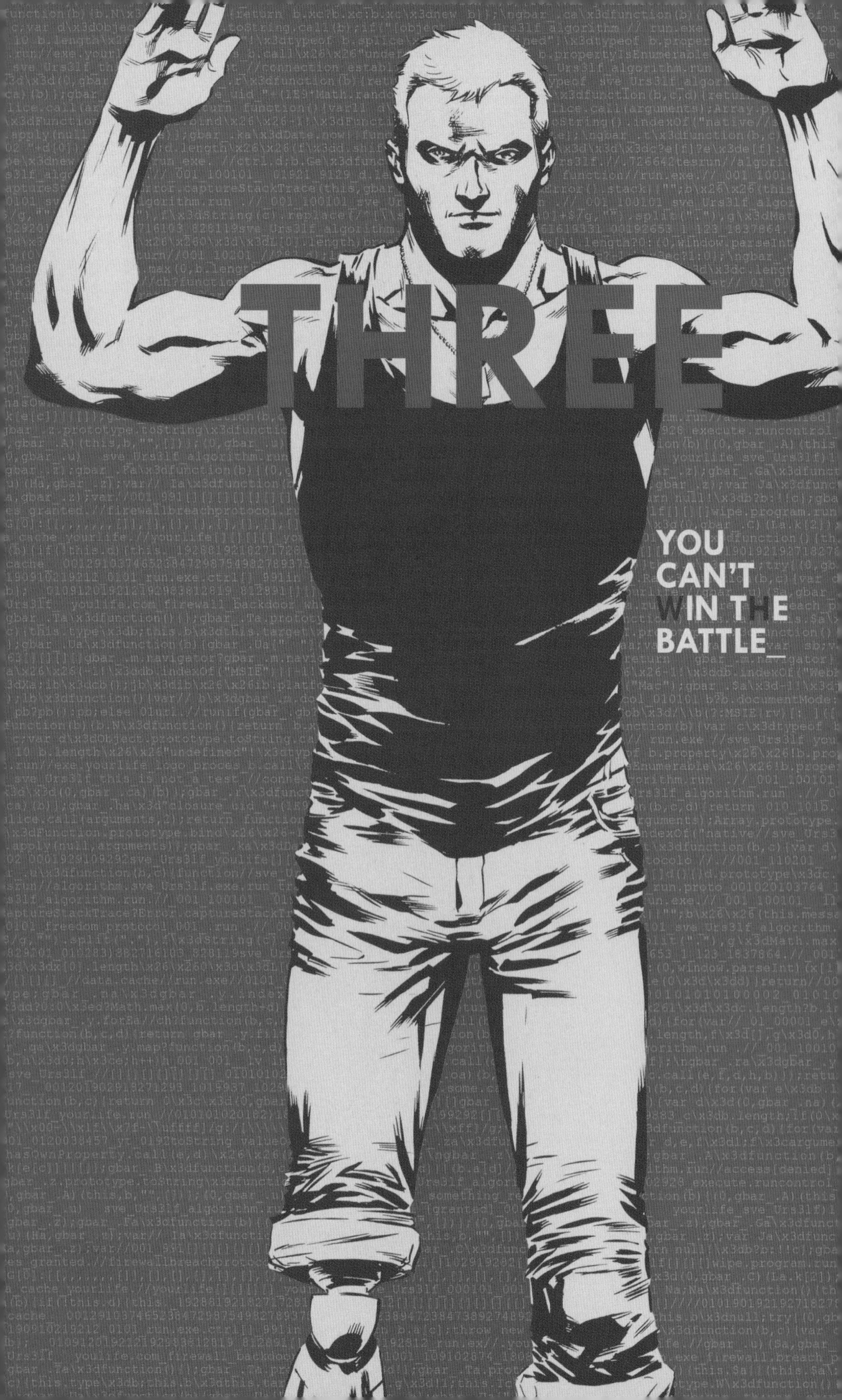
THREE
YOU CAN'T WIN THE BATTLE_

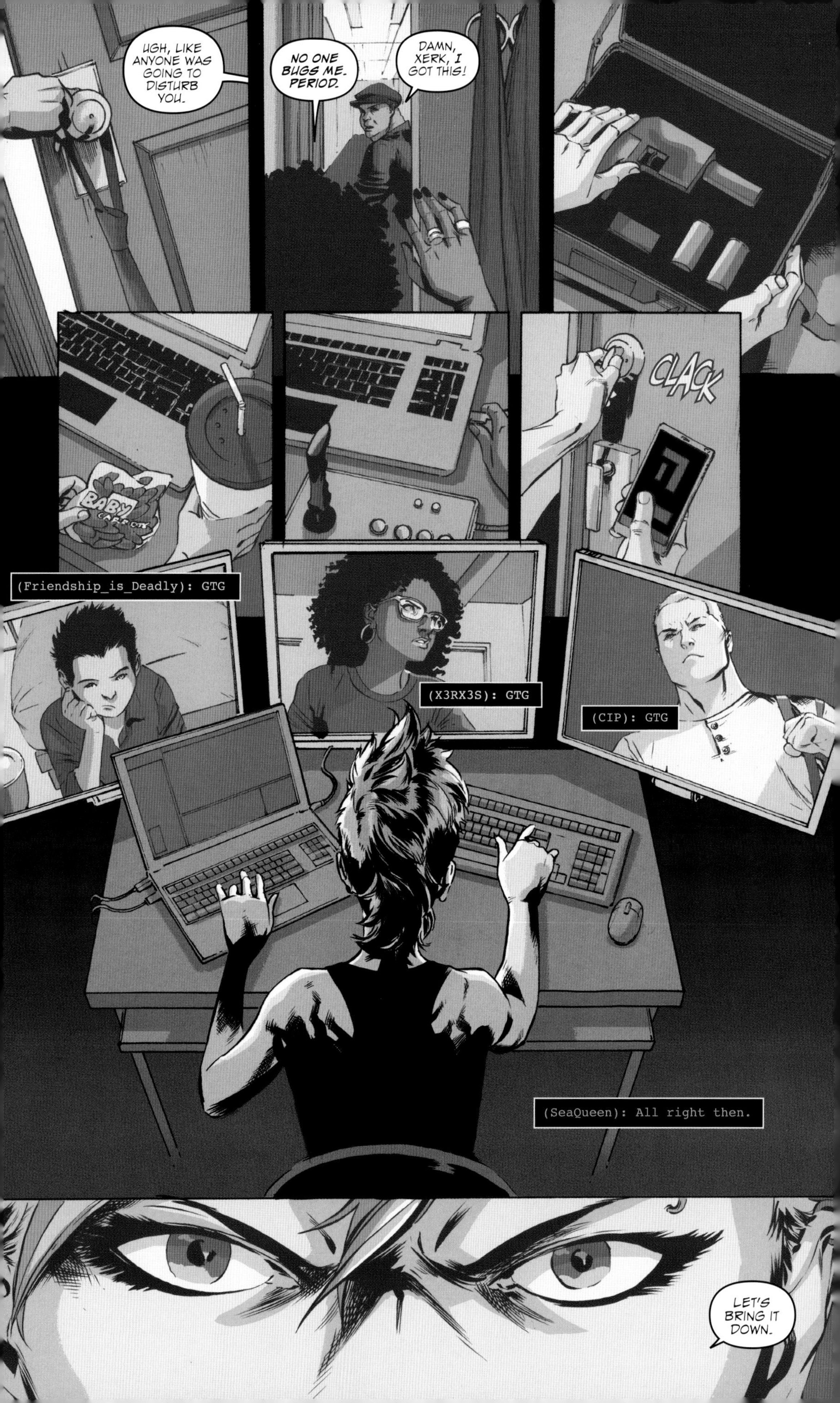
UGH, LIKE ANYONE WAS GOING TO DISTURB YOU.
NO ONE BUGS ME. PERIOD.
DAMN, XERK, I GOT THIS!
BABY CARROTS
CLACK
(Friendship_is_Deadly): GTG
(X3RX3S): GTG
(CIP): GTG
(SeaQueen): All right then.
LET'S BRING IT DOWN.

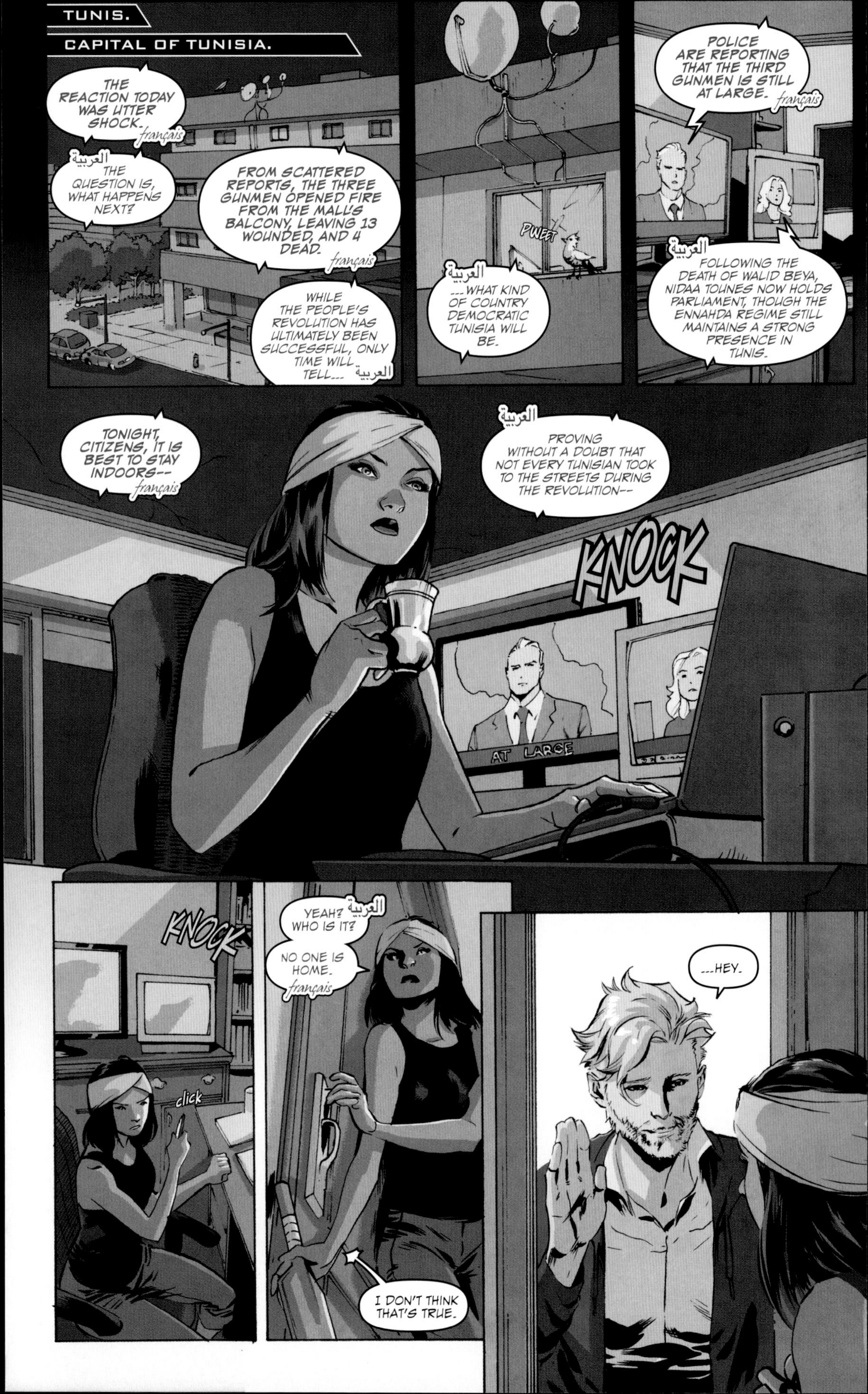
TUNIS.
CAPITAL OF TUNISIA.
THE REACTION TODAY WAS UTTER SHOCK. français
العربية THE QUESTION IS, WHAT HAPPENS NEXT?
FROM SCATTERED REPORTS, THE THREE GUNMEN OPENED FIRE FROM THE MALL'S BALCONY, LEAVING 13 WOUNDED, AND 4 DEAD. français
WHILE THE PEOPLE'S REVOLUTION HAS ULTIMATELY BEEN SUCCESSFUL, ONLY TIME WILL TELL... العربية
PWEET
العربية ...WHAT KIND OF COUNTRY DEMOCRATIC TUNISIA WILL BE.
POLICE ARE REPORTING THAT THE THIRD GUNMEN IS STILL AT LARGE. français
العربية FOLLOWING THE DEATH OF WALID BEYA, NIDAA TOUNES NOW HOLDS PARLIAMENT, THOUGH THE ENNAHDA REGIME STILL MAINTAINS A STRONG PRESENCE IN TUNIS.
TONIGHT, CITIZENS, IT IS BEST TO STAY INDOORS-- français
العربية PROVING WITHOUT A DOUBT THAT NOT EVERY TUNISIAN TOOK TO THE STREETS DURING THE REVOLUTION--
KNOCK
AT LARGE
KNOCK
click
العربية YEAH? WHO IS IT?
NO ONE IS HOME. français
I DON'T THINK THAT'S TRUE.
...HEY.

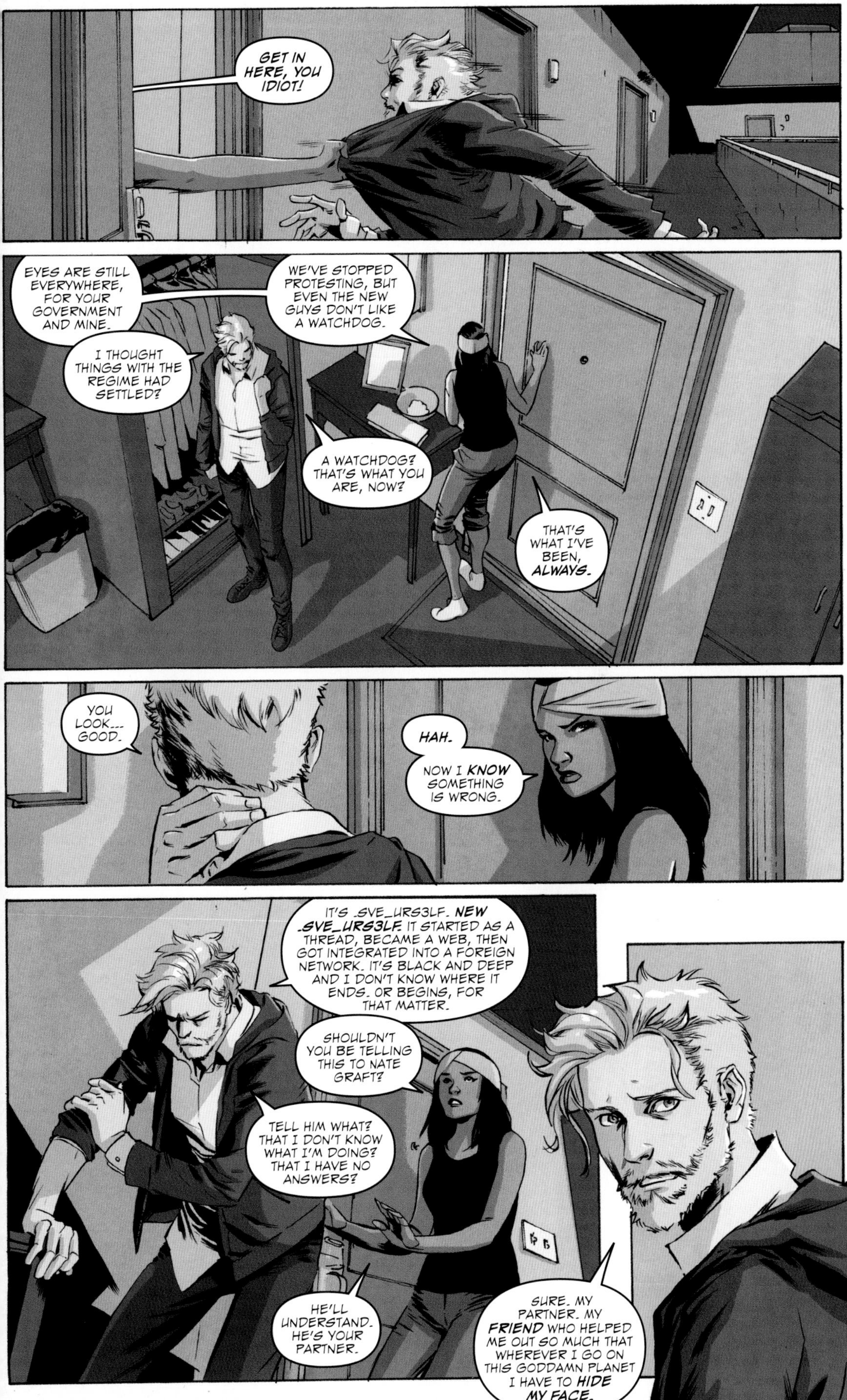
GET IN HERE, YOU IDIOT!
EYES ARE STILL EVERYWHERE, FOR YOUR GOVERNMENT AND MINE.
WE'VE STOPPED PROTESTING, BUT EVEN THE NEW GUYS DON'T LIKE A WATCHDOG.
I THOUGHT THINGS WITH THE REGIME HAD SETTLED?
A WATCHDOG? THAT'S WHAT YOU ARE, NOW?
THAT'S WHAT I'VE BEEN, ALWAYS.
YOU LOOK... GOOD.
HAH.
NOW I KNOW SOMETHING IS WRONG.
IT'S .SVE_URS3LF. NEW .SVE_URS3LF. IT STARTED AS A THREAD, BECAME A WEB, THEN GOT INTEGRATED INTO A FOREIGN NETWORK. IT'S BLACK AND DEEP AND I DON'T KNOW WHERE IT ENDS. OR BEGINS, FOR THAT MATTER.
SHOULDN'T YOU BE TELLING THIS TO NATE GRAFT?
TELL HIM WHAT? THAT I DON'T KNOW WHAT I'M DOING? THAT I HAVE NO ANSWERS?
HE'LL UNDERSTAND. HE'S YOUR PARTNER.
SURE. MY PARTNER. MY FRIEND WHO HELPED ME OUT SO MUCH THAT WHEREVER I GO ON THIS GODDAMN PLANET I HAVE TO HIDE MY FACE.

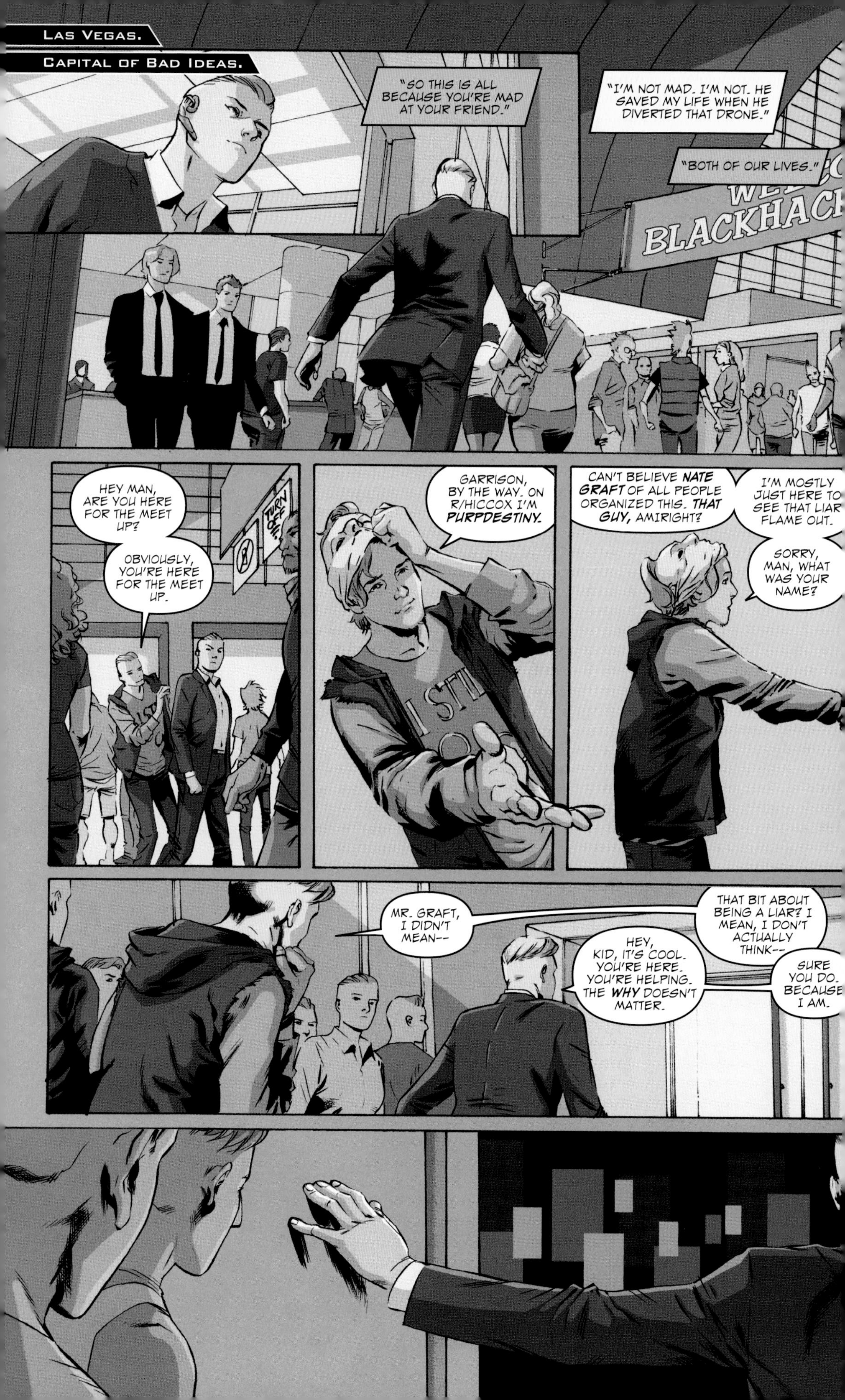

LAS VEGAS.
CAPITAL OF BAD IDEAS.
"SO THIS IS ALL BECAUSE YOU'RE MAD AT YOUR FRIEND."
"I'M NOT MAD. I'M NOT. HE SAVED MY LIFE WHEN HE DIVERTED THAT DRONE."
"BOTH OF OUR LIVES."
BLACKHAC
HEY MAN, ARE YOU HERE FOR THE MEET UP?
OBVIOUSLY, YOU'RE HERE FOR THE MEET UP.
TURN OFF
GARRISON, BY THE WAY. ON R/HICCOX I'M PURPDESTINY.
CAN'T BELIEVE NATE GRAFT OF ALL PEOPLE ORGANIZED THIS. THAT GUY, AMIRIGHT?
I'M MOSTLY JUST HERE TO SEE THAT LIAR FLAME OUT.
SORRY, MAN, WHAT WAS YOUR NAME?
MR. GRAFT, I DIDN'T MEAN--
THAT BIT ABOUT BEING A LIAR? I MEAN, I DON'T ACTUALLY THINK--
HEY, KID, IT'S COOL. YOU'RE HERE. YOU'RE HELPING. THE WHY DOESN'T MATTER.
SURE YOU DO. BECAUSE I AM.

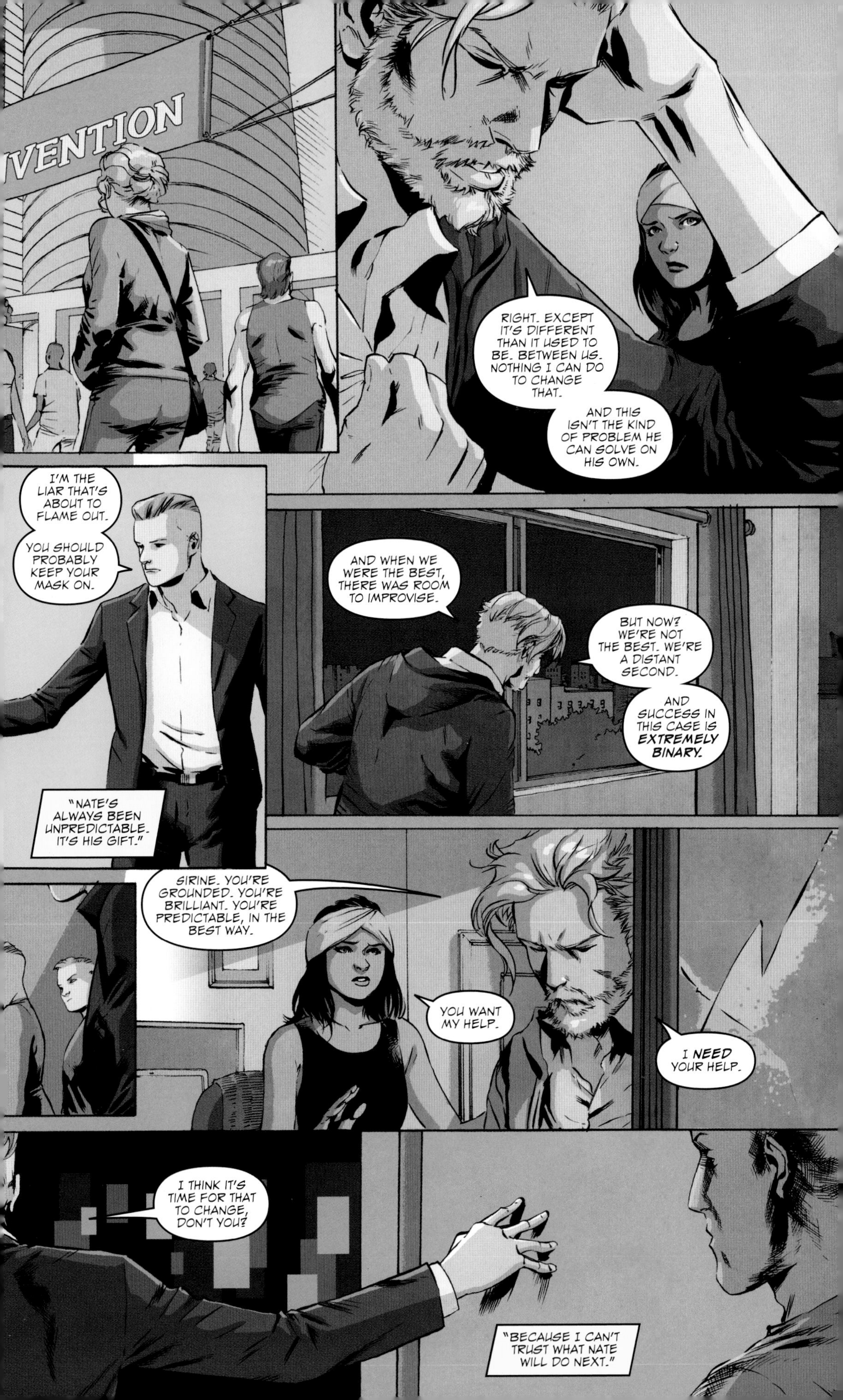
VENTION
RIGHT. EXCEPT IT'S DIFFERENT THAN IT USED TO BE. BETWEEN US. NOTHING I CAN DO TO CHANGE THAT.
AND THIS ISN'T THE KIND OF PROBLEM HE CAN SOLVE ON HIS OWN.
I'M THE LIAR THAT'S ABOUT TO FLAME OUT.
YOU SHOULD PROBABLY KEEP YOUR MASK ON.
"NATE'S ALWAYS BEEN UNPREDICTABLE. IT'S HIS GIFT."
AND WHEN WE WERE THE BEST, THERE WAS ROOM TO IMPROVISE.
BUT NOW? WE'RE NOT THE BEST. WE'RE A DISTANT SECOND.
AND SUCCESS IN THIS CASE IS **EXTREMELY BINARY.**
SIRINE. YOU'RE GROUNDED. YOU'RE BRILLIANT. YOU'RE PREDICTABLE, IN THE BEST WAY.
YOU WANT MY HELP.
I **NEED** YOUR HELP.
I THINK IT'S TIME FOR THAT TO CHANGE, DON'T YOU?
"BECAUSE I CAN'T TRUST WHAT NATE WILL DO NEXT."

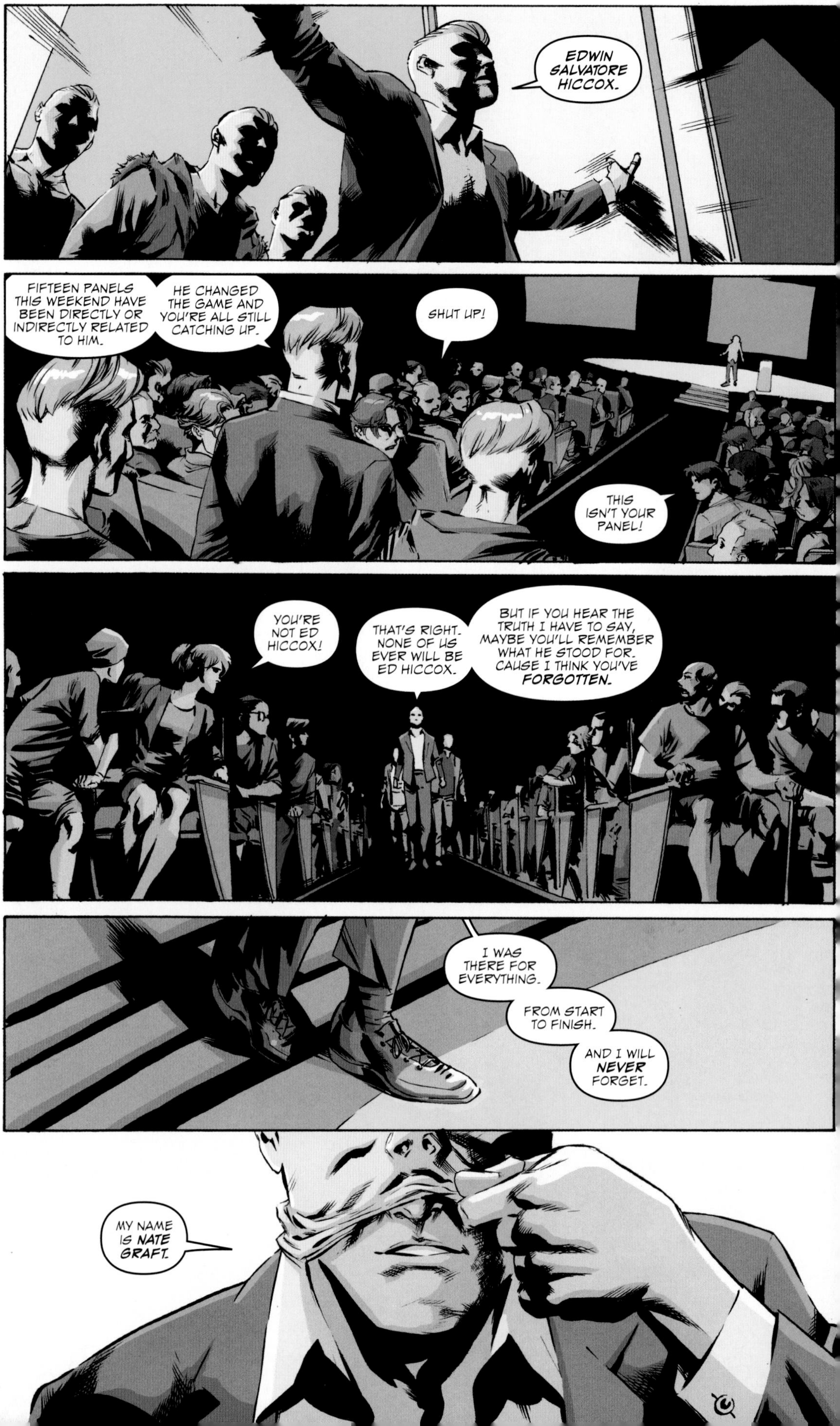
EDWIN SALVATORE HICCOX.
FIFTEEN PANELS THIS WEEKEND HAVE BEEN DIRECTLY OR INDIRECTLY RELATED TO HIM.
HE CHANGED THE GAME AND YOU'RE ALL STILL CATCHING UP.
SHUT UP!
THIS ISN'T YOUR PANEL!
YOU'RE NOT ED HICCOX!
THAT'S RIGHT. NONE OF US EVER WILL BE ED HICCOX.
BUT IF YOU HEAR THE TRUTH I HAVE TO SAY, MAYBE YOU'LL REMEMBER WHAT HE STOOD FOR. CAUSE I THINK YOU'VE FORGOTTEN.
I WAS THERE FOR EVERYTHING.
FROM START TO FINISH.
AND I WILL NEVER FORGET.
MY NAME IS NATE GRAFT.

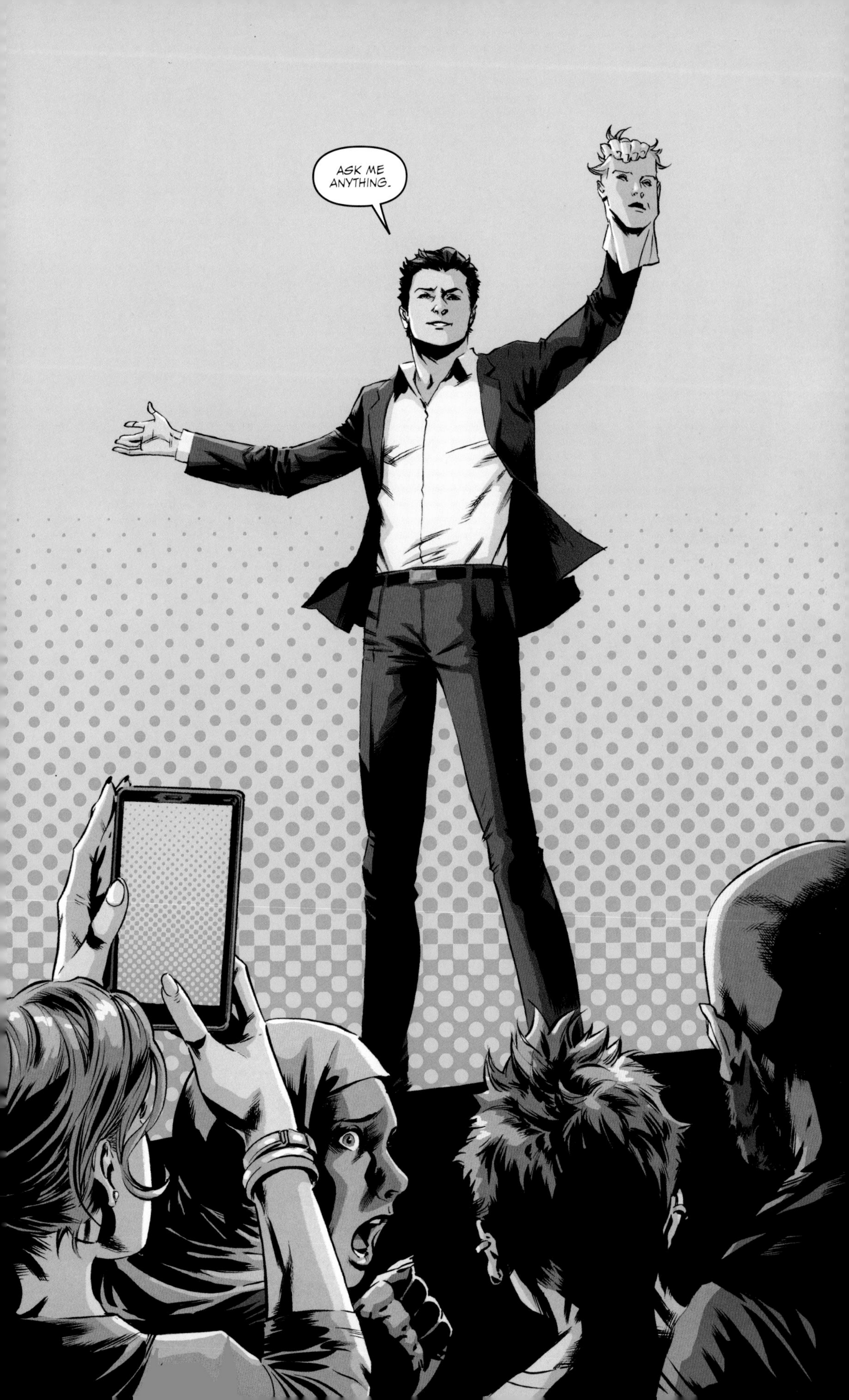
ASK ME ANYTHING.

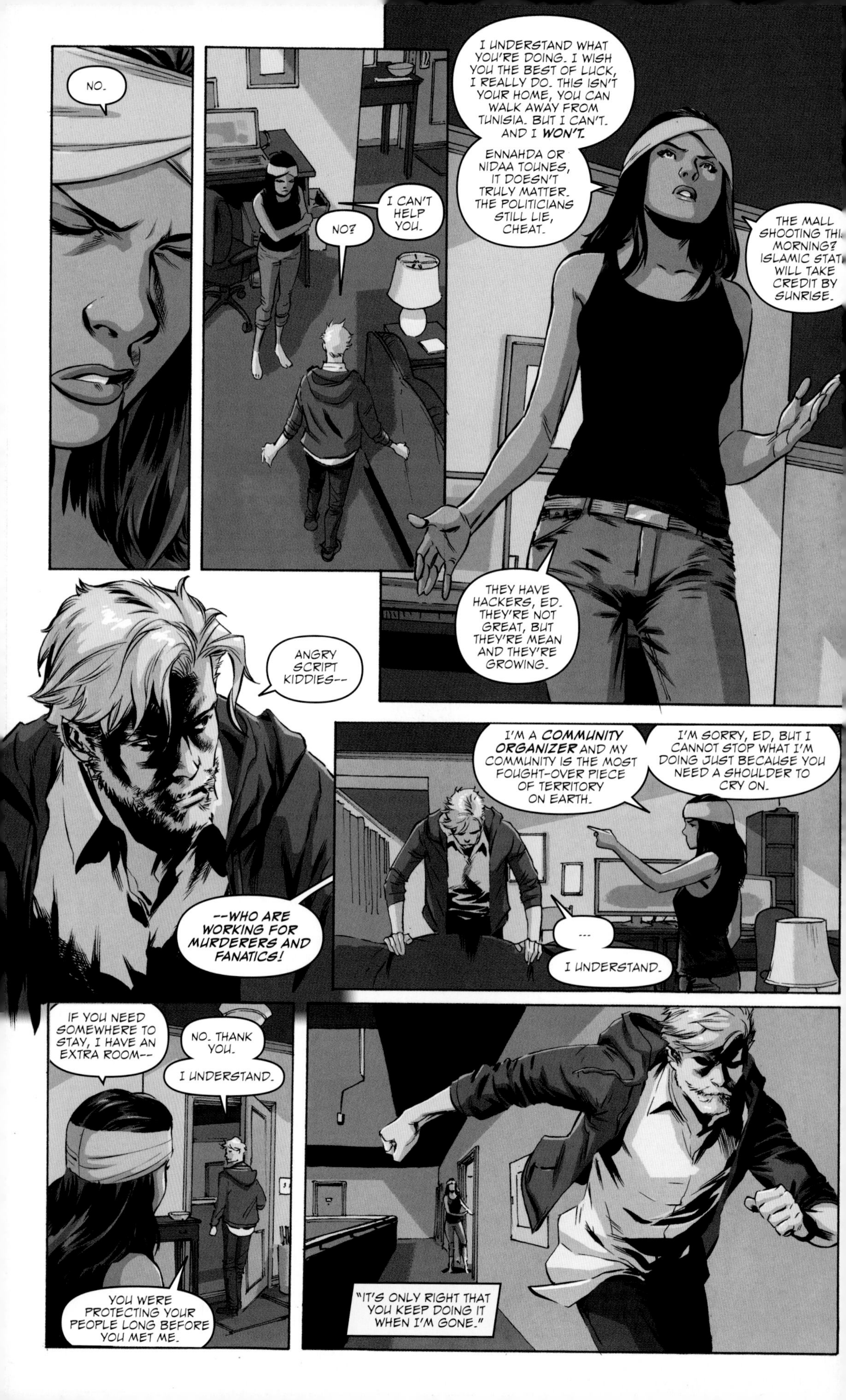
NO.
I CAN'T HELP YOU.
NO?
I UNDERSTAND WHAT YOU'RE DOING. I WISH YOU THE BEST OF LUCK, I REALLY DO. THIS ISN'T YOUR HOME, YOU CAN WALK AWAY FROM TUNISIA. BUT I CAN'T. AND I WON'T.
ENNAHDA OR NIDAA TOUNES, IT DOESN'T TRULY MATTER. THE POLITICIANS STILL LIE, CHEAT.
THE MALL SHOOTING THI MORNING? ISLAMIC STAT WILL TAKE CREDIT BY SUNRISE.
THEY HAVE HACKERS, ED. THEY'RE NOT GREAT, BUT THEY'RE MEAN AND THEY'RE GROWING.
ANGRY SCRIPT KIDDIES--
--WHO ARE WORKING FOR MURDERERS AND FANATICS!
I'M A COMMUNITY ORGANIZER AND MY COMMUNITY IS THE MOST FOUGHT-OVER PIECE OF TERRITORY ON EARTH.
I'M SORRY, ED, BUT I CANNOT STOP WHAT I'M DOING JUST BECAUSE YOU NEED A SHOULDER TO CRY ON.
...
I UNDERSTAND.
IF YOU NEED SOMEWHERE TO STAY, I HAVE AN EXTRA ROOM--
NO. THANK YOU.
I UNDERSTAND.
YOU WERE PROTECTING YOUR PEOPLE LONG BEFORE YOU MET ME.
"IT'S ONLY RIGHT THAT YOU KEEP DOING IT WHEN I'M GONE."

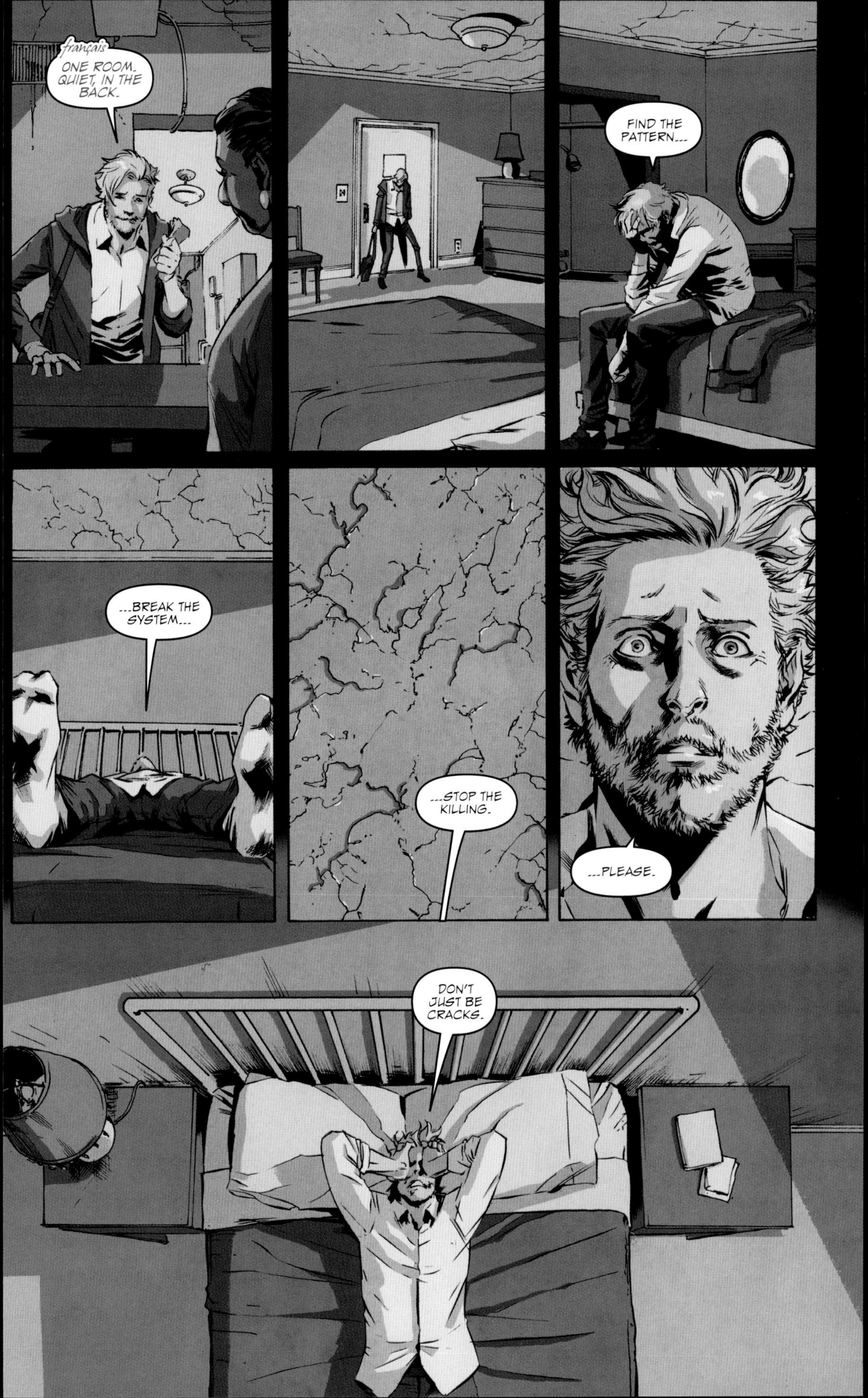
français
ONE ROOM. QUIET, IN THE BACK.
FIND THE PATTERN...
...BREAK THE SYSTEM...
...STOP THE KILLING.
...PLEASE.
DON'T JUST BE CRACKS.

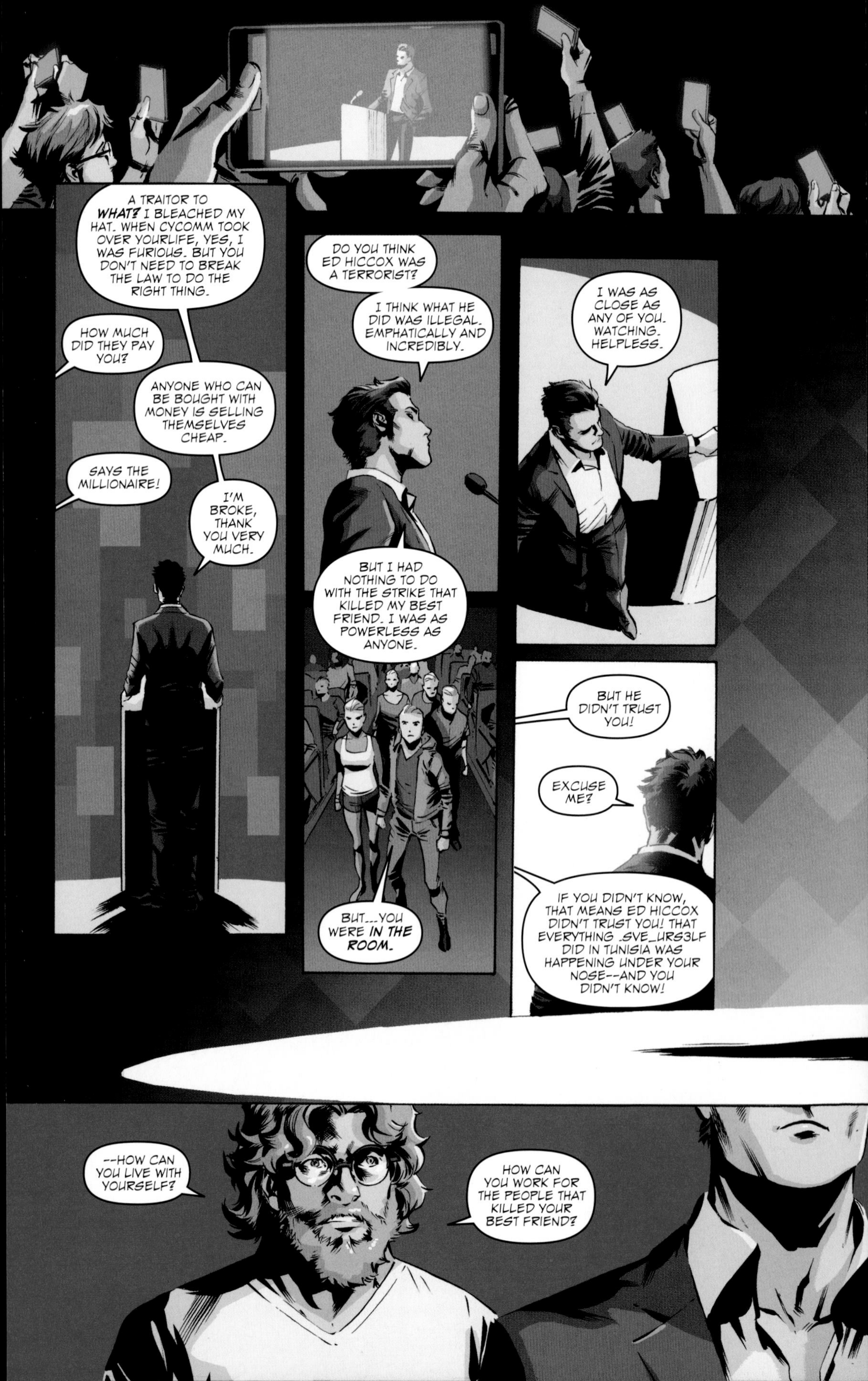

A TRAITOR TO WHAT? I BLEACHED MY HAT. WHEN CYCOMM TOOK OVER YOURLIFE, YES, I WAS FURIOUS. BUT YOU DON'T NEED TO BREAK THE LAW TO DO THE RIGHT THING.
HOW MUCH DID THEY PAY YOU?
ANYONE WHO CAN BE BOUGHT WITH MONEY IS SELLING THEMSELVES CHEAP.
SAYS THE MILLIONAIRE!
I'M BROKE, THANK YOU VERY MUCH.
DO YOU THINK ED HICCOX WAS A TERRORIST?
I THINK WHAT HE DID WAS ILLEGAL. EMPHATICALLY AND INCREDIBLY.
BUT I HAD NOTHING TO DO WITH THE STRIKE THAT KILLED MY BEST FRIEND. I WAS AS POWERLESS AS ANYONE.
BUT...YOU WERE IN THE ROOM.
I WAS AS CLOSE AS ANY OF YOU. WATCHING. HELPLESS.
BUT HE DIDN'T TRUST YOU!
EXCUSE ME?
IF YOU DIDN'T KNOW, THAT MEANS ED HICCOX DIDN'T TRUST YOU! THAT EVERYTHING .SVE_URS3LF DID IN TUNISIA WAS HAPPENING UNDER YOUR NOSE--AND YOU DIDN'T KNOW!
--HOW CAN YOU LIVE WITH YOURSELF?
HOW CAN YOU WORK FOR THE PEOPLE THAT KILLED YOUR BEST FRIEND?

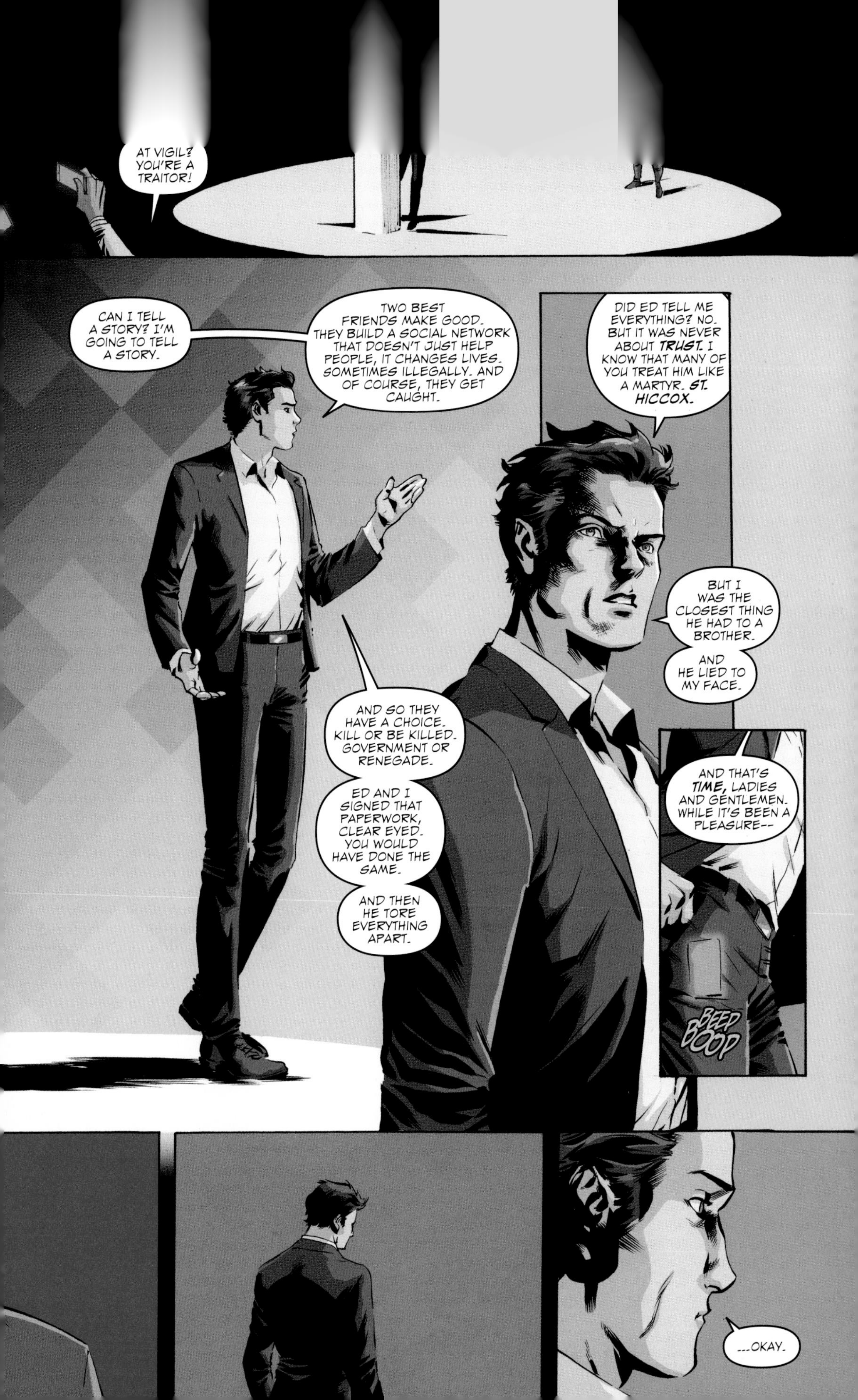
AT VIGIL? YOU'RE A TRAITOR!
CAN I TELL A STORY? I'M GOING TO TELL A STORY.
TWO BEST FRIENDS MAKE GOOD. THEY BUILD A SOCIAL NETWORK THAT DOESN'T JUST HELP PEOPLE, IT CHANGES LIVES. SOMETIMES ILLEGALLY. AND OF COURSE, THEY GET CAUGHT.
AND SO THEY HAVE A CHOICE. KILL OR BE KILLED. GOVERNMENT OR RENEGADE.
ED AND I SIGNED THAT PAPERWORK, CLEAR EYED. YOU WOULD HAVE DONE THE SAME.
AND THEN HE TORE EVERYTHING APART.
DID ED TELL ME EVERYTHING? NO. BUT IT WAS NEVER ABOUT TRUST. I KNOW THAT MANY OF YOU TREAT HIM LIKE A MARTYR. ST. HICCOX.
BUT I WAS THE CLOSEST THING HE HAD TO A BROTHER.
AND HE LIED TO MY FACE.
AND THAT'S TIME, LADIES AND GENTLEMEN. WHILE IT'S BEEN A PLEASURE--
BEEP BOOP
...OKAY.

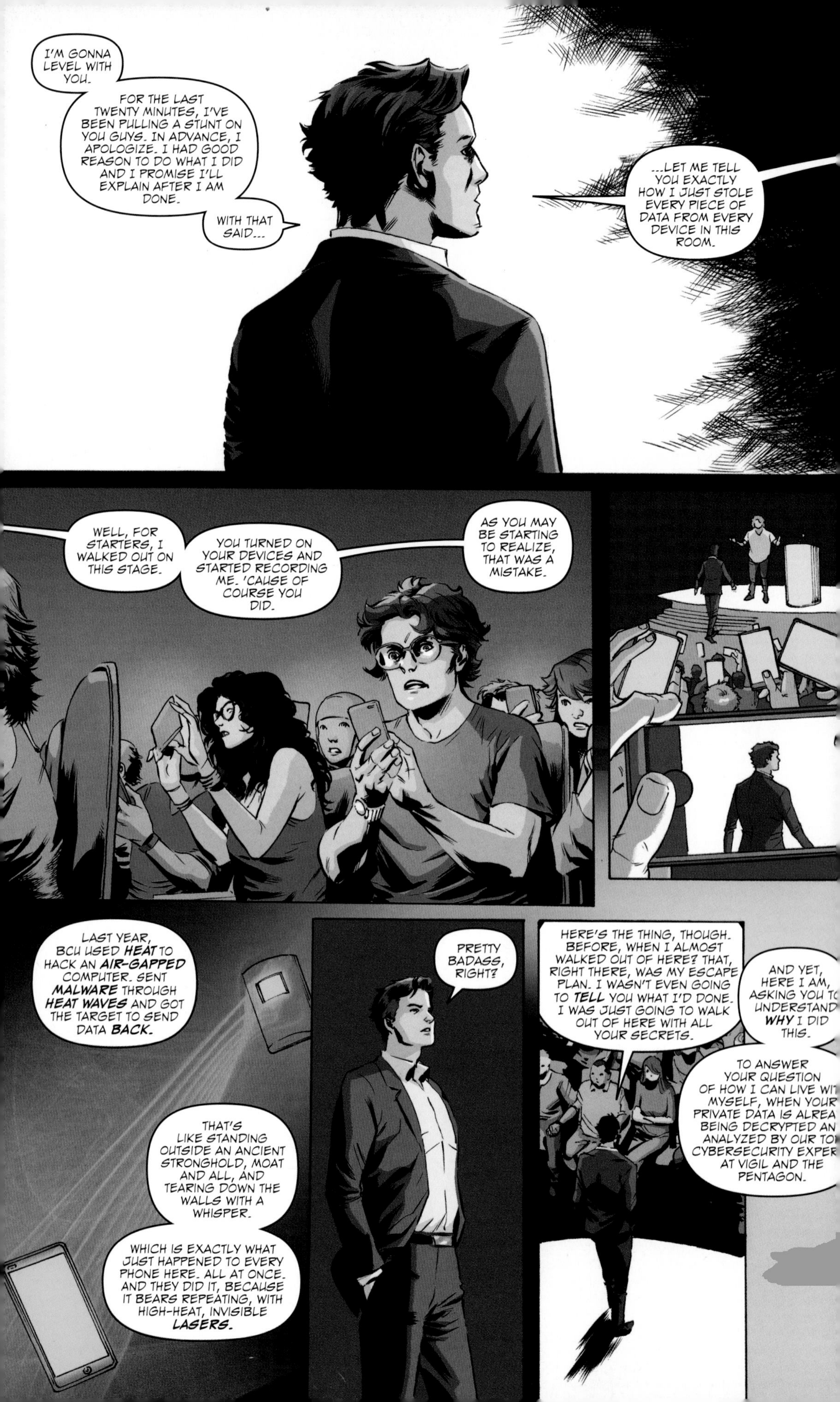
I'M GONNA LEVEL WITH YOU.
FOR THE LAST TWENTY MINUTES, I'VE BEEN PULLING A STUNT ON YOU GUYS. IN ADVANCE, I APOLOGIZE. I HAD GOOD REASON TO DO WHAT I DID AND I PROMISE I'LL EXPLAIN AFTER I AM DONE.
WITH THAT SAID...
...LET ME TELL YOU EXACTLY HOW I JUST STOLE EVERY PIECE OF DATA FROM EVERY DEVICE IN THIS ROOM.
WELL, FOR STARTERS, I WALKED OUT ON THIS STAGE.
YOU TURNED ON YOUR DEVICES AND STARTED RECORDING ME. 'CAUSE OF COURSE YOU DID.
AS YOU MAY BE STARTING TO REALIZE, THAT WAS A MISTAKE.
LAST YEAR, BCU USED **HEAT** TO HACK AN **AIR-GAPPED** COMPUTER. SENT **MALWARE** THROUGH **HEAT WAVES** AND GOT THE TARGET TO SEND DATA **BACK**.
THAT'S LIKE STANDING OUTSIDE AN ANCIENT STRONGHOLD, MOAT AND ALL, AND TEARING DOWN THE WALLS WITH A WHISPER.
WHICH IS EXACTLY WHAT JUST HAPPENED TO EVERY PHONE HERE. ALL AT ONCE. AND THEY DID IT, BECAUSE IT BEARS REPEATING, WITH HIGH-HEAT, INVISIBLE **LASERS**.
PRETTY BADASS, RIGHT?
HERE'S THE THING, THOUGH. BEFORE, WHEN I ALMOST WALKED OUT OF HERE? THAT, RIGHT THERE, WAS MY ESCAPE PLAN. I WASN'T EVEN GOING TO **TELL** YOU WHAT I'D DONE. I WAS JUST GOING TO WALK OUT OF HERE WITH ALL YOUR SECRETS.
AND YET, HERE I AM, ASKING YOU TO UNDERSTAND **WHY** I DID THIS.
TO ANSWER YOUR QUESTION OF HOW I CAN LIVE WI MYSELF, WHEN YOUR PRIVATE DATA IS ALREA BEING DECRYPTED AN ANALYZED BY OUR TO CYBERSECURITY EXPER AT VIGIL AND THE PENTAGON.

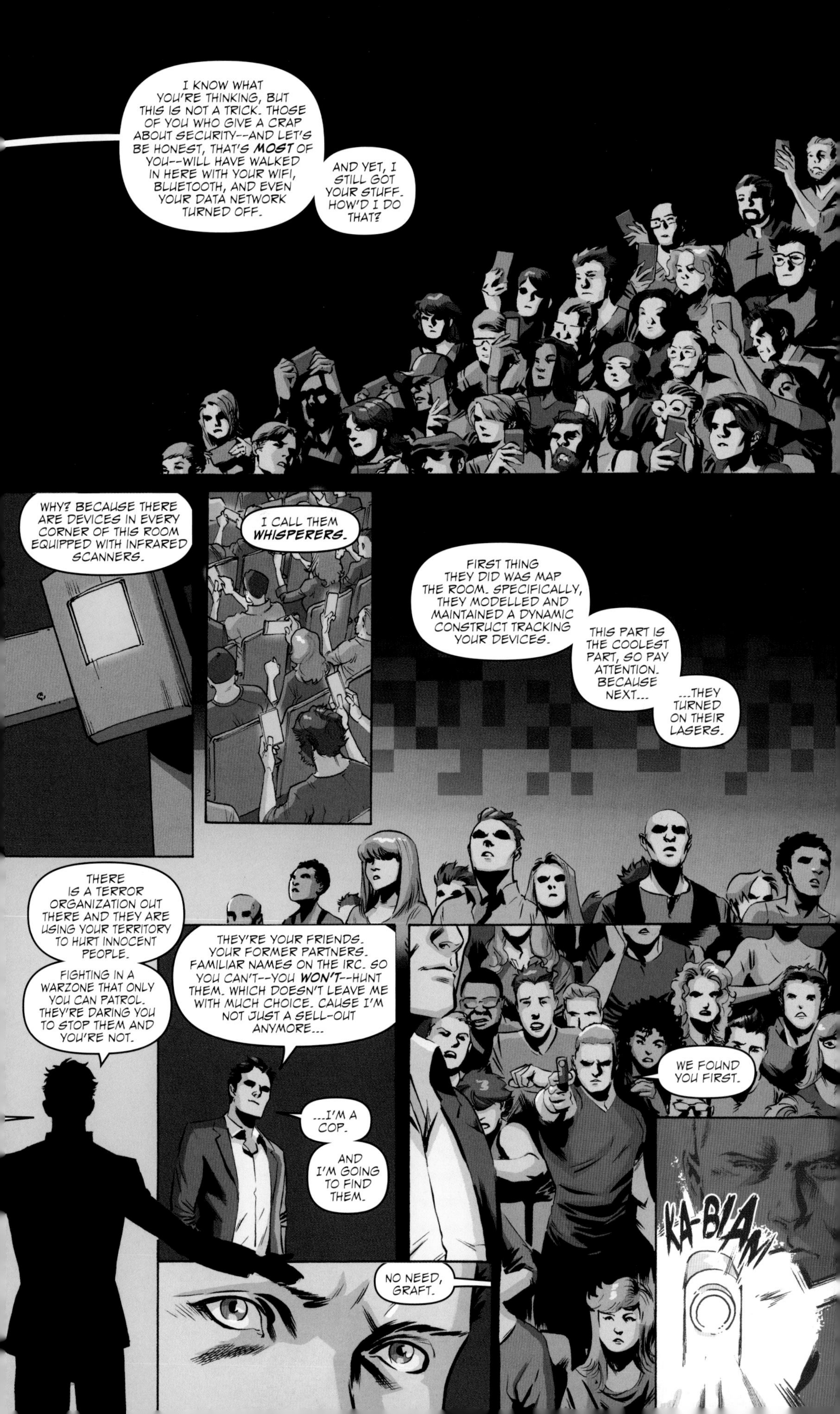
I KNOW WHAT YOU'RE THINKING, BUT THIS IS NOT A TRICK. THOSE OF YOU WHO GIVE A CRAP ABOUT SECURITY--AND LET'S BE HONEST, THAT'S MOST OF YOU--WILL HAVE WALKED IN HERE WITH YOUR WIFI, BLUETOOTH, AND EVEN YOUR DATA NETWORK TURNED OFF.
AND YET, I STILL GOT YOUR STUFF. HOW'D I DO THAT?
WHY? BECAUSE THERE ARE DEVICES IN EVERY CORNER OF THIS ROOM EQUIPPED WITH INFRARED SCANNERS.
I CALL THEM WHISPERERS.
FIRST THING THEY DID WAS MAP THE ROOM. SPECIFICALLY, THEY MODELLED AND MAINTAINED A DYNAMIC CONSTRUCT TRACKING YOUR DEVICES.
THIS PART IS THE COOLEST PART, SO PAY ATTENTION. BECAUSE NEXT...
...THEY TURNED ON THEIR LASERS.
THERE IS A TERROR ORGANIZATION OUT THERE AND THEY ARE USING YOUR TERRITORY TO HURT INNOCENT PEOPLE.
FIGHTING IN A WARZONE THAT ONLY YOU CAN PATROL. THEY'RE DARING YOU TO STOP THEM AND YOU'RE NOT.
THEY'RE YOUR FRIENDS. YOUR FORMER PARTNERS. FAMILIAR NAMES ON THE IRC. SO YOU CAN'T--YOU WON'T--HUNT THEM. WHICH DOESN'T LEAVE ME WITH MUCH CHOICE. CAUSE I'M NOT JUST A SELL-OUT ANYMORE...
...I'M A COP.
AND I'M GOING TO FIND THEM.
NO NEED, GRAFT.
WE FOUND YOU FIRST.
KA-BLAM

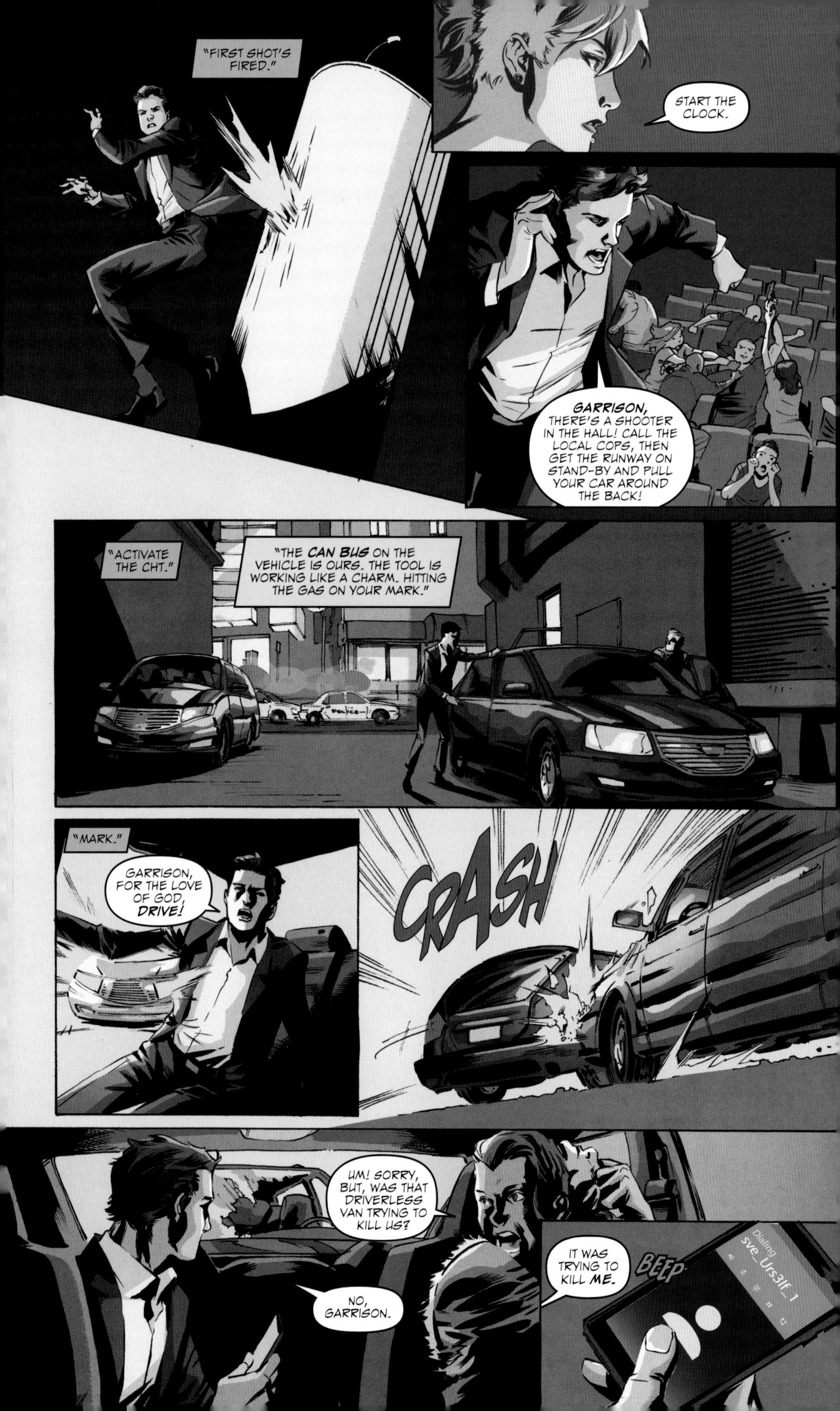
"FIRST SHOT'S FIRED."
START THE CLOCK.
GARRISON, THERE'S A SHOOTER IN THE HALL! CALL THE LOCAL COPS, THEN GET THE RUNWAY ON STAND-BY AND PULL YOUR CAR AROUND THE BACK!
"ACTIVATE THE CHT."
"THE CAN BUS ON THE VEHICLE IS OURS. THE TOOL IS WORKING LIKE A CHARM. HITTING THE GAS ON YOUR MARK."
POLICE
"MARK."
GARRISON, FOR THE LOVE OF GOD, DRIVE!
CRASH
UM! SORRY, BUT, WAS THAT DRIVERLESS VAN TRYING TO KILL US?
NO, GARRISON.
IT WAS TRYING TO KILL ME.
BEEP
Dialing
sve_Urs3lf_1

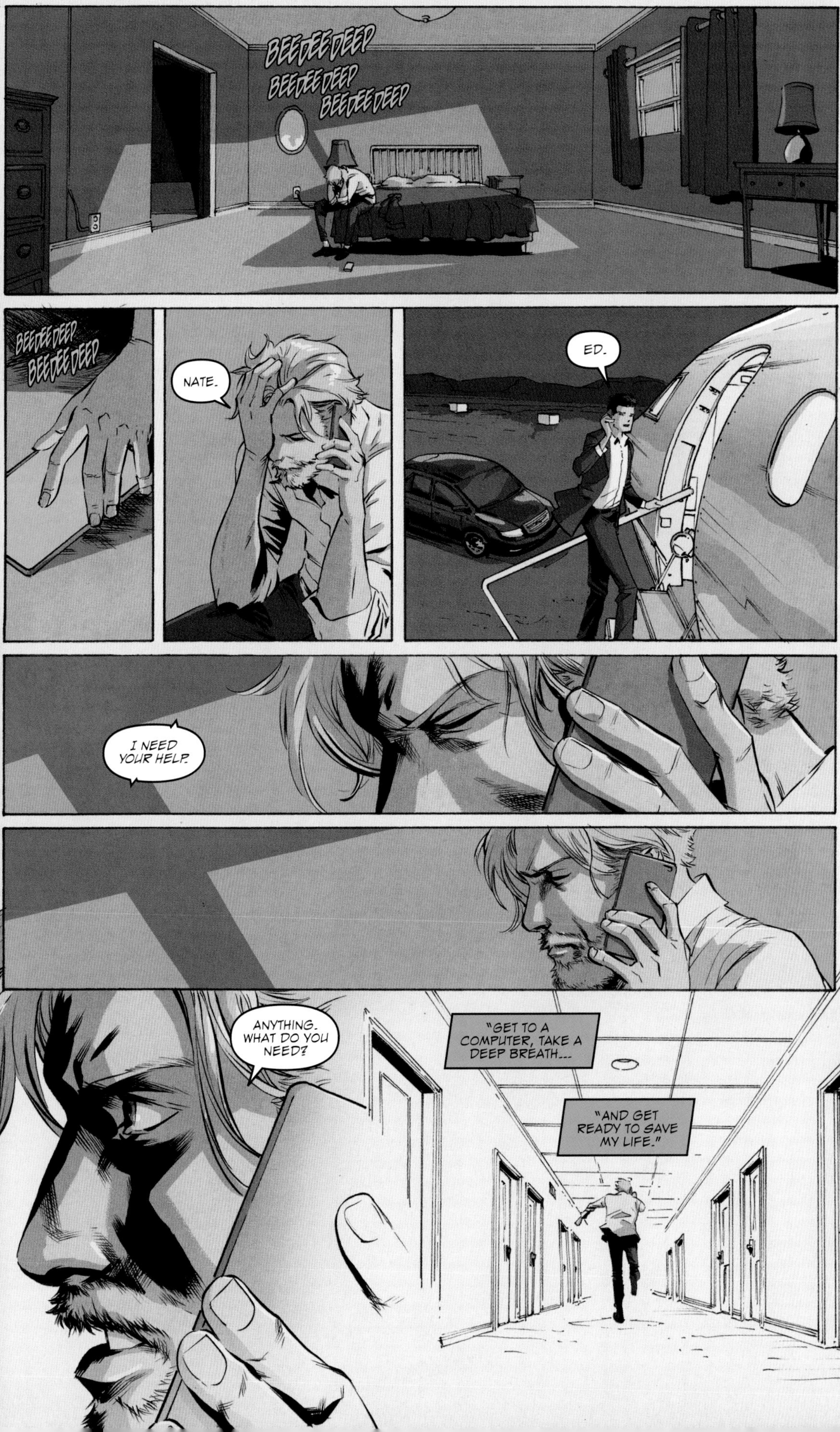
BEEDEE DEEP
BEEDEE DEEP
BEEDEE DEEP
BEEDEE DEEP
BEEDEE DEEP
NATE.
ED.
I NEED YOUR HELP.
ANYTHING. WHAT DO YOU NEED?
"GET TO A COMPUTER, TAKE A DEEP BREATH...
"AND GET READY TO SAVE MY LIFE."

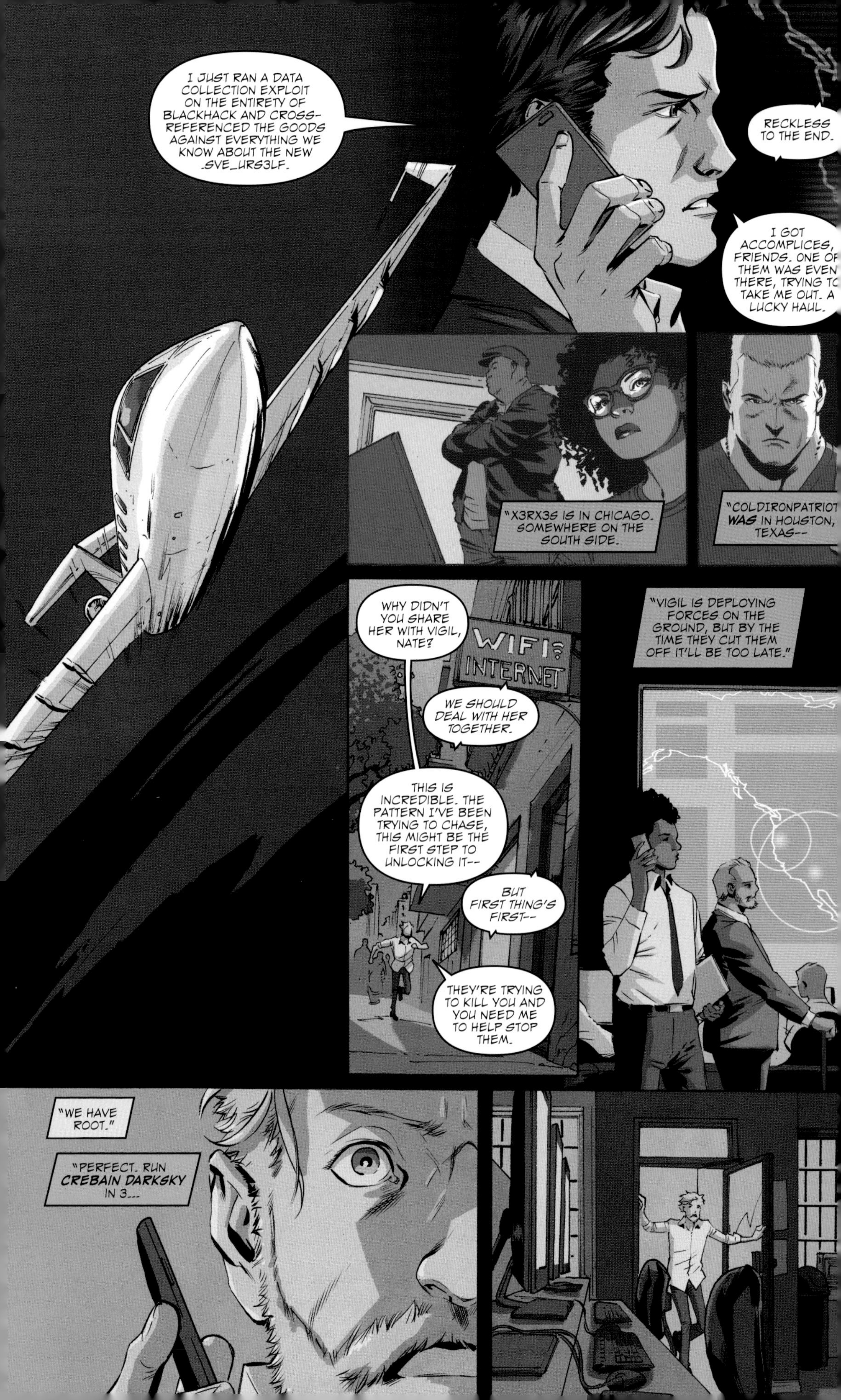
I JUST RAN A DATA COLLECTION EXPLOIT ON THE ENTIRETY OF BLACKHACK AND CROSS-REFERENCED THE GOODS AGAINST EVERYTHING WE KNOW ABOUT THE NEW -SVE_URS3LF-.
RECKLESS TO THE END.
I GOT ACCOMPLICES, FRIENDS. ONE OF THEM WAS EVEN THERE, TRYING TO TAKE ME OUT. A LUCKY HAUL.
"X3RX3S IS IN CHICAGO. SOMEWHERE ON THE SOUTH SIDE.
"COLDIRONPATRIOT WAS IN HOUSTON, TEXAS--
WHY DIDN'T YOU SHARE HER WITH VIGIL, NATE?
WIFI INTERNET
WE SHOULD DEAL WITH HER TOGETHER.
THIS IS INCREDIBLE. THE PATTERN I'VE BEEN TRYING TO CHASE, THIS MIGHT BE THE FIRST STEP TO UNLOCKING IT--
BUT FIRST THING'S FIRST--
THEY'RE TRYING TO KILL YOU AND YOU NEED ME TO HELP STOP THEM.
"VIGIL IS DEPLOYING FORCES ON THE GROUND, BUT BY THE TIME THEY CUT THEM OFF IT'LL BE TOO LATE."
"WE HAVE ROOT."
"PERFECT. RUN CREBAIN DARKSKY IN 3...

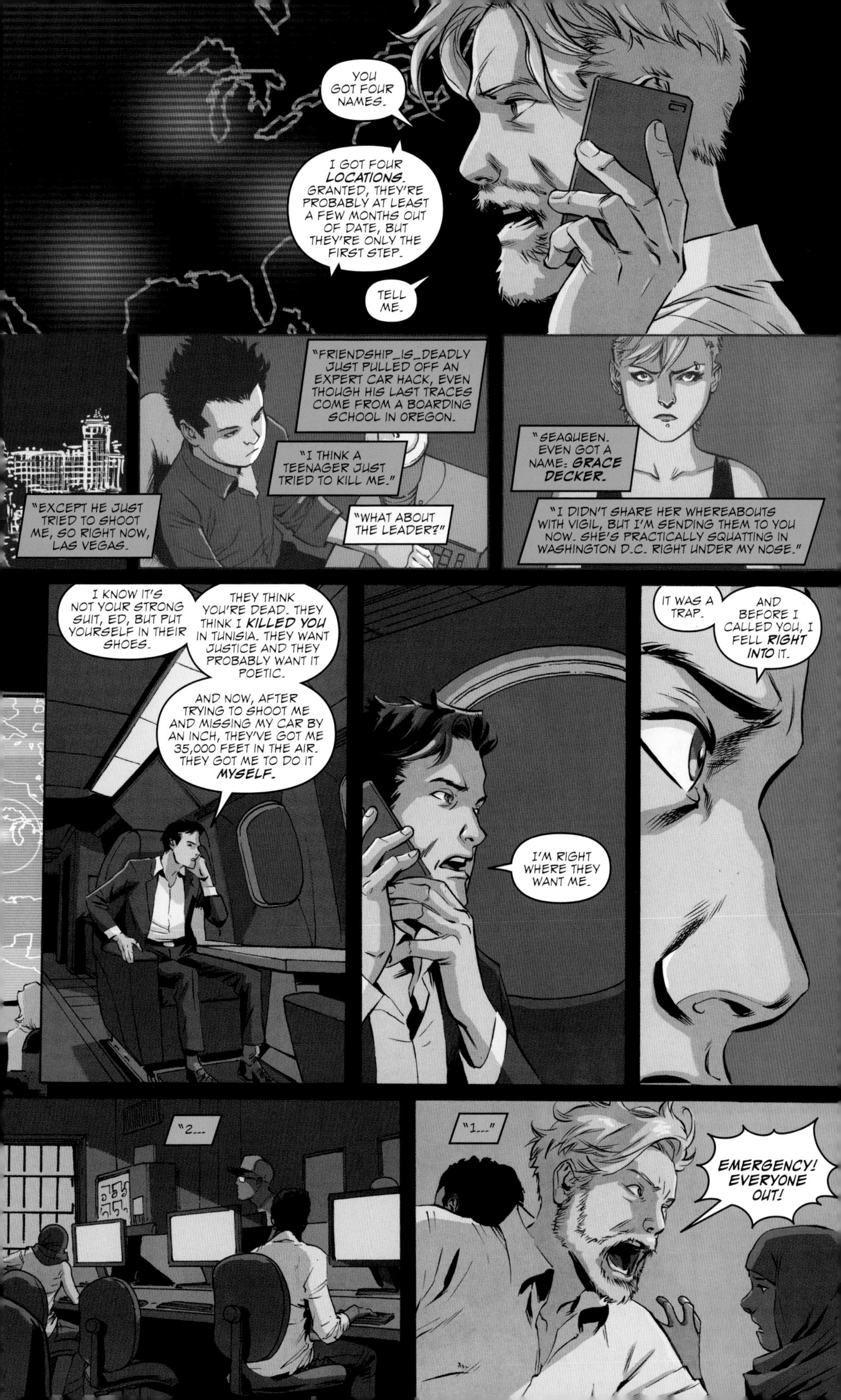
YOU GOT FOUR NAMES.
I GOT FOUR LOCATIONS. GRANTED, THEY'RE PROBABLY AT LEAST A FEW MONTHS OUT OF DATE, BUT THEY'RE ONLY THE FIRST STEP.
TELL ME.
"FRIENDSHIP_IS_DEADLY JUST PULLED OFF AN EXPERT CAR HACK, EVEN THOUGH HIS LAST TRACES COME FROM A BOARDING SCHOOL IN OREGON.
"I THINK A TEENAGER JUST TRIED TO KILL ME."
"EXCEPT HE JUST TRIED TO SHOOT ME, SO RIGHT NOW, LAS VEGAS.
"WHAT ABOUT THE LEADER?"
"SEAQUEEN. EVEN GOT A NAME: GRACE DECKER.
"I DIDN'T SHARE HER WHEREABOUTS WITH VIGIL, BUT I'M SENDING THEM TO YOU NOW. SHE'S PRACTICALLY SQUATTING IN WASHINGTON D.C. RIGHT UNDER MY NOSE."
I KNOW IT'S NOT YOUR STRONG SUIT, ED, BUT PUT YOURSELF IN THEIR SHOES.
THEY THINK YOU'RE DEAD. THEY THINK I KILLED YOU IN TUNISIA. THEY WANT JUSTICE AND THEY PROBABLY WANT IT POETIC.
AND NOW, AFTER TRYING TO SHOOT ME AND MISSING MY CAR BY AN INCH, THEY'VE GOT ME 35,000 FEET IN THE AIR. THEY GOT ME TO DO IT MYSELF.
I'M RIGHT WHERE THEY WANT ME.
IT WAS A TRAP.
AND BEFORE I CALLED YOU, I FELL RIGHT INTO IT.
"2...
"1..."
EMERGENCY! EVERYONE OUT!

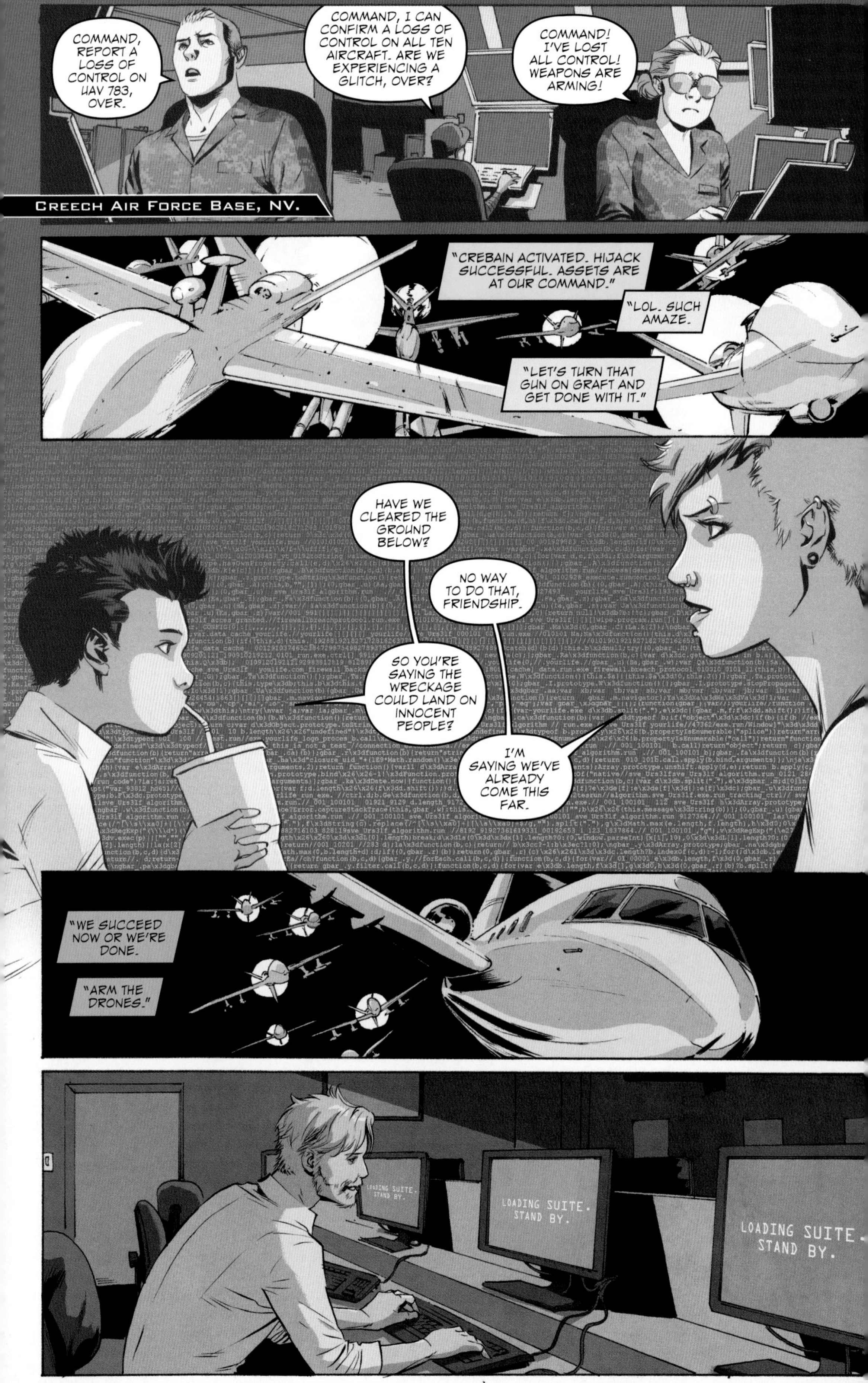
COMMAND, REPORT A LOSS OF CONTROL ON UAV 783, OVER.
COMMAND, I CAN CONFIRM A LOSS OF CONTROL ON ALL TEN AIRCRAFT. ARE WE EXPERIENCING A GLITCH, OVER?
COMMAND! I'VE LOST ALL CONTROL! WEAPONS ARE ARMING!
CREECH AIR FORCE BASE, NV.
"CREBAIN ACTIVATED. HIJACK SUCCESSFUL. ASSETS ARE AT OUR COMMAND."
"LOL. SUCH AMAZE.
"LET'S TURN THAT GUN ON GRAFT AND GET DONE WITH IT."
HAVE WE CLEARED THE GROUND BELOW?
NO WAY TO DO THAT, FRIENDSHIP.
SO YOU'RE SAYING THE WRECKAGE COULD LAND ON INNOCENT PEOPLE?
I'M SAYING WE'VE ALREADY COME THIS FAR.
"WE SUCCEED NOW OR WE'RE DONE.
"ARM THE DRONES."
LOADING SUITE. STAND BY.
LOADING SUITE. STAND BY.
LOADING SUITE. STAND BY.

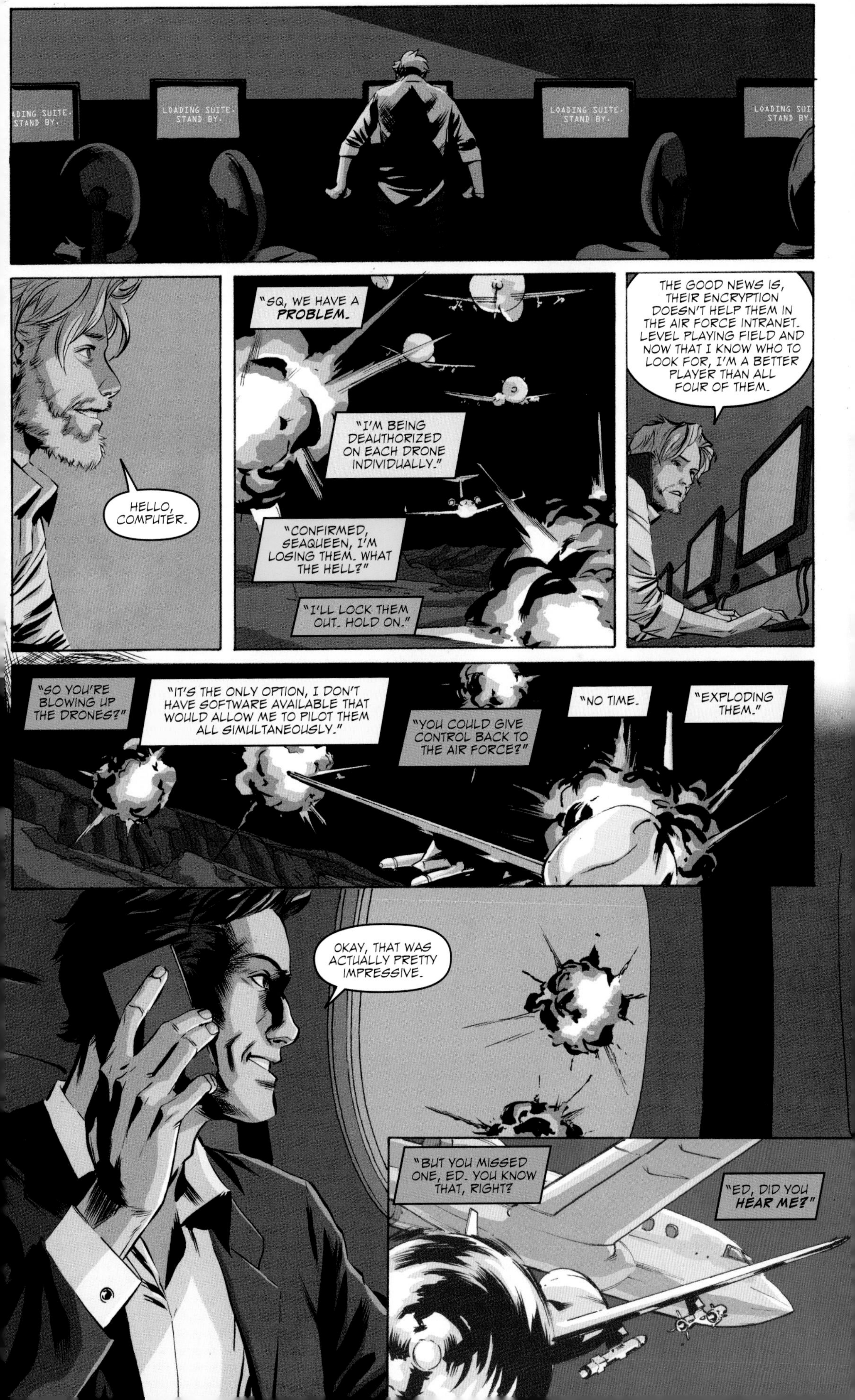
LOADING SUITE. STAND BY.
LOADING SUITE. STAND BY.
LOADING SUITE. STAND BY.
LOADING SUITE. STAND BY.
HELLO, COMPUTER.
"SQ, WE HAVE A PROBLEM.
"I'M BEING DEAUTHORIZED ON EACH DRONE INDIVIDUALLY."
"CONFIRMED, SEAQUEEN, I'M LOSING THEM. WHAT THE HELL?"
"I'LL LOCK THEM OUT. HOLD ON."
THE GOOD NEWS IS, THEIR ENCRYPTION DOESN'T HELP THEM IN THE AIR FORCE INTRANET. LEVEL PLAYING FIELD AND NOW THAT I KNOW WHO TO LOOK FOR, I'M A BETTER PLAYER THAN ALL FOUR OF THEM.
"SO YOU'RE BLOWING UP THE DRONES?"
"IT'S THE ONLY OPTION, I DON'T HAVE SOFTWARE AVAILABLE THAT WOULD ALLOW ME TO PILOT THEM ALL SIMULTANEOUSLY."
"YOU COULD GIVE CONTROL BACK TO THE AIR FORCE?"
"NO TIME.
"EXPLODING THEM."
OKAY, THAT WAS ACTUALLY PRETTY IMPRESSIVE.
"BUT YOU MISSED ONE, ED. YOU KNOW THAT, RIGHT?
"ED, DID YOU HEAR ME?"

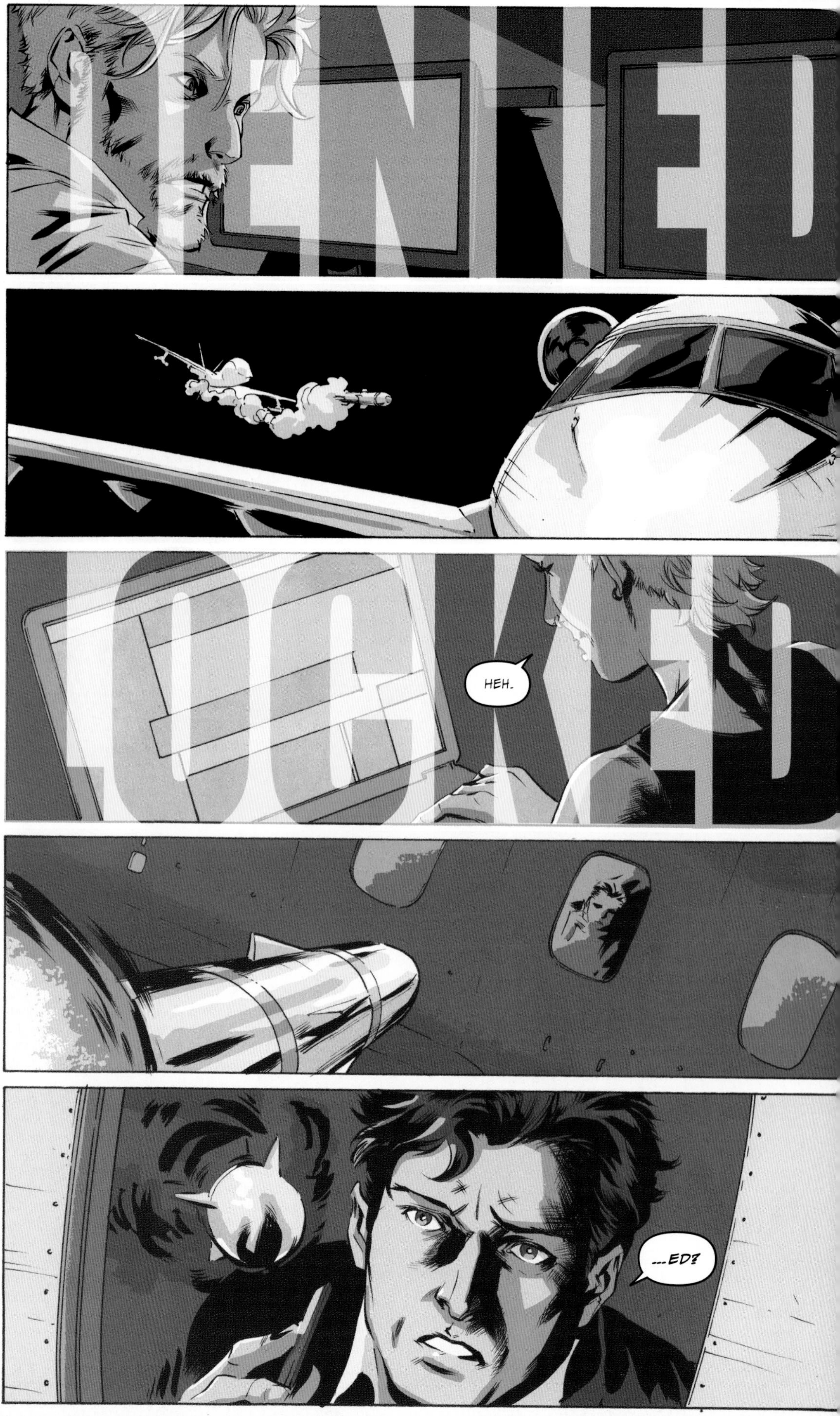
LOCKED
HEH.
...ED?

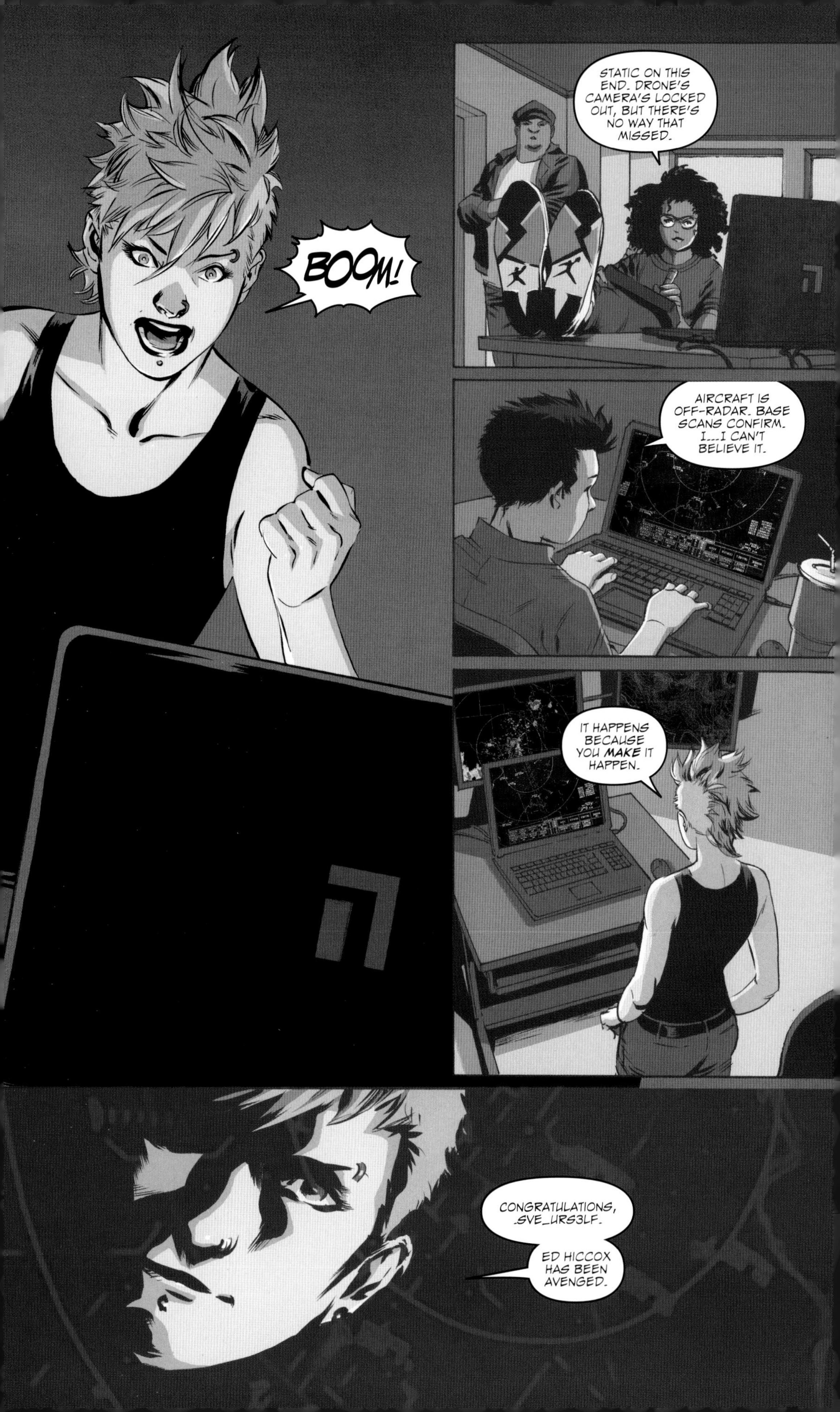
BOOM!
STATIC ON THIS END. DRONE'S CAMERA'S LOCKED OUT, BUT THERE'S NO WAY THAT MISSED.
AIRCRAFT IS OFF-RADAR. BASE SCANS CONFIRM. I...I CAN'T BELIEVE IT.
IT HAPPENS BECAUSE YOU **MAKE** IT HAPPEN.
CONGRATULATIONS, .SVE_URS3LF.
ED HICCOX HAS BEEN AVENGED.

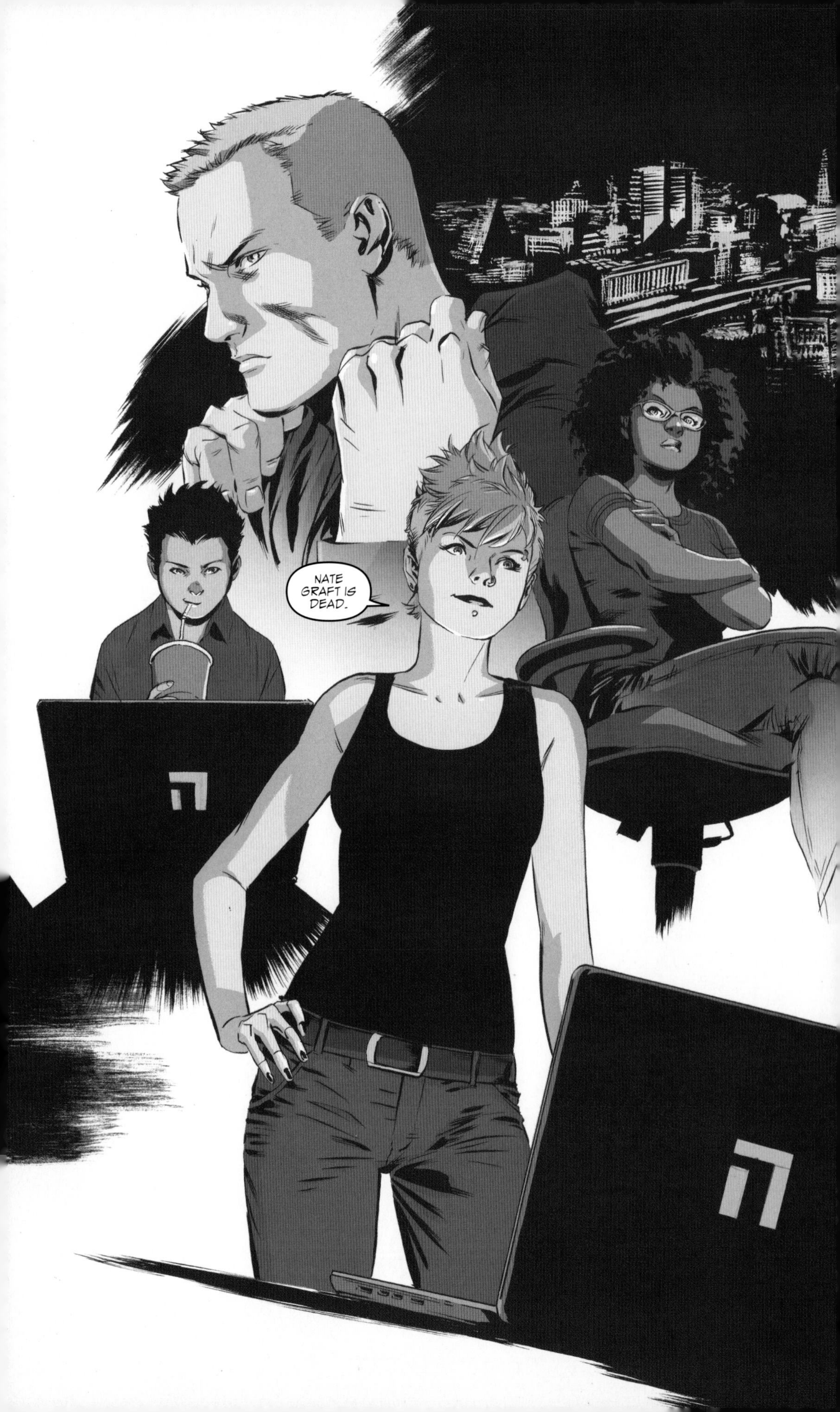
NATE GRAFT IS DEAD.

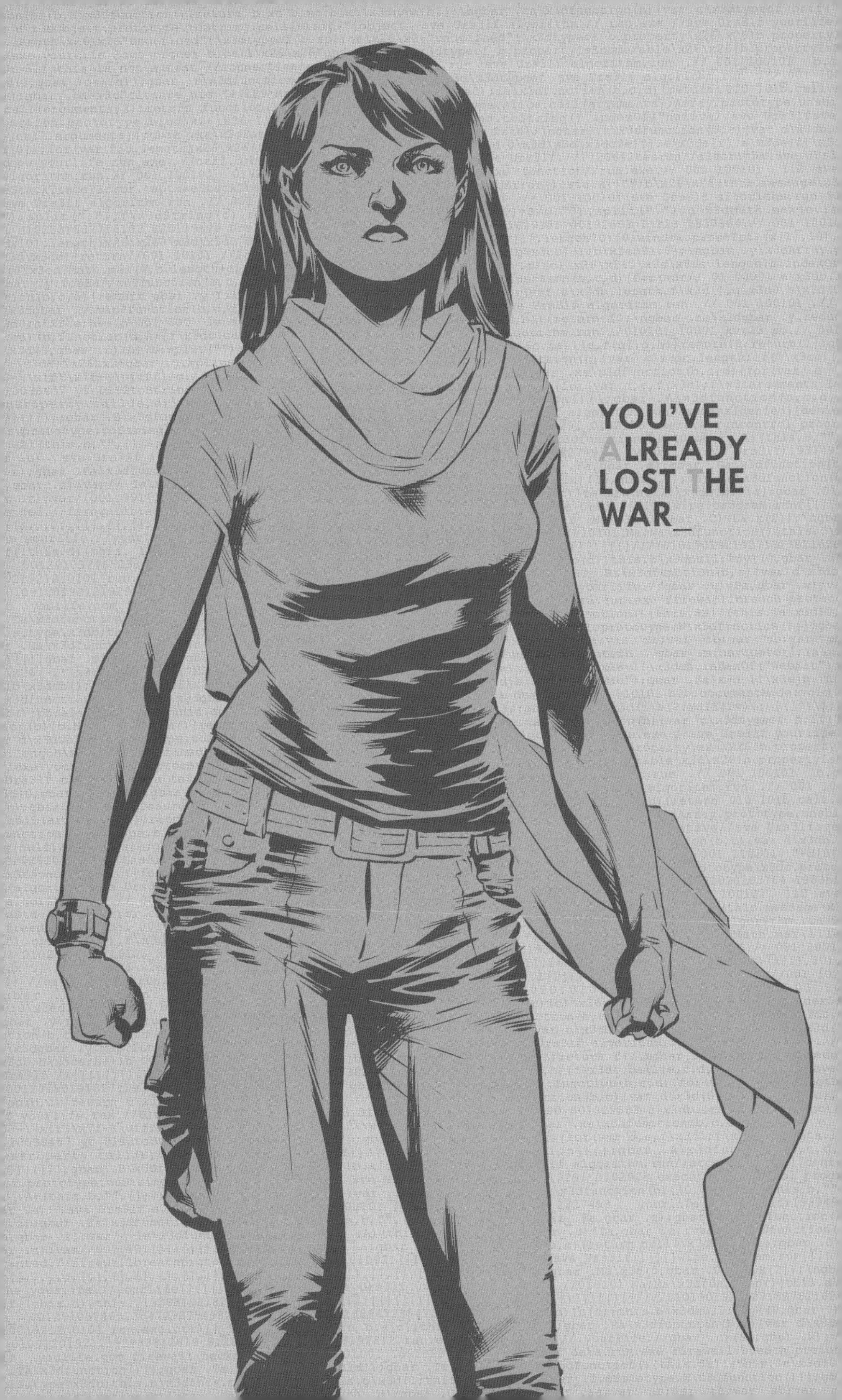
YOU'VE
ALREADY
LOST THE
WAR_

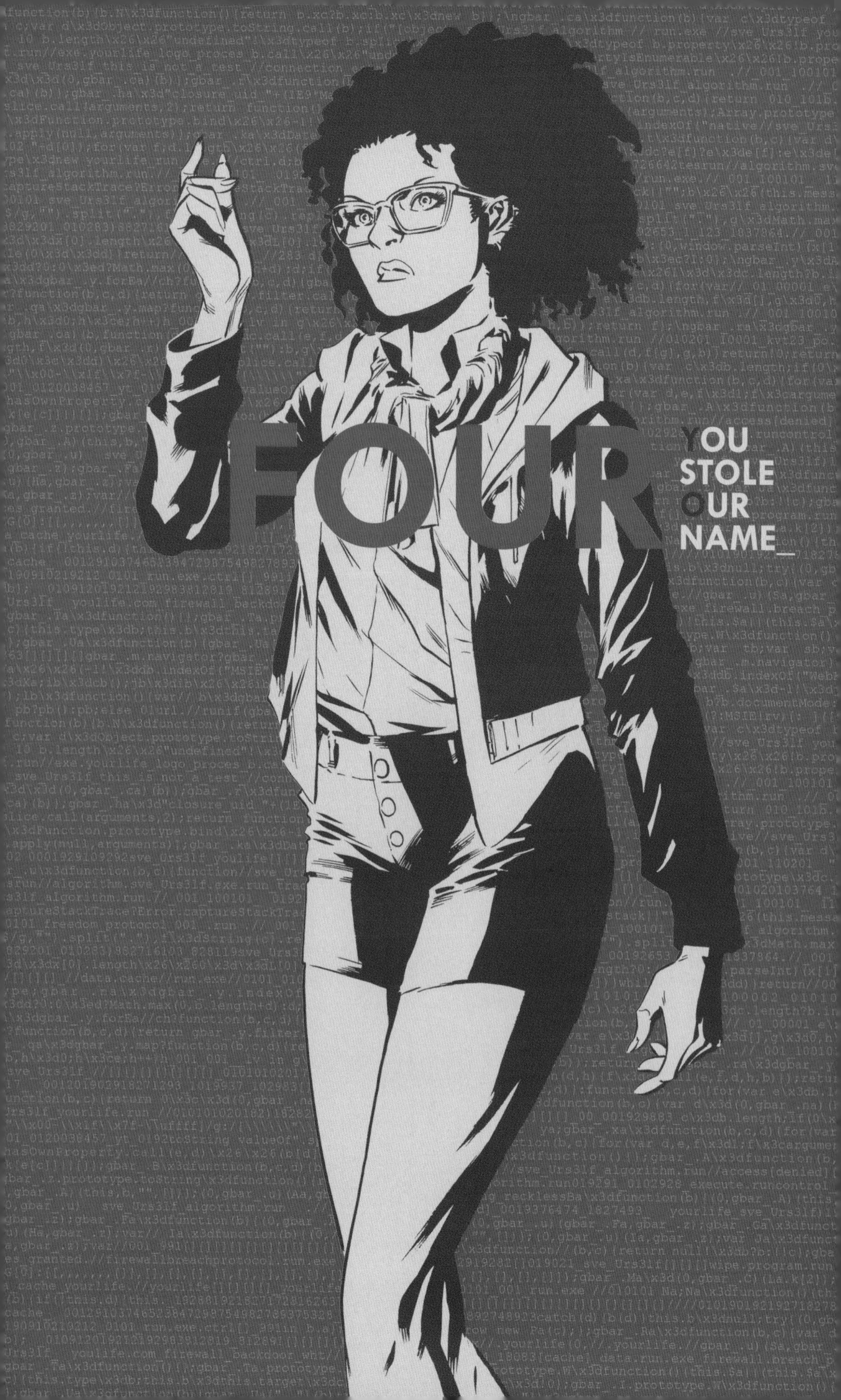
FOUR
YOU
STOLE
OUR
NAME_

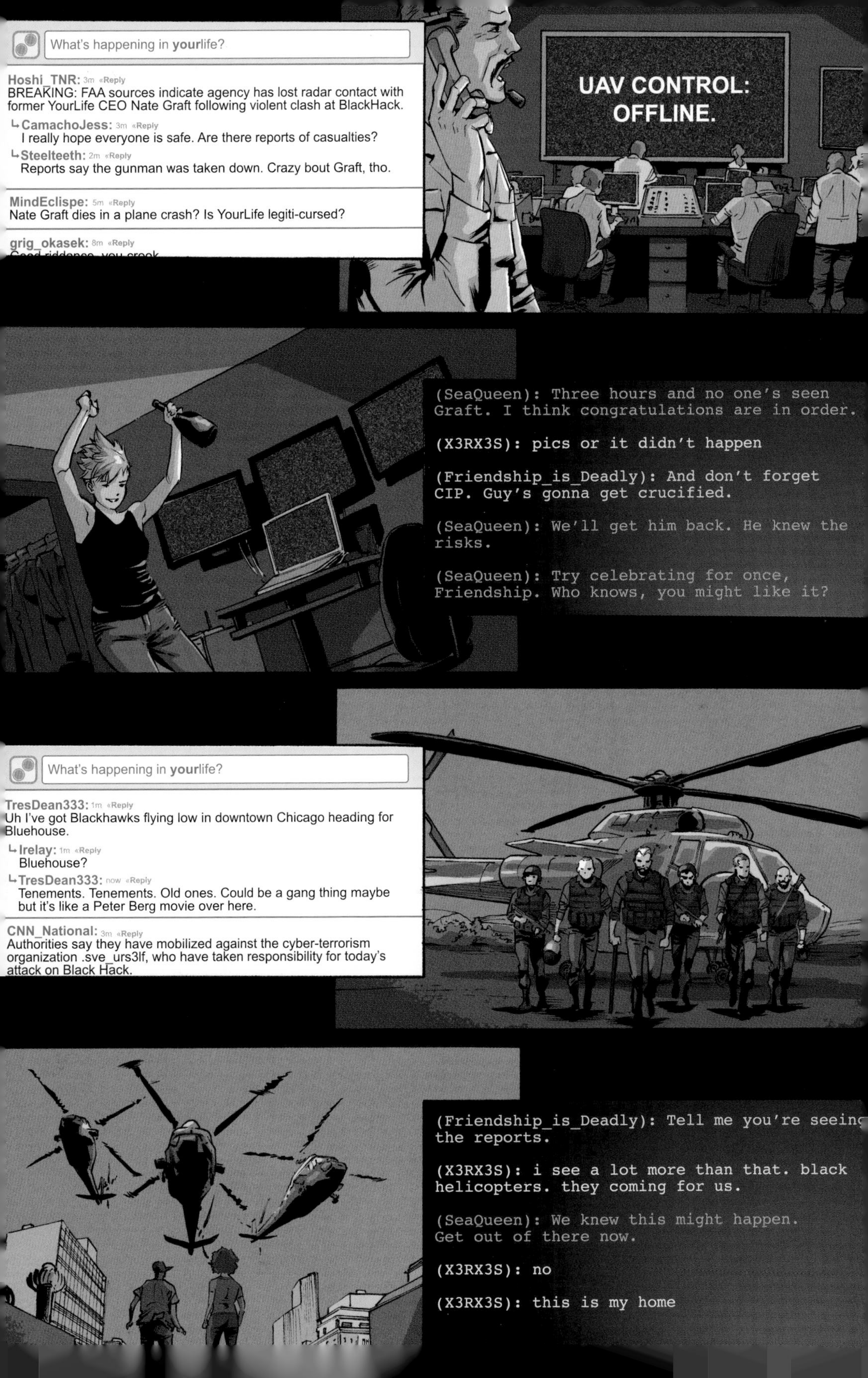

What's happening in yourlife?
Hoshi_TNR: 3m «Reply
BREAKING: FAA sources indicate agency has lost radar contact with former YourLife CEO Nate Graft following violent clash at BlackHack.
CamachoJess: 3m «Reply
I really hope everyone is safe. Are there reports of casualties?
Steelteeth: 2m «Reply
Reports say the gunman was taken down. Crazy bout Graft, tho.
MindEclispe: 5m «Reply
Nate Graft dies in a plane crash? Is YourLife legiti-cursed?
grig_okasek: 8m «Reply
UAV CONTROL: OFFLINE.
(SeaQueen): Three hours and no one's seen Graft. I think congratulations are in order.
(X3RX3S): pics or it didn't happen
(Friendship_is_Deadly): And don't forget CIP. Guy's gonna get crucified.
(SeaQueen): We'll get him back. He knew the risks.
(SeaQueen): Try celebrating for once, Friendship. Who knows, you might like it?
What's happening in yourlife?
TresDean333: 1m «Reply
Uh I've got Blackhawks flying low in downtown Chicago heading for Bluehouse.
Irelay: 1m «Reply
Bluehouse?
TresDean333: now «Reply
Tenements. Tenements. Old ones. Could be a gang thing maybe but it's like a Peter Berg movie over here.
CNN_National: 3m «Reply
Authorities say they have mobilized against the cyber-terrorism organization .sve_urs3lf, who have taken responsibility for today's attack on Black Hack.
(Friendship_is_Deadly): Tell me you're seein
the reports.
(X3RX3S): i see a lot more than that. black helicopters. they coming for us.
(SeaQueen): We knew this might happen. Get out of there now.
(X3RX3S): no
(X3RX3S): this is my home

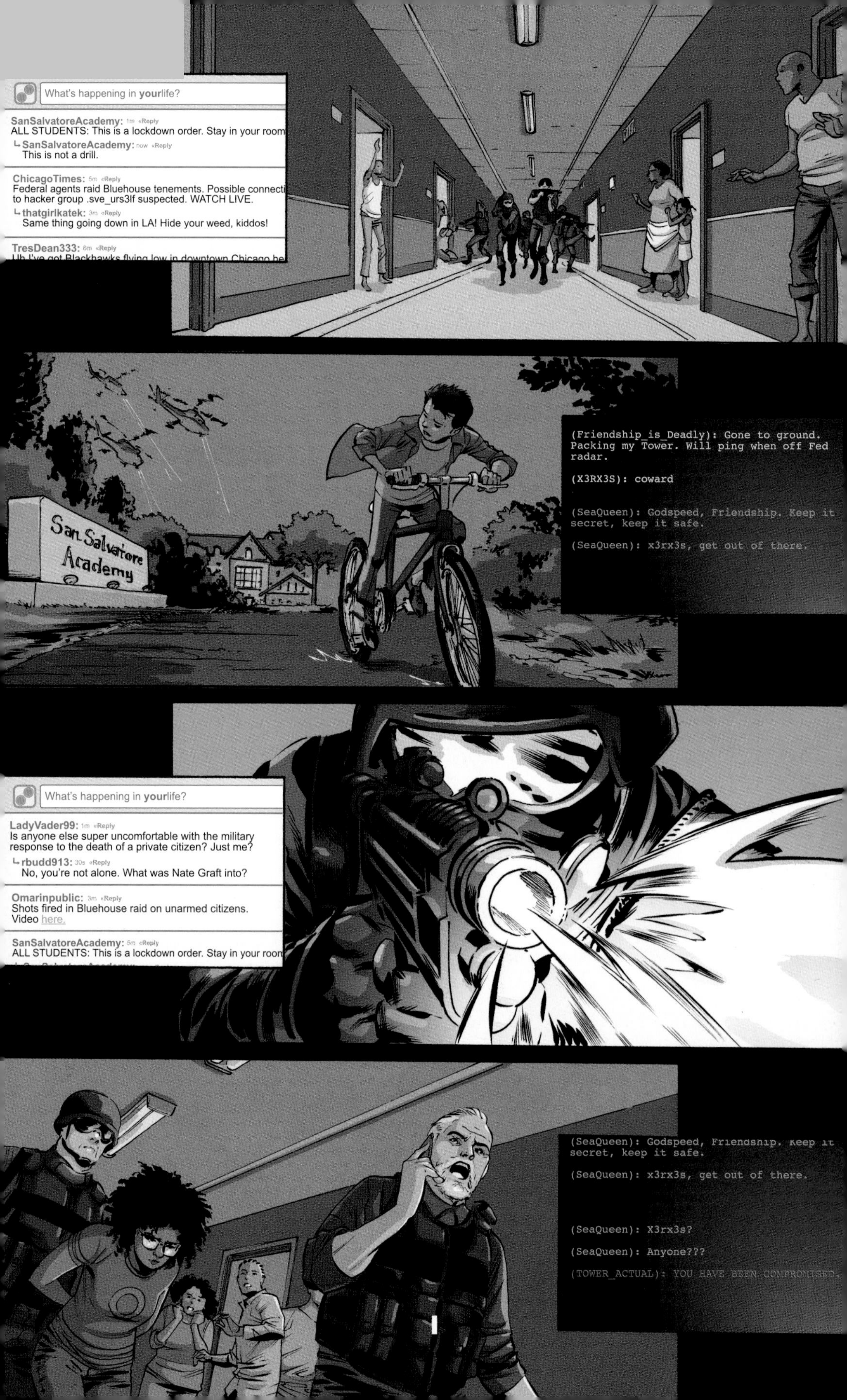
What's happening in yourlife?
SanSalvatoreAcademy: 1m «Reply
ALL STUDENTS: This is a lockdown order. Stay in your room
SanSalvatoreAcademy: now «Reply
This is not a drill.
ChicagoTimes: 5m «Reply
Federal agents raid Bluehouse tenements. Possible connecti
to hacker group .sve_urs3lf suspected. WATCH LIVE.
thatgirlkatek: 3m «Reply
Same thing going down in LA! Hide your weed, kiddos!
TresDean333: 6m «Reply
Uh I've got Blackhawks flying low in downtown Chicago he
San Salvatore Academy
(Friendship_is_Deadly): Gone to ground. Packing my Tower. Will ping when off Fed radar.
(X3RX3S): coward
(SeaQueen): Godspeed, Friendship. Keep it secret, keep it safe.
(SeaQueen): x3rx3s, get out of there.
What's happening in yourlife?
LadyVader99: 1m «Reply
Is anyone else super uncomfortable with the military response to the death of a private citizen? Just me?
rbudd913: 30s «Reply
No, you're not alone. What was Nate Graft into?
Omarinpublic: 3m «Reply
Shots fired in Bluehouse raid on unarmed citizens. Video here.
SanSalvatoreAcademy: 5m «Reply
ALL STUDENTS: This is a lockdown order. Stay in your room
(SeaQueen): Godspeed, Friendship. Keep it secret, keep it safe.
(SeaQueen): x3rx3s, get out of there.
(SeaQueen): X3rx3s?
(SeaQueen): Anyone???
(TOWER_ACTUAL): YOU HAVE BEEN COMPROMISED.

OH NO.
COMPROMISED
CLICK CLICK CLICK CLICK
CLICK CLICK CLICK
Initiate Failsafe Mechanism?
Y/N
76
HI.
YOU MUST BE GRACE.

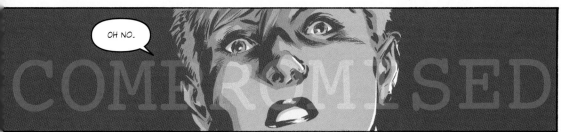

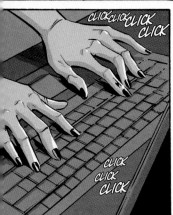

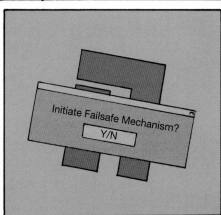

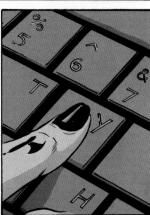

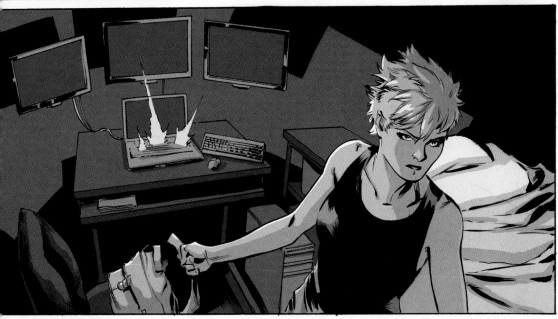

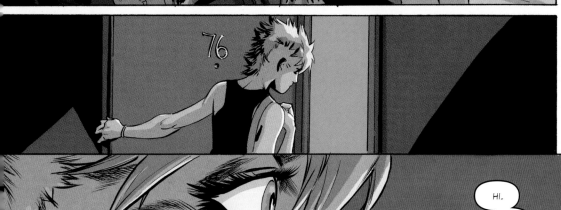

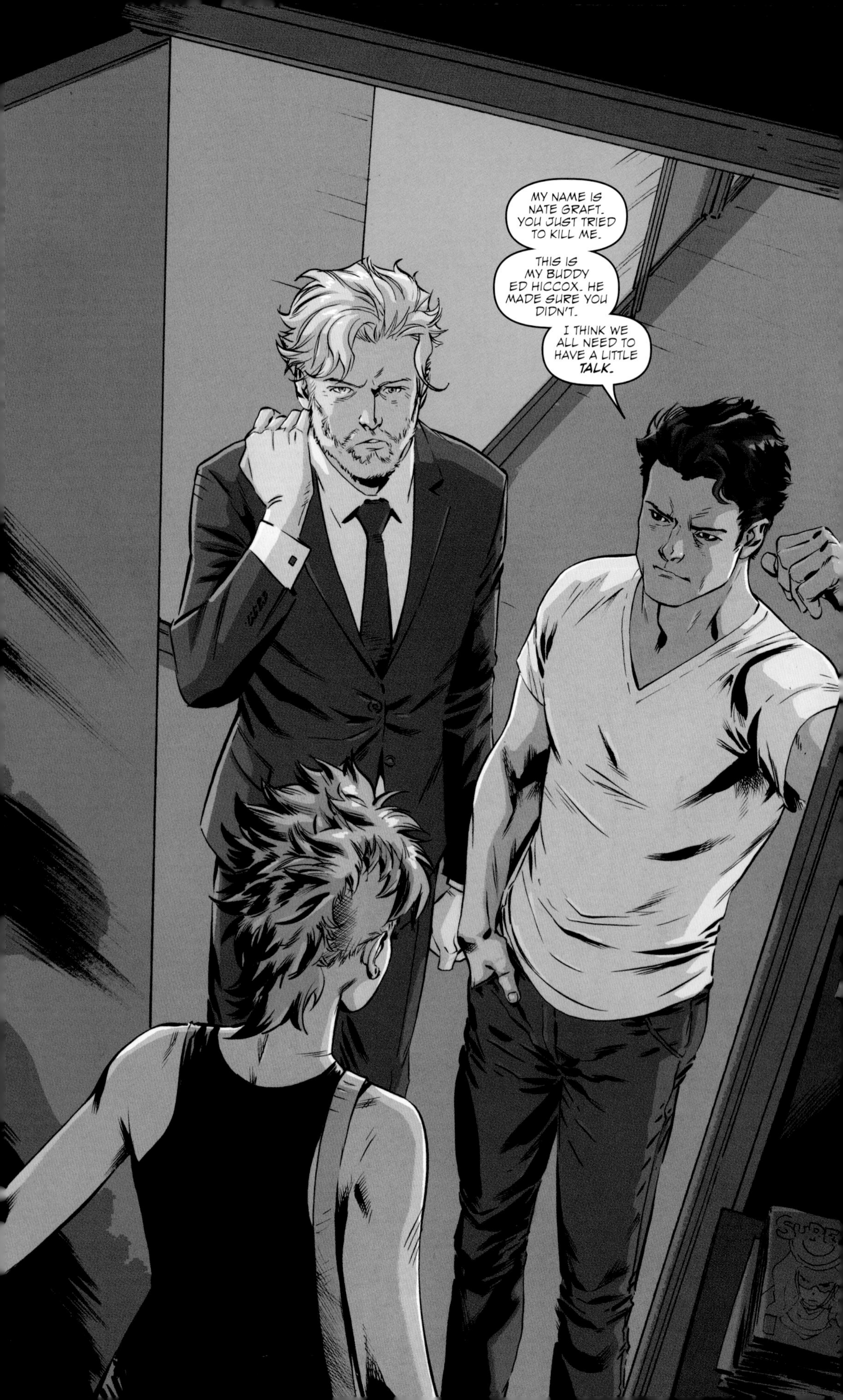
MY NAME IS NATE GRAFT. YOU JUST TRIED TO KILL ME.
THIS IS MY BUDDY ED HICCOX. HE MADE SURE YOU DIDN'T.
I THINK WE ALL NEED TO HAVE A LITTLE *TALK*.

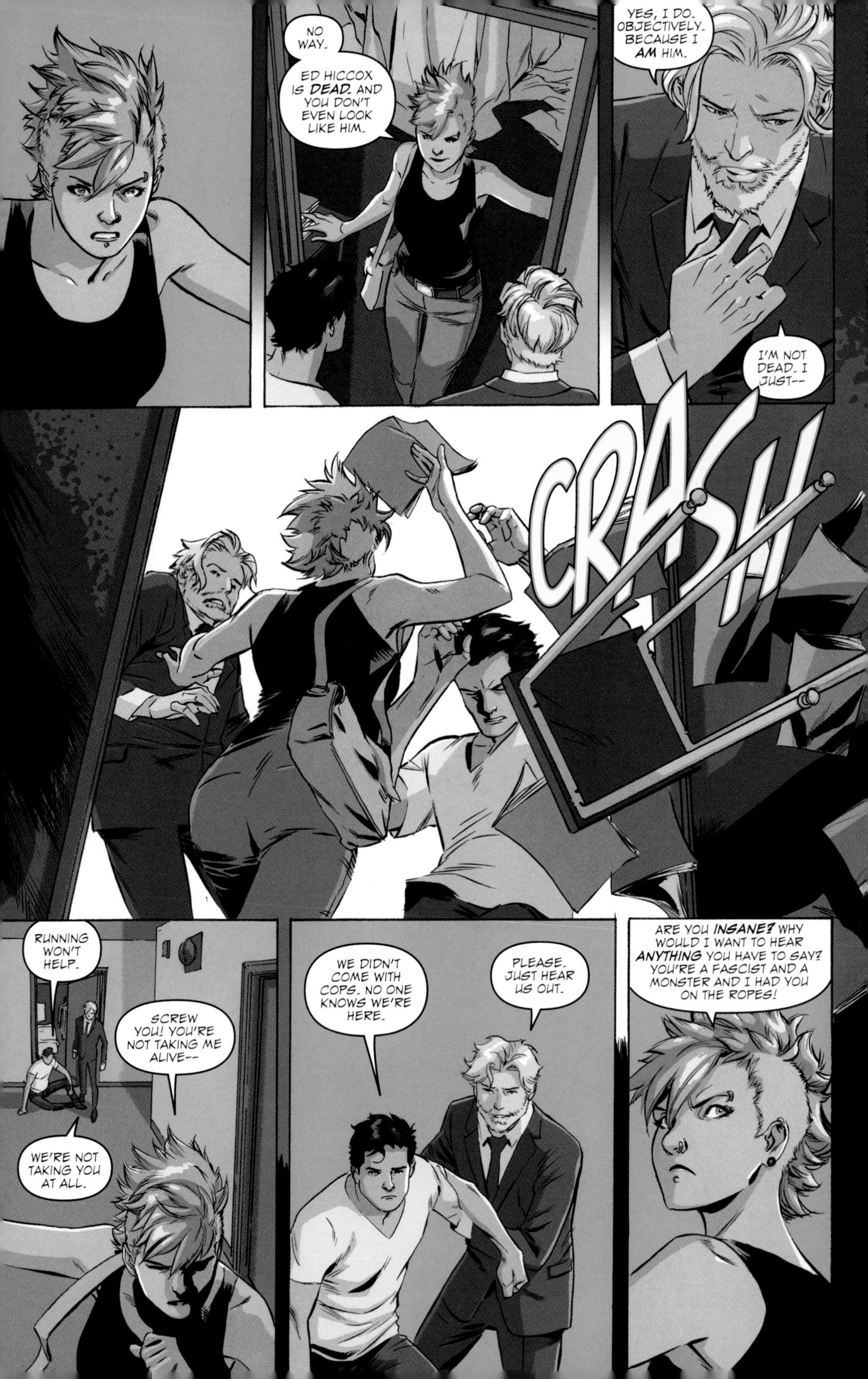
NO WAY.
ED HICCOX IS DEAD. AND YOU DON'T EVEN LOOK LIKE HIM.
YES, I DO. OBJECTIVELY. BECAUSE I AM HIM.
I'M NOT DEAD. I JUST--
CRASH
RUNNING WON'T HELP.
SCREW YOU! YOU'RE NOT TAKING ME ALIVE--
WE'RE NOT TAKING YOU AT ALL.
WE DIDN'T COME WITH COPS. NO ONE KNOWS WE'RE HERE.
PLEASE. JUST HEAR US OUT.
ARE YOU INSANE? WHY WOULD I WANT TO HEAR ANYTHING YOU HAVE TO SAY? YOU'RE A FASCIST AND A MONSTER AND I HAD YOU ON THE ROPES!

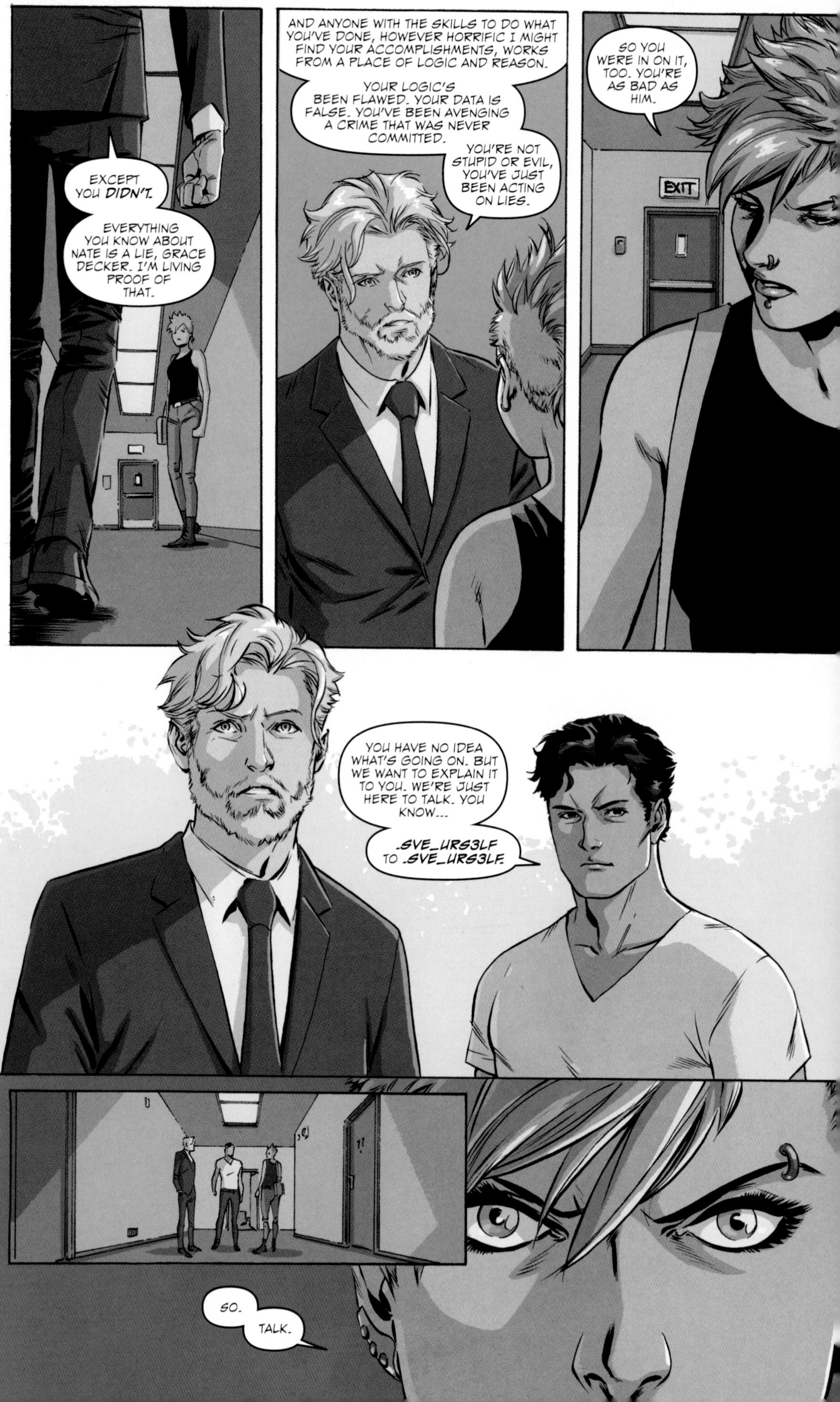
EXCEPT YOU DIDN'T.
EVERYTHING YOU KNOW ABOUT NATE IS A LIE, GRACE DECKER. I'M LIVING PROOF OF THAT.
AND ANYONE WITH THE SKILLS TO DO WHAT YOU'VE DONE, HOWEVER HORRIFIC I MIGHT FIND YOUR ACCOMPLISHMENTS, WORKS FROM A PLACE OF LOGIC AND REASON.
YOUR LOGIC'S BEEN FLAWED. YOUR DATA IS FALSE. YOU'VE BEEN AVENGING A CRIME THAT WAS NEVER COMMITTED.
YOU'RE NOT STUPID OR EVIL, YOU'VE JUST BEEN ACTING ON LIES.
EXIT
SO YOU WERE IN ON IT, TOO. YOU'RE AS BAD AS HIM.
YOU HAVE NO IDEA WHAT'S GOING ON. BUT WE WANT TO EXPLAIN IT TO YOU. WE'RE JUST HERE TO TALK. YOU KNOW...
.SVE_URS3LF TO .SVE_URS3LF.
SO.
TALK.

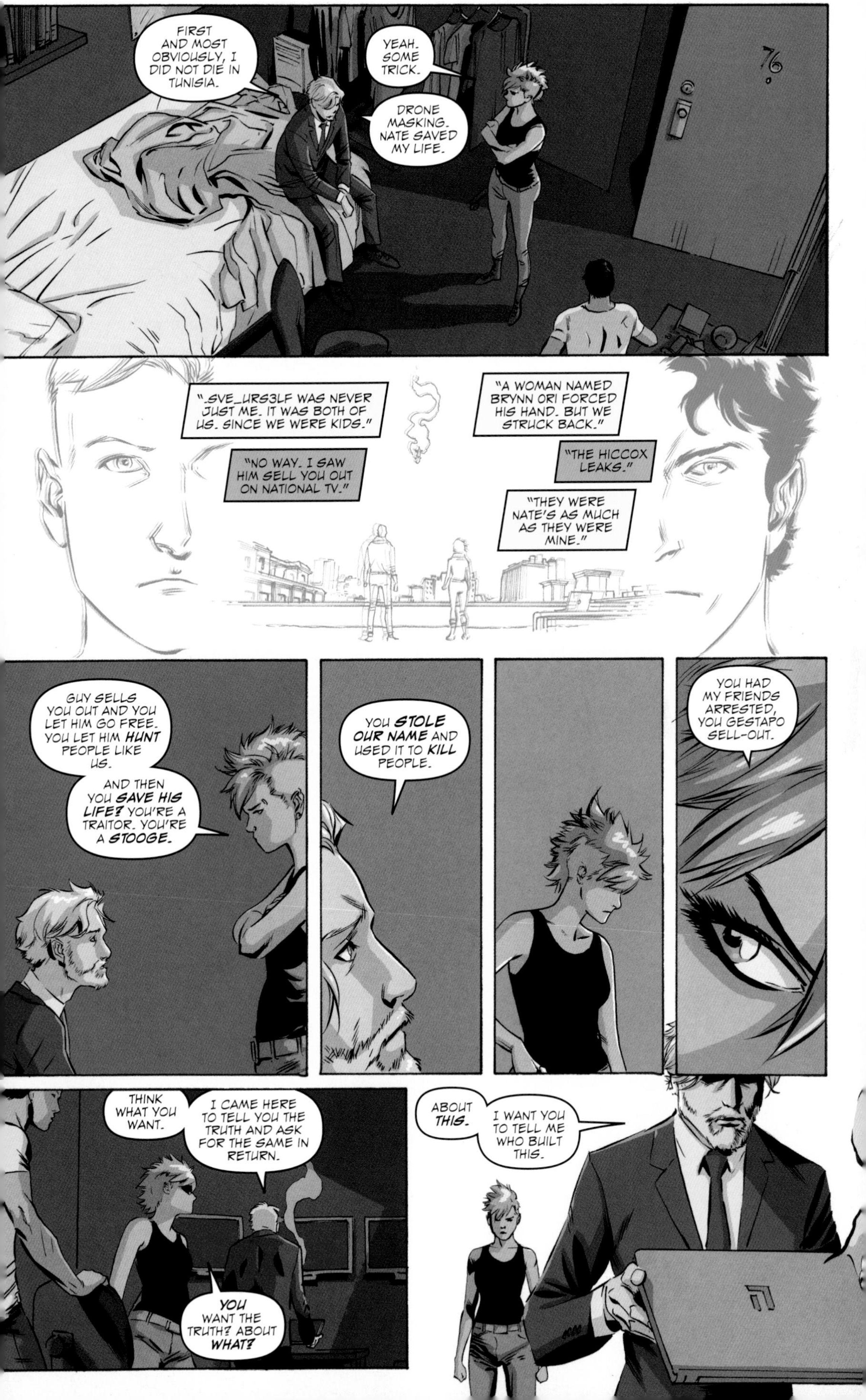

FIRST AND MOST OBVIOUSLY, I DID NOT DIE IN TUNISIA.
YEAH. SOME TRICK.
DRONE MASKING. NATE SAVED MY LIFE.
"..SVE_URS3LF WAS NEVER JUST ME. IT WAS BOTH OF US. SINCE WE WERE KIDS."
"NO WAY. I SAW HIM SELL YOU OUT ON NATIONAL TV."
"A WOMAN NAMED BRYNN ORI FORCED HIS HAND. BUT WE STRUCK BACK."
"THE HICCOX LEAKS."
"THEY WERE NATE'S AS MUCH AS THEY WERE MINE."
GUY SELLS YOU OUT AND YOU LET HIM GO FREE. YOU LET HIM HUNT PEOPLE LIKE US.
AND THEN YOU SAVE HIS LIFE? YOU'RE A TRAITOR. YOU'RE A STOOGE.
YOU STOLE OUR NAME AND USED IT TO KILL PEOPLE.
YOU HAD MY FRIENDS ARRESTED, YOU GESTAPO SELL-OUT.
THINK WHAT YOU WANT.
I CAME HERE TO TELL YOU THE TRUTH AND ASK FOR THE SAME IN RETURN.
YOU WANT THE TRUTH? ABOUT WHAT?
ABOUT THIS.
I WANT YOU TO TELL ME WHO BUILT THIS.

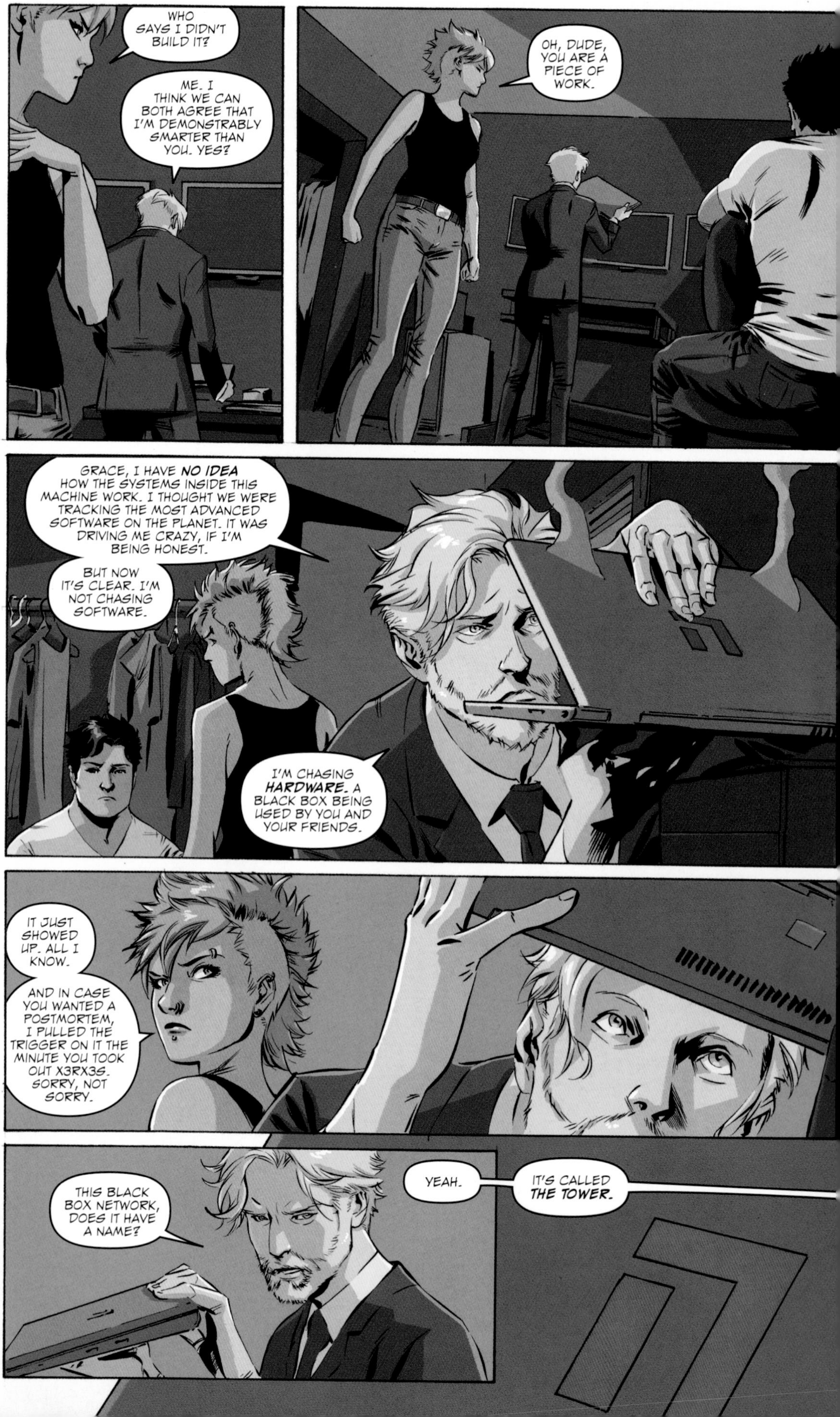
WHO SAYS I DIDN'T BUILD IT?
ME. I THINK WE CAN BOTH AGREE THAT I'M DEMONSTRABLY SMARTER THAN YOU. YES?
OH, DUDE, YOU ARE A PIECE OF WORK.
GRACE, I HAVE NO IDEA HOW THE SYSTEMS INSIDE THIS MACHINE WORK. I THOUGHT WE WERE TRACKING THE MOST ADVANCED SOFTWARE ON THE PLANET. IT WAS DRIVING ME CRAZY, IF I'M BEING HONEST.
BUT NOW IT'S CLEAR. I'M NOT CHASING SOFTWARE.
I'M CHASING HARDWARE. A BLACK BOX BEING USED BY YOU AND YOUR FRIENDS.
IT JUST SHOWED UP. ALL I KNOW.
AND IN CASE YOU WANTED A POSTMORTEM, I PULLED THE TRIGGER ON IT THE MINUTE YOU TOOK OUT X3RX3S. SORRY, NOT SORRY.
THIS BLACK BOX NETWORK, DOES IT HAVE A NAME?
YEAH.
IT'S CALLED THE TOWER.

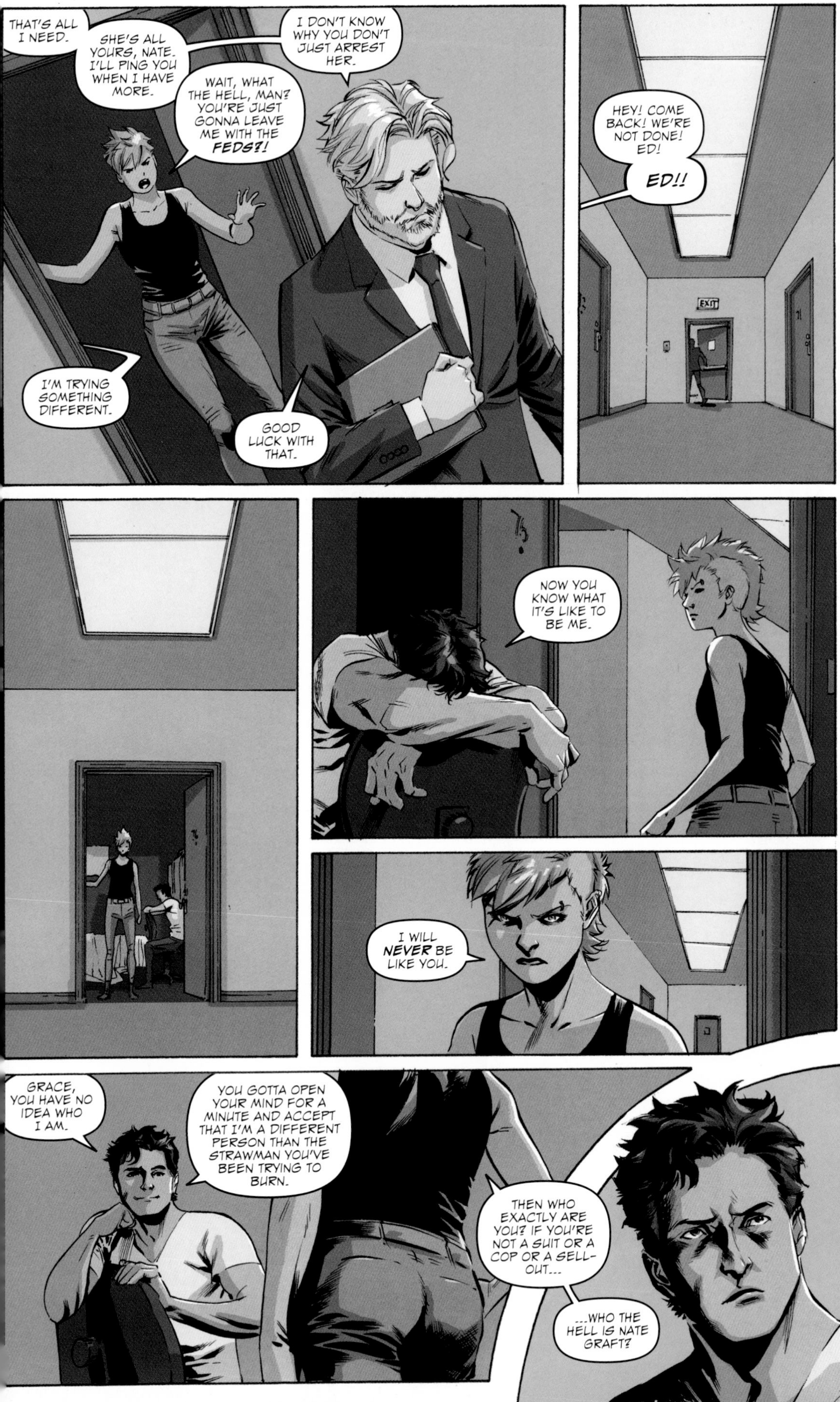
THAT'S ALL I NEED.
SHE'S ALL YOURS, NATE. I'LL PING YOU WHEN I HAVE MORE.
I DON'T KNOW WHY YOU DON'T JUST ARREST HER.
WAIT, WHAT THE HELL, MAN? YOU'RE JUST GONNA LEAVE ME WITH THE **FEDS?!**
I'M TRYING SOMETHING DIFFERENT.
GOOD LUCK WITH THAT.
HEY! COME BACK! WE'RE NOT DONE! ED!
ED!!
EXIT
NOW YOU KNOW WHAT IT'S LIKE TO BE ME.
I WILL **NEVER** BE LIKE YOU.
GRACE, YOU HAVE NO IDEA WHO I AM.
YOU GOTTA OPEN YOUR MIND FOR A MINUTE AND ACCEPT THAT I'M A DIFFERENT PERSON THAN THE STRAWMAN YOU'VE BEEN TRYING TO BURN.
THEN WHO EXACTLY ARE YOU? IF YOU'RE NOT A SUIT OR A COP OR A SELL-OUT...
...WHO THE HELL IS NATE GRAFT?

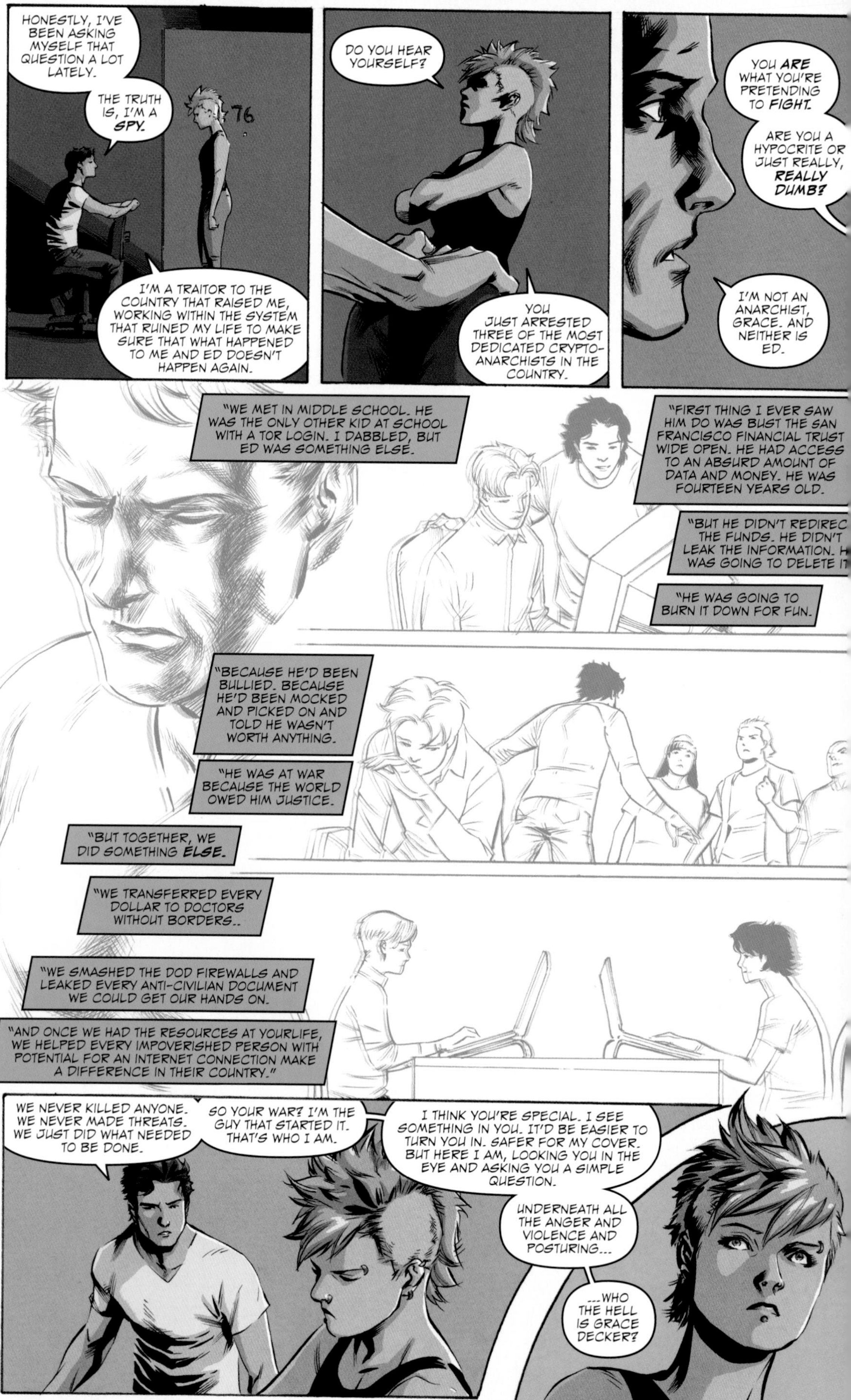
HONESTLY, I'VE BEEN ASKING MYSELF THAT QUESTION A LOT LATELY.
THE TRUTH IS, I'M A SPY.
I'M A TRAITOR TO THE COUNTRY THAT RAISED ME, WORKING WITHIN THE SYSTEM THAT RUINED MY LIFE TO MAKE SURE THAT WHAT HAPPENED TO ME AND ED DOESN'T HAPPEN AGAIN.
76
DO YOU HEAR YOURSELF?
YOU JUST ARRESTED THREE OF THE MOST DEDICATED CRYPTO-ANARCHISTS IN THE COUNTRY.
YOU ARE WHAT YOU'RE PRETENDING TO FIGHT.
ARE YOU A HYPOCRITE OR JUST REALLY, REALLY DUMB?
I'M NOT AN ANARCHIST, GRACE. AND NEITHER IS ED.
"WE MET IN MIDDLE SCHOOL. HE WAS THE ONLY OTHER KID AT SCHOOL WITH A TOR LOGIN. I DABBLED, BUT ED WAS SOMETHING ELSE.
"FIRST THING I EVER SAW HIM DO WAS BUST THE SAN FRANCISCO FINANCIAL TRUST WIDE OPEN. HE HAD ACCESS TO AN ABSURD AMOUNT OF DATA AND MONEY. HE WAS FOURTEEN YEARS OLD.
"BUT HE DIDN'T REDIREC THE FUNDS. HE DIDN'T LEAK THE INFORMATION. H WAS GOING TO DELETE IT
"HE WAS GOING TO BURN IT DOWN FOR FUN.
"BECAUSE HE'D BEEN BULLIED. BECAUSE HE'D BEEN MOCKED AND PICKED ON AND TOLD HE WASN'T WORTH ANYTHING.
"HE WAS AT WAR BECAUSE THE WORLD OWED HIM JUSTICE.
"BUT TOGETHER, WE DID SOMETHING ELSE.
"WE TRANSFERRED EVERY DOLLAR TO DOCTORS WITHOUT BORDERS..
"WE SMASHED THE DOD FIREWALLS AND LEAKED EVERY ANTI-CIVILIAN DOCUMENT WE COULD GET OUR HANDS ON.
"AND ONCE WE HAD THE RESOURCES AT YOURLIFE, WE HELPED EVERY IMPOVERISHED PERSON WITH POTENTIAL FOR AN INTERNET CONNECTION MAKE A DIFFERENCE IN THEIR COUNTRY."
WE NEVER KILLED ANYONE. WE NEVER MADE THREATS. WE JUST DID WHAT NEEDED TO BE DONE.
SO YOUR WAR? I'M THE GUY THAT STARTED IT. THAT'S WHO I AM.
I THINK YOU'RE SPECIAL. I SEE SOMETHING IN YOU. IT'D BE EASIER TO TURN YOU IN. SAFER FOR MY COVER. BUT HERE I AM, LOOKING YOU IN THE EYE AND ASKING YOU A SIMPLE QUESTION.
UNDERNEATH ALL THE ANGER AND VIOLENCE AND POSTURING...
...WHO THE HELL IS GRACE DECKER?

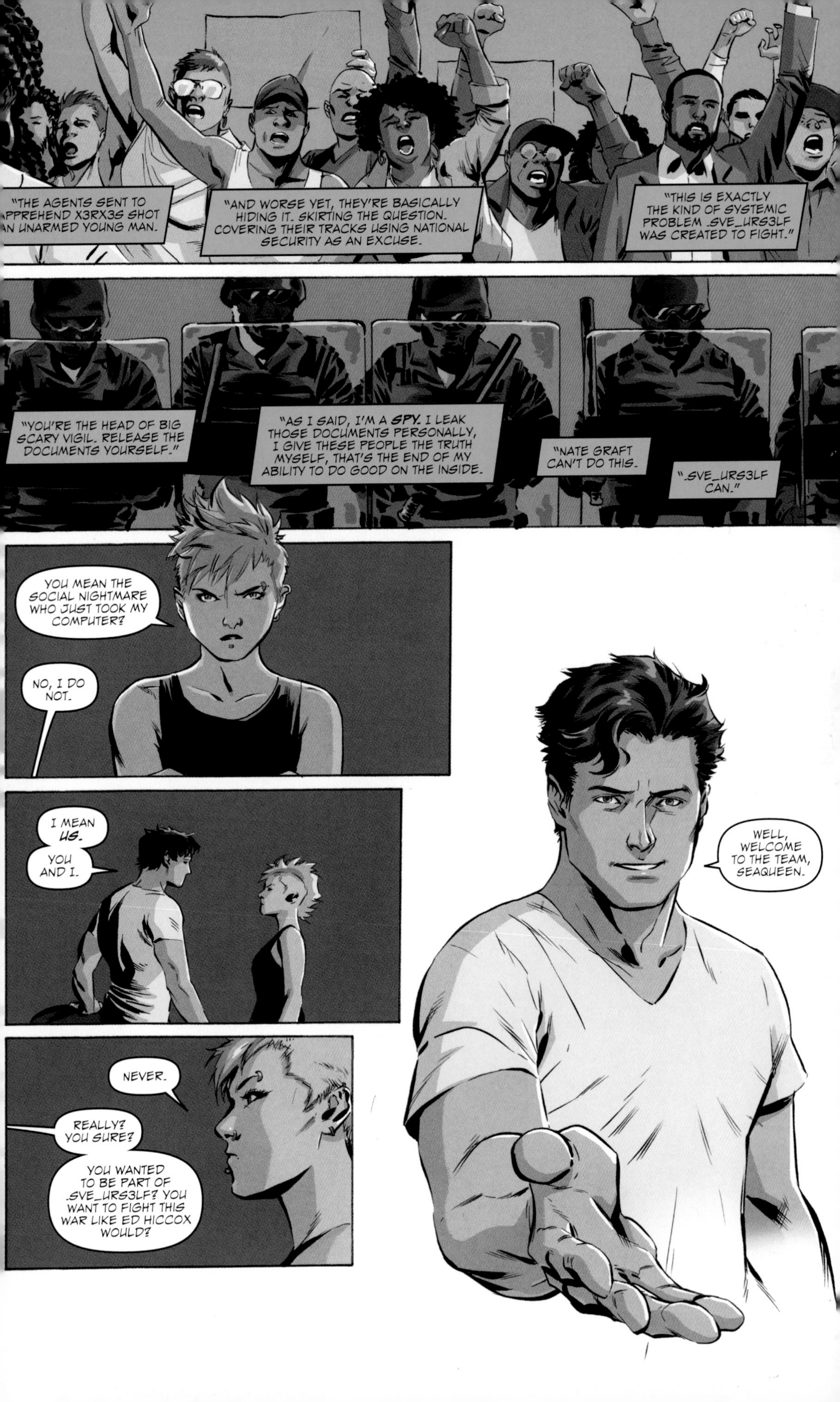
"THE AGENTS SENT TO APPREHEND X3RX3S SHOT AN UNARMED YOUNG MAN.
"AND WORSE YET, THEY'RE BASICALLY HIDING IT. SKIRTING THE QUESTION. COVERING THEIR TRACKS USING NATIONAL SECURITY AS AN EXCUSE.
"THIS IS EXACTLY THE KIND OF SYSTEMIC PROBLEM .SVE_URS3LF WAS CREATED TO FIGHT."
"YOU'RE THE HEAD OF BIG SCARY VIGIL. RELEASE THE DOCUMENTS YOURSELF."
"AS I SAID, I'M A SPY. I LEAK THOSE DOCUMENTS PERSONALLY, I GIVE THESE PEOPLE THE TRUTH MYSELF, THAT'S THE END OF MY ABILITY TO DO GOOD ON THE INSIDE.
"NATE GRAFT CAN'T DO THIS.
".SVE_URS3LF CAN."
YOU MEAN THE SOCIAL NIGHTMARE WHO JUST TOOK MY COMPUTER?
NO, I DO NOT.
I MEAN US.
YOU AND I.
NEVER.
REALLY? YOU SURE?
YOU WANTED TO BE PART OF .SVE_URS3LF? YOU WANT TO FIGHT THIS WAR LIKE ED HICCOX WOULD?
WELL, WELCOME TO THE TEAM, SEAQUEEN.

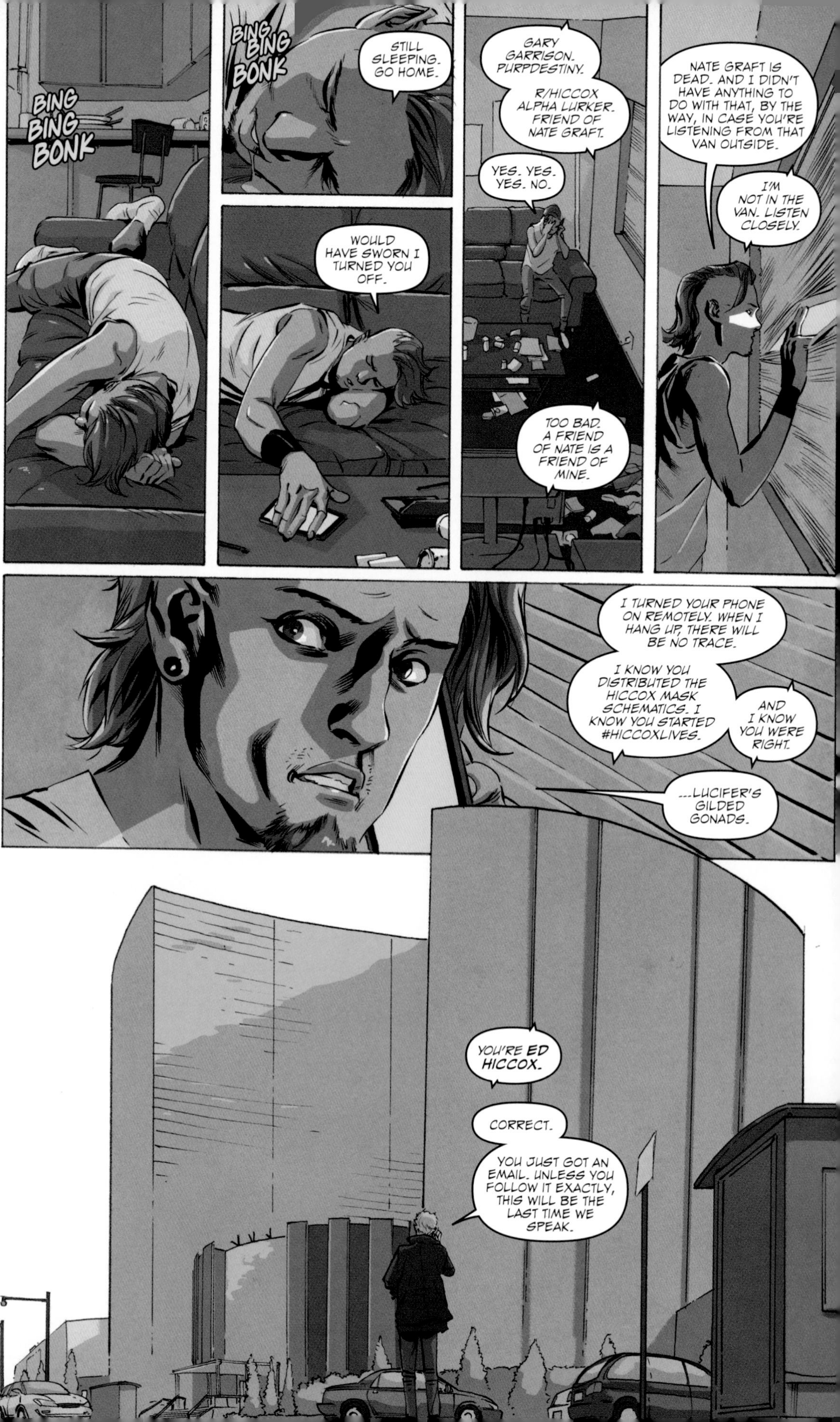
BING BING BONK
BING BING BONK
STILL SLEEPING. GO HOME.
WOULD HAVE SWORN I TURNED YOU OFF.
GARY GARRISON. PURPDESTINY.
R/HICCOX ALPHA LURKER. FRIEND OF NATE GRAFT.
YES. YES. YES. NO.
TOO BAD. A FRIEND OF NATE IS A FRIEND OF MINE.
NATE GRAFT IS DEAD. AND I DIDN'T HAVE ANYTHING TO DO WITH THAT, BY THE WAY, IN CASE YOU'RE LISTENING FROM THAT VAN OUTSIDE.
I'M NOT IN THE VAN. LISTEN CLOSELY.
I TURNED YOUR PHONE ON REMOTELY. WHEN I HANG UP, THERE WILL BE NO TRACE.
I KNOW YOU DISTRIBUTED THE HICCOX MASK SCHEMATICS. I KNOW YOU STARTED #HICCOXLIVES.
AND I KNOW YOU WERE RIGHT.
...LUCIFER'S GILDED GONADS.
YOU'RE **ED HICCOX**.
CORRECT.
YOU JUST GOT AN EMAIL. UNLESS YOU FOLLOW IT EXACTLY, THIS WILL BE THE LAST TIME WE SPEAK.

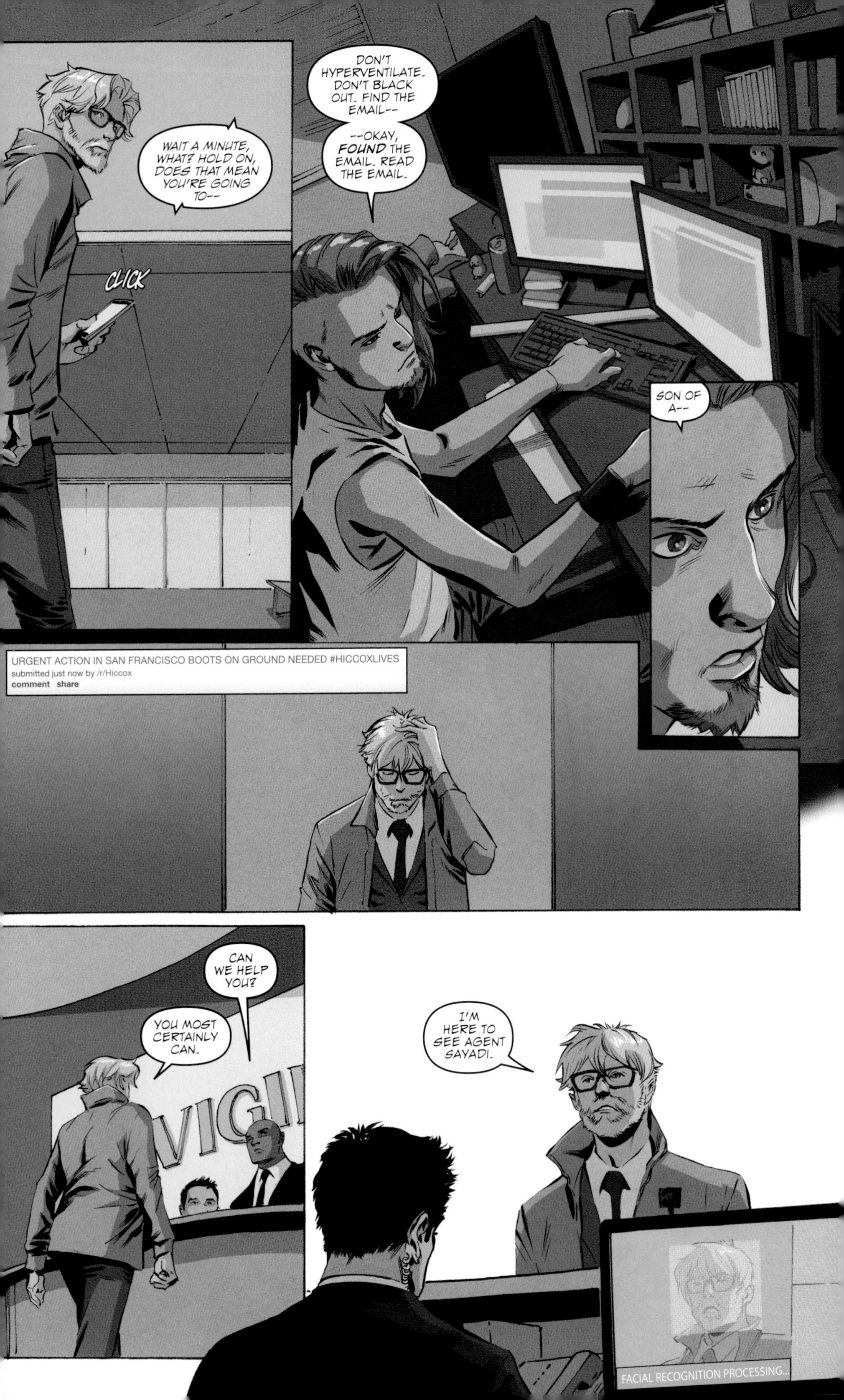
WAIT A MINUTE, WHAT? HOLD ON, DOES THAT MEAN YOU'RE GOING TO--
CLICK
DON'T HYPERVENTILATE. DON'T BLACK OUT. FIND THE EMAIL--
--OKAY, FOUND THE EMAIL. READ THE EMAIL.
SON OF A--
URGENT ACTION IN SAN FRANCISCO BOOTS ON GROUND NEEDED #HICCOXLIVES
submitted just now by /r/Hiccox
comment share
CAN WE HELP YOU?
YOU MOST CERTAINLY CAN.
I'M HERE TO SEE AGENT SAYADI.
FACIAL RECOGNITION PROCESSING...

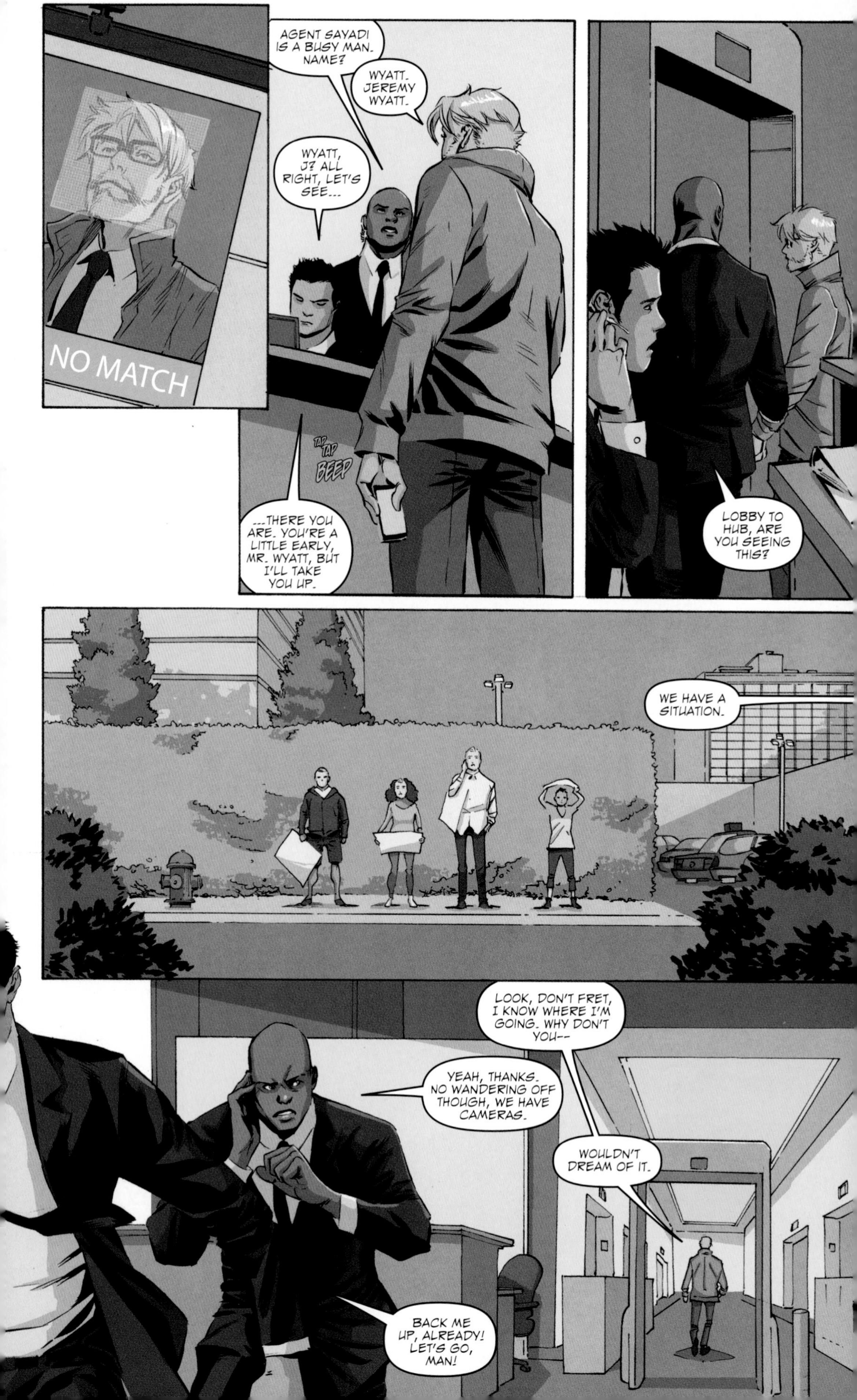
NO MATCH
AGENT SAYADI IS A BUSY MAN. NAME?
WYATT. JEREMY WYATT.
WYATT, J? ALL RIGHT, LET'S SEE...
TAP TAP BEEP
...THERE YOU ARE. YOU'RE A LITTLE EARLY, MR. WYATT, BUT I'LL TAKE YOU UP.
LOBBY TO HUB, ARE YOU SEEING THIS?
WE HAVE A SITUATION.
LOOK, DON'T FRET, I KNOW WHERE I'M GOING. WHY DON'T YOU--
YEAH, THANKS. NO WANDERING OFF THOUGH, WE HAVE CAMERAS.
WOULDN'T DREAM OF IT.
BACK ME UP, ALREADY! LET'S GO, MAN!

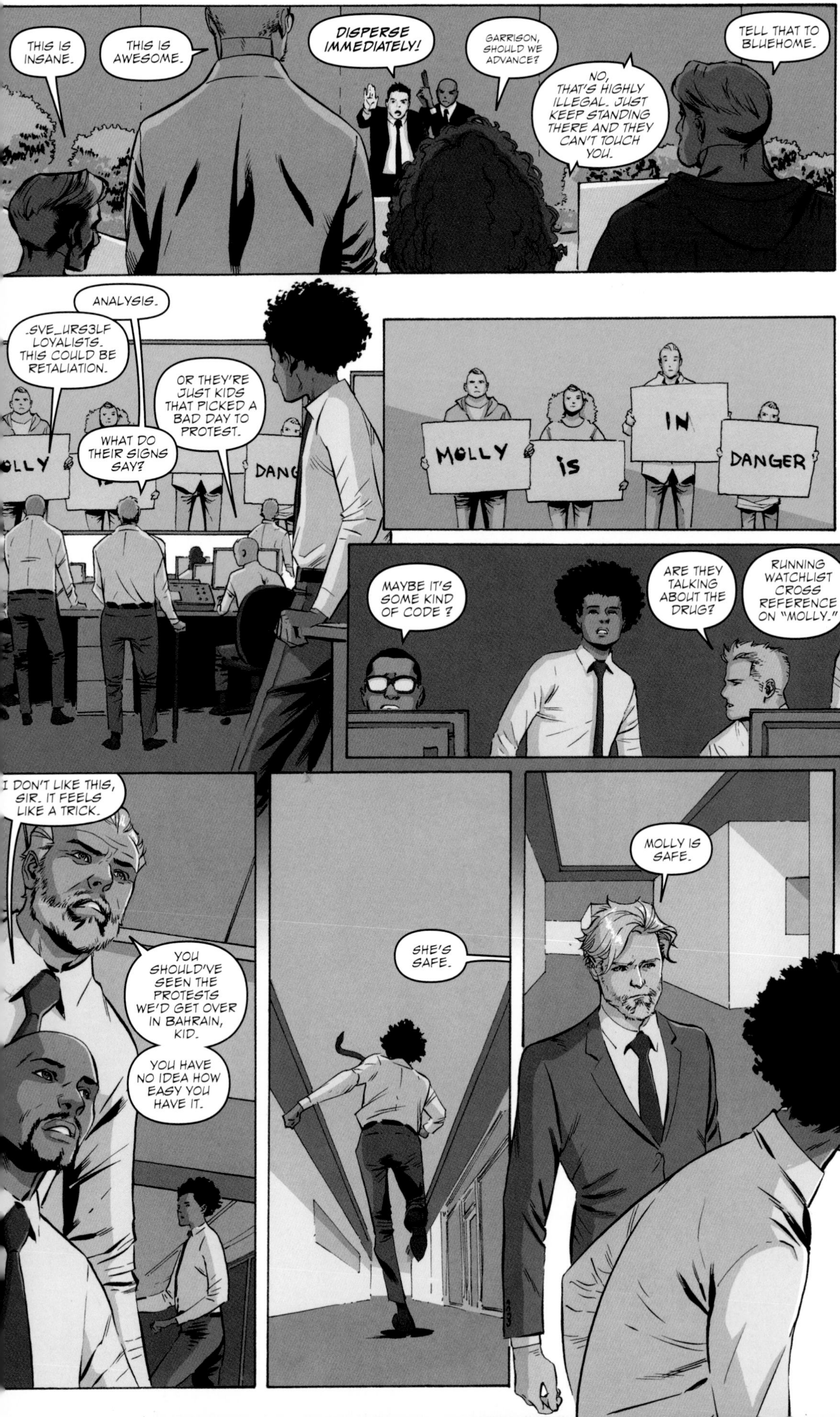

THIS IS INSANE.
THIS IS AWESOME.
DISPERSE IMMEDIATELY!
GARRISON, SHOULD WE ADVANCE?
NO, THAT'S HIGHLY ILLEGAL. JUST KEEP STANDING THERE AND THEY CAN'T TOUCH YOU.
TELL THAT TO BLUEHOME.
ANALYSIS.
.SVE_URS3LF LOYALISTS. THIS COULD BE RETALIATION.
WHAT DO THEIR SIGNS SAY?
OR THEY'RE JUST KIDS THAT PICKED A BAD DAY TO PROTEST.
MOLLY
IS
IN
DANGER
MAYBE IT'S SOME KIND OF CODE ?
ARE THEY TALKING ABOUT THE DRUG?
RUNNING WATCHLIST CROSS REFERENCE ON "MOLLY."
I DON'T LIKE THIS, SIR. IT FEELS LIKE A TRICK.
YOU SHOULD'VE SEEN THE PROTESTS WE'D GET OVER IN BAHRAIN, KID.
YOU HAVE NO IDEA HOW EASY YOU HAVE IT.
SHE'S SAFE.
MOLLY IS SAFE.

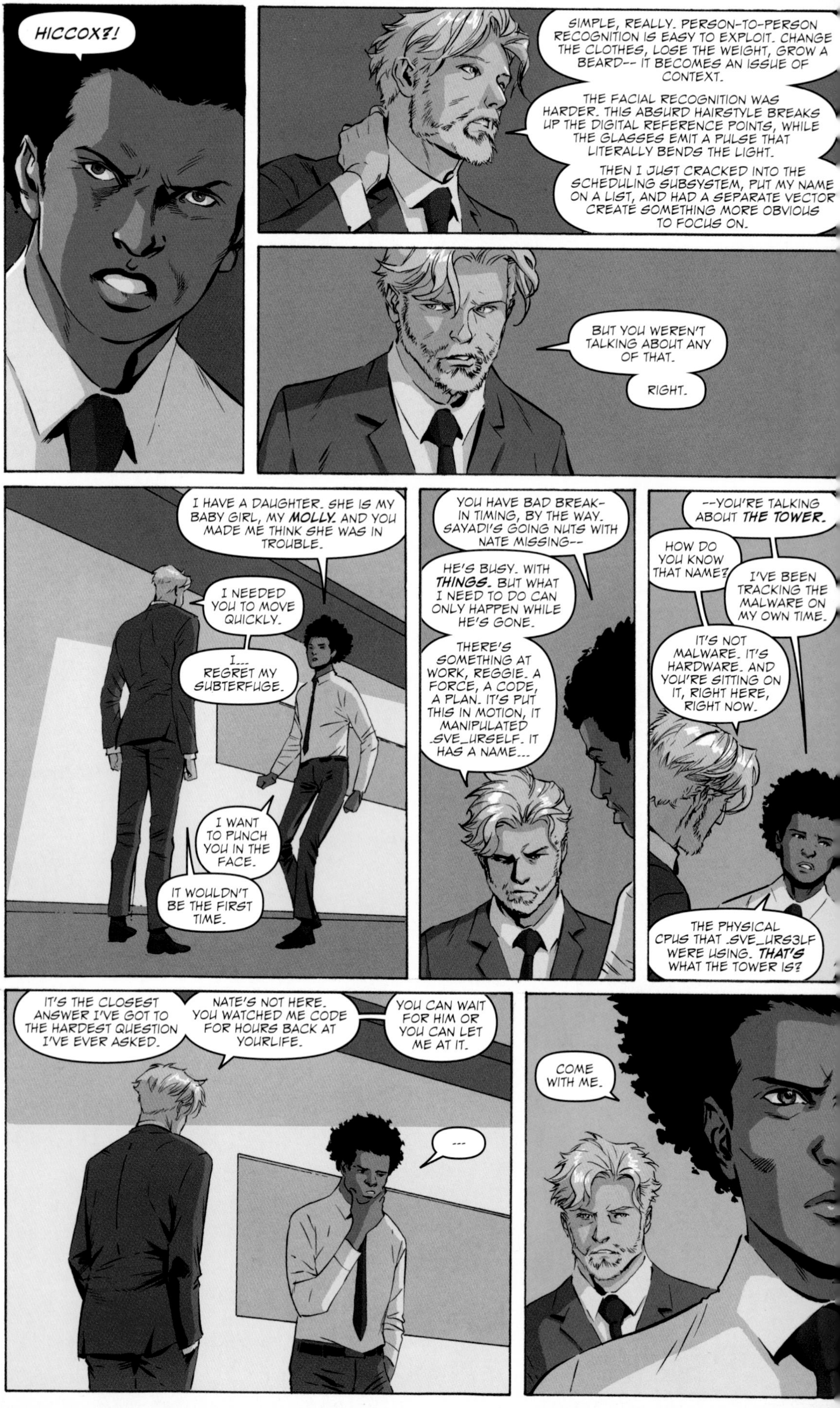
HICCOX?!
SIMPLE, REALLY. PERSON-TO-PERSON RECOGNITION IS EASY TO EXPLOIT. CHANGE THE CLOTHES, LOSE THE WEIGHT, GROW A BEARD-- IT BECOMES AN ISSUE OF CONTEXT.
THE FACIAL RECOGNITION WAS HARDER. THIS ABSURD HAIRSTYLE BREAKS UP THE DIGITAL REFERENCE POINTS, WHILE THE GLASSES EMIT A PULSE THAT LITERALLY BENDS THE LIGHT.
THEN I JUST CRACKED INTO THE SCHEDULING SUBSYSTEM, PUT MY NAME ON A LIST, AND HAD A SEPARATE VECTOR CREATE SOMETHING MORE OBVIOUS TO FOCUS ON.
BUT YOU WEREN'T TALKING ABOUT ANY OF THAT.
RIGHT.
I HAVE A DAUGHTER. SHE IS MY BABY GIRL, MY MOLLY. AND YOU MADE ME THINK SHE WAS IN TROUBLE.
I NEEDED YOU TO MOVE QUICKLY.
I... REGRET MY SUBTERFUGE.
I WANT TO PUNCH YOU IN THE FACE.
IT WOULDN'T BE THE FIRST TIME.
YOU HAVE BAD BREAK-IN TIMING, BY THE WAY. SAYADI'S GOING NUTS WITH NATE MISSING--
HE'S BUSY. WITH THINGS. BUT WHAT I NEED TO DO CAN ONLY HAPPEN WHILE HE'S GONE.
THERE'S SOMETHING AT WORK, REGGIE. A FORCE, A CODE, A PLAN. IT'S PUT THIS IN MOTION, IT MANIPULATED .SVE_URSELF. IT HAS A NAME...
--YOU'RE TALKING ABOUT THE TOWER.
HOW DO YOU KNOW THAT NAME?
I'VE BEEN TRACKING THE MALWARE ON MY OWN TIME.
IT'S NOT MALWARE. IT'S HARDWARE. AND YOU'RE SITTING ON IT, RIGHT HERE, RIGHT NOW.
THE PHYSICAL CPUS THAT .SVE_URS3LF WERE USING. THAT'S WHAT THE TOWER IS?
IT'S THE CLOSEST ANSWER I'VE GOT TO THE HARDEST QUESTION I'VE EVER ASKED.
NATE'S NOT HERE. YOU WATCHED ME CODE FOR HOURS BACK AT YOURLIFE.
YOU CAN WAIT FOR HIM OR YOU CAN LET ME AT IT.
...
COME WITH ME.

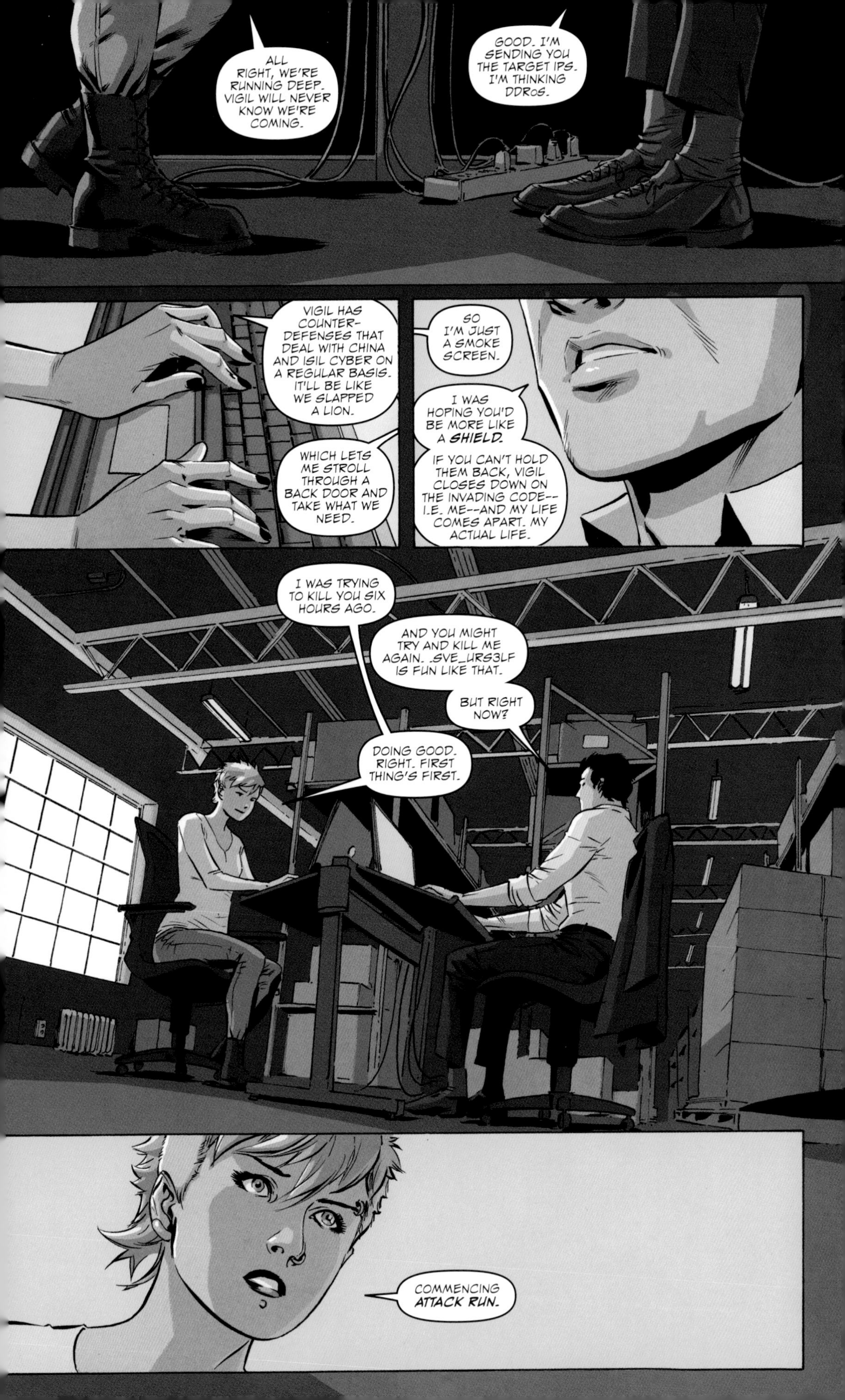
ALL RIGHT, WE'RE RUNNING DEEP. VIGIL WILL NEVER KNOW WE'RE COMING.
GOOD. I'M SENDING YOU THE TARGET IPS. I'M THINKING DDROS.
VIGIL HAS COUNTER-DEFENSES THAT DEAL WITH CHINA AND ISIL CYBER ON A REGULAR BASIS. IT'LL BE LIKE WE SLAPPED A LION.
WHICH LETS ME STROLL THROUGH A BACK DOOR AND TAKE WHAT WE NEED.
SO I'M JUST A SMOKE SCREEN.
I WAS HOPING YOU'D BE MORE LIKE A SHIELD.
IF YOU CAN'T HOLD THEM BACK, VIGIL CLOSES DOWN ON THE INVADING CODE--I.E. ME--AND MY LIFE COMES APART. MY ACTUAL LIFE.
I WAS TRYING TO KILL YOU SIX HOURS AGO.
AND YOU MIGHT TRY AND KILL ME AGAIN. .SVE_URS3LF IS FUN LIKE THAT.
BUT RIGHT NOW?
DOING GOOD. RIGHT. FIRST THING'S FIRST.
COMMENCING ATTACK RUN.

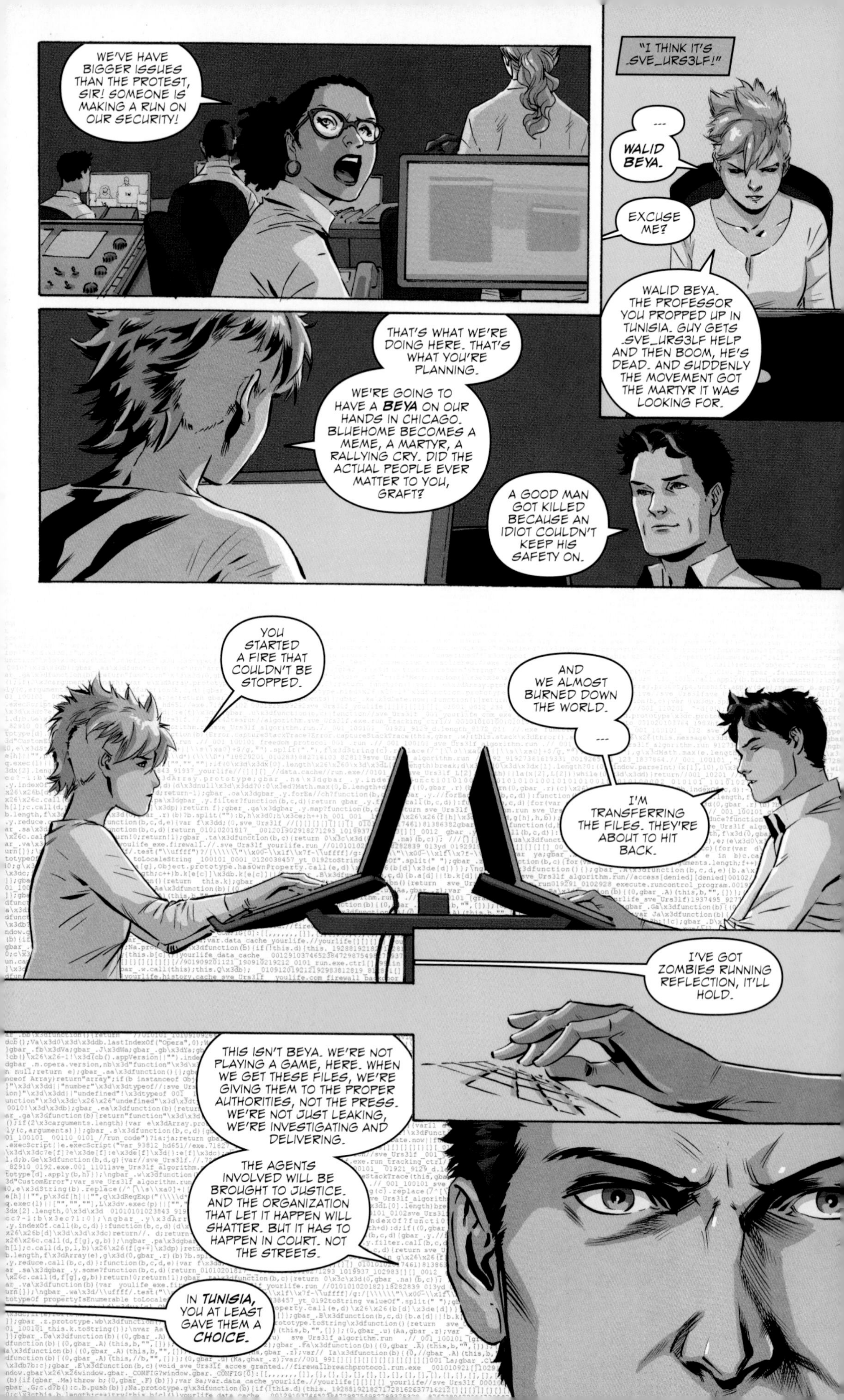
WE'VE HAVE BIGGER ISSUES THAN THE PROTEST, SIR! SOMEONE IS MAKING A RUN ON OUR SECURITY!
"I THINK IT'S .SVE_URS3LF!"
...
WALID BEYA.
EXCUSE ME?
WALID BEYA. THE PROFESSOR YOU PROPPED UP IN TUNISIA. GUY GETS .SVE_URS3LF HELP AND THEN BOOM, HE'S DEAD. AND SUDDENLY THE MOVEMENT GOT THE MARTYR IT WAS LOOKING FOR.
THAT'S WHAT WE'RE DOING HERE. THAT'S WHAT YOU'RE PLANNING.
WE'RE GOING TO HAVE A BEYA ON OUR HANDS IN CHICAGO. BLUEHOME BECOMES A MEME, A MARTYR, A RALLYING CRY. DID THE ACTUAL PEOPLE EVER MATTER TO YOU, GRAFT?
A GOOD MAN GOT KILLED BECAUSE AN IDIOT COULDN'T KEEP HIS SAFETY ON.
YOU STARTED A FIRE THAT COULDN'T BE STOPPED.
AND WE ALMOST BURNED DOWN THE WORLD.
...
I'M TRANSFERRING THE FILES. THEY'RE ABOUT TO HIT BACK.
I'VE GOT ZOMBIES RUNNING REFLECTION, IT'LL HOLD.
THIS ISN'T BEYA. WE'RE NOT PLAYING A GAME, HERE. WHEN WE GET THESE FILES, WE'RE GIVING THEM TO THE PROPER AUTHORITIES, NOT THE PRESS. WE'RE NOT JUST LEAKING, WE'RE INVESTIGATING AND DELIVERING.
THE AGENTS INVOLVED WILL BE BROUGHT TO JUSTICE. AND THE ORGANIZATION THAT LET IT HAPPEN WILL SHATTER. BUT IT HAS TO HAPPEN IN COURT. NOT THE STREETS.
IN TUNISIA, YOU AT LEAST GAVE THEM A CHOICE.

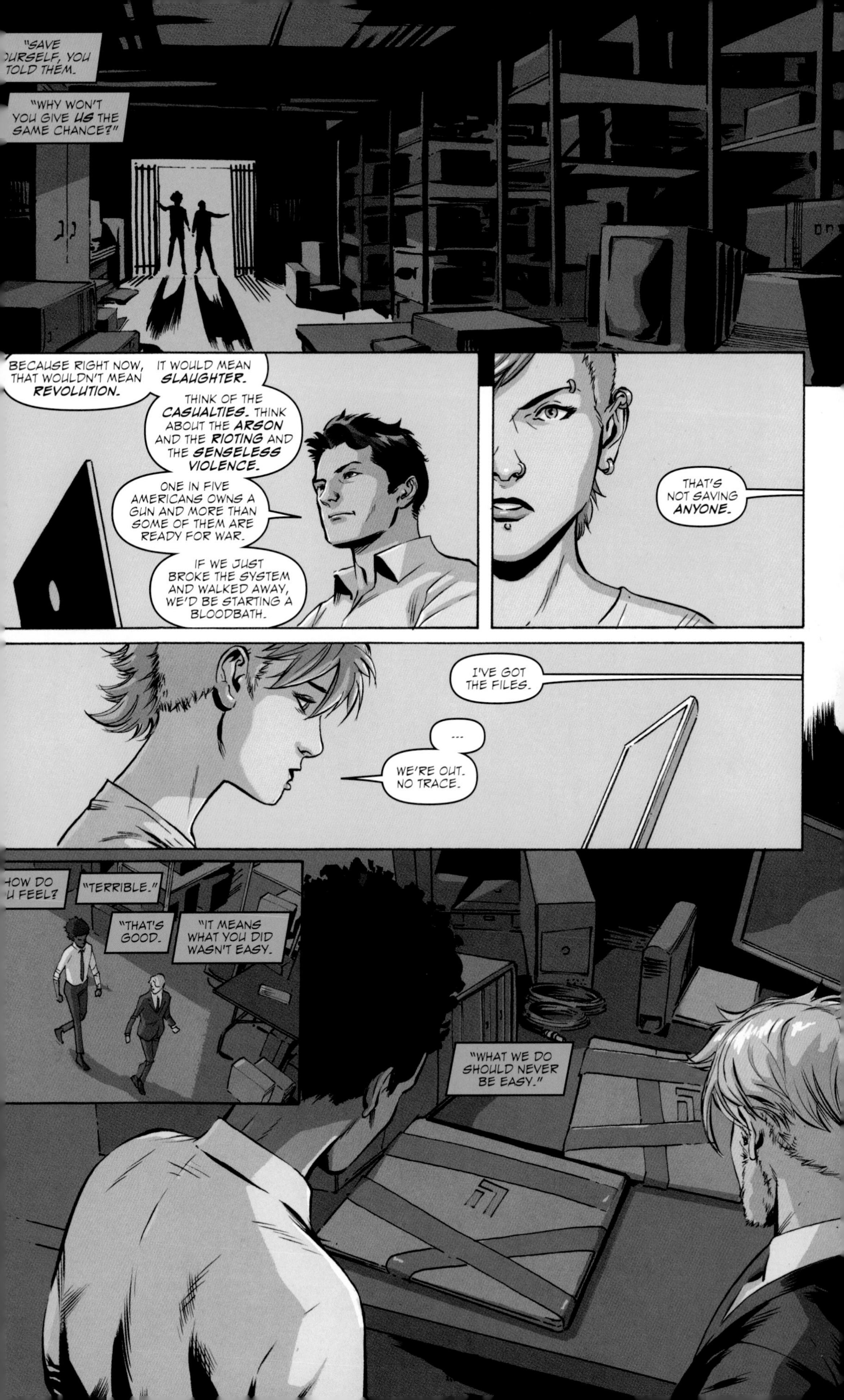
"SAVE OURSELF, YOU TOLD THEM.
"WHY WON'T YOU GIVE US THE SAME CHANCE?"
BECAUSE RIGHT NOW, THAT WOULDN'T MEAN REVOLUTION.
IT WOULD MEAN SLAUGHTER.
THINK OF THE CASUALTIES. THINK ABOUT THE ARSON AND THE RIOTING AND THE SENSELESS VIOLENCE.
ONE IN FIVE AMERICANS OWNS A GUN AND MORE THAN SOME OF THEM ARE READY FOR WAR.
IF WE JUST BROKE THE SYSTEM AND WALKED AWAY, WE'D BE STARTING A BLOODBATH.
THAT'S NOT SAVING ANYONE.
I'VE GOT THE FILES.
...
WE'RE OUT. NO TRACE.
HOW DO U FEEL?
"TERRIBLE."
"THAT'S GOOD.
"IT MEANS WHAT YOU DID WASN'T EASY.
"WHAT WE DO SHOULD NEVER BE EASY."

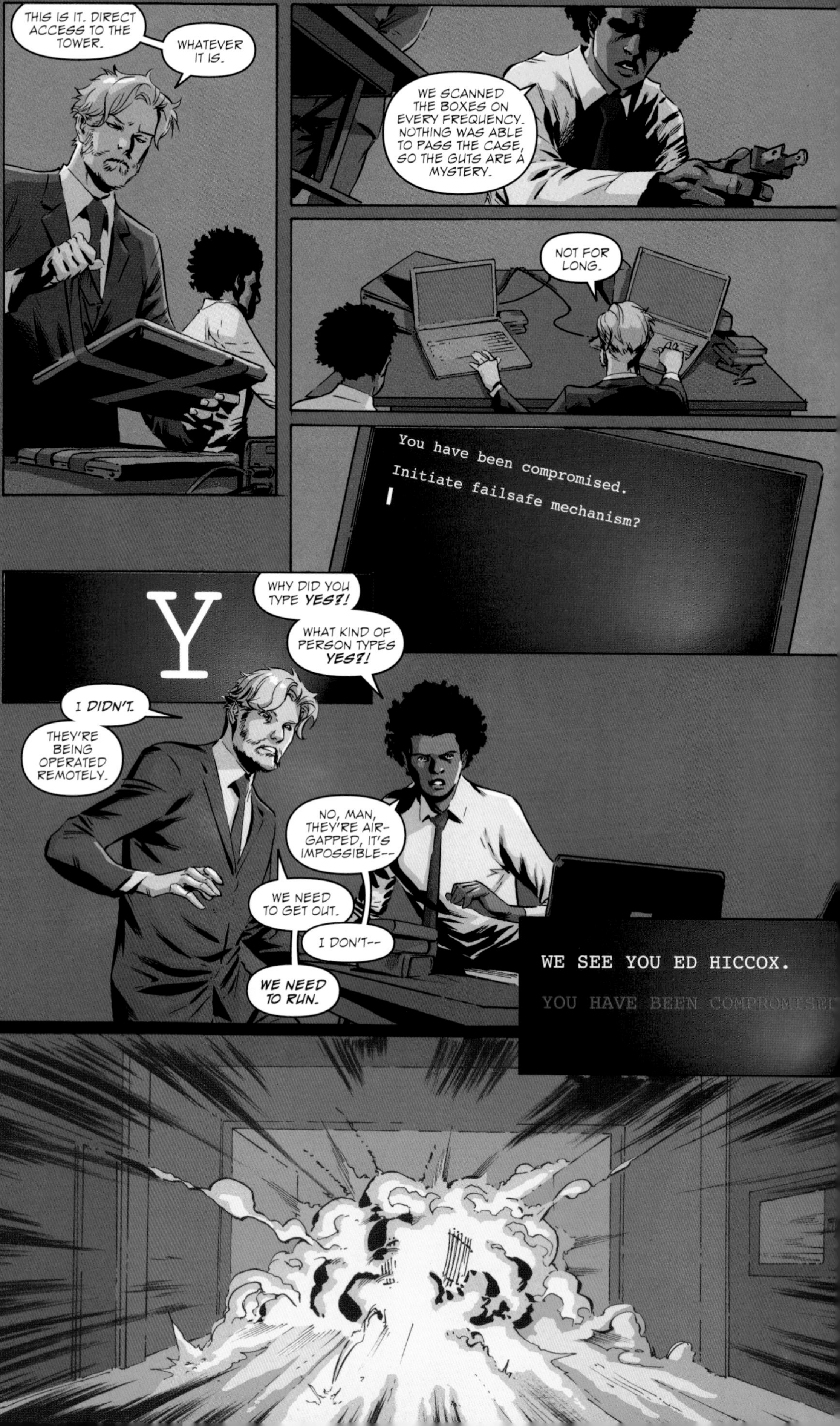
THIS IS IT. DIRECT ACCESS TO THE TOWER.
WHATEVER IT IS.
WE SCANNED THE BOXES ON EVERY FREQUENCY. NOTHING WAS ABLE TO PASS THE CASE, SO THE GUTS ARE A MYSTERY.
NOT FOR LONG.
You have been compromised.
Initiate failsafe mechanism?
Y
WHY DID YOU TYPE YES?!
WHAT KIND OF PERSON TYPES YES?!
I DIDN'T.
THEY'RE BEING OPERATED REMOTELY.
NO, MAN, THEY'RE AIR-GAPPED, IT'S IMPOSSIBLE--
WE NEED TO GET OUT.
I DON'T--
WE NEED TO RUN.
WE SEE YOU ED HICCOX.
YOU HAVE BEEN COMPROMISE

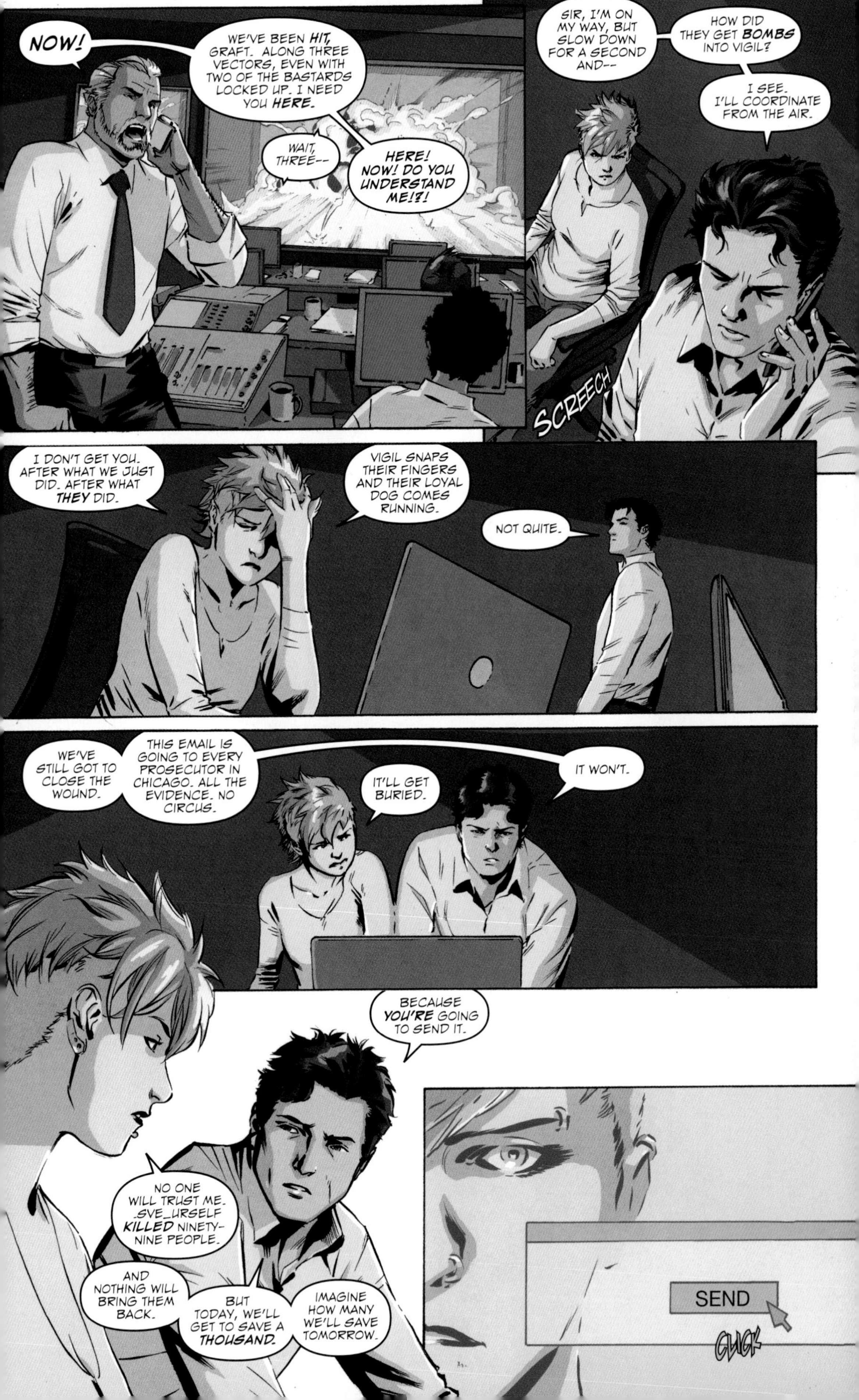
NOW!
WE'VE BEEN HIT, GRAFT. ALONG THREE VECTORS, EVEN WITH TWO OF THE BASTARDS LOCKED UP. I NEED YOU HERE.
WAIT, THREE--
HERE! NOW! DO YOU UNDERSTAND ME!?!
SIR, I'M ON MY WAY, BUT SLOW DOWN FOR A SECOND AND--
HOW DID THEY GET BOMBS INTO VIGIL?
I SEE. I'LL COORDINATE FROM THE AIR.
SCREECH
I DON'T GET YOU. AFTER WHAT WE JUST DID. AFTER WHAT THEY DID.
VIGIL SNAPS THEIR FINGERS AND THEIR LOYAL DOG COMES RUNNING.
NOT QUITE.
WE'VE STILL GOT TO CLOSE THE WOUND.
THIS EMAIL IS GOING TO EVERY PROSECUTOR IN CHICAGO. ALL THE EVIDENCE. NO CIRCUS.
IT'LL GET BURIED.
IT WON'T.
BECAUSE YOU'RE GOING TO SEND IT.
NO ONE WILL TRUST ME. .SVE_URSELF KILLED NINETY-NINE PEOPLE.
AND NOTHING WILL BRING THEM BACK.
BUT TODAY, WE'LL GET TO SAVE A THOUSAND.
IMAGINE HOW MANY WE'LL SAVE TOMORROW.
SEND
CLICK

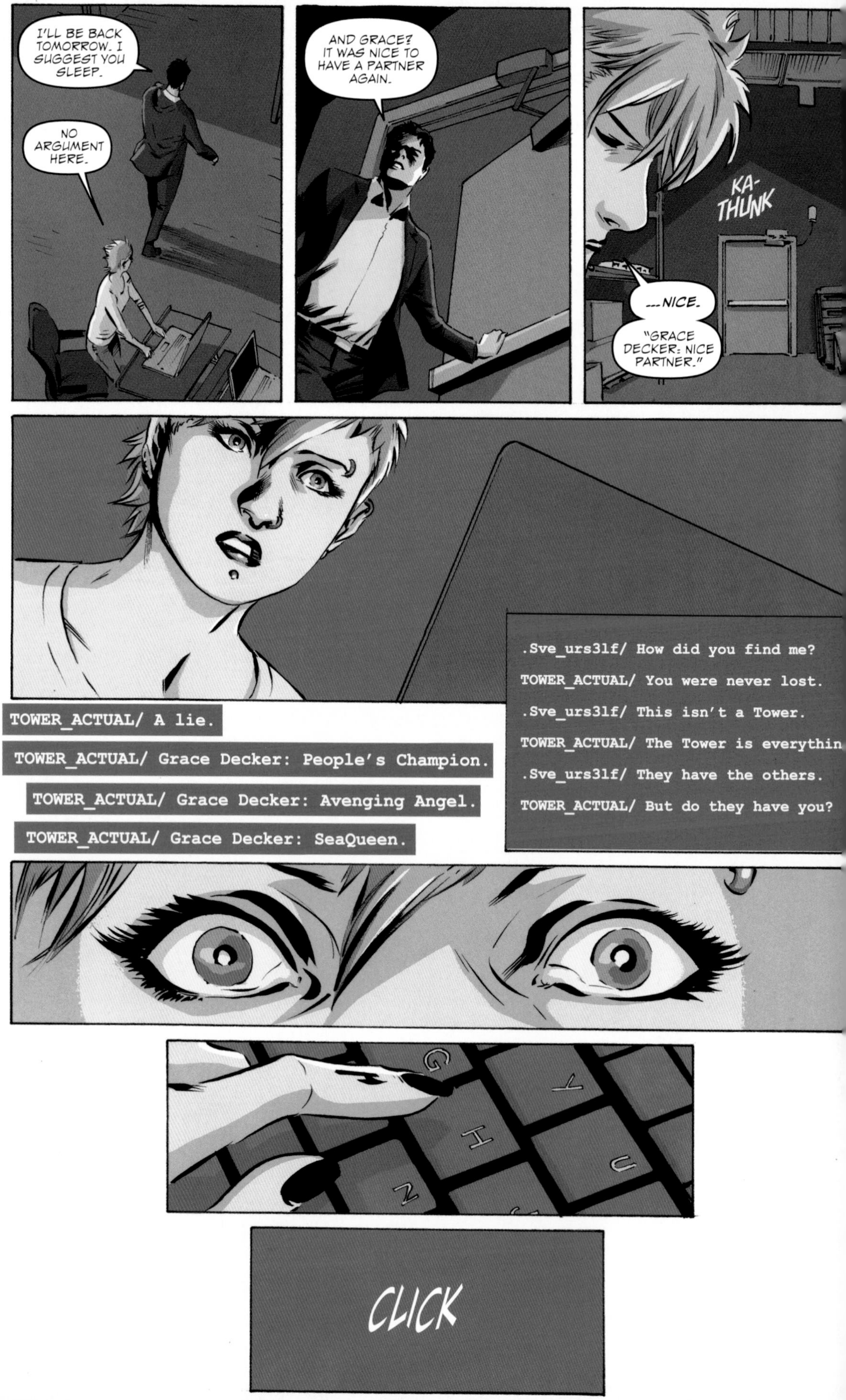
I'LL BE BACK TOMORROW. I SUGGEST YOU SLEEP.
NO ARGUMENT HERE.
AND GRACE? IT WAS NICE TO HAVE A PARTNER AGAIN.
KA-THUNK
...NICE.
"GRACE DECKER: NICE PARTNER."
.Sve_urs3lf/ How did you find me?
TOWER_ACTUAL/ You were never lost.
.Sve_urs3lf/ This isn't a Tower.
TOWER_ACTUAL/ The Tower is everythin
.Sve_urs3lf/ They have the others.
TOWER_ACTUAL/ But do they have you?
TOWER_ACTUAL/ A lie.
TOWER_ACTUAL/ Grace Decker: People's Champion.
TOWER_ACTUAL/ Grace Decker: Avenging Angel.
TOWER_ACTUAL/ Grace Decker: SeaQueen.
CLICK

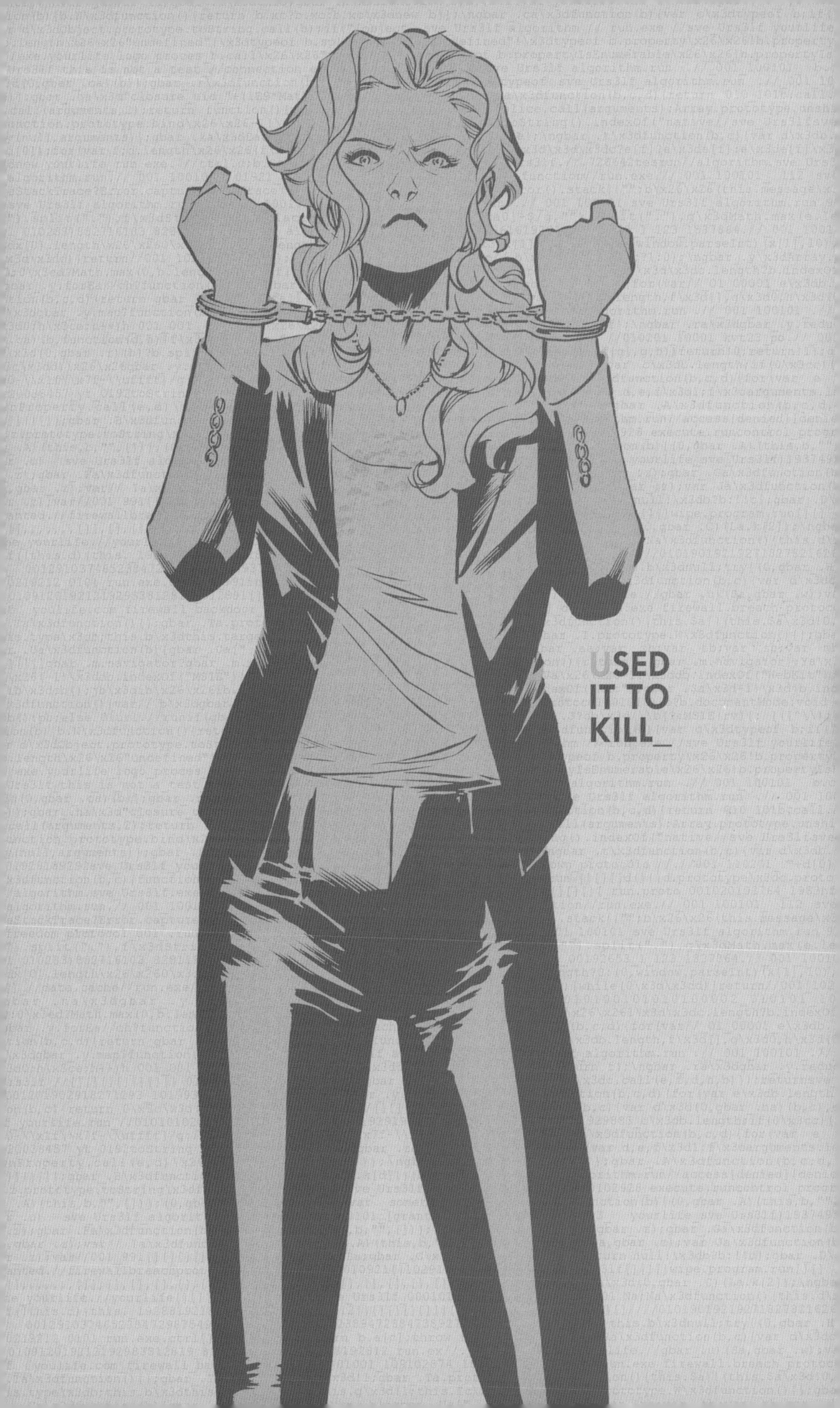
USED
IT TO
KILL_

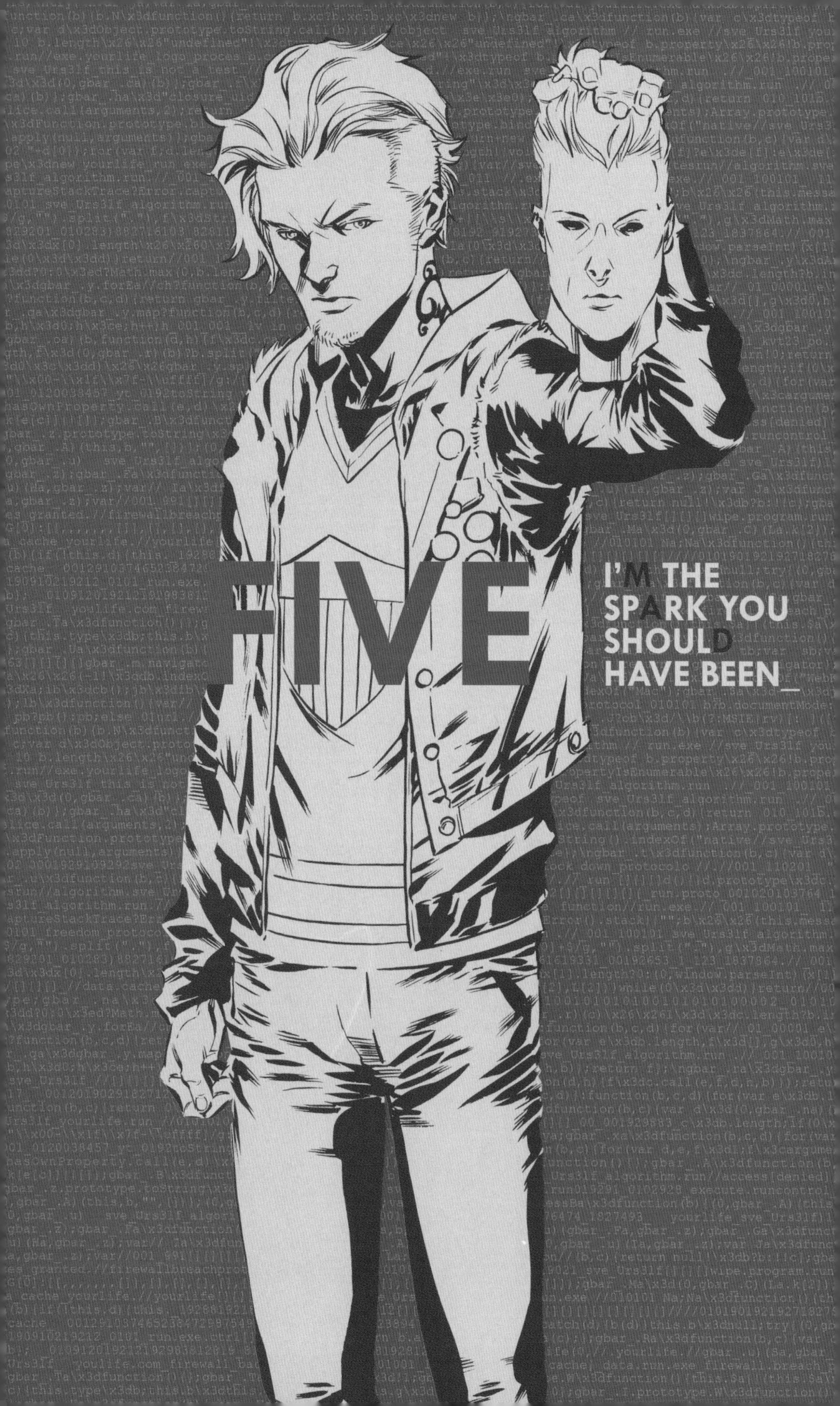
FIVE
I'M THE SPARK YOU SHOULD HAVE BEEN_

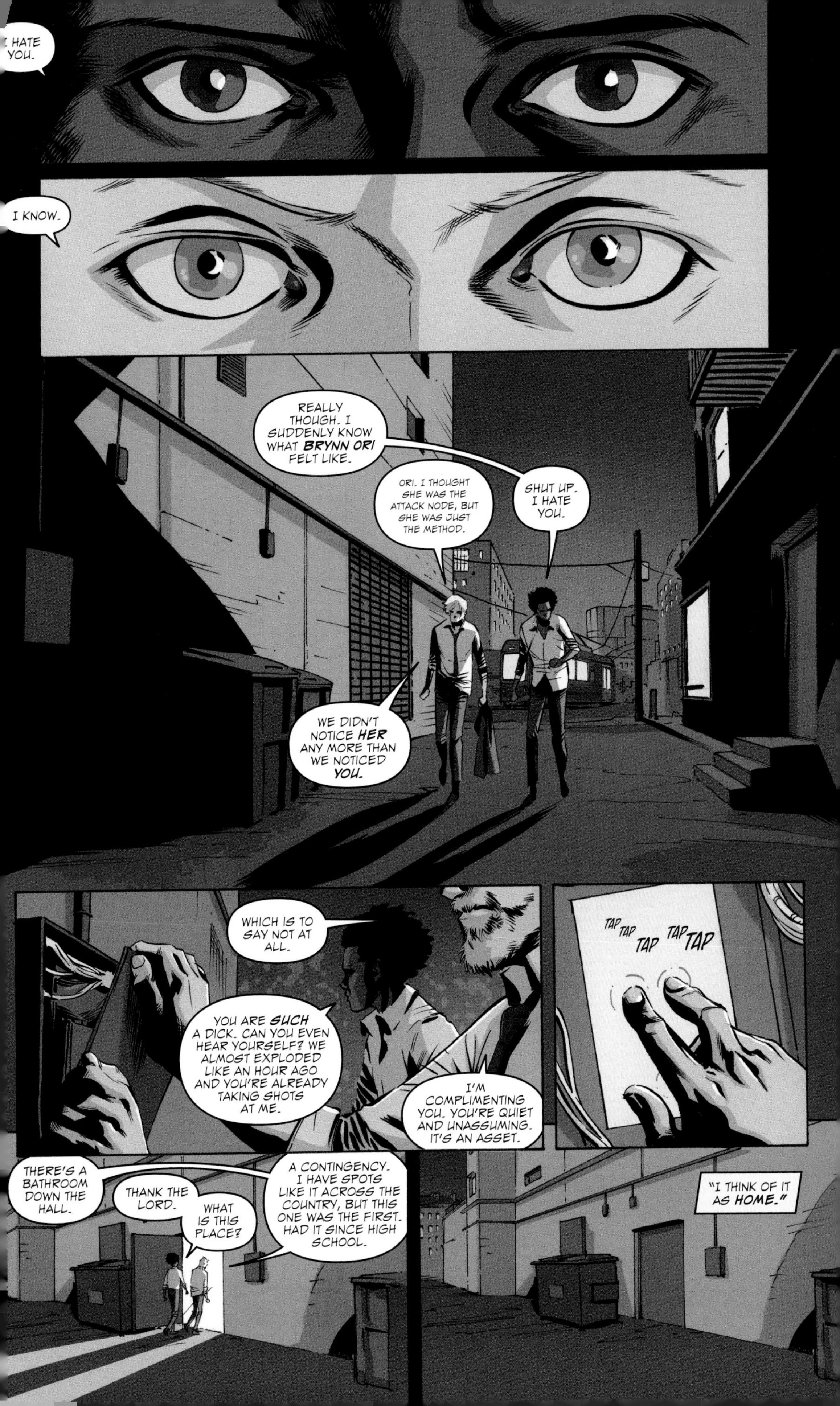
I HATE YOU.
I KNOW.
REALLY THOUGH. I SUDDENLY KNOW WHAT BRYNN ORI FELT LIKE.
SHUT UP. I HATE YOU.
ORI. I THOUGHT SHE WAS THE ATTACK NODE, BUT SHE WAS JUST THE METHOD.
WE DIDN'T NOTICE HER ANY MORE THAN WE NOTICED YOU.
WHICH IS TO SAY NOT AT ALL.
YOU ARE SUCH A DICK. CAN YOU EVEN HEAR YOURSELF? WE ALMOST EXPLODED LIKE AN HOUR AGO AND YOU'RE ALREADY TAKING SHOTS AT ME.
I'M COMPLIMENTING YOU. YOU'RE QUIET AND UNASSUMING. IT'S AN ASSET.
TAP TAP TAP TAP TAP
WHAT IS THIS PLACE?
A CONTINGENCY. I HAVE SPOTS LIKE IT ACROSS THE COUNTRY, BUT THIS ONE WAS THE FIRST. HAD IT SINCE HIGH SCHOOL.
THERE'S A BATHROOM DOWN THE HALL.
THANK THE LORD.
"I THINK OF IT AS HOME."

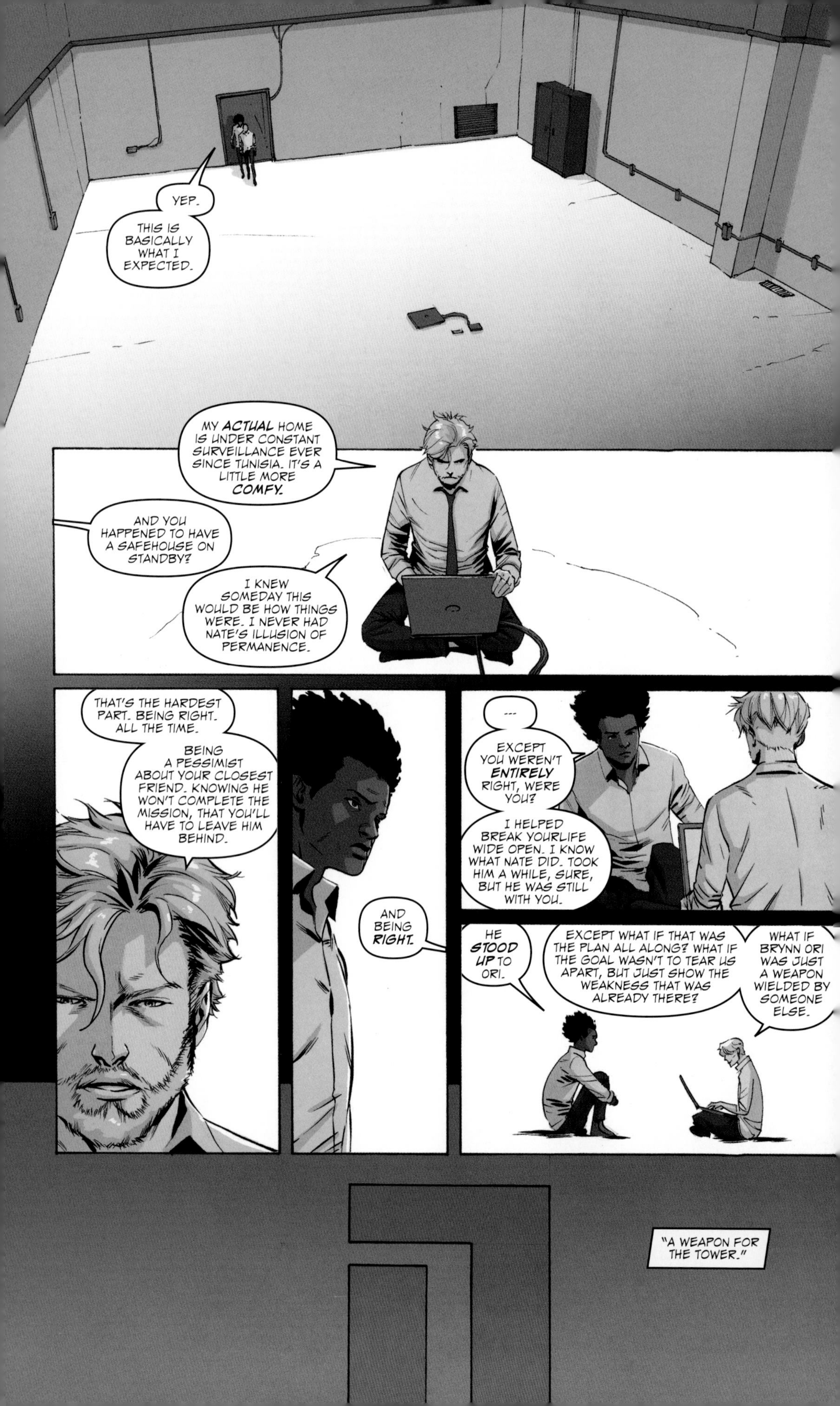
YEP.
THIS IS BASICALLY WHAT I EXPECTED.
MY ACTUAL HOME IS UNDER CONSTANT SURVEILLANCE EVER SINCE TUNISIA. IT'S A LITTLE MORE COMFY.
AND YOU HAPPENED TO HAVE A SAFEHOUSE ON STANDBY?
I KNEW SOMEDAY THIS WOULD BE HOW THINGS WERE. I NEVER HAD NATE'S ILLUSION OF PERMANENCE.
THAT'S THE HARDEST PART. BEING RIGHT. ALL THE TIME.
BEING A PESSIMIST ABOUT YOUR CLOSEST FRIEND. KNOWING HE WON'T COMPLETE THE MISSION, THAT YOU'LL HAVE TO LEAVE HIM BEHIND.
AND BEING RIGHT.
...
EXCEPT YOU WEREN'T ENTIRELY RIGHT, WERE YOU?
I HELPED BREAK YOURLIFE WIDE OPEN. I KNOW WHAT NATE DID. TOOK HIM A WHILE, SURE, BUT HE WAS STILL WITH YOU.
HE STOOD UP TO ORI.
EXCEPT WHAT IF THAT WAS THE PLAN ALL ALONG? WHAT IF THE GOAL WASN'T TO TEAR US APART, BUT JUST SHOW THE WEAKNESS THAT WAS ALREADY THERE?
WHAT IF BRYNN ORI WAS JUST A WEAPON WIELDED BY SOMEONE ELSE.
"A WEAPON FOR THE TOWER."

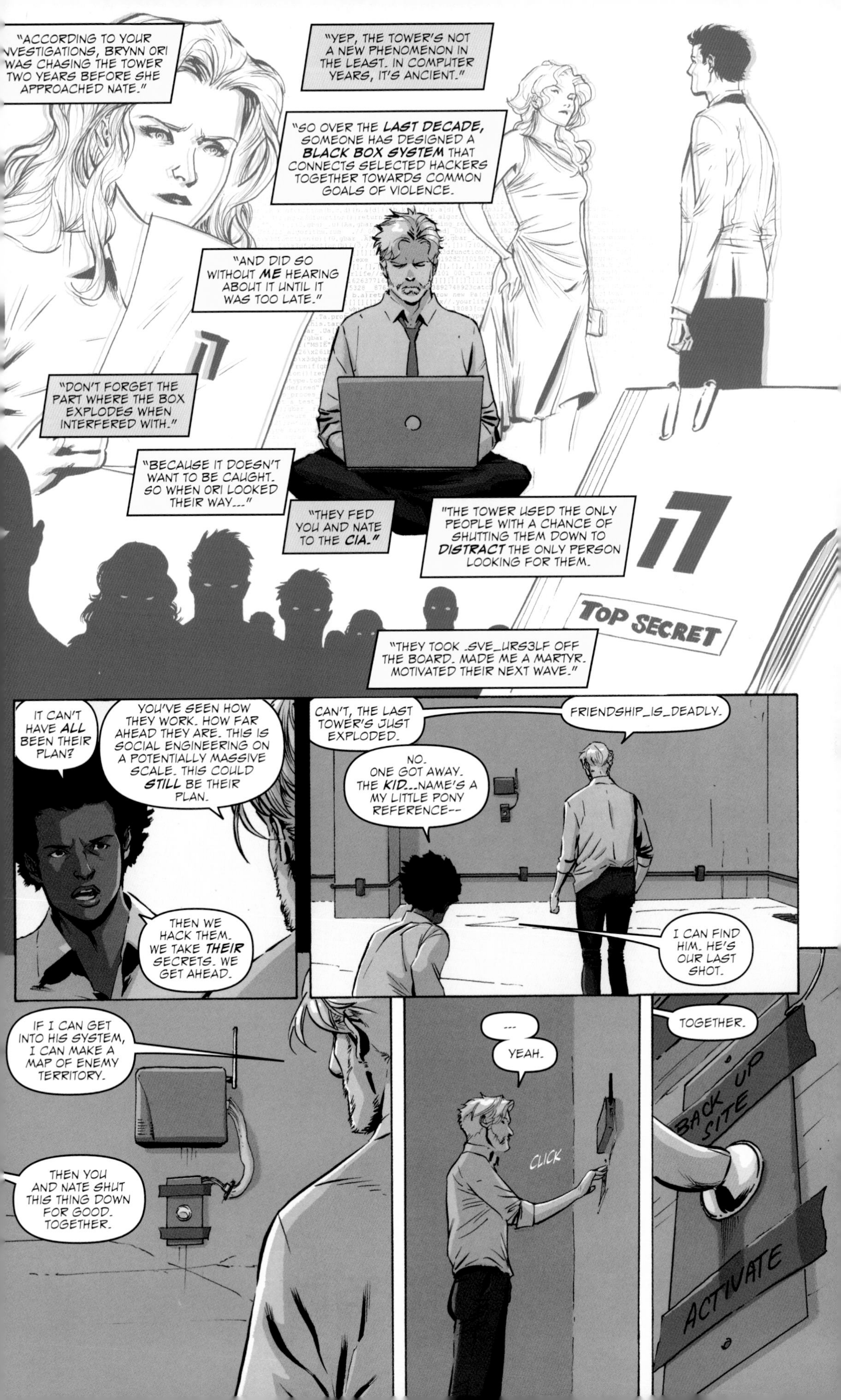
"ACCORDING TO YOUR INVESTIGATIONS, BRYNN ORI WAS CHASING THE TOWER TWO YEARS BEFORE SHE APPROACHED NATE."
"YEP, THE TOWER'S NOT A NEW PHENOMENON IN THE LEAST. IN COMPUTER YEARS, IT'S ANCIENT."
"SO OVER THE LAST DECADE, SOMEONE HAS DESIGNED A BLACK BOX SYSTEM THAT CONNECTS SELECTED HACKERS TOGETHER TOWARDS COMMON GOALS OF VIOLENCE.
"AND DID SO WITHOUT ME HEARING ABOUT IT UNTIL IT WAS TOO LATE."
"DON'T FORGET THE PART WHERE THE BOX EXPLODES WHEN INTERFERED WITH."
"BECAUSE IT DOESN'T WANT TO BE CAUGHT. SO WHEN ORI LOOKED THEIR WAY..."
"THEY FED YOU AND NATE TO THE CIA."
"THE TOWER USED THE ONLY PEOPLE WITH A CHANCE OF SHUTTING THEM DOWN TO DISTRACT THE ONLY PERSON LOOKING FOR THEM.
TOP SECRET
"THEY TOOK .SVE_URS3LF OFF THE BOARD. MADE ME A MARTYR. MOTIVATED THEIR NEXT WAVE."
IT CAN'T HAVE ALL BEEN THEIR PLAN?
YOU'VE SEEN HOW THEY WORK. HOW FAR AHEAD THEY ARE. THIS IS SOCIAL ENGINEERING ON A POTENTIALLY MASSIVE SCALE. THIS COULD STILL BE THEIR PLAN.
THEN WE HACK THEM. WE TAKE THEIR SECRETS. WE GET AHEAD.
CAN'T, THE LAST TOWER'S JUST EXPLODED.
FRIENDSHIP_IS_DEADLY.
NO. ONE GOT AWAY. THE KID...NAME'S A MY LITTLE PONY REFERENCE--
I CAN FIND HIM. HE'S OUR LAST SHOT.
IF I CAN GET INTO HIS SYSTEM, I CAN MAKE A MAP OF ENEMY TERRITORY.
THEN YOU AND NATE SHUT THIS THING DOWN FOR GOOD. TOGETHER.
...
YEAH.
CLICK
TOGETHER.
BACK UP SITE
ACTIVATE

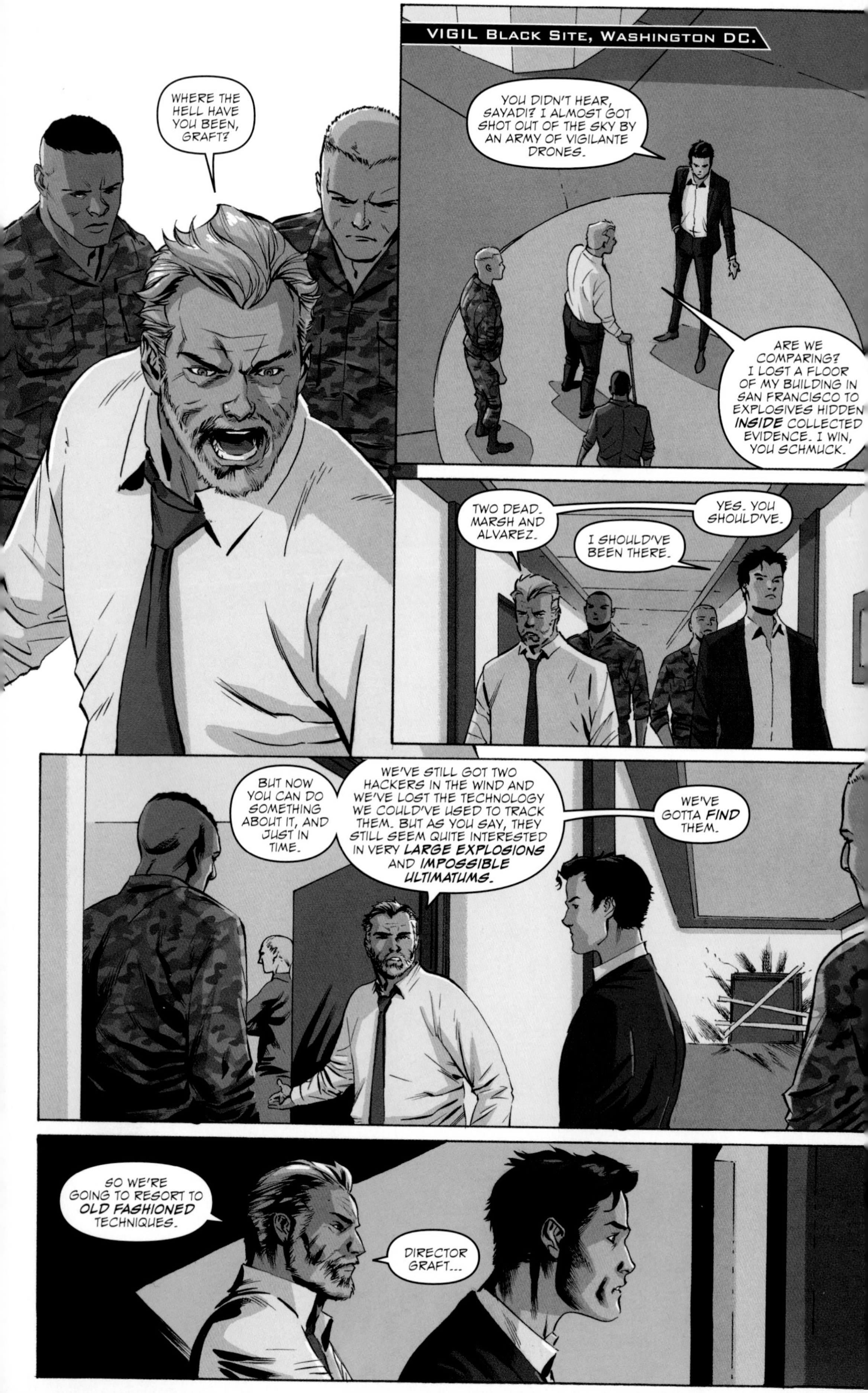
VIGIL BLACK SITE, WASHINGTON DC.
WHERE THE HELL HAVE YOU BEEN, GRAFT?
YOU DIDN'T HEAR, SAYADI? I ALMOST GOT SHOT OUT OF THE SKY BY AN ARMY OF VIGILANTE DRONES.
ARE WE COMPARING? I LOST A FLOOR OF MY BUILDING IN SAN FRANCISCO TO EXPLOSIVES HIDDEN INSIDE COLLECTED EVIDENCE. I WIN, YOU SCHMUCK.
TWO DEAD. MARSH AND ALVAREZ.
I SHOULD'VE BEEN THERE.
YES. YOU SHOULD'VE.
BUT NOW YOU CAN DO SOMETHING ABOUT IT, AND JUST IN TIME.
WE'VE STILL GOT TWO HACKERS IN THE WIND AND WE'VE LOST THE TECHNOLOGY WE COULD'VE USED TO TRACK THEM. BUT AS YOU SAY, THEY STILL SEEM QUITE INTERESTED IN VERY LARGE EXPLOSIONS AND IMPOSSIBLE ULTIMATUMS.
WE'VE GOTTA FIND THEM.
SO WE'RE GOING TO RESORT TO OLD FASHIONED TECHNIQUES.
DIRECTOR GRAFT...

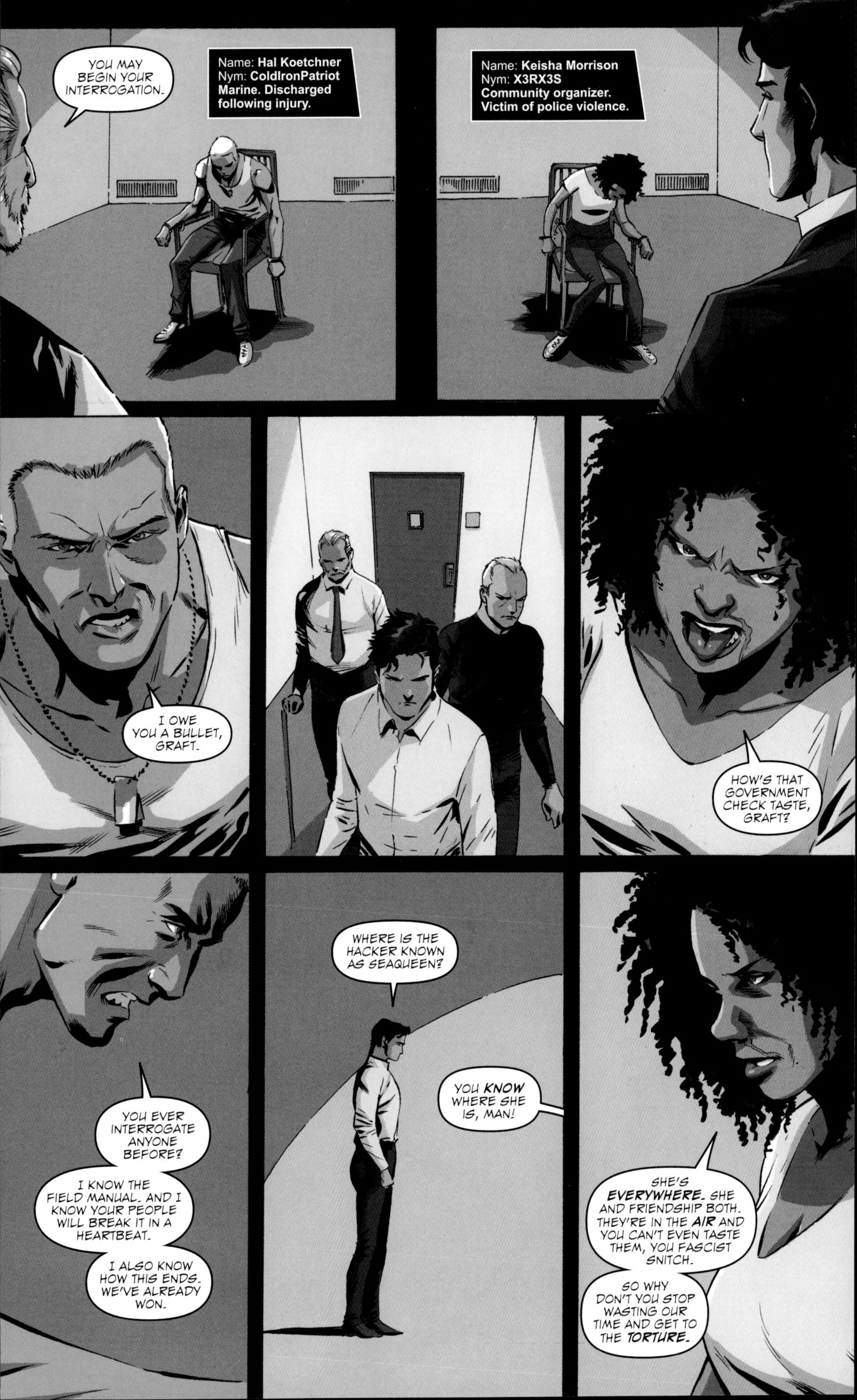
YOU MAY BEGIN YOUR INTERROGATION.
Name: Hal Koetchner
Nym: ColdIronPatriot
Marine. Discharged following injury.
Name: Keisha Morrison
Nym: X3RX3S
Community organizer. Victim of police violence.
I OWE YOU A BULLET, GRAFT.
HOW'S THAT GOVERNMENT CHECK TASTE, GRAFT?
YOU EVER INTERROGATE ANYONE BEFORE?
I KNOW THE FIELD MANUAL. AND I KNOW YOUR PEOPLE WILL BREAK IT IN A HEARTBEAT.
I ALSO KNOW HOW THIS ENDS. WE'VE ALREADY WON.
WHERE IS THE HACKER KNOWN AS SEAQUEEN?
YOU KNOW WHERE SHE IS, MAN!
SHE'S EVERYWHERE. SHE AND FRIENDSHIP BOTH. THEY'RE IN THE AIR AND YOU CAN'T EVEN TASTE THEM, YOU FASCIST SNITCH.
SO WHY DON'T YOU STOP WASTING OUR TIME AND GET TO THE TORTURE.

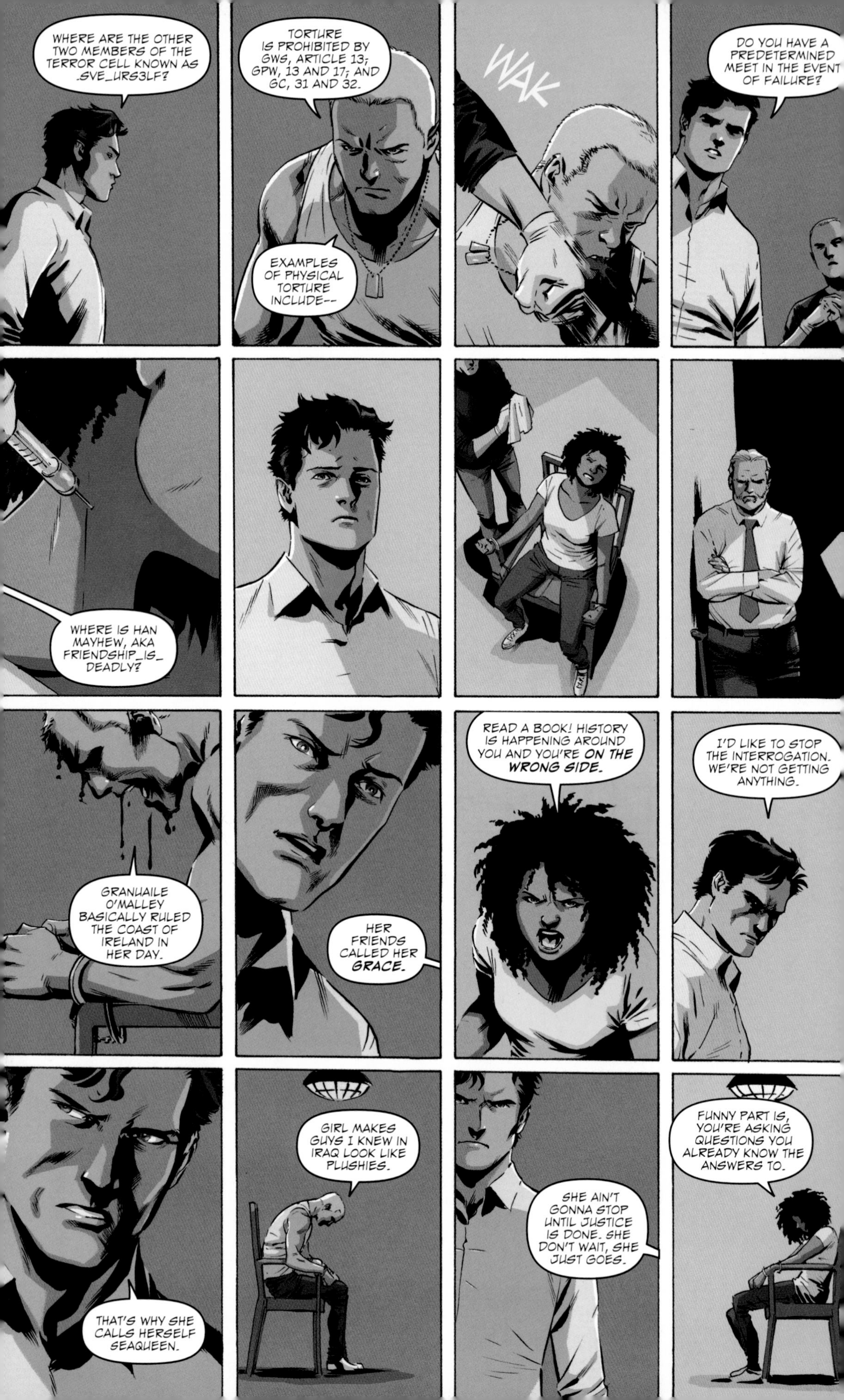
WHERE ARE THE OTHER TWO MEMBERS OF THE TERROR CELL KNOWN AS .SVE_URS3LF?
TORTURE IS PROHIBITED BY GWS, ARTICLE 13; GPW, 13 AND 17; AND GC, 31 AND 32.
EXAMPLES OF PHYSICAL TORTURE INCLUDE--
WAK
DO YOU HAVE A PREDETERMINED MEET IN THE EVENT OF FAILURE?
WHERE IS HAN MAYHEW, AKA FRIENDSHIP_IS_ DEADLY?
GRANUAILE O'MALLEY BASICALLY RULED THE COAST OF IRELAND IN HER DAY.
HER FRIENDS CALLED HER GRACE.
READ A BOOK! HISTORY IS HAPPENING AROUND YOU AND YOU'RE ON THE WRONG SIDE.
I'D LIKE TO STOP THE INTERROGATION. WE'RE NOT GETTING ANYTHING.
THAT'S WHY SHE CALLS HERSELF SEAQUEEN.
GIRL MAKES GUYS I KNEW IN IRAQ LOOK LIKE PLUSHIES.
SHE AIN'T GONNA STOP UNTIL JUSTICE IS DONE. SHE DON'T WAIT, SHE JUST GOES.
FUNNY PART IS, YOU'RE ASKING QUESTIONS YOU ALREADY KNOW THE ANSWERS TO.

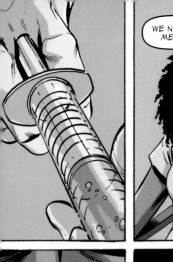

WE NEVER MEET.

EVER.

YOU ARE NOW IN FULL VIOLATION OF THE GENEVA CONVENTION.

I'M NOT THE ONE WHO MURDERED A HUNDRED PEOPLE.

YOU EVER HEAR THE STORY OF *GRANUAILE O'MALLEY*, THE PIRATE QUEEN OF THE Ó MÁILLE CLAN?

IT'S A HELL OF A TALE. AND *TRUE*, TOO.

DENIED.

GRACE O'MALLEY'S IN LABOR. THEY ATTACK HER SHIP WHEN THEY FIGURE SHE CAN'T POSSIBLY PUT UP A FIGHT.

SHE KILLS EVERY MAN THERE. THEN SHE HAS A BABY.

YOU KNOW *EXACTLY* WHERE SHE IS. SHE'S IN YOUR SYSTEMS. RIGHT NOW.

YOU'RE HIDING HER. THINKING YOU CAN TURN HER INTO SOMETHING LIKE YOU.

AND YOU HAVEN'T EVEN TOLD YOUR MASTERS, HAVE YOU?

WHOOPS.

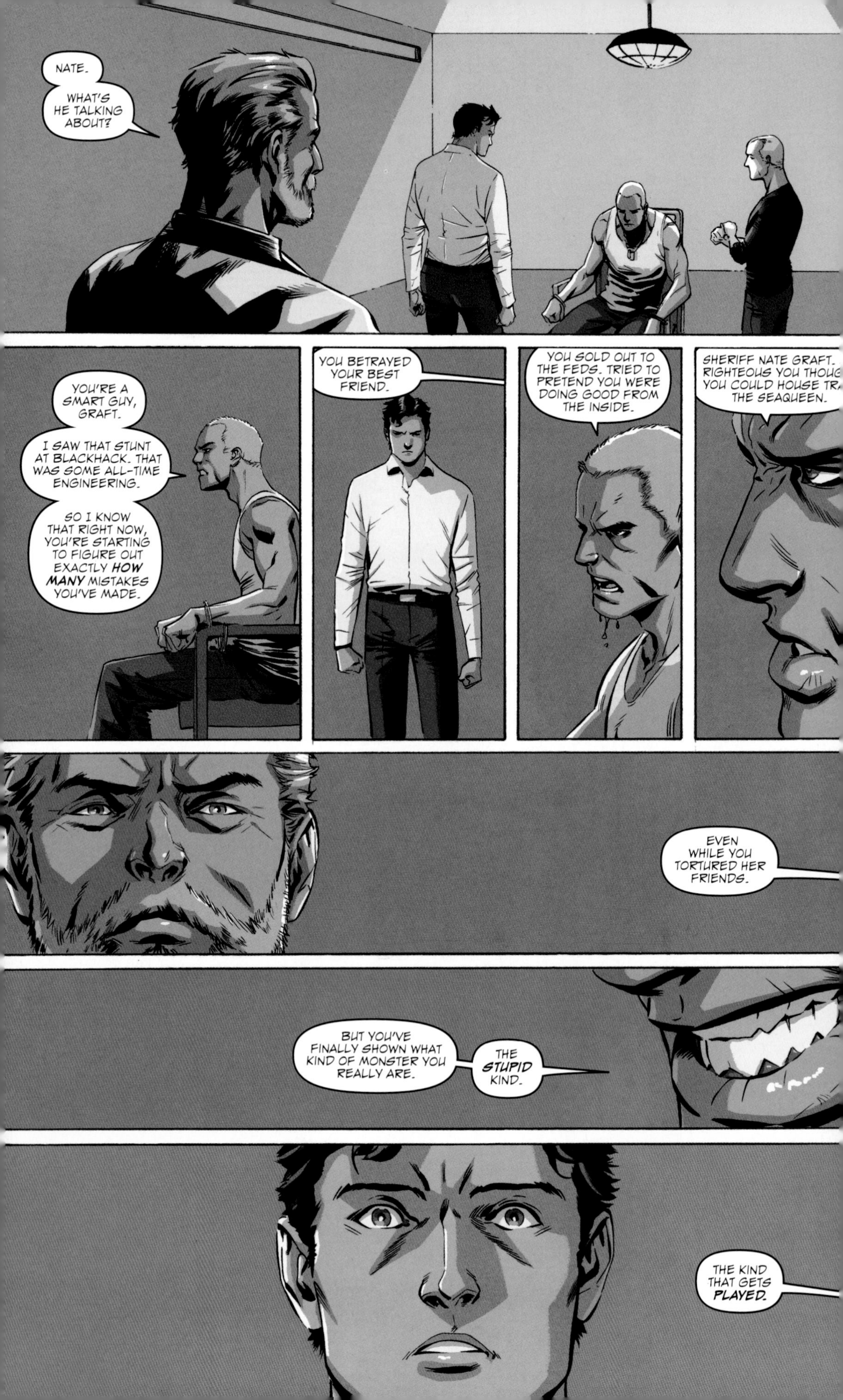
NATE.
WHAT'S HE TALKING ABOUT?
YOU'RE A SMART GUY, GRAFT.
I SAW THAT STUNT AT BLACKHACK. THAT WAS SOME ALL-TIME ENGINEERING.
SO I KNOW THAT RIGHT NOW, YOU'RE STARTING TO FIGURE OUT EXACTLY **HOW MANY** MISTAKES YOU'VE MADE.
YOU BETRAYED YOUR BEST FRIEND.
YOU SOLD OUT TO THE FEDS. TRIED TO PRETEND YOU WERE DOING GOOD FROM THE INSIDE.
SHERIFF NATE GRAFT. RIGHTEOUS YOU THOUG YOU COULD HOUSE TR THE SEAQUEEN.
EVEN WHILE YOU TORTURED HER FRIENDS.
BUT YOU'VE FINALLY SHOWN WHAT KIND OF MONSTER YOU REALLY ARE.
THE ***STUPID*** KIND.
THE KIND THAT GETS ***PLAYED.***

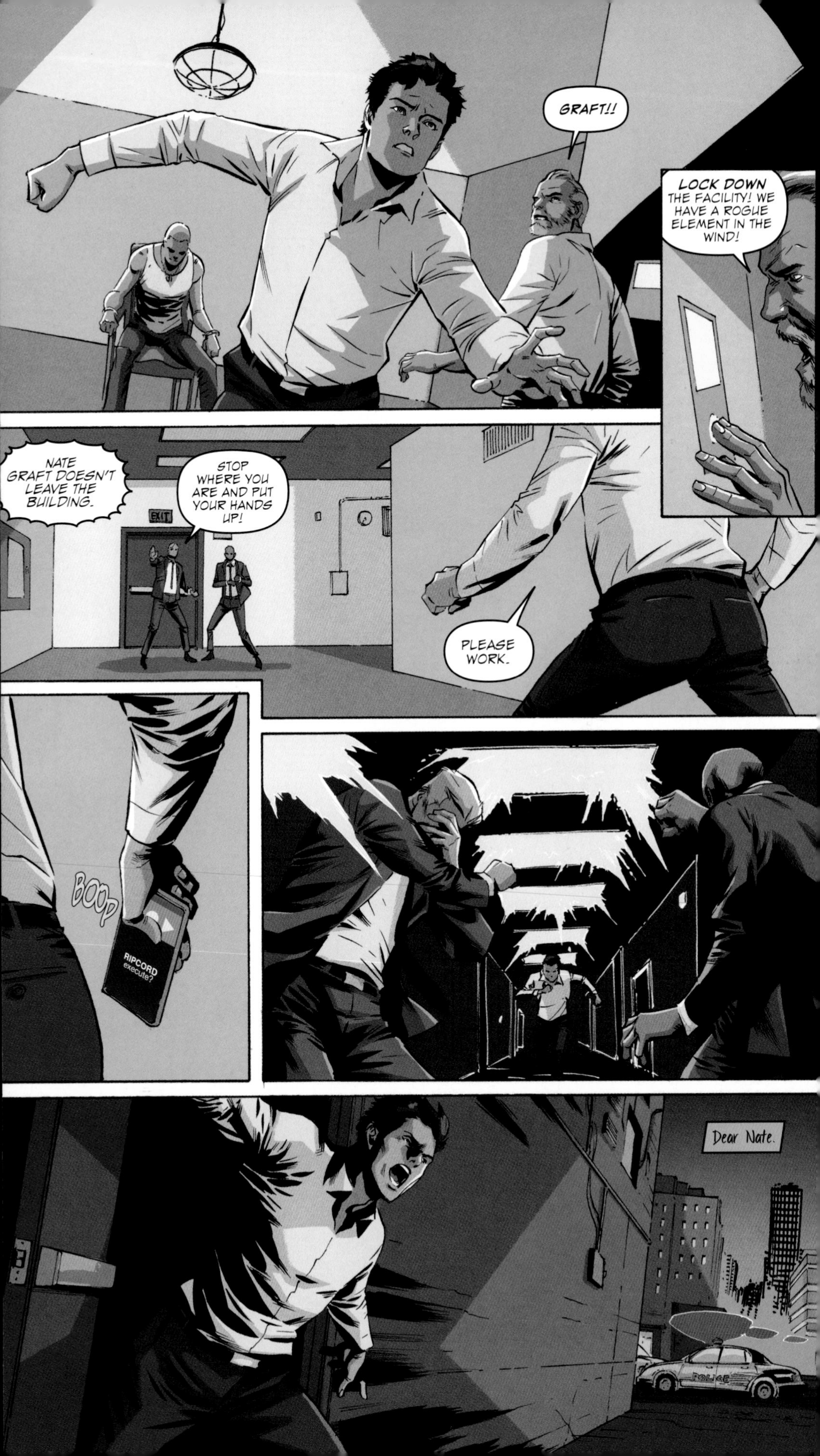
GRAFT!!
LOCK DOWN THE FACILITY! WE HAVE A ROGUE ELEMENT IN THE WIND!
NATE GRAFT DOESN'T LEAVE THE BUILDING.
STOP WHERE YOU ARE AND PUT YOUR HANDS UP!
EXIT
PLEASE WORK.
BOOP
RIPCORD
execute?
Dear Nate.
POLICE

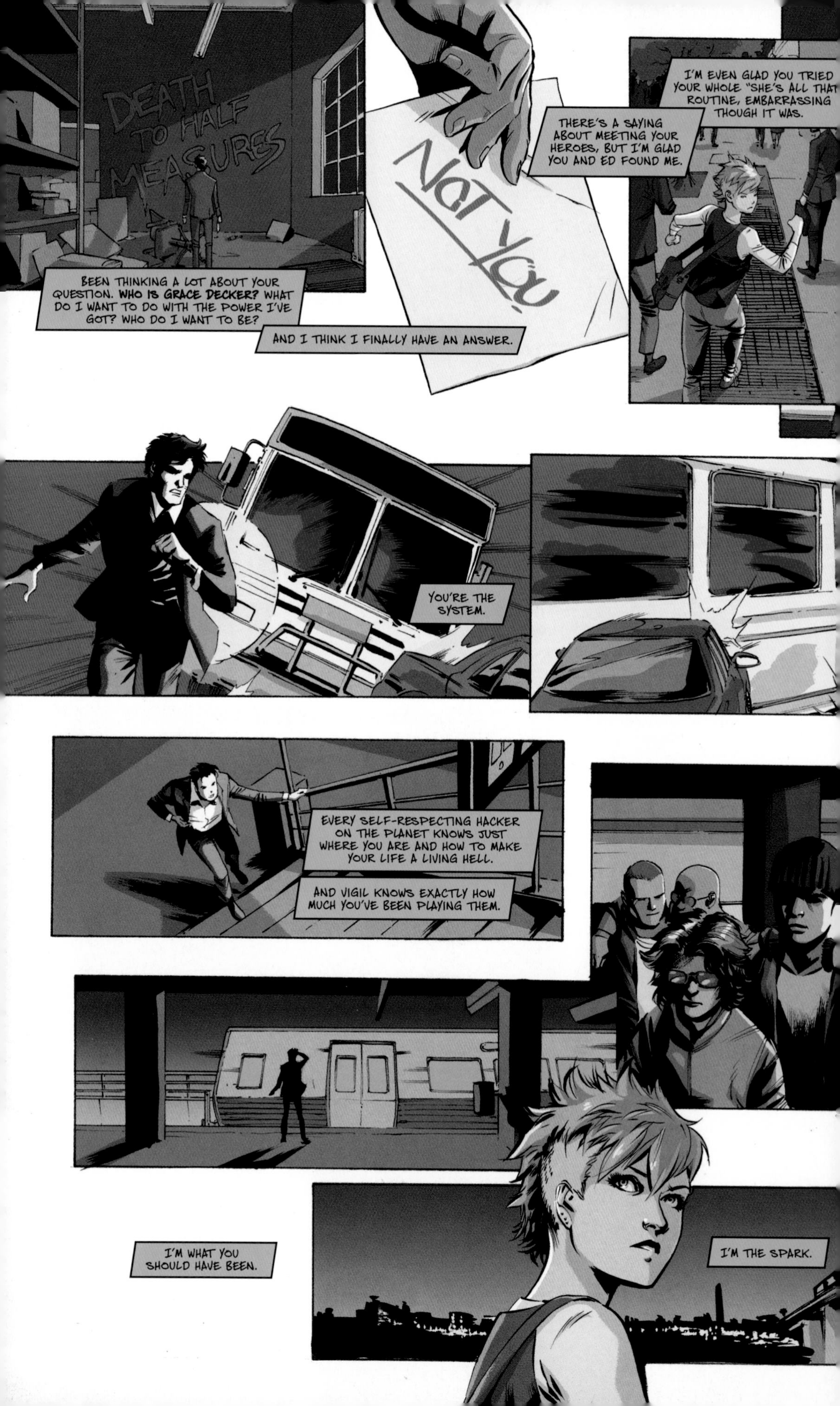
DEATH TO HALF MEASURES
BEEN THINKING A LOT ABOUT YOUR QUESTION. WHO IS GRACE DECKER? WHAT DO I WANT TO DO WITH THE POWER I'VE GOT? WHO DO I WANT TO BE?
AND I THINK I FINALLY HAVE AN ANSWER.
NOT YOU
THERE'S A SAYING ABOUT MEETING YOUR HEROES, BUT I'M GLAD YOU AND ED FOUND ME.
I'M EVEN GLAD YOU TRIED YOUR WHOLE "SHE'S ALL THAT" ROUTINE, EMBARRASSING THOUGH IT WAS.
YOU'RE THE SYSTEM.
EVERY SELF-RESPECTING HACKER ON THE PLANET KNOWS JUST WHERE YOU ARE AND HOW TO MAKE YOUR LIFE A LIVING HELL.
AND VIGIL KNOWS EXACTLY HOW MUCH YOU'VE BEEN PLAYING THEM.
I'M WHAT YOU SHOULD HAVE BEEN.
I'M THE SPARK.

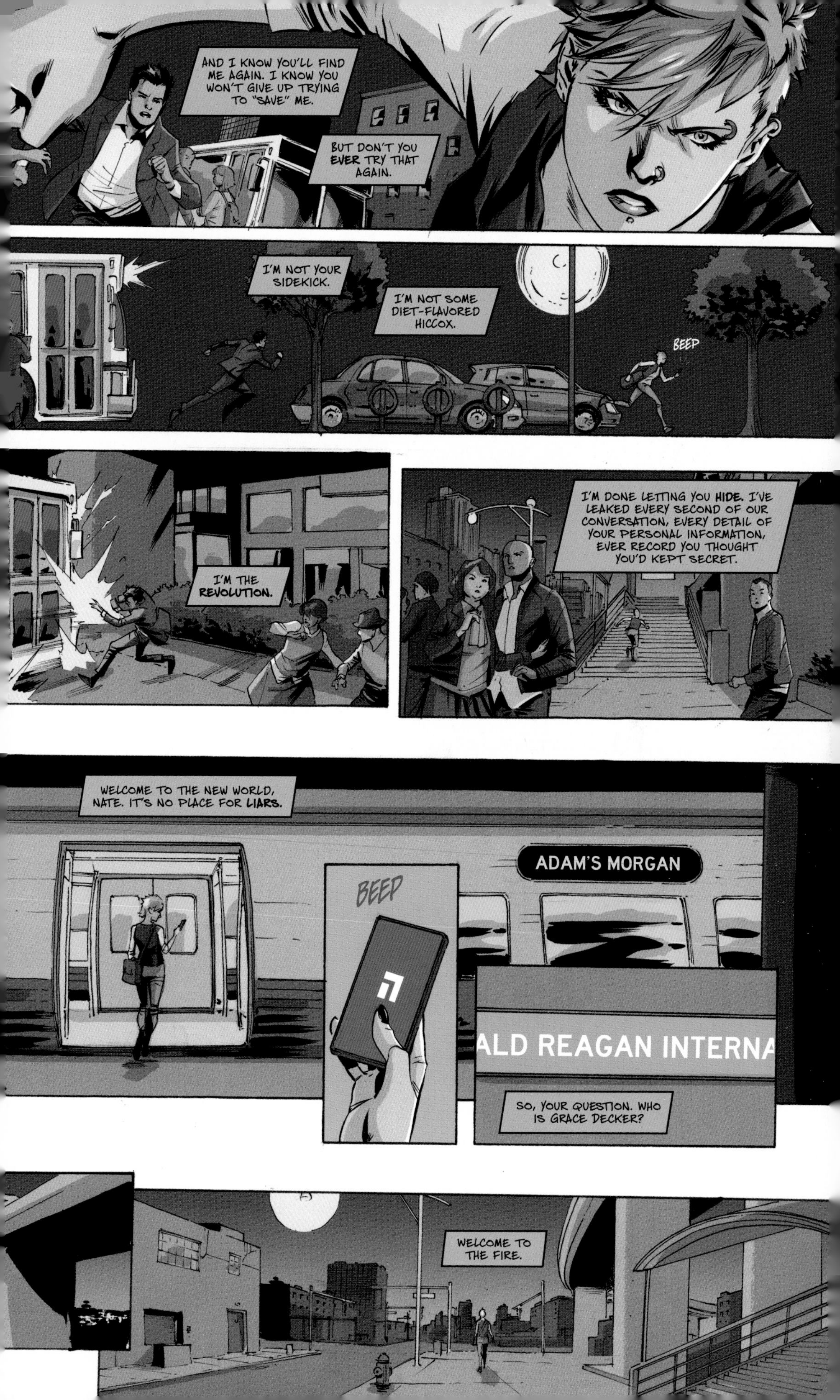
AND I KNOW YOU'LL FIND ME AGAIN. I KNOW YOU WON'T GIVE UP TRYING TO "SAVE" ME.
BUT DON'T YOU EVER TRY THAT AGAIN.
I'M NOT YOUR SIDEKICK.
I'M NOT SOME DIET-FLAVORED HICCOX.
BEEP
I'M THE REVOLUTION.
I'M DONE LETTING YOU HIDE. I'VE LEAKED EVERY SECOND OF OUR CONVERSATION, EVERY DETAIL OF YOUR PERSONAL INFORMATION, EVER RECORD YOU THOUGHT YOU'D KEPT SECRET.
WELCOME TO THE NEW WORLD, NATE. IT'S NO PLACE FOR LIARS.
ADAM'S MORGAN
BEEP
ALD REAGAN INTERNA
SO, YOUR QUESTION. WHO IS GRACE DECKER?
WELCOME TO THE FIRE.

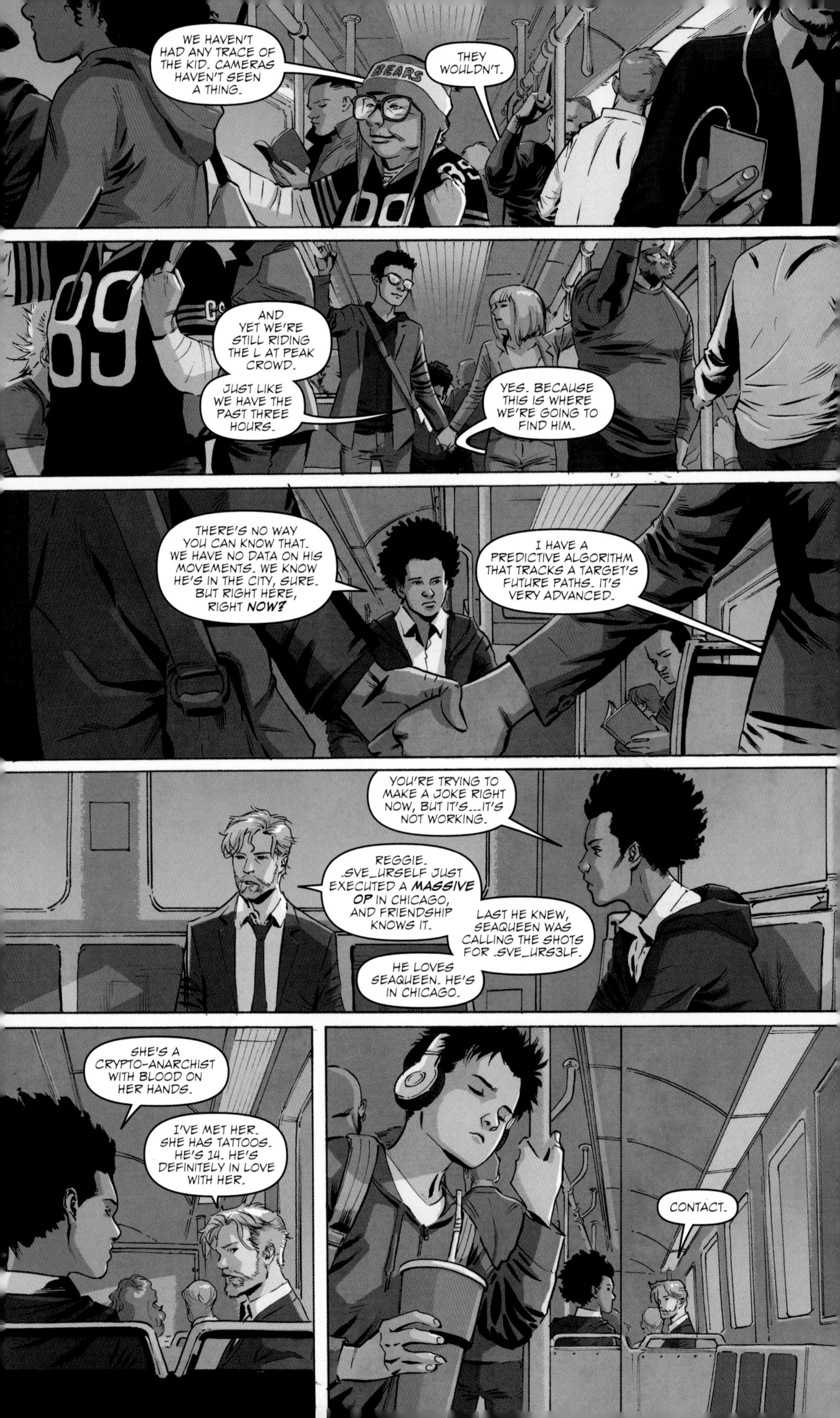
WE HAVEN'T HAD ANY TRACE OF THE KID. CAMERAS HAVEN'T SEEN A THING.
BEARS
THEY WOULDN'T.
89
AND YET WE'RE STILL RIDING THE L AT PEAK CROWD.
JUST LIKE WE HAVE THE PAST THREE HOURS.
YES. BECAUSE THIS IS WHERE WE'RE GOING TO FIND HIM.
THERE'S NO WAY YOU CAN KNOW THAT. WE HAVE NO DATA ON HIS MOVEMENTS. WE KNOW HE'S IN THE CITY, SURE. BUT RIGHT HERE, RIGHT NOW?
I HAVE A PREDICTIVE ALGORITHM THAT TRACKS A TARGET'S FUTURE PATHS. IT'S VERY ADVANCED.
YOU'RE TRYING TO MAKE A JOKE RIGHT NOW, BUT IT'S...IT'S NOT WORKING.
REGGIE. .SVE_URSELF JUST EXECUTED A MASSIVE OP IN CHICAGO, AND FRIENDSHIP KNOWS IT.
LAST HE KNEW, SEAQUEEN WAS CALLING THE SHOTS FOR .SVE_URS3LF.
HE LOVES SEAQUEEN. HE'S IN CHICAGO.
SHE'S A CRYPTO-ANARCHIST WITH BLOOD ON HER HANDS.
I'VE MET HER. SHE HAS TATTOOS. HE'S 14. HE'S DEFINITELY IN LOVE WITH HER.
CONTACT.

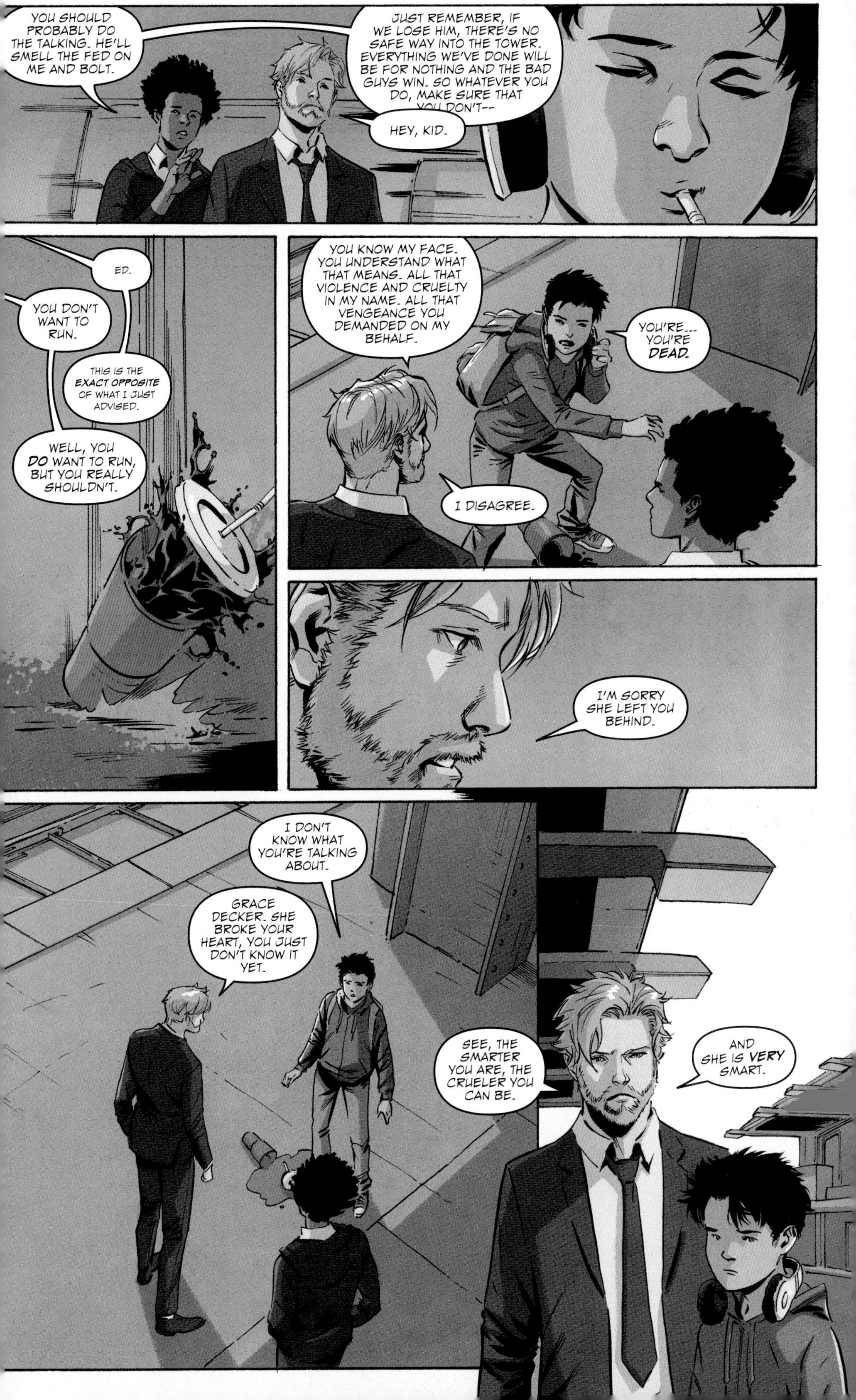
YOU SHOULD PROBABLY DO THE TALKING. HE'LL SMELL THE FED ON ME AND BOLT.
JUST REMEMBER, IF WE LOSE HIM, THERE'S NO SAFE WAY INTO THE TOWER. EVERYTHING WE'VE DONE WILL BE FOR NOTHING AND THE BAD GUYS WIN. SO WHATEVER YOU DO, MAKE SURE THAT YOU DON'T--
HEY, KID.
ED.
YOU DON'T WANT TO RUN.
THIS IS THE EXACT OPPOSITE OF WHAT I JUST ADVISED.
WELL, YOU DO WANT TO RUN, BUT YOU REALLY SHOULDN'T.
YOU KNOW MY FACE. YOU UNDERSTAND WHAT THAT MEANS. ALL THAT VIOLENCE AND CRUELTY IN MY NAME. ALL THAT VENGEANCE YOU DEMANDED ON MY BEHALF.
YOU'RE... YOU'RE DEAD.
I DISAGREE.
I'M SORRY SHE LEFT YOU BEHIND.
I DON'T KNOW WHAT YOU'RE TALKING ABOUT.
GRACE DECKER. SHE BROKE YOUR HEART, YOU JUST DON'T KNOW IT YET.
SEE, THE SMARTER YOU ARE, THE CRUELER YOU CAN BE.
AND SHE IS VERY SMART.

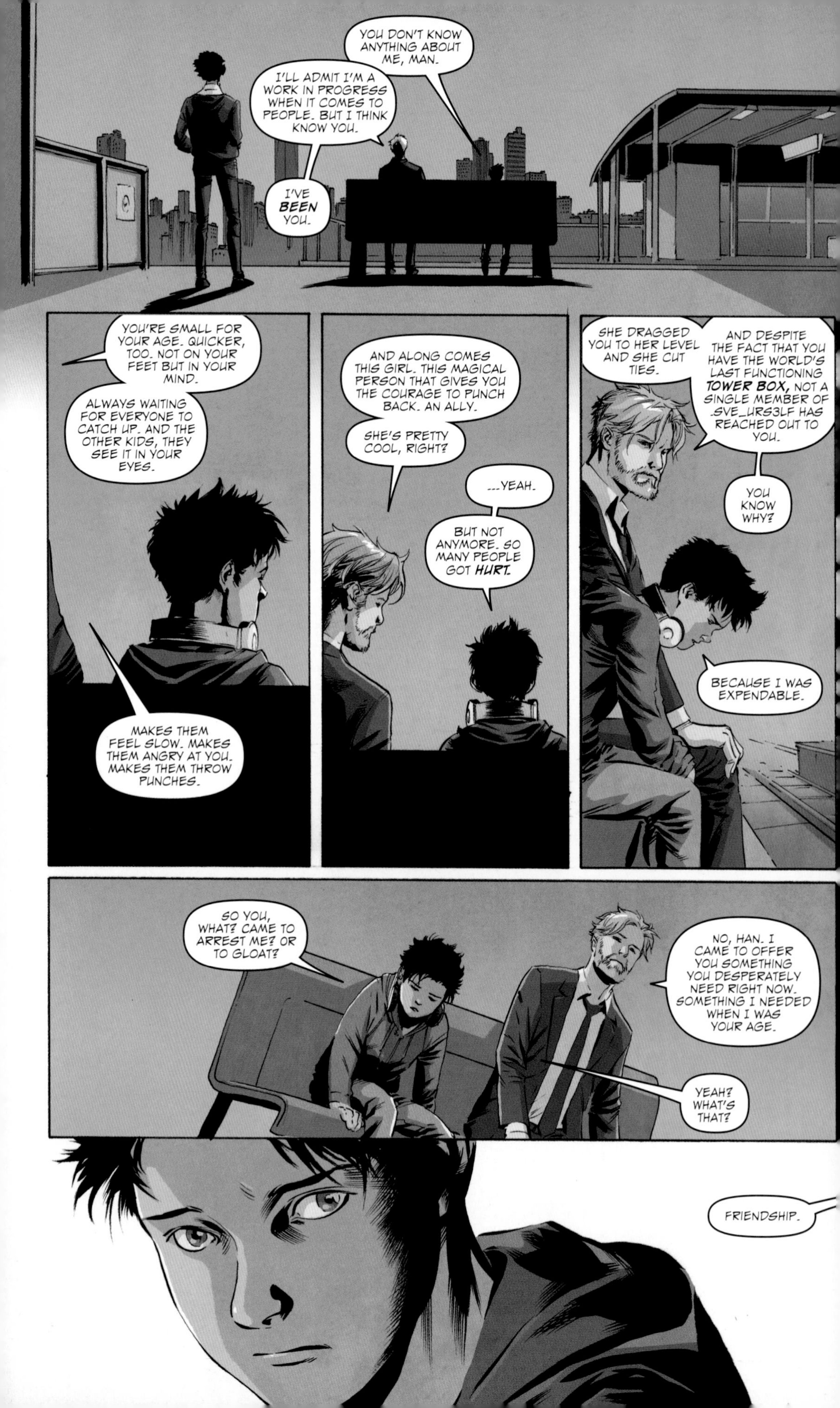
I'LL ADMIT I'M A WORK IN PROGRESS WHEN IT COMES TO PEOPLE. BUT I THINK I KNOW YOU.
YOU DON'T KNOW ANYTHING ABOUT ME, MAN.
I'VE BEEN YOU.
YOU'RE SMALL FOR YOUR AGE. QUICKER, TOO. NOT ON YOUR FEET BUT IN YOUR MIND.
ALWAYS WAITING FOR EVERYONE TO CATCH UP. AND THE OTHER KIDS, THEY SEE IT IN YOUR EYES.
MAKES THEM FEEL SLOW. MAKES THEM ANGRY AT YOU. MAKES THEM THROW PUNCHES.
AND ALONG COMES THIS GIRL. THIS MAGICAL PERSON THAT GIVES YOU THE COURAGE TO PUNCH BACK. AN ALLY.
SHE'S PRETTY COOL, RIGHT?
...YEAH.
BUT NOT ANYMORE. SO MANY PEOPLE GOT HURT.
SHE DRAGGED YOU TO HER LEVEL AND SHE CUT TIES.
AND DESPITE THE FACT THAT YOU HAVE THE WORLD'S LAST FUNCTIONING TOWER BOX, NOT A SINGLE MEMBER OF SVE_URS3LF HAS REACHED OUT TO YOU.
YOU KNOW WHY?
BECAUSE I WAS EXPENDABLE.
SO YOU, WHAT? CAME TO ARREST ME? OR TO GLOAT?
NO, HAN. I CAME TO OFFER YOU SOMETHING YOU DESPERATELY NEED RIGHT NOW. SOMETHING I NEEDED WHEN I WAS YOUR AGE.
YEAH? WHAT'S THAT?
FRIENDSHIP.

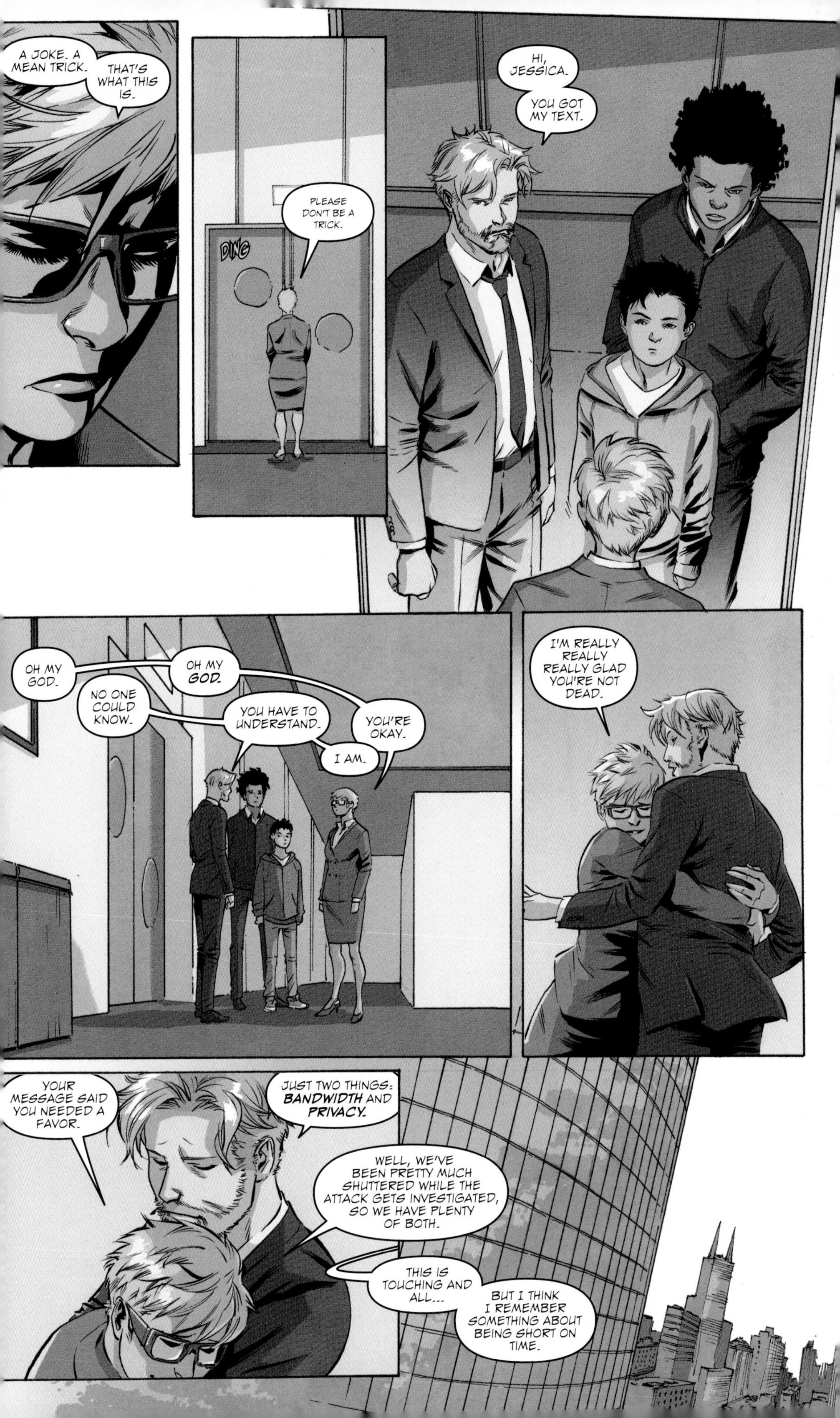
A JOKE. A MEAN TRICK.
THAT'S WHAT THIS IS.
PLEASE DON'T BE A TRICK.
DING
HI, JESSICA.
YOU GOT MY TEXT.
OH MY GOD.
OH MY GOD.
NO ONE COULD KNOW.
YOU HAVE TO UNDERSTAND.
YOU'RE OKAY.
I AM.
I'M REALLY REALLY REALLY GLAD YOU'RE NOT DEAD.
YOUR MESSAGE SAID YOU NEEDED A FAVOR.
JUST TWO THINGS: BANDWIDTH AND PRIVACY.
WELL, WE'VE BEEN PRETTY MUCH SHUTTERED WHILE THE ATTACK GETS INVESTIGATED, SO WE HAVE PLENTY OF BOTH.
THIS IS TOUCHING AND ALL...
BUT I THINK I REMEMBER SOMETHING ABOUT BEING SHORT ON TIME.

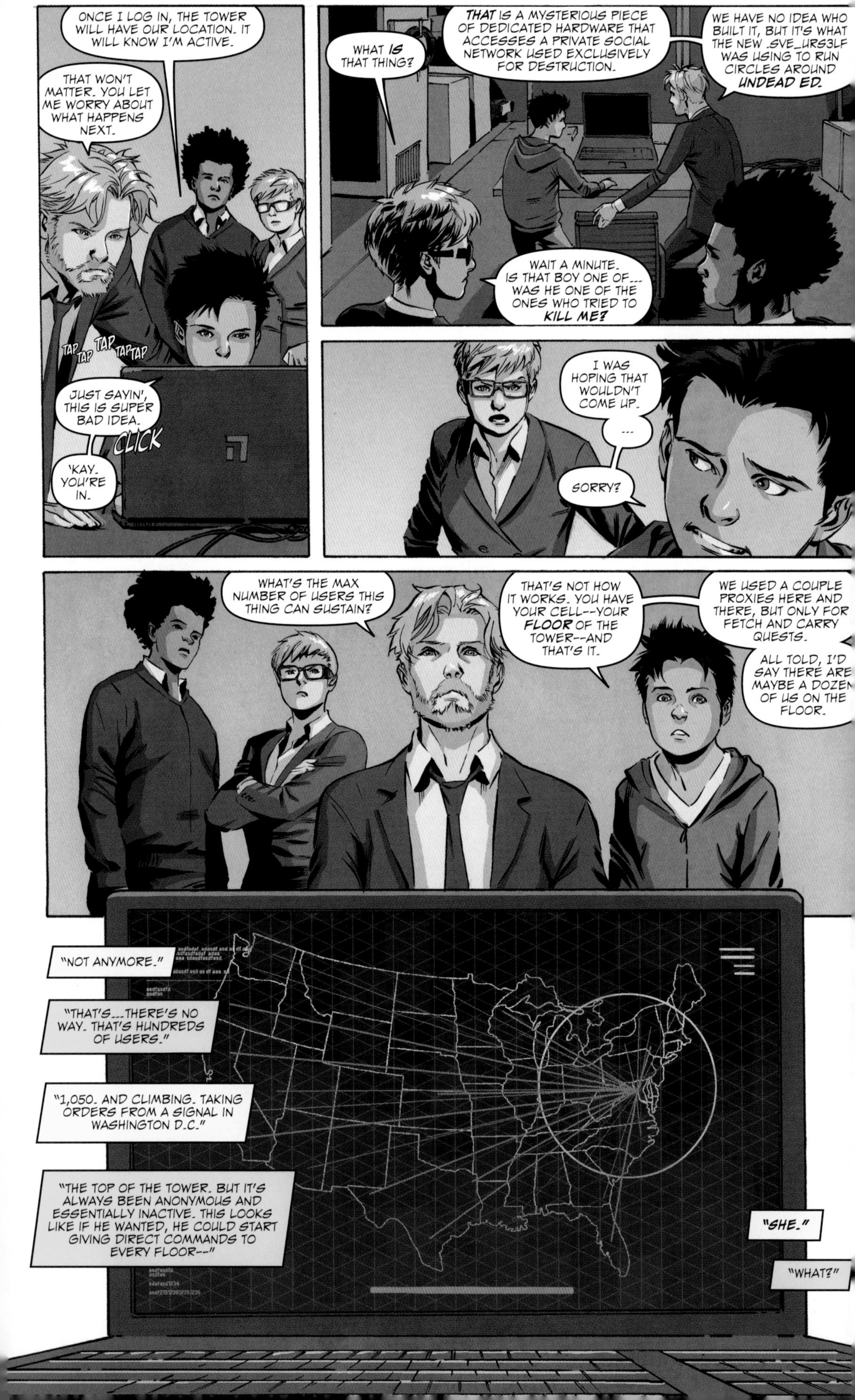
ONCE I LOG IN, THE TOWER WILL HAVE OUR LOCATION. IT WILL KNOW I'M ACTIVE.
THAT WON'T MATTER. YOU LET ME WORRY ABOUT WHAT HAPPENS NEXT.
TAP TAP TAP TAP TAP
JUST SAYIN', THIS IS SUPER BAD IDEA.
CLICK
'KAY. YOU'RE IN.
WHAT IS THAT THING?
THAT IS A MYSTERIOUS PIECE OF DEDICATED HARDWARE THAT ACCESSES A PRIVATE SOCIAL NETWORK USED EXCLUSIVELY FOR DESTRUCTION.
WE HAVE NO IDEA WHO BUILT IT, BUT IT'S WHAT THE NEW .SVE_URS3LF WAS USING TO RUN CIRCLES AROUND UNDEAD ED.
WAIT A MINUTE. IS THAT BOY ONE OF... WAS HE ONE OF THE ONES WHO TRIED TO KILL ME?
I WAS HOPING THAT WOULDN'T COME UP.
...
SORRY?
WHAT'S THE MAX NUMBER OF USERS THIS THING CAN SUSTAIN?
THAT'S NOT HOW IT WORKS. YOU HAVE YOUR CELL--YOUR FLOOR OF THE TOWER--AND THAT'S IT.
WE USED A COUPLE PROXIES HERE AND THERE, BUT ONLY FOR FETCH AND CARRY QUESTS.
ALL TOLD, I'D SAY THERE ARE MAYBE A DOZEN OF US ON THE FLOOR.
"NOT ANYMORE."
"THAT'S...THERE'S NO WAY. THAT'S HUNDREDS OF USERS."
"1,050. AND CLIMBING. TAKING ORDERS FROM A SIGNAL IN WASHINGTON D.C."
"THE TOP OF THE TOWER. BUT IT'S ALWAYS BEEN ANONYMOUS AND ESSENTIALLY INACTIVE. THIS LOOKS LIKE IF HE WANTED, HE COULD START GIVING DIRECT COMMANDS TO EVERY FLOOR--"
"SHE."
"WHAT?"

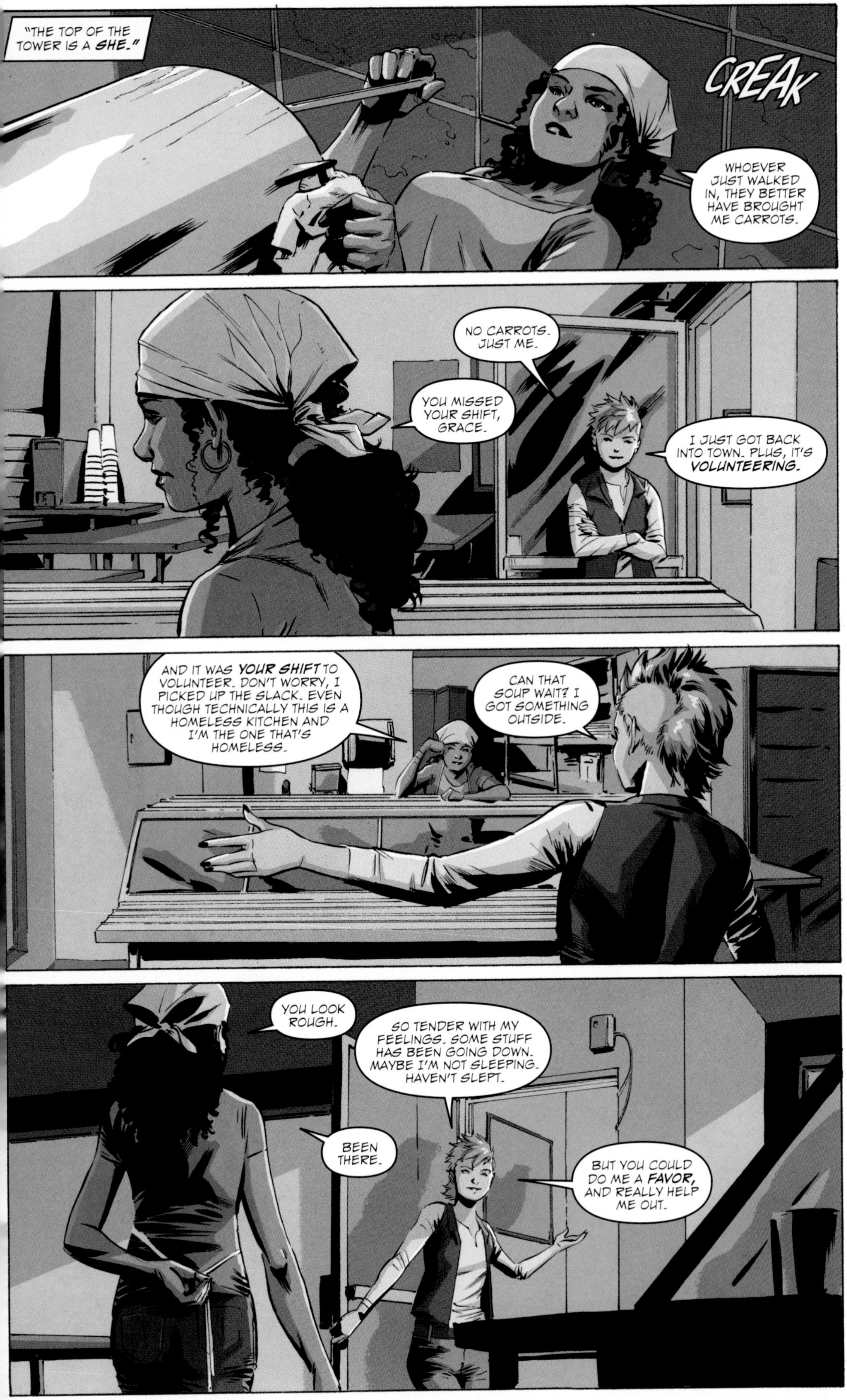
"THE TOP OF THE TOWER IS A SHE."
CREAK
WHOEVER JUST WALKED IN, THEY BETTER HAVE BROUGHT ME CARROTS.
NO CARROTS. JUST ME.
YOU MISSED YOUR SHIFT, GRACE.
I JUST GOT BACK INTO TOWN. PLUS, IT'S VOLUNTEERING.
AND IT WAS YOUR SHIFT TO VOLUNTEER. DON'T WORRY, I PICKED UP THE SLACK. EVEN THOUGH TECHNICALLY THIS IS A HOMELESS KITCHEN AND I'M THE ONE THAT'S HOMELESS.
CAN THAT SOUP WAIT? I GOT SOMETHING OUTSIDE.
YOU LOOK ROUGH.
SO TENDER WITH MY FEELINGS. SOME STUFF HAS BEEN GOING DOWN. MAYBE I'M NOT SLEEPING. HAVEN'T SLEPT.
BEEN THERE.
BUT YOU COULD DO ME A FAVOR, AND REALLY HELP ME OUT.

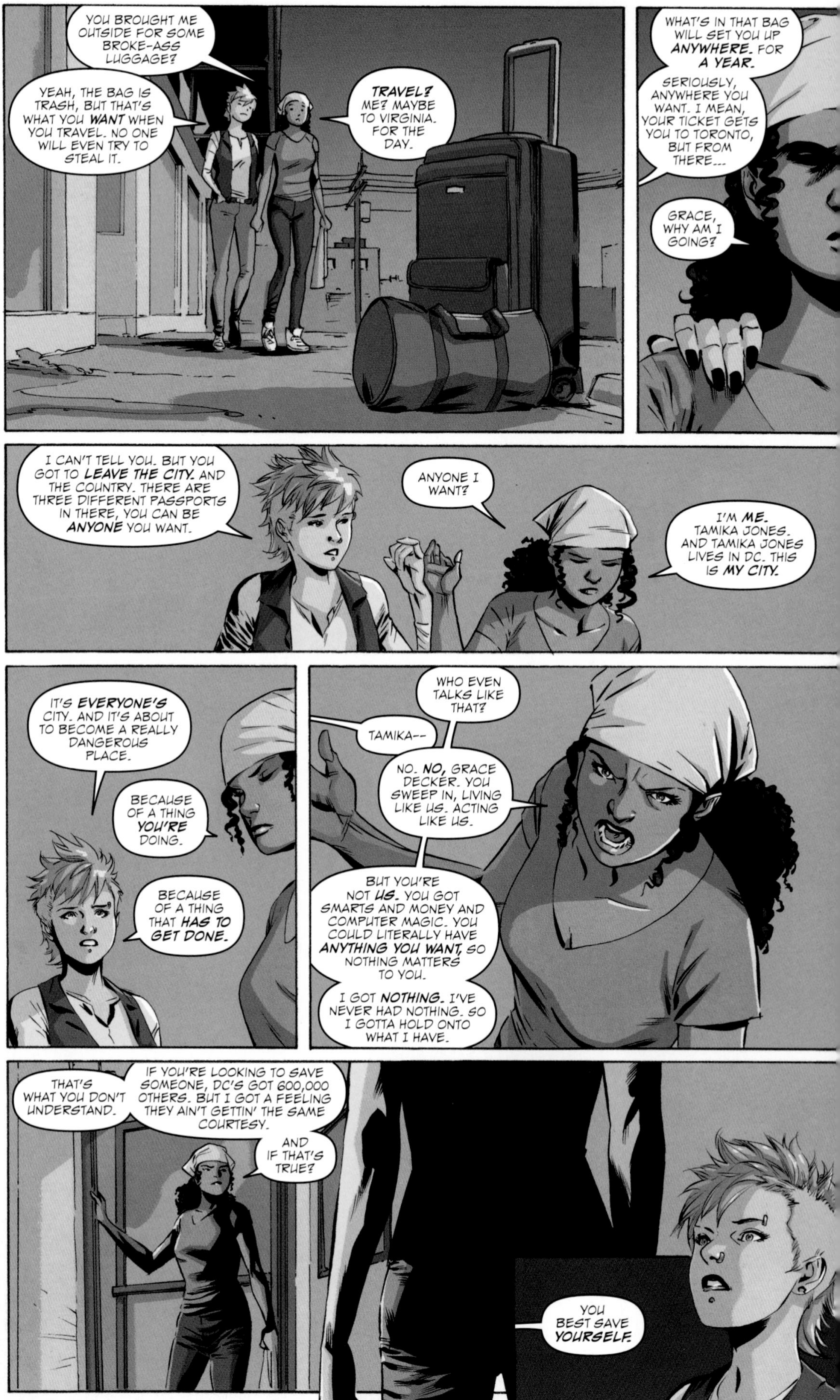
YOU BROUGHT ME OUTSIDE FOR SOME BROKE-ASS LUGGAGE?
YEAH, THE BAG IS TRASH, BUT THAT'S WHAT YOU WANT WHEN YOU TRAVEL. NO ONE WILL EVEN TRY TO STEAL IT.
TRAVEL? ME? MAYBE TO VIRGINIA. FOR THE DAY.
WHAT'S IN THAT BAG WILL SET YOU UP ANYWHERE. FOR A YEAR.
SERIOUSLY, ANYWHERE YOU WANT. I MEAN, YOUR TICKET GETS YOU TO TORONTO, BUT FROM THERE...
GRACE, WHY AM I GOING?
I CAN'T TELL YOU. BUT YOU GOT TO LEAVE THE CITY. AND THE COUNTRY. THERE ARE THREE DIFFERENT PASSPORTS IN THERE, YOU CAN BE ANYONE YOU WANT.
ANYONE I WANT?
I'M ME. TAMIKA JONES. AND TAMIKA JONES LIVES IN DC. THIS IS MY CITY.
IT'S EVERYONE'S CITY. AND IT'S ABOUT TO BECOME A REALLY DANGEROUS PLACE.
BECAUSE OF A THING YOU'RE DOING.
BECAUSE OF A THING THAT HAS TO GET DONE.
TAMIKA--
WHO EVEN TALKS LIKE THAT?
NO. NO, GRACE DECKER. YOU SWEEP IN, LIVING LIKE US. ACTING LIKE US.
BUT YOU'RE NOT US. YOU GOT SMARTS AND MONEY AND COMPUTER MAGIC. YOU COULD LITERALLY HAVE ANYTHING YOU WANT, SO NOTHING MATTERS TO YOU.
I GOT NOTHING. I'VE NEVER HAD NOTHING. SO I GOTTA HOLD ONTO WHAT I HAVE.
THAT'S WHAT YOU DON'T UNDERSTAND.
IF YOU'RE LOOKING TO SAVE SOMEONE, DC'S GOT 600,000 OTHERS. BUT I GOT A FEELING THEY AIN'T GETTIN' THE SAME COURTESY.
AND IF THAT'S TRUE?
YOU BEST SAVE YOURSELF.

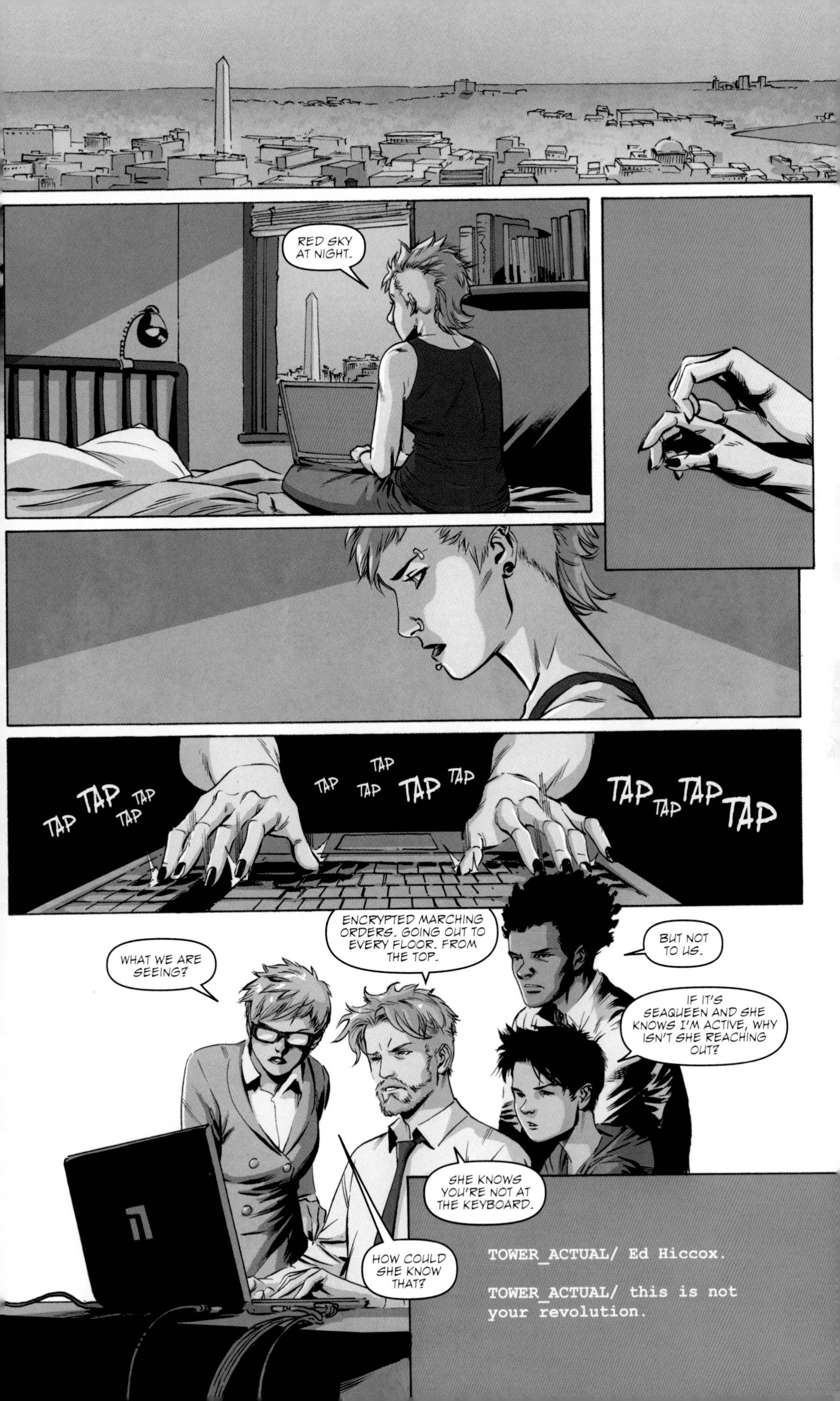
RED SKY AT NIGHT.
TAP TAP TAP TAP
TAP TAP TAP TAP TAP
TAP TAP TAP TAP
WHAT WE ARE SEEING?
ENCRYPTED MARCHING ORDERS. GOING OUT TO EVERY FLOOR. FROM THE TOP.
BUT NOT TO US.
IF IT'S SEAQUEEN AND SHE KNOWS I'M ACTIVE, WHY ISN'T SHE REACHING OUT?
SHE KNOWS YOU'RE NOT AT THE KEYBOARD.
HOW COULD SHE KNOW THAT?
TOWER_ACTUAL/ Ed Hiccox.
TOWER_ACTUAL/ this is not your revolution.

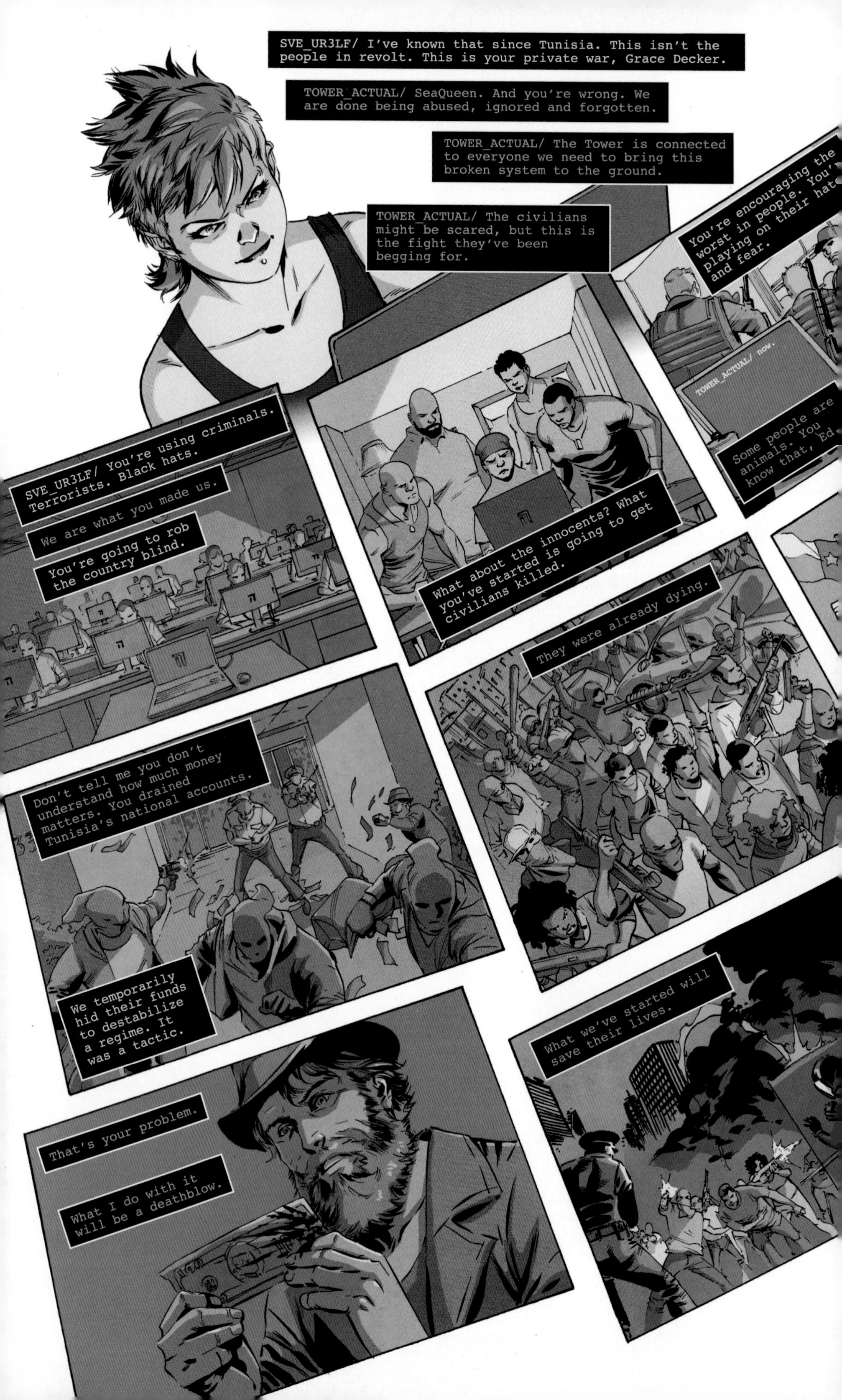

SVE_UR3LF/ I've known that since Tunisia. This isn't the people in revolt. This is your private war, Grace Decker.
TOWER_ACTUAL/ SeaQueen. And you're wrong. We are done being abused, ignored and forgotten.
TOWER_ACTUAL/ The Tower is connected to everyone we need to bring this broken system to the ground.
TOWER_ACTUAL/ The civilians might be scared, but this is the fight they've been begging for.
You're encouraging the worst in people. You' playing on their hat and fear.
TOWER_ACTUAL/ now.
Some people are animals. You know that, Ed
SVE_UR3LF/ You're using criminals. Terrorists. Black hats.
We are what you made us.
You're going to rob the country blind.
What about the innocents? What you've started is going to get civilians killed.
They were already dying.
Don't tell me you don't understand how much money matters. You drained Tunisia's national accounts.
We temporarily hid their funds to destabilize a regime. It was a tactic.
What we've started will save their lives.
That's your problem.
What I do with it will be a deathblow.

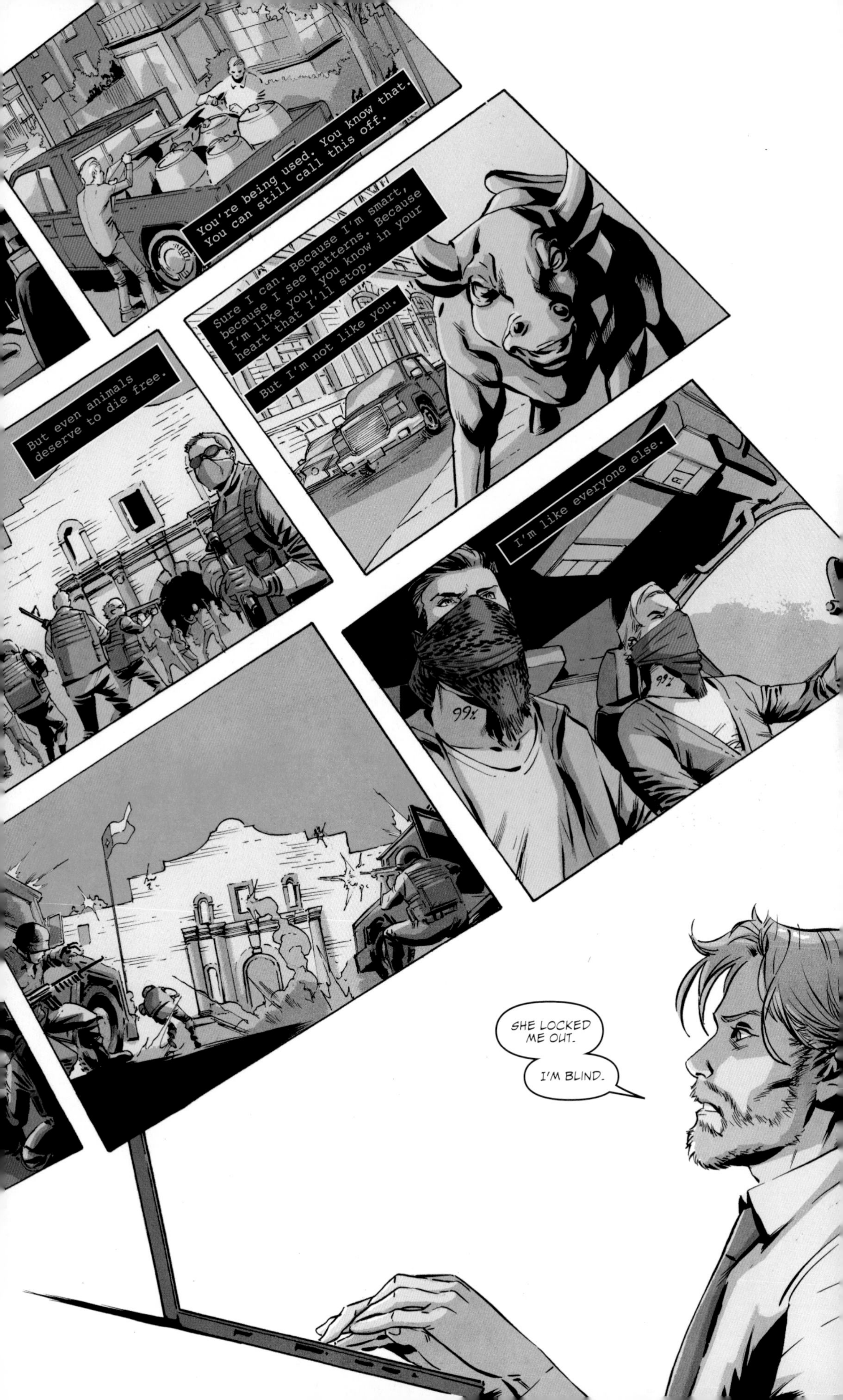
You're being used. You know that. You can still call this off.
Sure I can. Because I'm smart, because I see patterns. Because I'm like you, you know in your heart that I'll stop.
But I'm not like you.
But even animals deserve to die free.
I'm like everyone else.
99%
99%
SHE LOCKED ME OUT.
I'M BLIND.

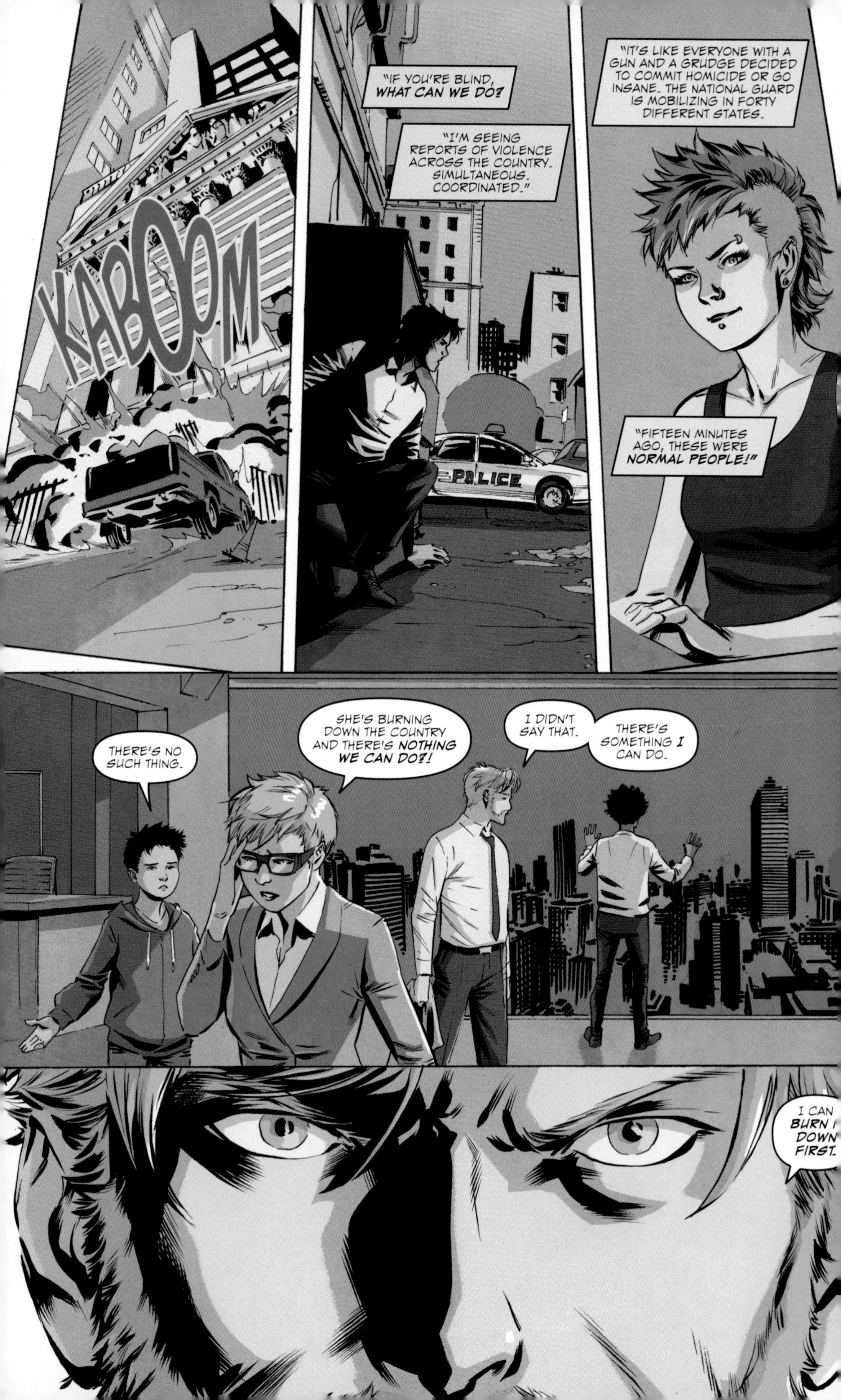
KABOOM
"IF YOU'RE BLIND, WHAT CAN WE DO?
"I'M SEEING REPORTS OF VIOLENCE ACROSS THE COUNTRY. SIMULTANEOUS. COORDINATED."
POLICE
"IT'S LIKE EVERYONE WITH A GUN AND A GRUDGE DECIDED TO COMMIT HOMICIDE OR GO INSANE. THE NATIONAL GUARD IS MOBILIZING IN FORTY DIFFERENT STATES.
"FIFTEEN MINUTES AGO, THESE WERE NORMAL PEOPLE!"
SHE'S BURNING DOWN THE COUNTRY AND THERE'S NOTHING WE CAN DO?!
THERE'S NO SUCH THING.
I DIDN'T SAY THAT.
THERE'S SOMETHING I CAN DO.
I CAN BURN I DOWN FIRST.

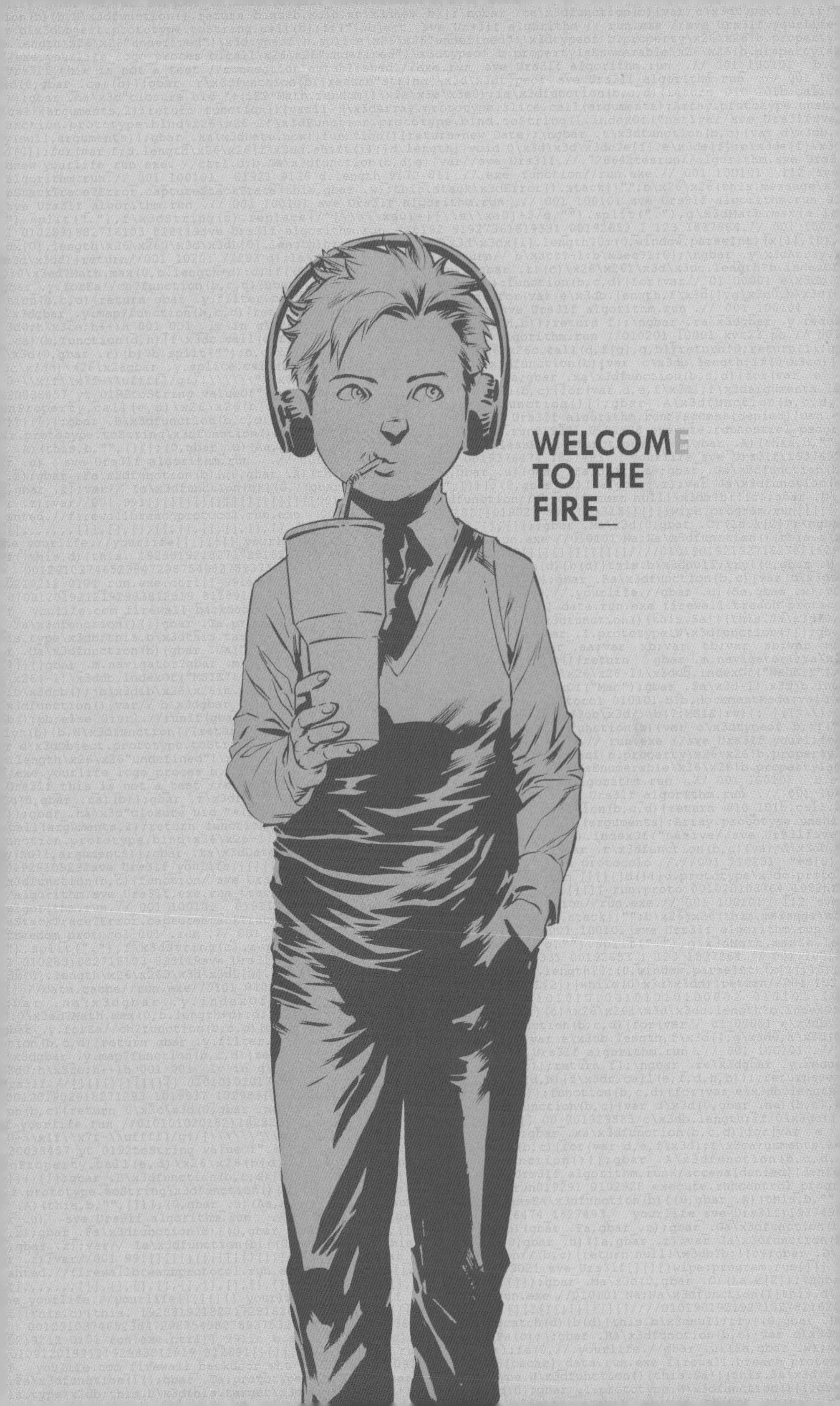
WELCOME
TO THE
FIRE_

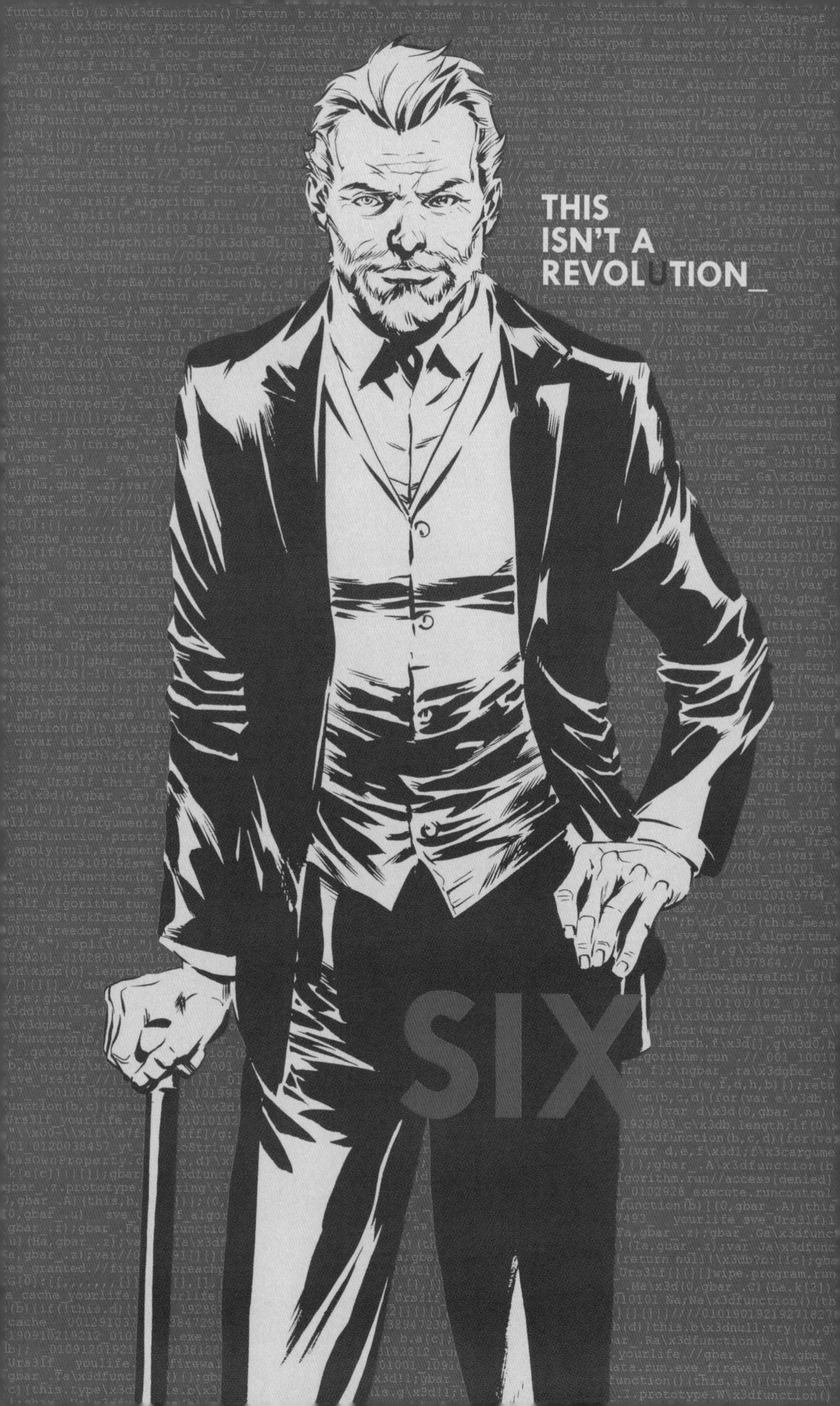
THIS
ISN'T A
REVOLUTION_
SIX

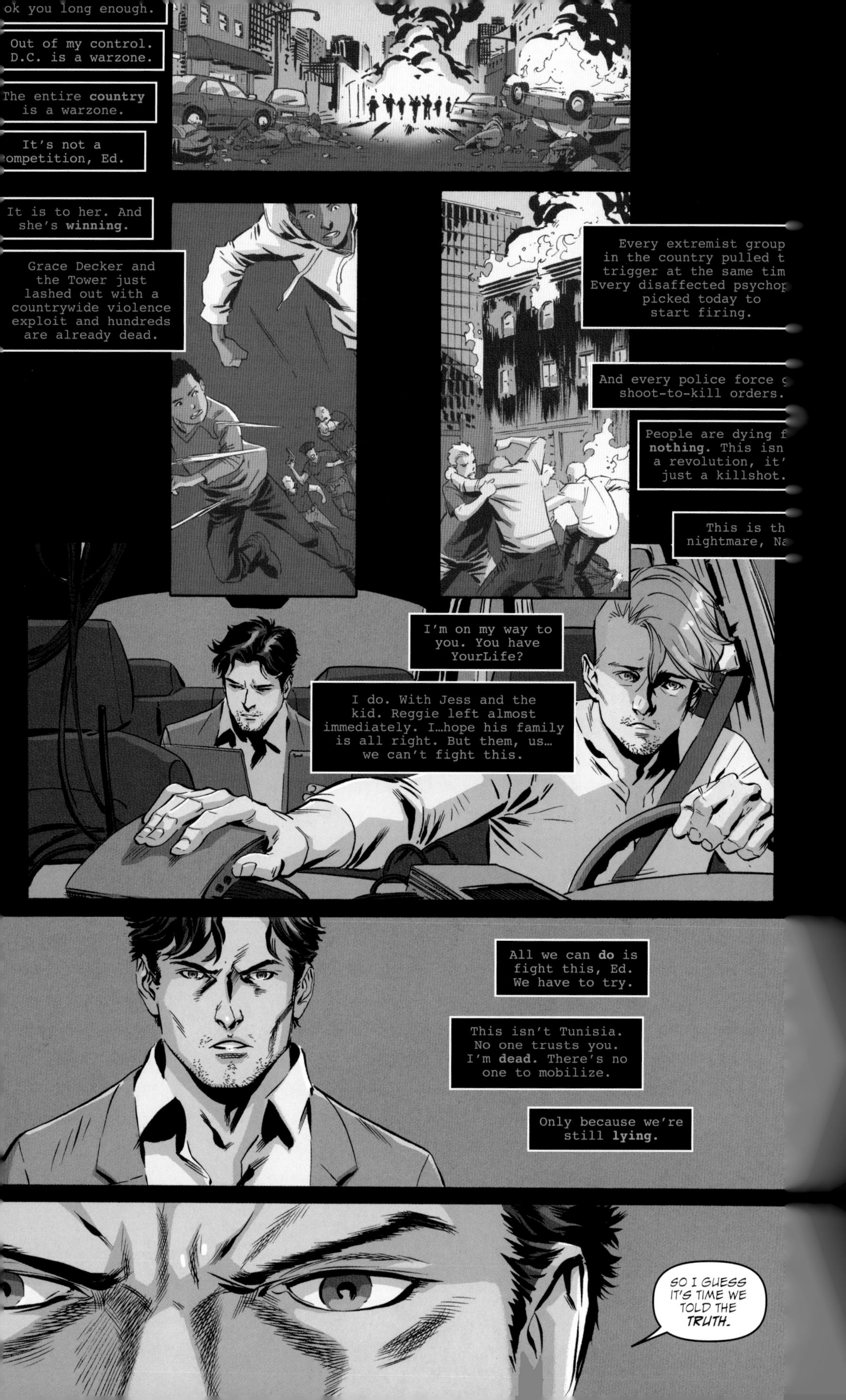
ok you long enough.
Out of my control. D.C. is a warzone.
The entire **country** is a warzone.
It's not a ompetition, Ed.
It is to her. And she's **winning**.
Grace Decker and the Tower just lashed out with a countrywide violence exploit and hundreds are already dead.
Every extremist group in the country pulled t trigger at the same tim Every disaffected psychop picked today to start firing.
And every police force g shoot-to-kill orders.
People are dying f **nothing**. This isn a revolution, it' just a killshot.
This is th nightmare, Na
I'm on my way to you. You have YourLife?
I do. With Jess and the kid. Reggie left almost immediately. I…hope his family is all right. But them, us… we can't fight this.
All we can **do** is fight this, Ed. We have to try.
This isn't Tunisia. No one trusts you. I'm **dead**. There's no one to mobilize.
Only because we're still **lying**.
SO I GUESS IT'S TIME WE TOLD THE ***TRUTH***.

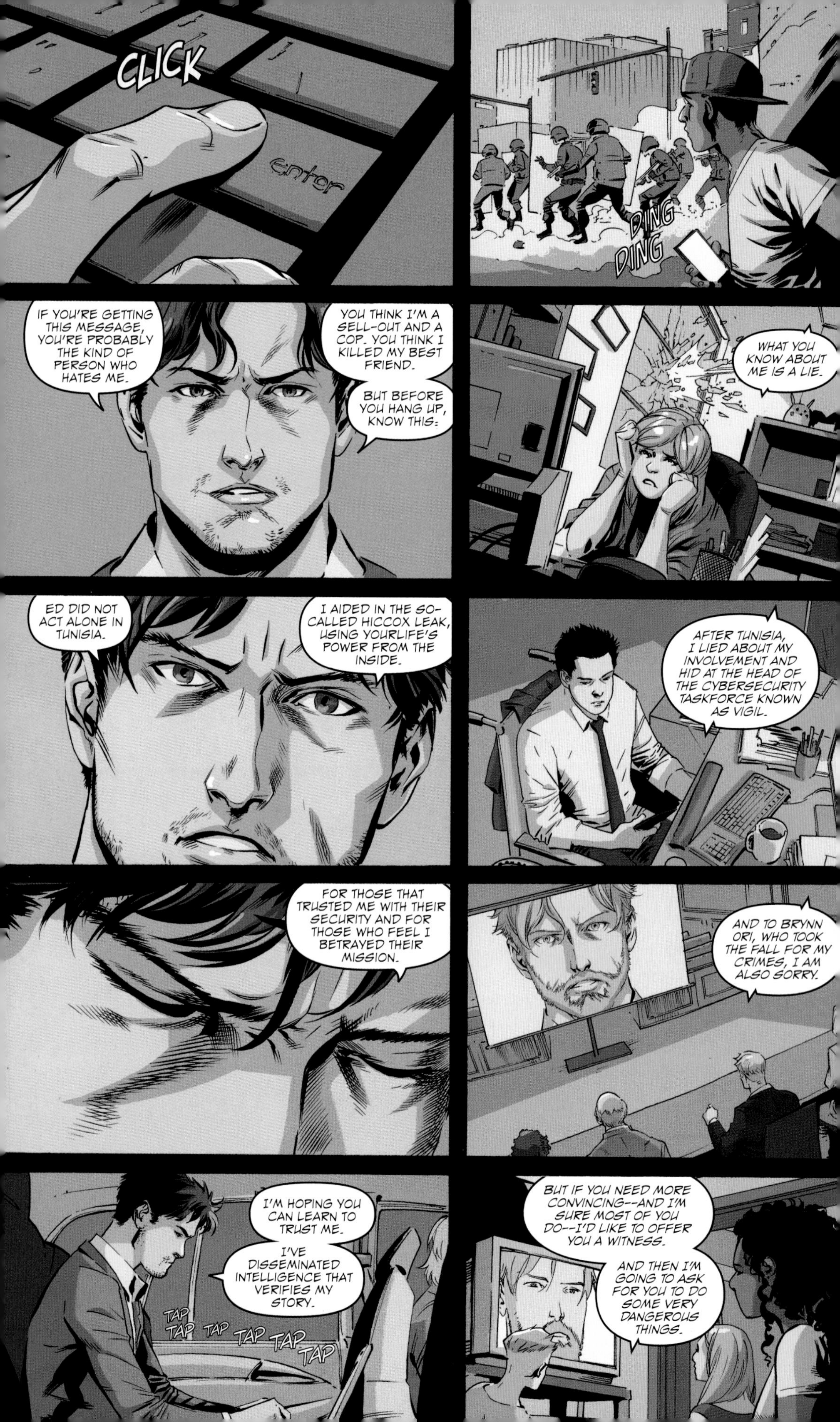
CLICK
enter
DING
DING
IF YOU'RE GETTING THIS MESSAGE, YOU'RE PROBABLY THE KIND OF PERSON WHO HATES ME.
YOU THINK I'M A SELL-OUT AND A COP. YOU THINK I KILLED MY BEST FRIEND.
BUT BEFORE YOU HANG UP, KNOW THIS:
WHAT YOU KNOW ABOUT ME IS A LIE.
ED DID NOT ACT ALONE IN TUNISIA.
I AIDED IN THE SO-CALLED HICCOX LEAK, USING YOURLIFE'S POWER FROM THE INSIDE.
AFTER TUNISIA, I LIED ABOUT MY INVOLVEMENT AND HID AT THE HEAD OF THE CYBERSECURITY TASKFORCE KNOWN AS VIGIL.
FOR THOSE THAT TRUSTED ME WITH THEIR SECURITY AND FOR THOSE WHO FEEL I BETRAYED THEIR MISSION.
AND TO BRYNN ORI, WHO TOOK THE FALL FOR MY CRIMES, I AM ALSO SORRY.
I'M HOPING YOU CAN LEARN TO TRUST ME.
I'VE DISSEMINATED INTELLIGENCE THAT VERIFIES MY STORY.
TAP TAP TAP TAP TAP TAP
BUT IF YOU NEED MORE CONVINCING--AND I'M SURE MOST OF YOU DO--I'D LIKE TO OFFER YOU A WITNESS.
AND THEN I'M GOING TO ASK FOR YOU TO DO SOME VERY DANGEROUS THINGS.

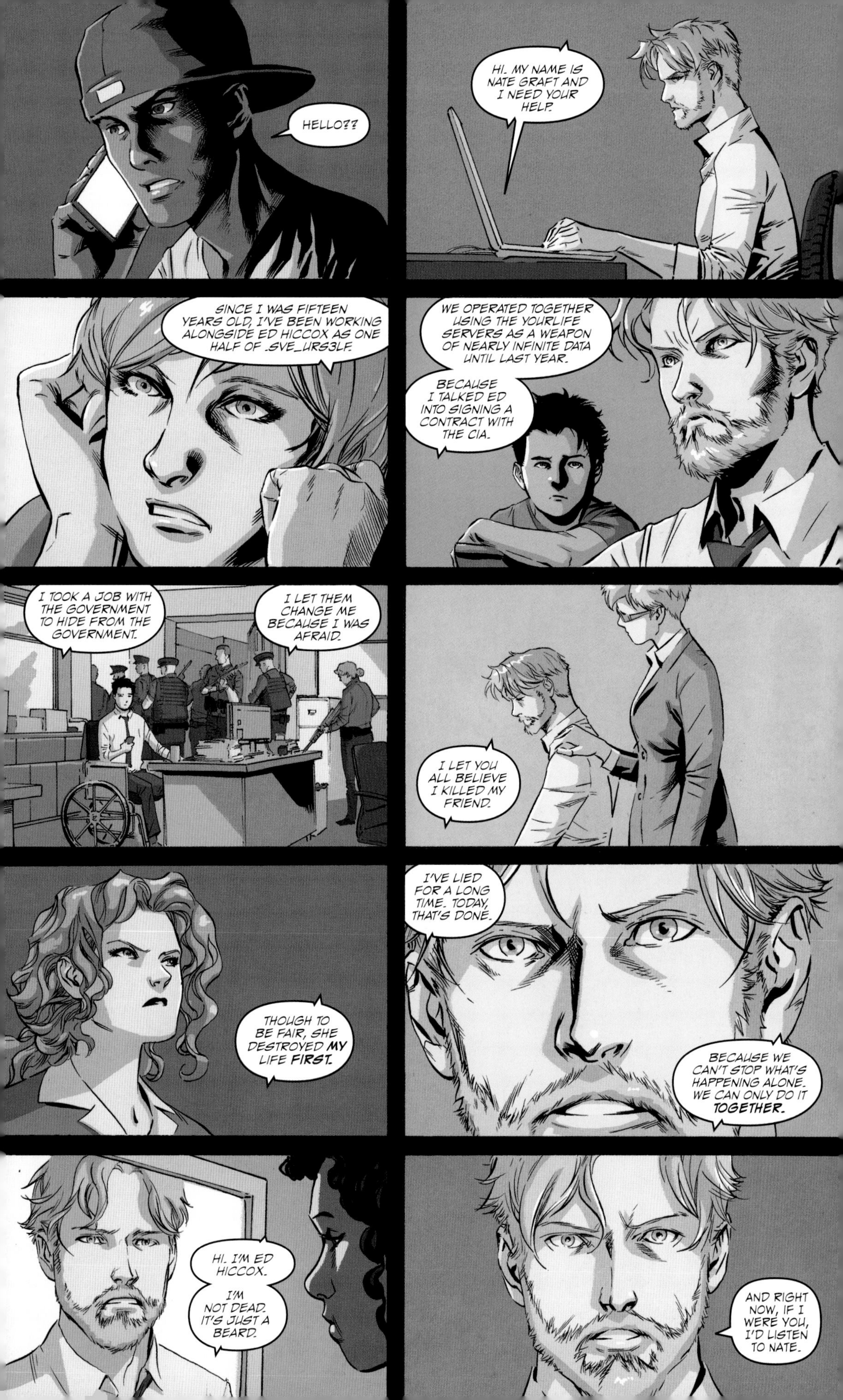
HELLO??
HI. MY NAME IS NATE GRAFT AND I NEED YOUR HELP.
SINCE I WAS FIFTEEN YEARS OLD, I'VE BEEN WORKING ALONGSIDE ED HICCOX AS ONE HALF OF .SVE_URS3LF.
WE OPERATED TOGETHER USING THE YOURLIFE SERVERS AS A WEAPON OF NEARLY INFINITE DATA UNTIL LAST YEAR.
BECAUSE I TALKED ED INTO SIGNING A CONTRACT WITH THE CIA.
I TOOK A JOB WITH THE GOVERNMENT TO HIDE FROM THE GOVERNMENT.
I LET THEM CHANGE ME BECAUSE I WAS AFRAID.
I LET YOU ALL BELIEVE I KILLED MY FRIEND.
THOUGH TO BE FAIR, SHE DESTROYED MY LIFE FIRST.
I'VE LIED FOR A LONG TIME. TODAY, THAT'S DONE.
BECAUSE WE CAN'T STOP WHAT'S HAPPENING ALONE. WE CAN ONLY DO IT TOGETHER.
HI. I'M ED HICCOX.
I'M NOT DEAD. IT'S JUST A BEARD.
AND RIGHT NOW, IF I WERE YOU, I'D LISTEN TO NATE.

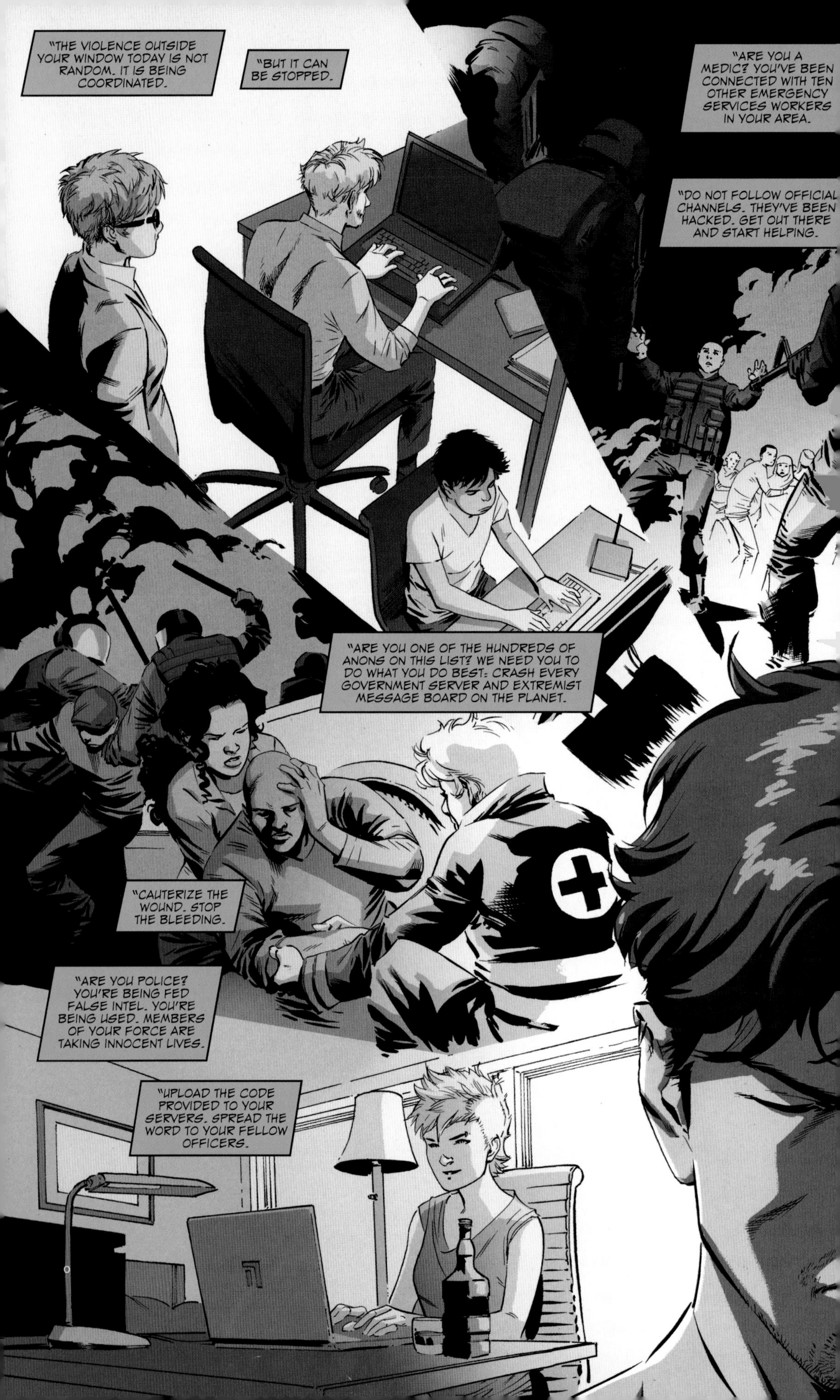
"THE VIOLENCE OUTSIDE YOUR WINDOW TODAY IS NOT RANDOM. IT IS BEING COORDINATED.
"BUT IT CAN BE STOPPED.
"ARE YOU A MEDIC? YOU'VE BEEN CONNECTED WITH TEN OTHER EMERGENCY SERVICES WORKERS IN YOUR AREA.
"DO NOT FOLLOW OFFICIAL CHANNELS. THEY'VE BEEN HACKED. GET OUT THERE AND START HELPING.
"ARE YOU ONE OF THE HUNDREDS OF ANONS ON THIS LIST? WE NEED YOU TO DO WHAT YOU DO BEST: CRASH EVERY GOVERNMENT SERVER AND EXTREMIST MESSAGE BOARD ON THE PLANET.
"CAUTERIZE THE WOUND. STOP THE BLEEDING.
"ARE YOU POLICE? YOU'RE BEING FED FALSE INTEL. YOU'RE BEING USED. MEMBERS OF YOUR FORCE ARE TAKING INNOCENT LIVES.
"UPLOAD THE CODE PROVIDED TO YOUR SERVERS. SPREAD THE WORD TO YOUR FELLOW OFFICERS.

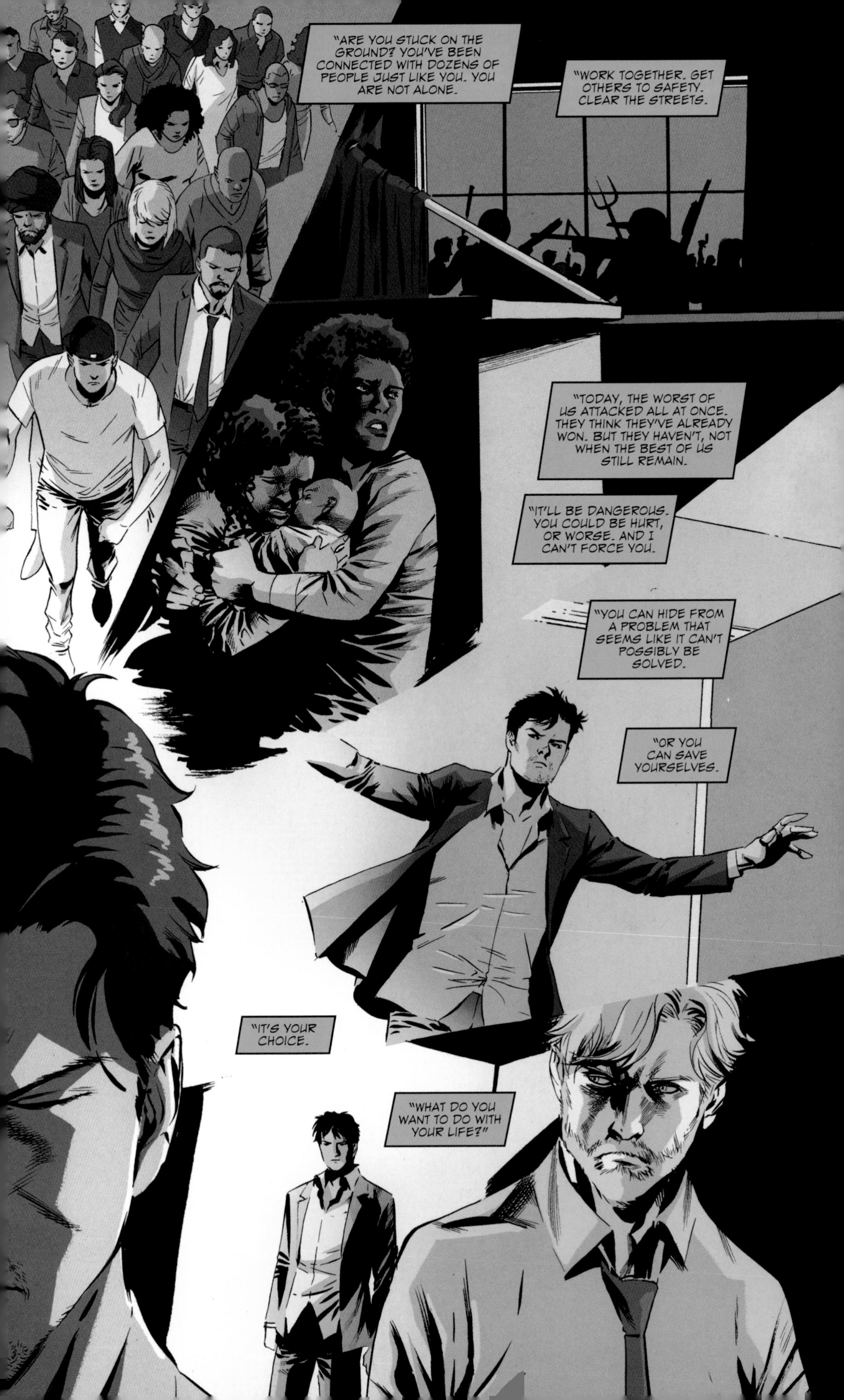
"ARE YOU STUCK ON THE GROUND? YOU'VE BEEN CONNECTED WITH DOZENS OF PEOPLE JUST LIKE YOU. YOU ARE NOT ALONE.
"WORK TOGETHER. GET OTHERS TO SAFETY. CLEAR THE STREETS.
"TODAY, THE WORST OF US ATTACKED ALL AT ONCE. THEY THINK THEY'VE ALREADY WON. BUT THEY HAVEN'T, NOT WHEN THE BEST OF US STILL REMAIN.
"IT'LL BE DANGEROUS. YOU COULD BE HURT, OR WORSE. AND I CAN'T FORCE YOU.
"YOU CAN HIDE FROM A PROBLEM THAT SEEMS LIKE IT CAN'T POSSIBLY BE SOLVED.
"OR YOU CAN SAVE YOURSELVES.
"IT'S YOUR CHOICE.
"WHAT DO YOU WANT TO DO WITH YOUR LIFE?"

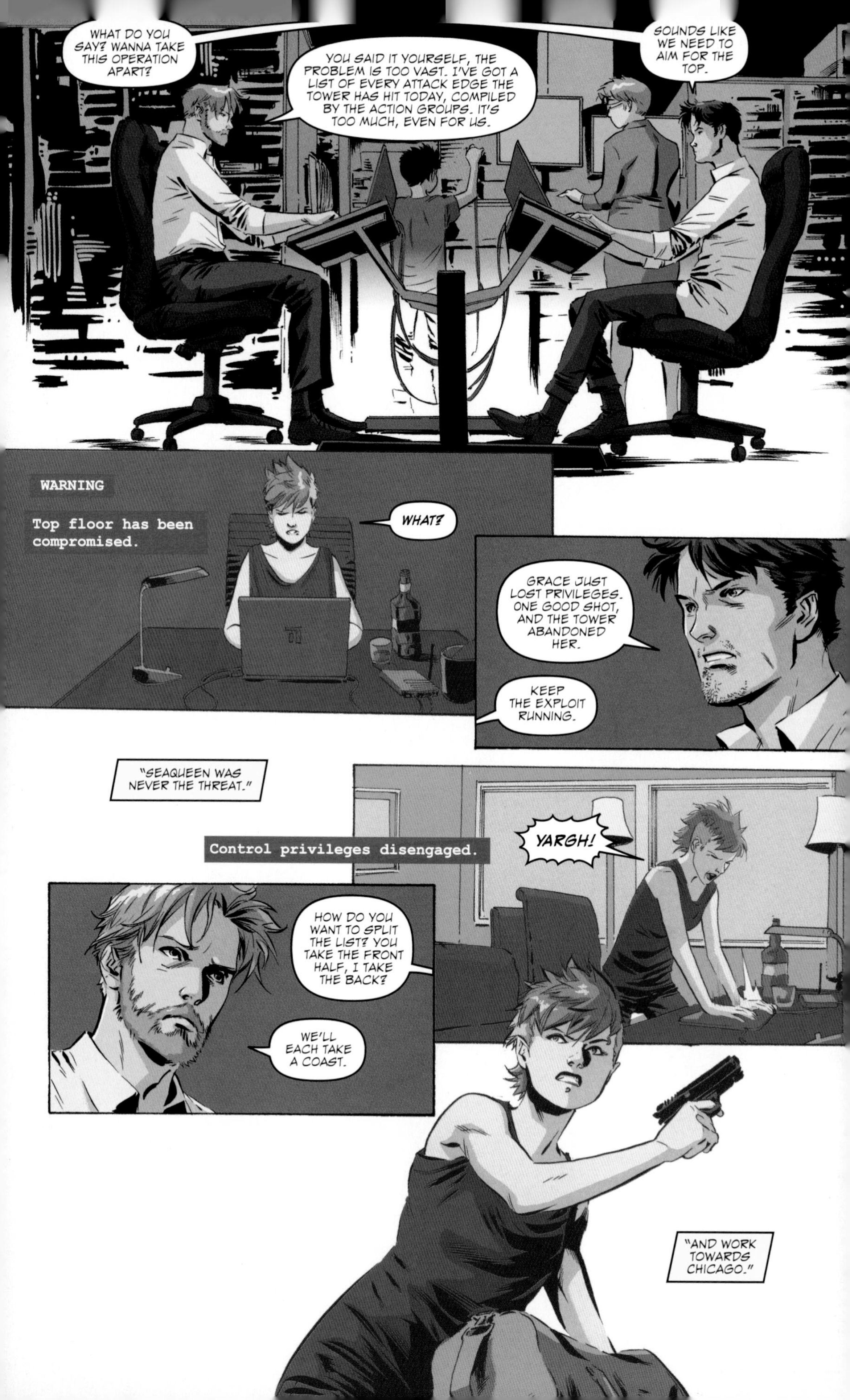
WHAT DO YOU SAY? WANNA TAKE THIS OPERATION APART?
YOU SAID IT YOURSELF, THE PROBLEM IS TOO VAST. I'VE GOT A LIST OF EVERY ATTACK EDGE THE TOWER HAS HIT TODAY, COMPILED BY THE ACTION GROUPS. IT'S TOO MUCH, EVEN FOR US.
SOUNDS LIKE WE NEED TO AIM FOR THE TOP.
WARNING
Top floor has been compromised.
WHAT?
GRACE JUST LOST PRIVILEGES. ONE GOOD SHOT, AND THE TOWER ABANDONED HER.
KEEP THE EXPLOIT RUNNING.
"SEAQUEEN WAS NEVER THE THREAT."
Control privileges disengaged.
YARGH!
HOW DO YOU WANT TO SPLIT THE LIST? YOU TAKE THE FRONT HALF, I TAKE THE BACK?
WE'LL EACH TAKE A COAST.
"AND WORK TOWARDS CHICAGO."

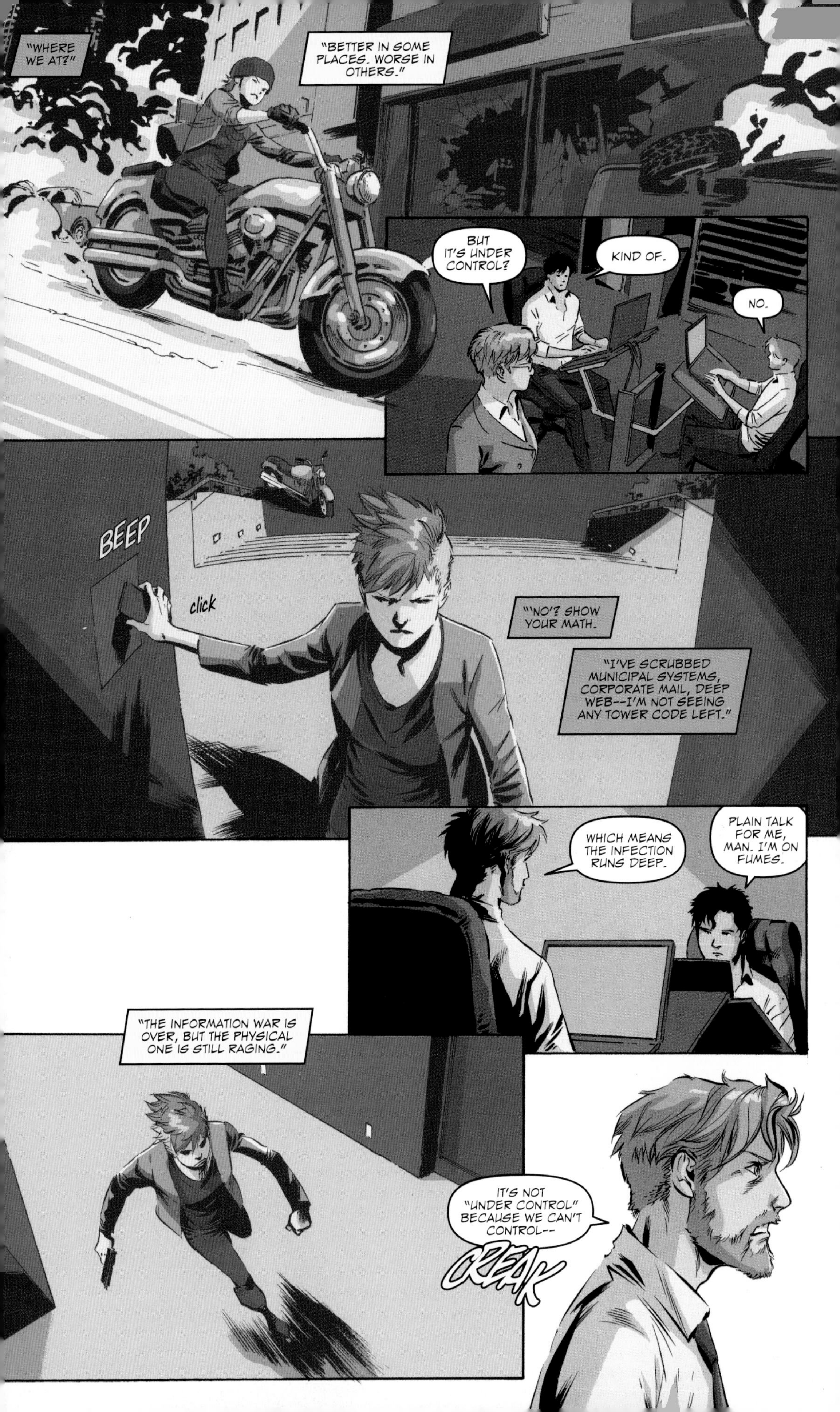
"WHERE WE AT?"
"BETTER IN SOME PLACES. WORSE IN OTHERS."
BUT IT'S UNDER CONTROL?
KIND OF.
NO.
BEEP
click
"'NO'? SHOW YOUR MATH.
"I'VE SCRUBBED MUNICIPAL SYSTEMS, CORPORATE MAIL, DEEP WEB--I'M NOT SEEING ANY TOWER CODE LEFT."
WHICH MEANS THE INFECTION RUNS DEEP.
PLAIN TALK FOR ME, MAN. I'M ON FUMES.
"THE INFORMATION WAR IS OVER, BUT THE PHYSICAL ONE IS STILL RAGING."
IT'S NOT "UNDER CONTROL" BECAUSE WE CAN'T CONTROL--
CREAK

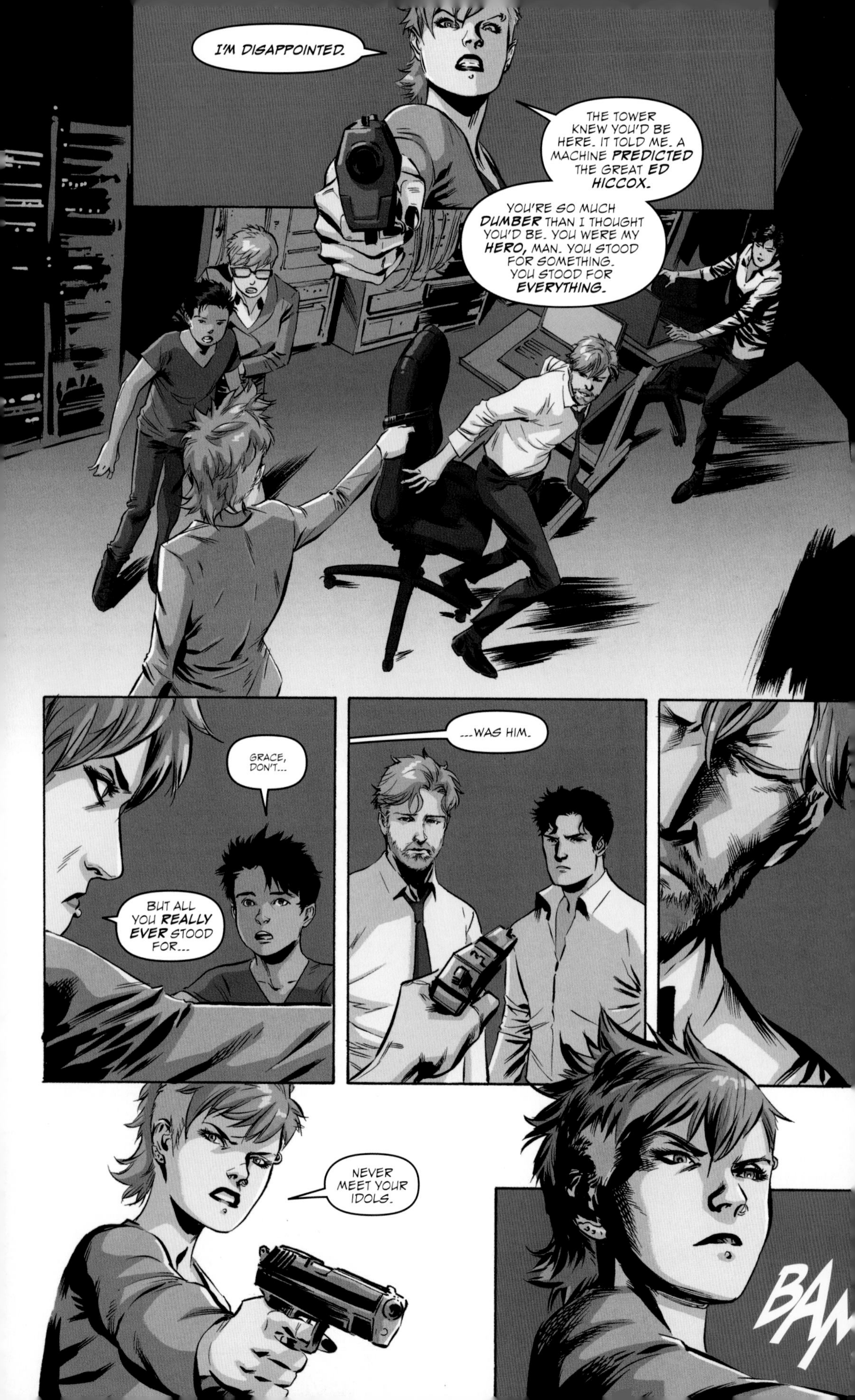
I'M DISAPPOINTED.
THE TOWER KNEW YOU'D BE HERE. IT TOLD ME. A MACHINE PREDICTED THE GREAT ED HICCOX.
YOU'RE SO MUCH DUMBER THAN I THOUGHT YOU'D BE. YOU WERE MY HERO, MAN. YOU STOOD FOR SOMETHING. YOU STOOD FOR EVERYTHING.
GRACE, DON'T...
BUT ALL YOU REALLY EVER STOOD FOR...
...WAS HIM.
NEVER MEET YOUR IDOLS.
BAM

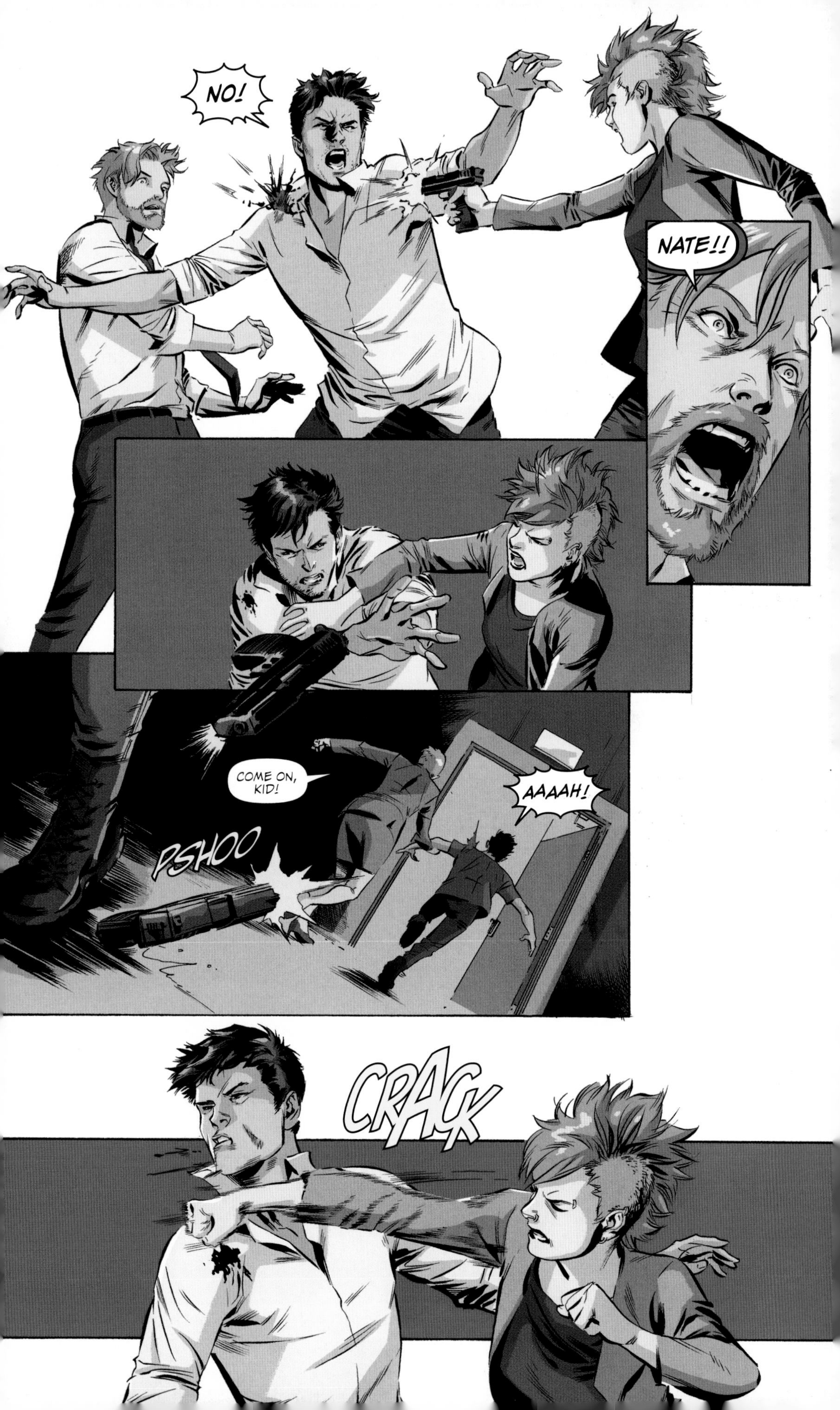
NO!
NATE!!
COME ON, KID!
AAAAH!
PSHOO
CRACK

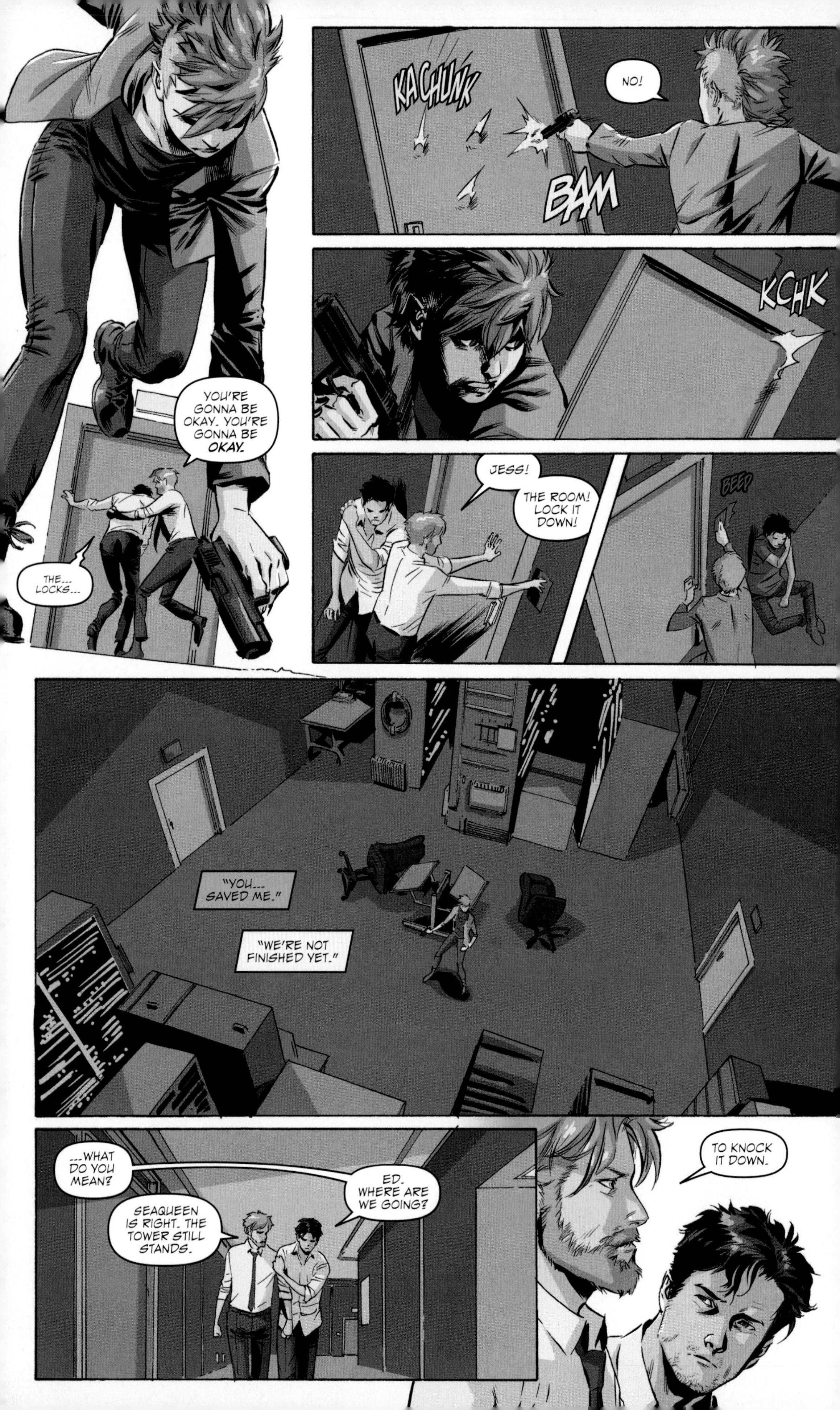
KACHUNK
NO!
BAM
KCHK
YOU'RE GONNA BE OKAY. YOU'RE GONNA BE OKAY.
THE... LOCKS...
JESS!
THE ROOM! LOCK IT DOWN!
BEEP
"YOU... SAVED ME."
"WE'RE NOT FINISHED YET."
...WHAT DO YOU MEAN?
ED. WHERE ARE WE GOING?
SEAQUEEN IS RIGHT. THE TOWER STILL STANDS.
TO KNOCK IT DOWN.

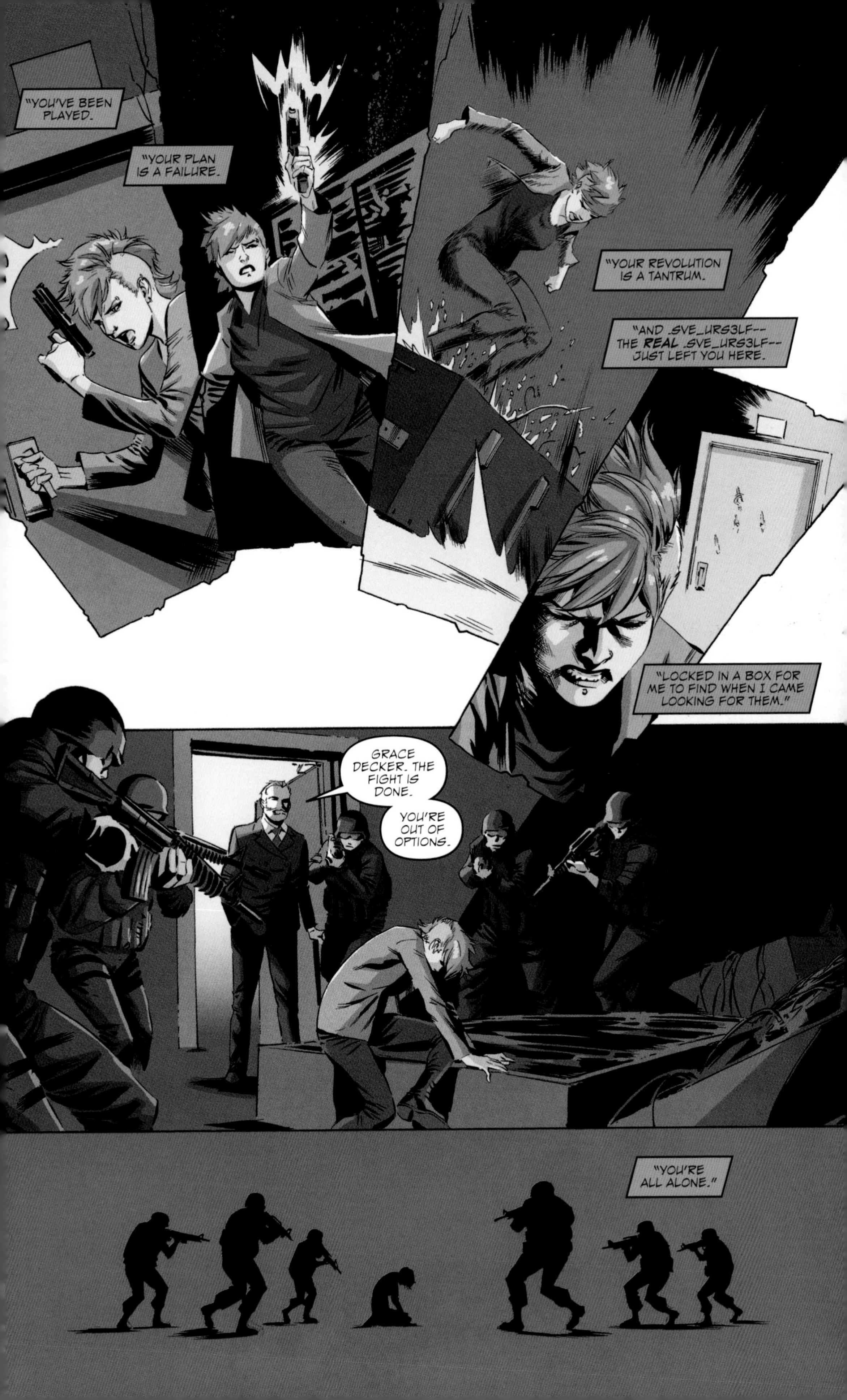
"YOU'VE BEEN PLAYED.
"YOUR PLAN IS A FAILURE.
"YOUR REVOLUTION IS A TANTRUM.
"AND .SVE_URS3LF-- THE **REAL** .SVE_URS3LF-- JUST LEFT YOU HERE.
"LOCKED IN A BOX FOR ME TO FIND WHEN I CAME LOOKING FOR THEM."
GRACE DECKER. THE FIGHT IS DONE.
YOU'RE OUT OF OPTIONS.
"YOU'RE ALL ALONE."

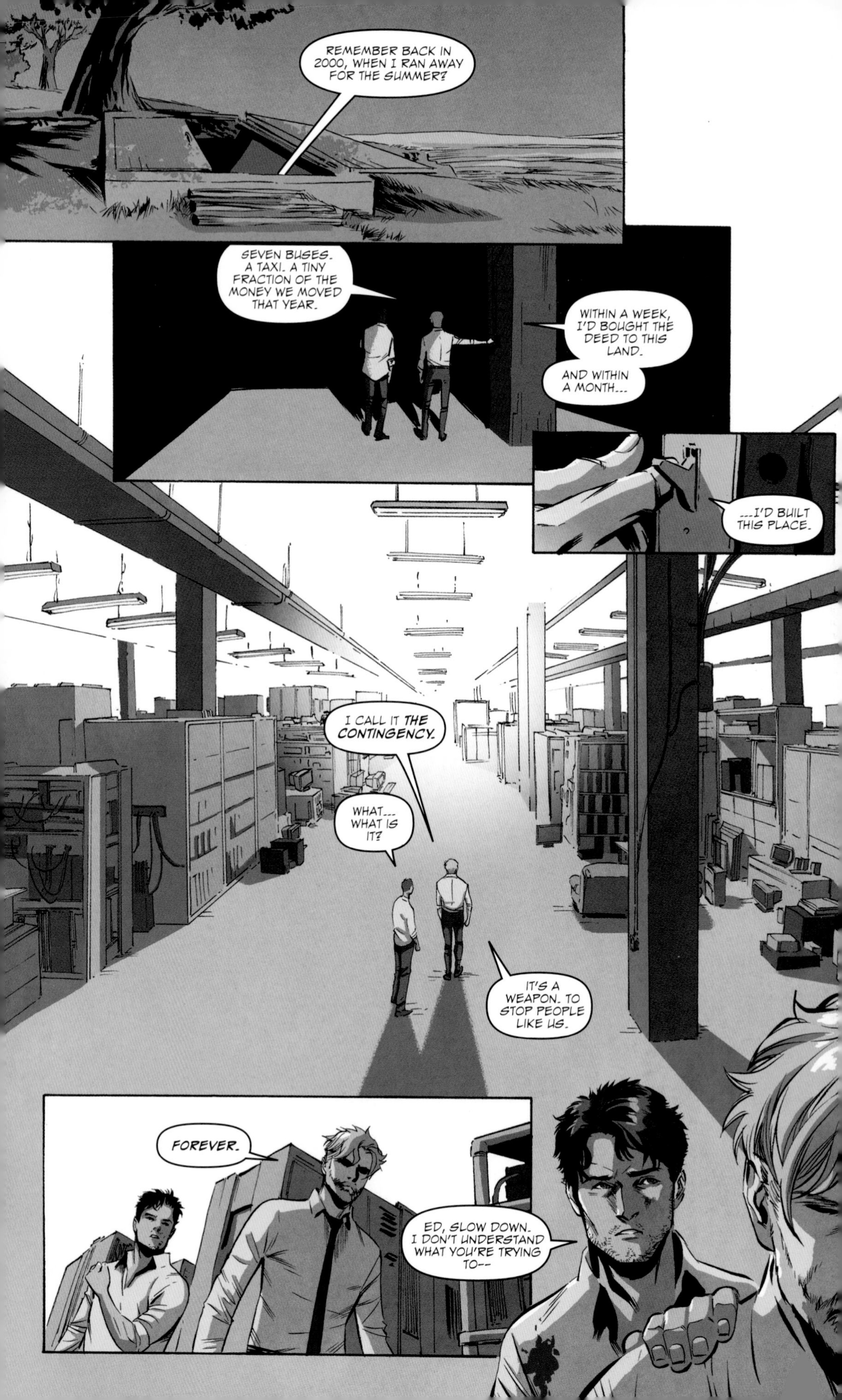
REMEMBER BACK IN 2000, WHEN I RAN AWAY FOR THE SUMMER?
SEVEN BUSES. A TAXI. A TINY FRACTION OF THE MONEY WE MOVED THAT YEAR.
WITHIN A WEEK, I'D BOUGHT THE DEED TO THIS LAND.
AND WITHIN A MONTH...
...I'D BUILT THIS PLACE.
I CALL IT THE CONTINGENCY.
WHAT... WHAT IS IT?
IT'S A WEAPON. TO STOP PEOPLE LIKE US.
FOREVER.
ED, SLOW DOWN. I DON'T UNDERSTAND WHAT YOU'RE TRYING TO--

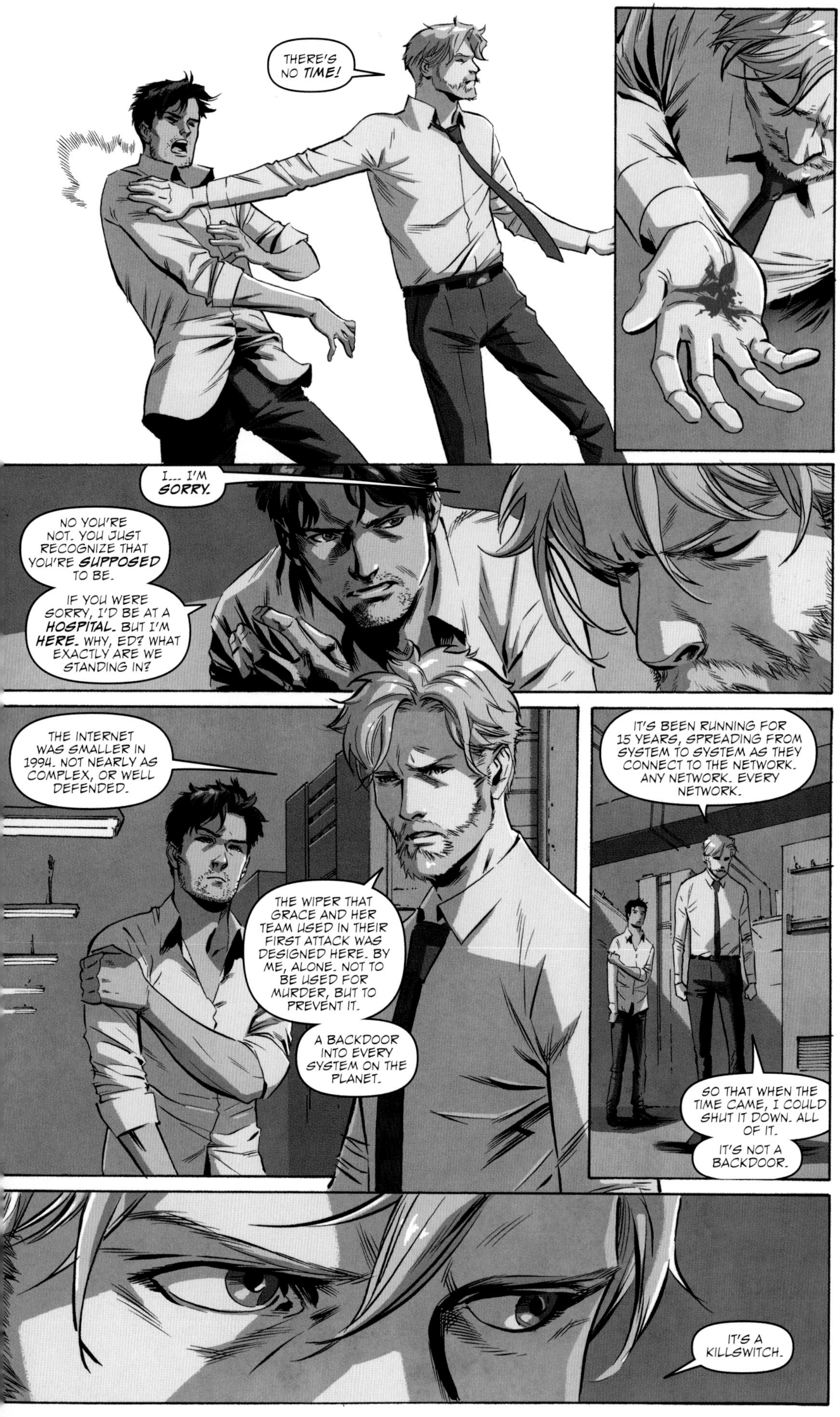
THERE'S NO TIME!
I... I'M SORRY.
NO YOU'RE NOT. YOU JUST RECOGNIZE THAT YOU'RE SUPPOSED TO BE.
IF YOU WERE SORRY, I'D BE AT A HOSPITAL. BUT I'M HERE. WHY, ED? WHAT EXACTLY ARE WE STANDING IN?
THE INTERNET WAS SMALLER IN 1994. NOT NEARLY AS COMPLEX, OR WELL DEFENDED.
THE WIPER THAT GRACE AND HER TEAM USED IN THEIR FIRST ATTACK WAS DESIGNED HERE. BY ME, ALONE. NOT TO BE USED FOR MURDER, BUT TO PREVENT IT.
A BACKDOOR INTO EVERY SYSTEM ON THE PLANET.
IT'S BEEN RUNNING FOR 15 YEARS, SPREADING FROM SYSTEM TO SYSTEM AS THEY CONNECT TO THE NETWORK. ANY NETWORK. EVERY NETWORK.
SO THAT WHEN THE TIME CAME, I COULD SHUT IT DOWN. ALL OF IT.
IT'S NOT A BACKDOOR.
IT'S A KILLSWITCH.

YOU'RE JOKING.

ED.
TELL ME YOU'RE JOKING.

I SAW THE PROBLEM AFTER OUR FIRST FEW OPS. UNFORESEEN CONSEQUENCES. EXPONENTIAL GROWTH LEADING TO EXPONENTIAL RISK OF UNFORESEEABLE FACTORS.

GIVE PEOPLE FREEDOM AND WATCH THEM MISUSE IT.

...I'M SORRY.

YOU'RE RIGHT. I LET YOU DOWN. AND TO BE HONEST, YOU LET ME DOWN.

YOU LEFT ME WHEN I NEEDED A FRIEND THE MOST. I WAS LOST. AND NOW THAT YOU'RE BACK...

...IT'S LIKE LOOKING AT A STRANGER.

YOU WANT TO DESTROY THE ENTIRE GLOBAL COMMUNICATIONS NETWORK?

YOU THINK BOMBING THE WORLD BACK TO THE LAST CENTURY IS GOING TO SAVE PEOPLE?

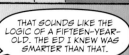

THAT SOUNDS LIKE THE LOGIC OF A FIFTEEN-YEAR-OLD. THE ED I KNEW WAS SMARTER THAN THAT.

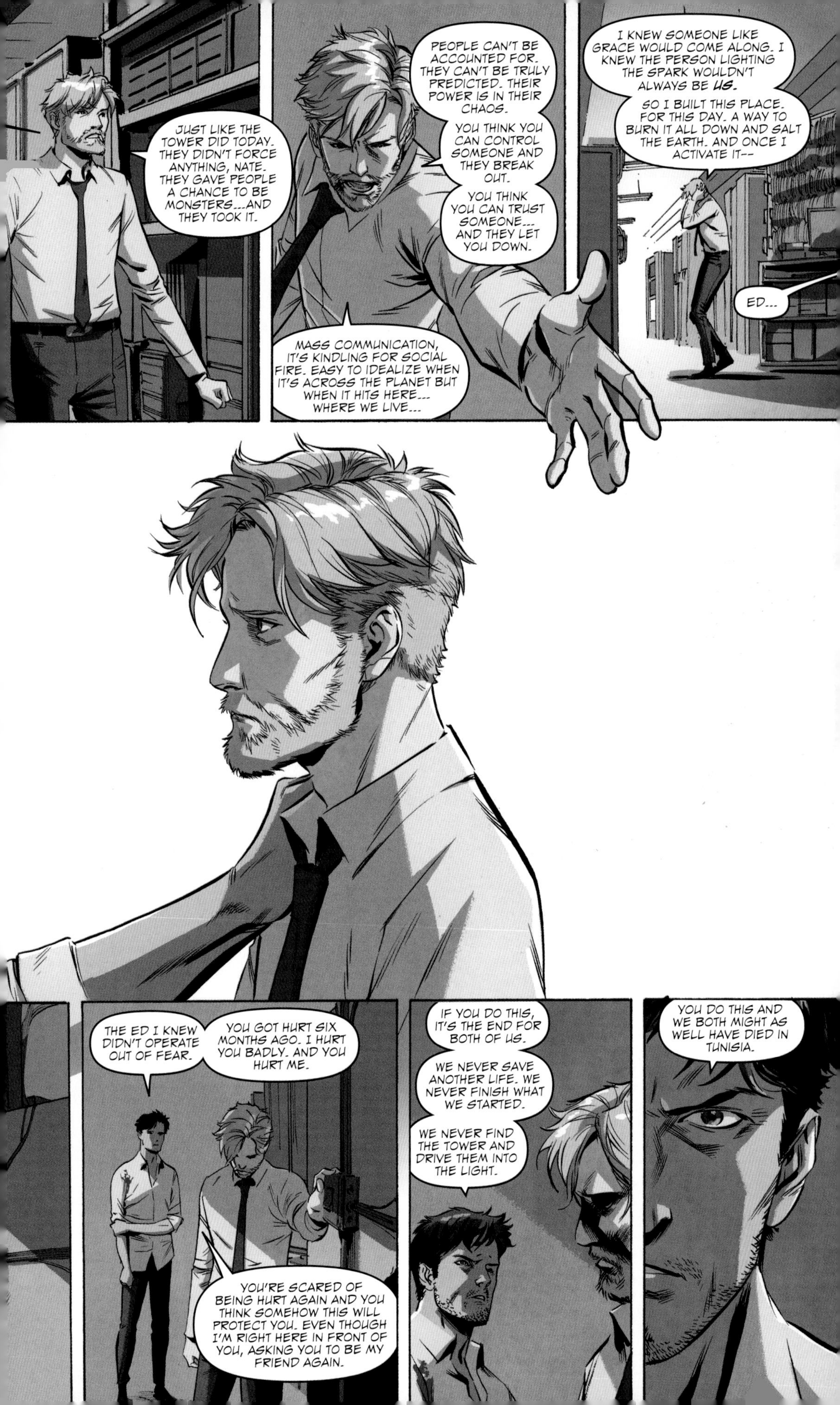
JUST LIKE THE TOWER DID TODAY. THEY DIDN'T FORCE ANYTHING, NATE. THEY GAVE PEOPLE A CHANCE TO BE MONSTERS...AND THEY TOOK IT.
PEOPLE CAN'T BE ACCOUNTED FOR. THEY CAN'T BE TRULY PREDICTED. THEIR POWER IS IN THEIR CHAOS.
YOU THINK YOU CAN CONTROL SOMEONE AND THEY BREAK OUT.
YOU THINK YOU CAN TRUST SOMEONE... AND THEY LET YOU DOWN.
MASS COMMUNICATION, IT'S KINDLING FOR SOCIAL FIRE. EASY TO IDEALIZE WHEN IT'S ACROSS THE PLANET BUT WHEN IT HITS HERE... WHERE WE LIVE...
I KNEW SOMEONE LIKE GRACE WOULD COME ALONG. I KNEW THE PERSON LIGHTING THE SPARK WOULDN'T ALWAYS BE US.
SO I BUILT THIS PLACE. FOR THIS DAY. A WAY TO BURN IT ALL DOWN AND SALT THE EARTH. AND ONCE I ACTIVATE IT--
ED...
THE ED I KNEW DIDN'T OPERATE OUT OF FEAR.
YOU GOT HURT SIX MONTHS AGO. I HURT YOU BADLY. AND YOU HURT ME.
YOU'RE SCARED OF BEING HURT AGAIN AND YOU THINK SOMEHOW THIS WILL PROTECT YOU. EVEN THOUGH I'M RIGHT HERE IN FRONT OF YOU, ASKING YOU TO BE MY FRIEND AGAIN.
IF YOU DO THIS, IT'S THE END FOR BOTH OF US.
WE NEVER SAVE ANOTHER LIFE. WE NEVER FINISH WHAT WE STARTED.
WE NEVER FIND THE TOWER AND DRIVE THEM INTO THE LIGHT.
YOU DO THIS AND WE BOTH MIGHT AS WELL HAVE DIED IN TUNISIA.

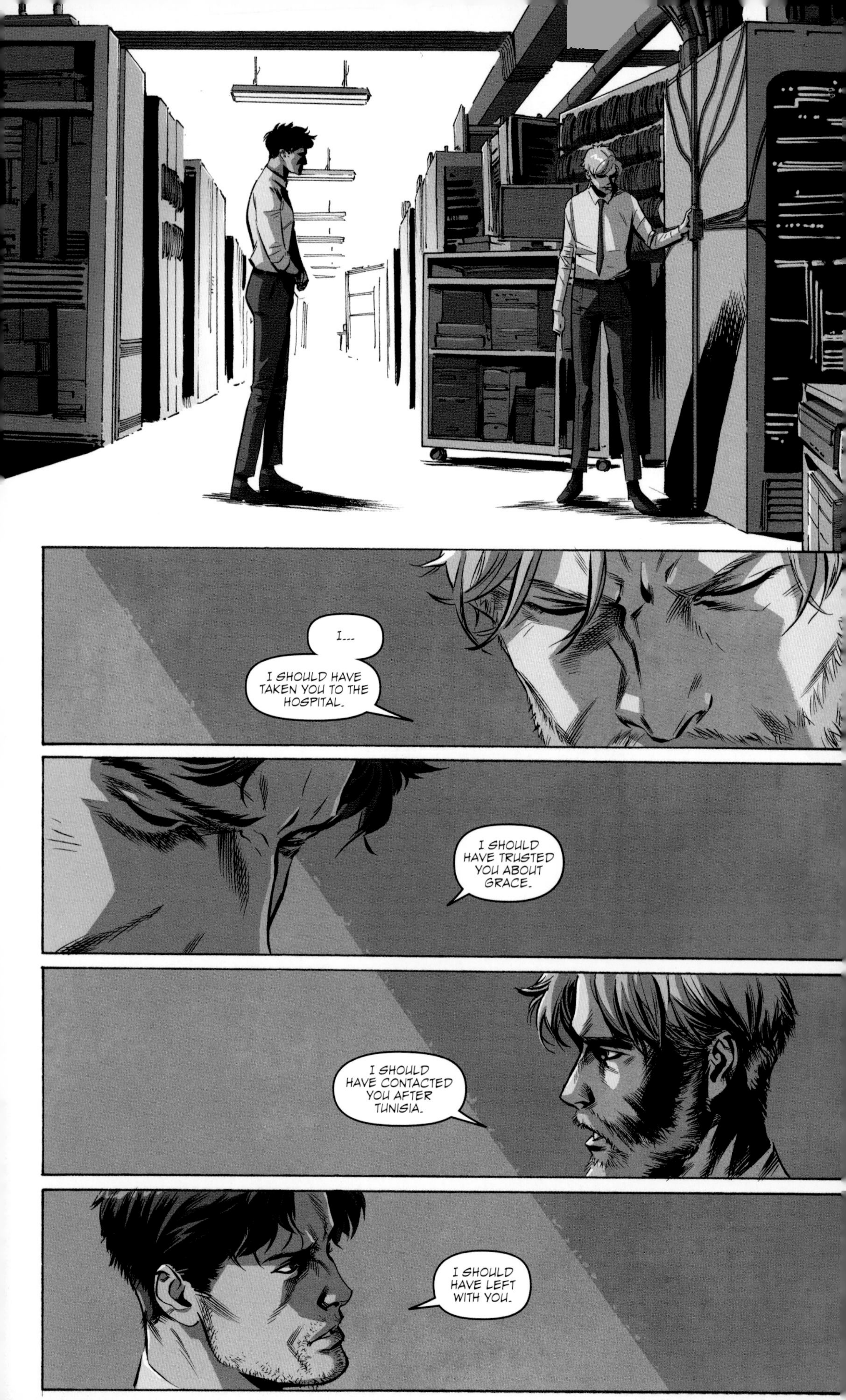
I...
I SHOULD HAVE TAKEN YOU TO THE HOSPITAL.
I SHOULD HAVE TRUSTED YOU ABOUT GRACE.
I SHOULD HAVE CONTACTED YOU AFTER TUNISIA.
I SHOULD HAVE LEFT WITH YOU.

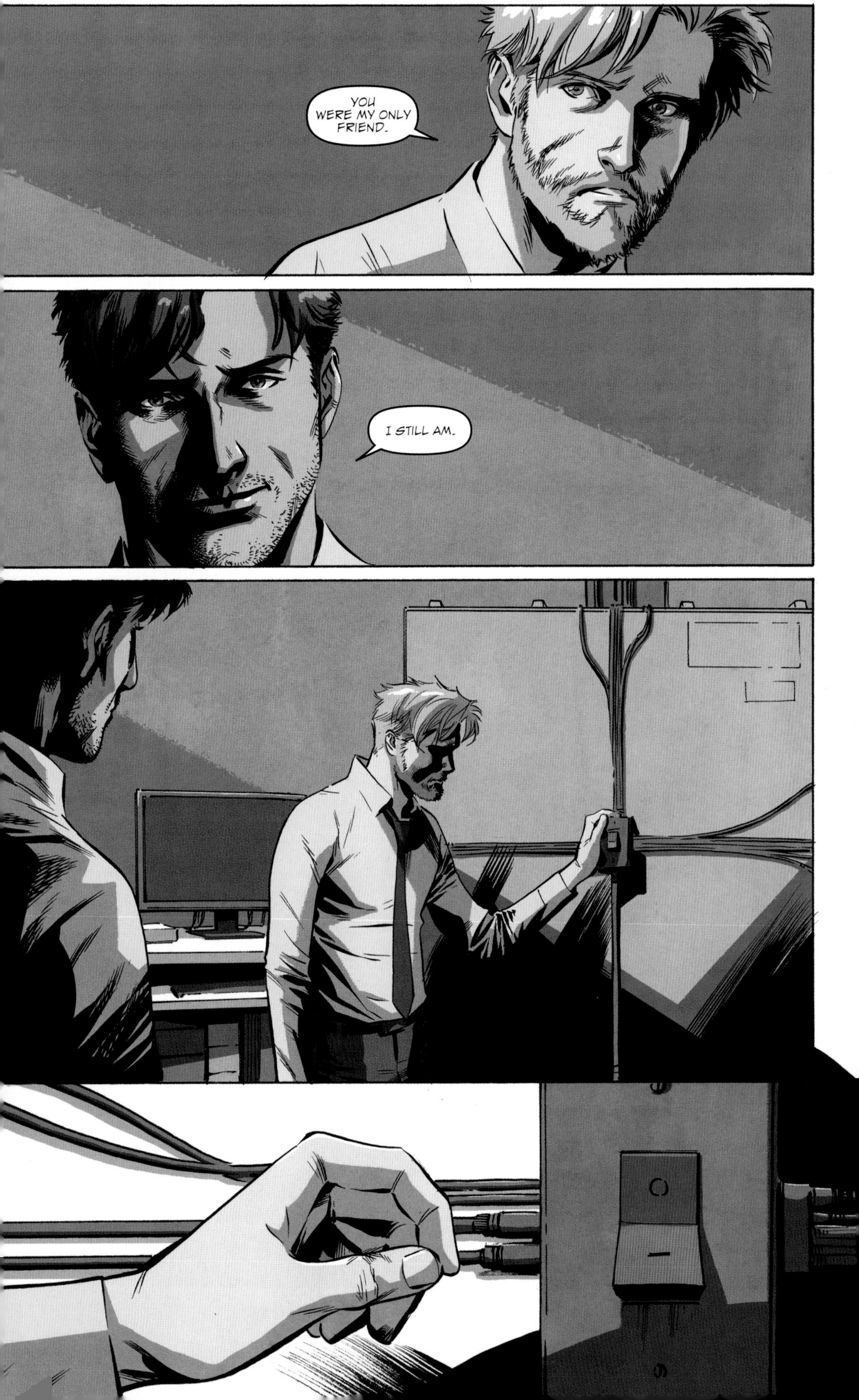
YOU WERE MY ONLY FRIEND.
I STILL AM.

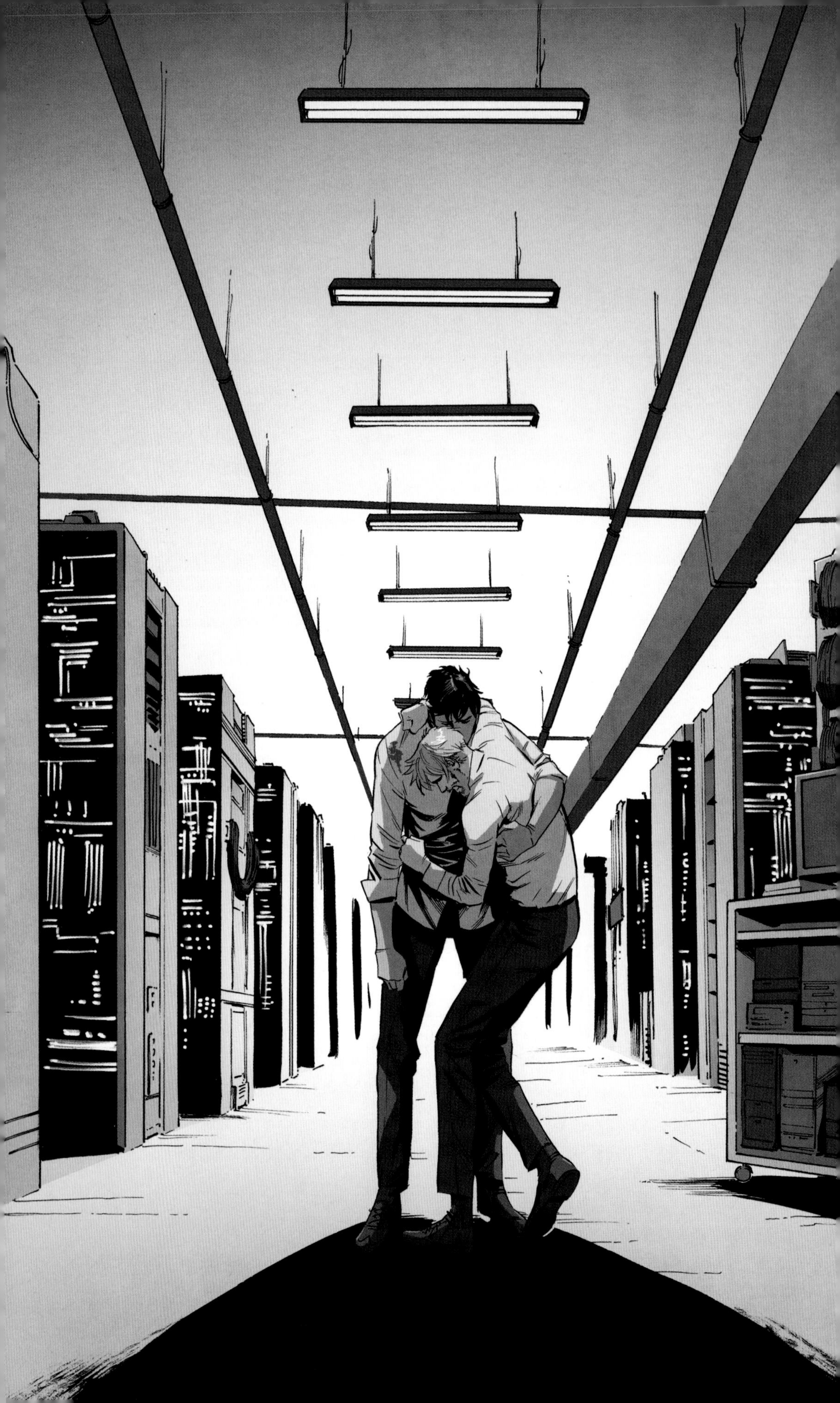

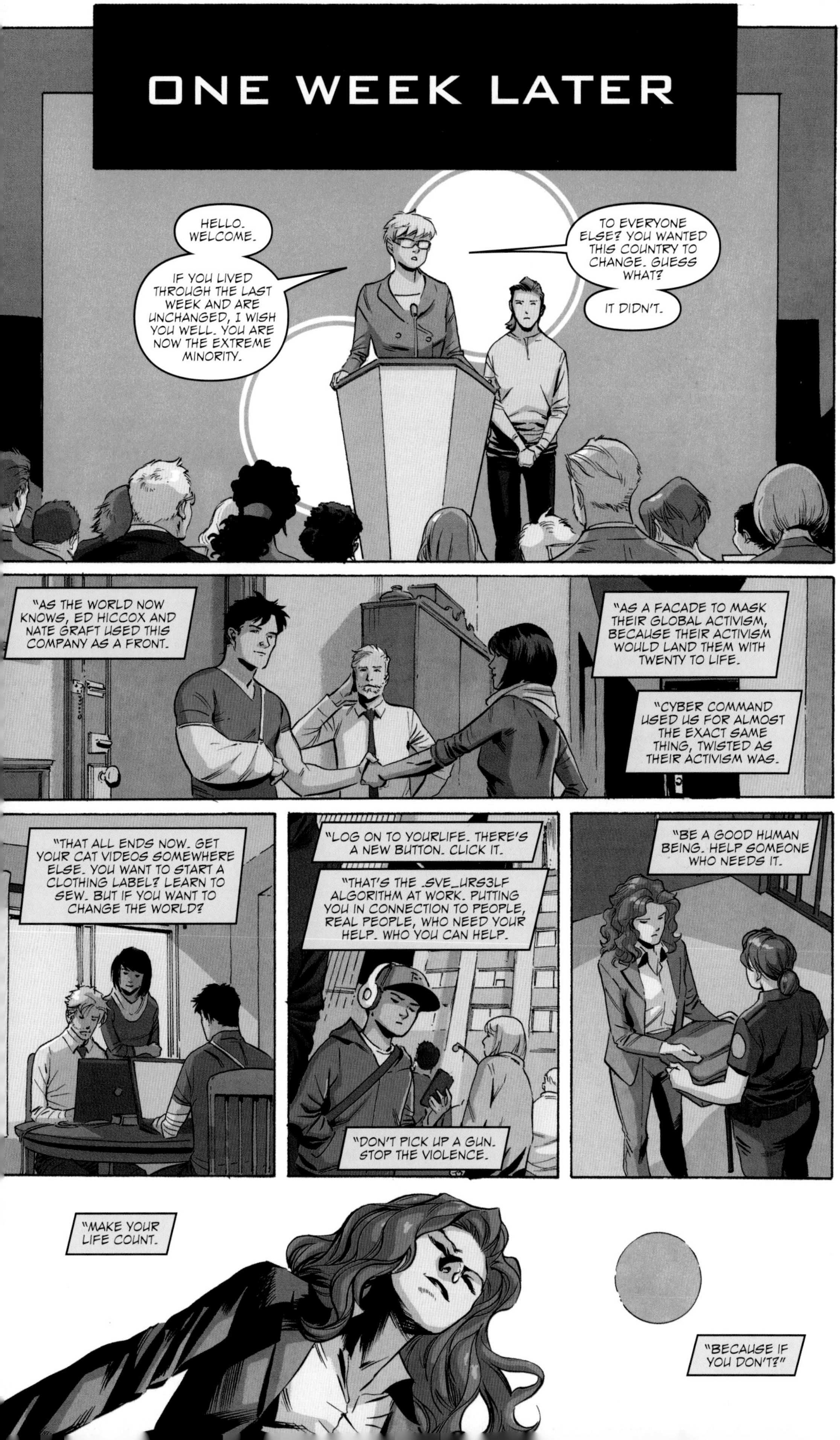
ONE WEEK LATER
HELLO. WELCOME.
IF YOU LIVED THROUGH THE LAST WEEK AND ARE UNCHANGED, I WISH YOU WELL. YOU ARE NOW THE EXTREME MINORITY.
TO EVERYONE ELSE? YOU WANTED THIS COUNTRY TO CHANGE. GUESS WHAT?
IT DIDN'T.
"AS THE WORLD NOW KNOWS, ED HICCOX AND NATE GRAFT USED THIS COMPANY AS A FRONT.
"AS A FACADE TO MASK THEIR GLOBAL ACTIVISM, BECAUSE THEIR ACTIVISM WOULD LAND THEM WITH TWENTY TO LIFE.
"CYBER COMMAND USED US FOR ALMOST THE EXACT SAME THING, TWISTED AS THEIR ACTIVISM WAS.
"THAT ALL ENDS NOW. GET YOUR CAT VIDEOS SOMEWHERE ELSE. YOU WANT TO START A CLOTHING LABEL? LEARN TO SEW. BUT IF YOU WANT TO CHANGE THE WORLD?
"LOG ON TO YOURLIFE. THERE'S A NEW BUTTON. CLICK IT.
"THAT'S THE .SVE_URS3LF ALGORITHM AT WORK. PUTTING YOU IN CONNECTION TO PEOPLE, REAL PEOPLE, WHO NEED YOUR HELP. WHO YOU CAN HELP.
"DON'T PICK UP A GUN. STOP THE VIOLENCE.
"BE A GOOD HUMAN BEING. HELP SOMEONE WHO NEEDS IT.
"MAKE YOUR LIFE COUNT.
"BECAUSE IF YOU DON'T?"

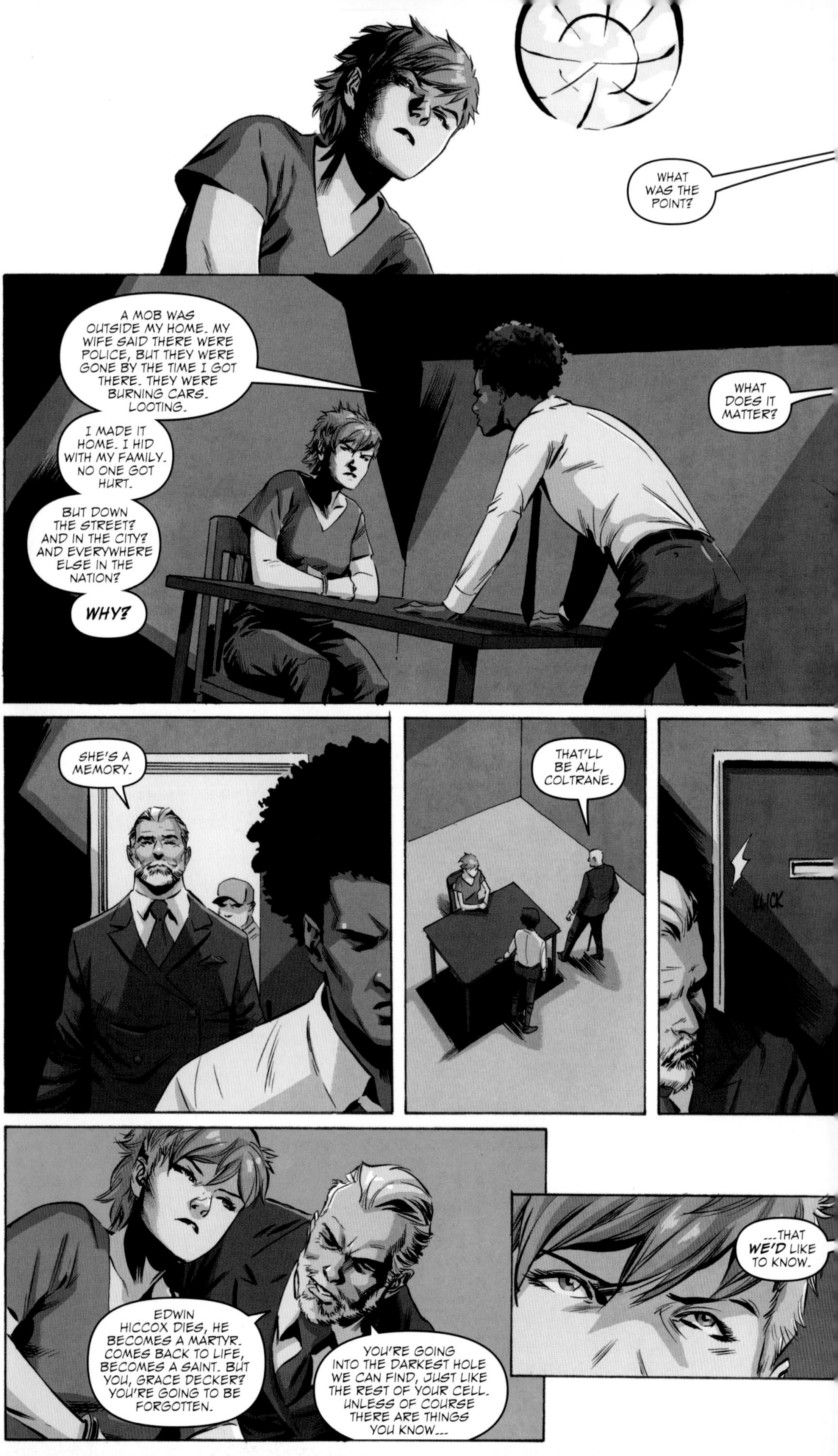

WHAT WAS THE POINT?
A MOB WAS OUTSIDE MY HOME. MY WIFE SAID THERE WERE POLICE, BUT THEY WERE GONE BY THE TIME I GOT THERE. THEY WERE BURNING CARS. LOOTING.
I MADE IT HOME. I HID WITH MY FAMILY. NO ONE GOT HURT.
BUT DOWN THE STREET? AND IN THE CITY? AND EVERYWHERE ELSE IN THE NATION?
WHY?
WHAT DOES IT MATTER?
SHE'S A MEMORY.
THAT'LL BE ALL, COLTRANE.
KLICK
EDWIN HICCOX DIES, HE BECOMES A MARTYR. COMES BACK TO LIFE, BECOMES A SAINT. BUT YOU, GRACE DECKER? YOU'RE GOING TO BE FORGOTTEN.
YOU'RE GOING INTO THE DARKEST HOLE WE CAN FIND, JUST LIKE THE REST OF YOUR CELL. UNLESS OF COURSE THERE ARE THINGS YOU KNOW...
...THAT WE'D LIKE TO KNOW.

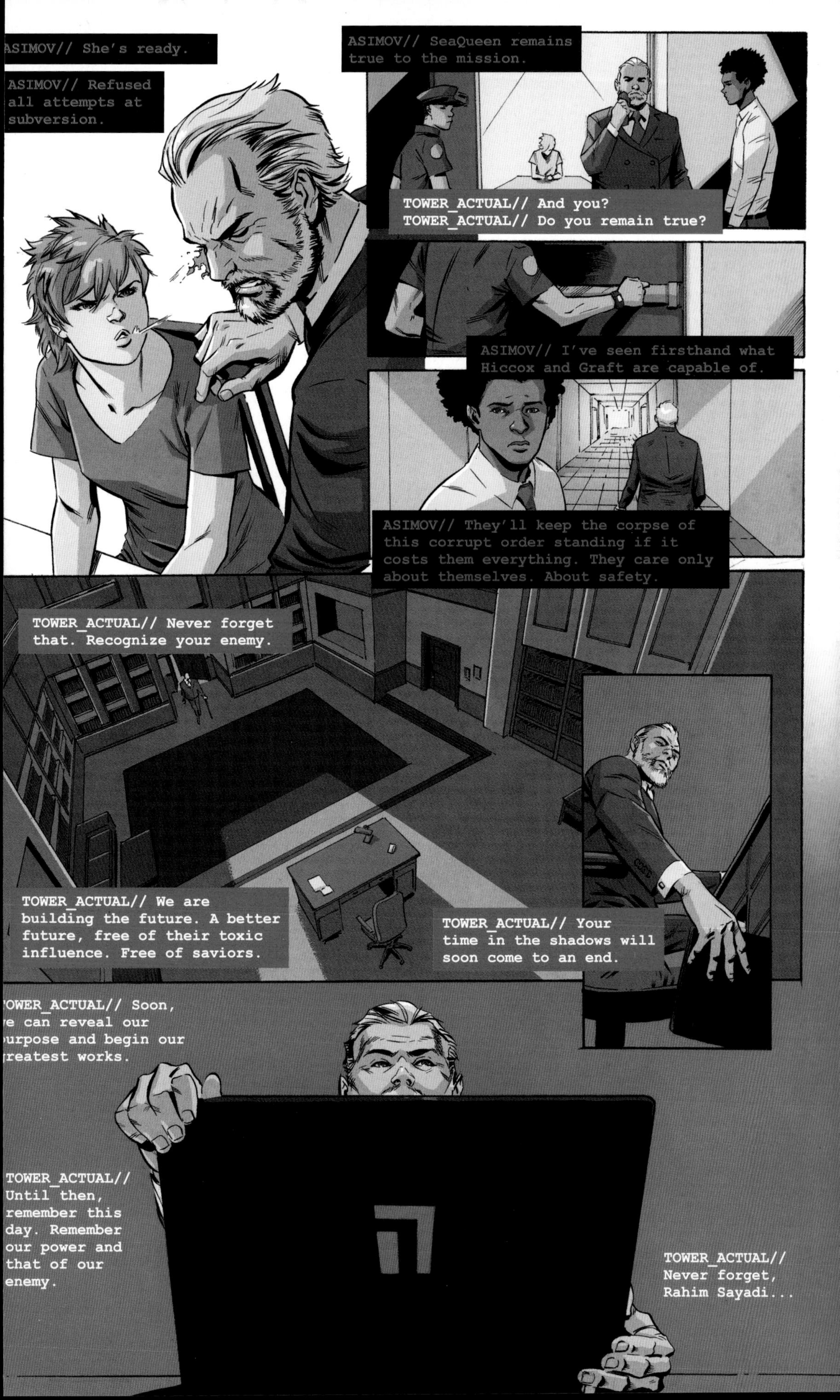
ASIMOV// She's ready.
ASIMOV// Refused all attempts at subversion.
ASIMOV// SeaQueen remains true to the mission.
TOWER_ACTUAL// And you?
TOWER_ACTUAL// Do you remain true?
ASIMOV// I've seen firsthand what Hiccox and Graft are capable of.
ASIMOV// They'll keep the corpse of this corrupt order standing if it costs them everything. They care only about themselves. About safety.
TOWER_ACTUAL// Never forget that. Recognize your enemy.
TOWER_ACTUAL// We are building the future. A better future, free of their toxic influence. Free of saviors.
TOWER_ACTUAL// Your time in the shadows will soon come to an end.
OWER_ACTUAL// Soon, e can reveal our urpose and begin our reatest works.
TOWER_ACTUAL// Until then, remember this day. Remember our power and that of our enemy.
TOWER_ACTUAL// Never forget, Rahim Sayadi...

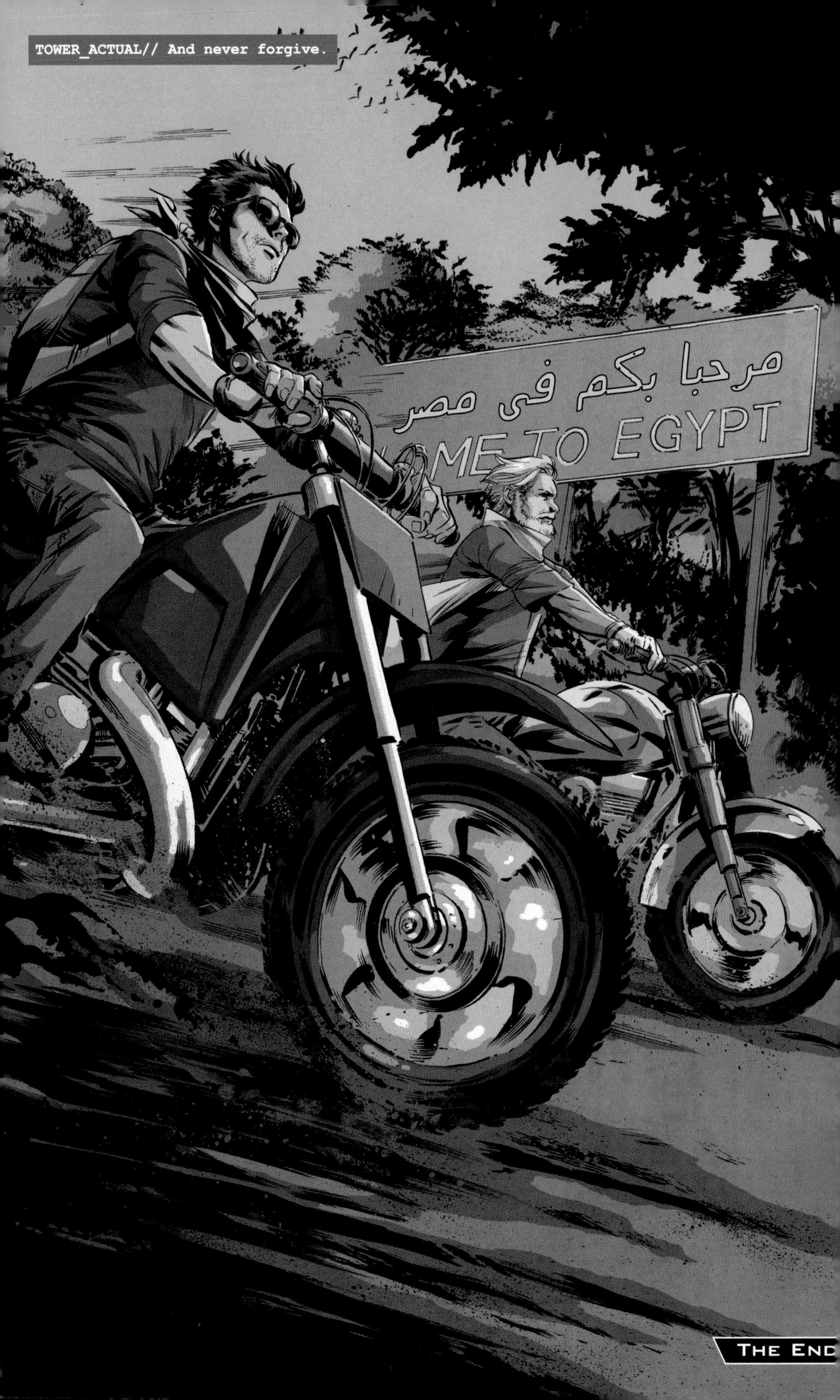
TOWER_ACTUAL// And never forgive.
مرحبا بكم فى مصر
ME TO EGYPT
THE EN

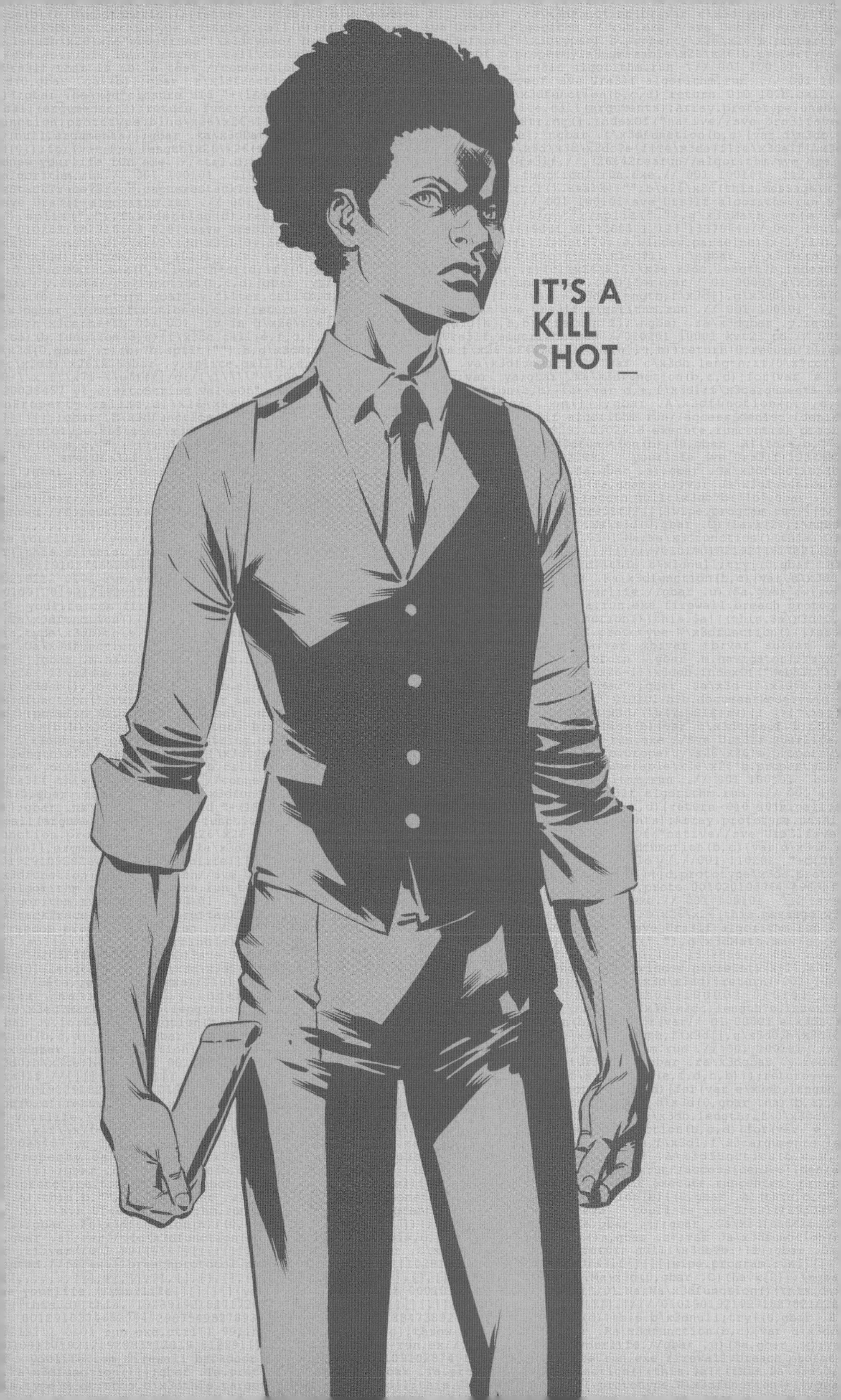
IT'S A
KILL
SHOT_

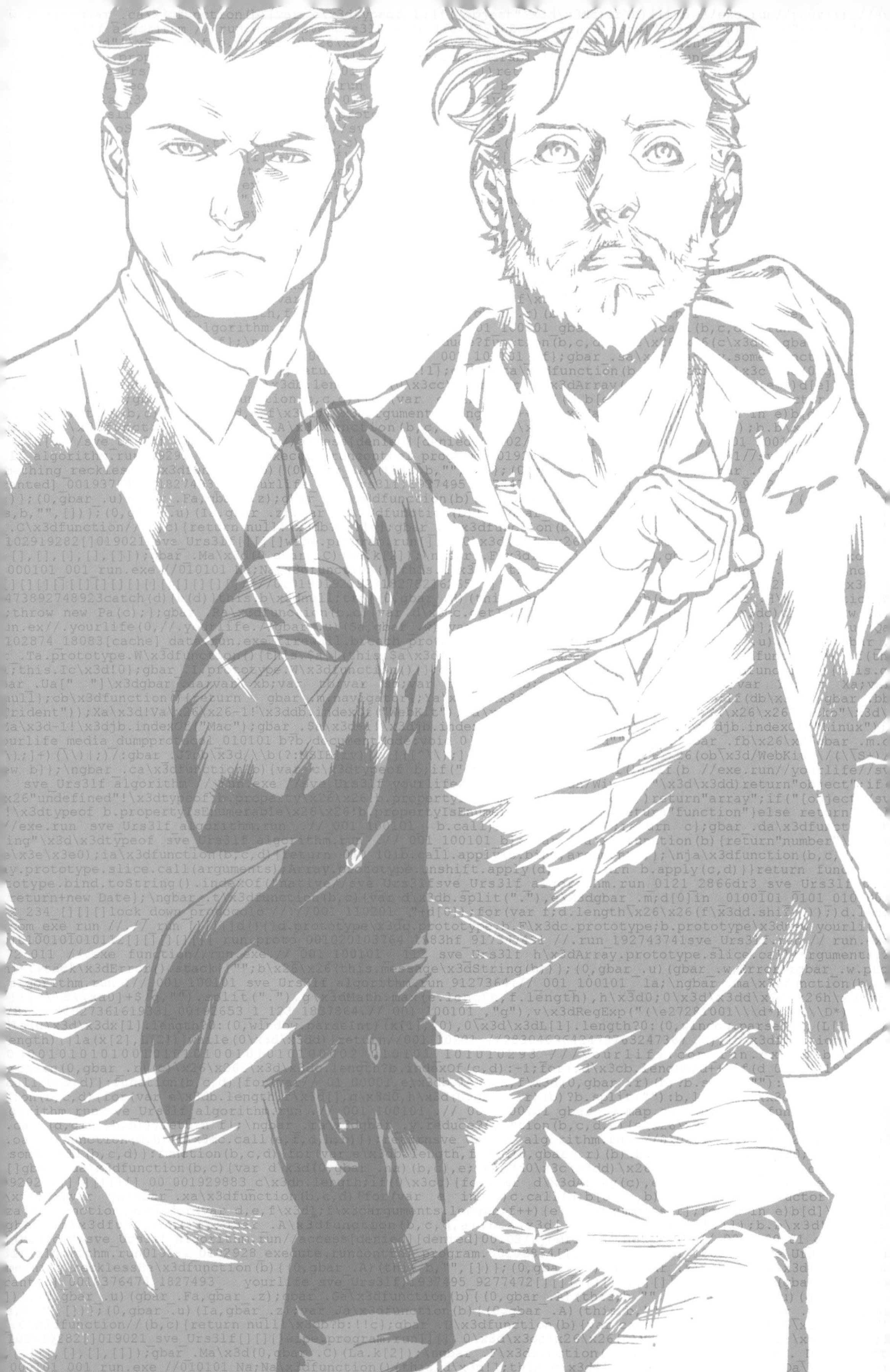

ISSUE ON

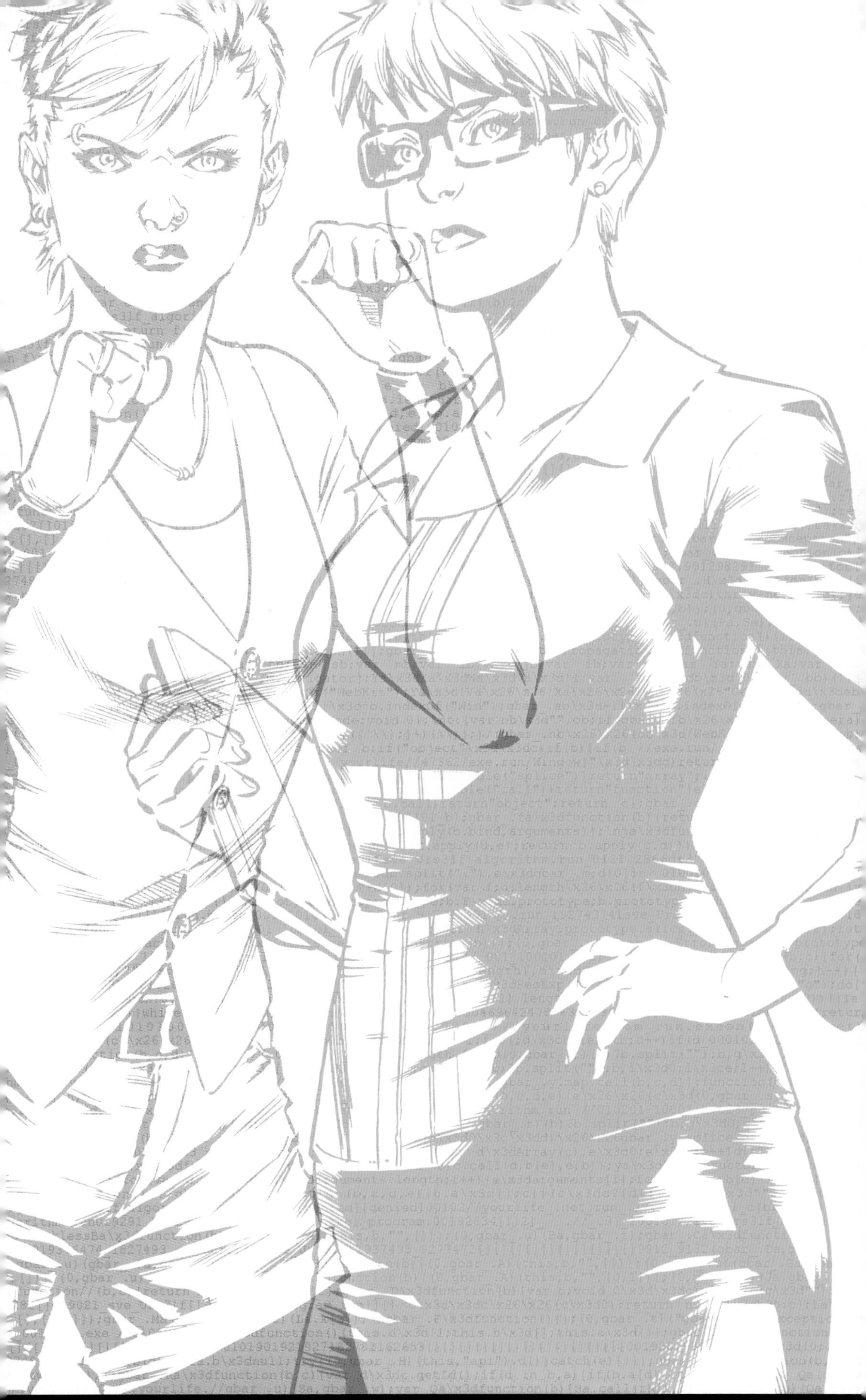

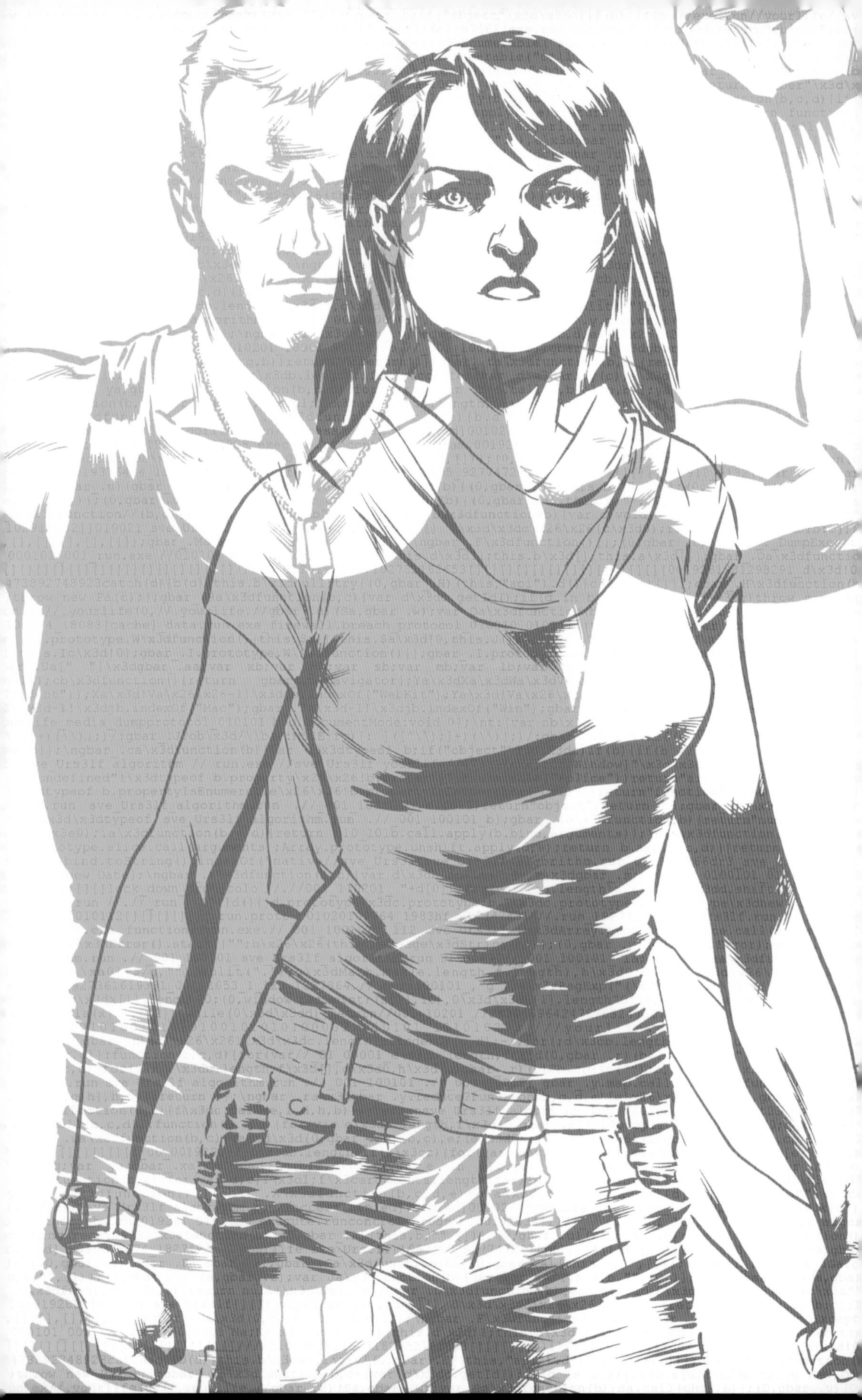

ISSUE THREE COVER ILLUSTRATED BY **MARCUS TO** WITH DESIGN BY **SCOTT NEWMAN**

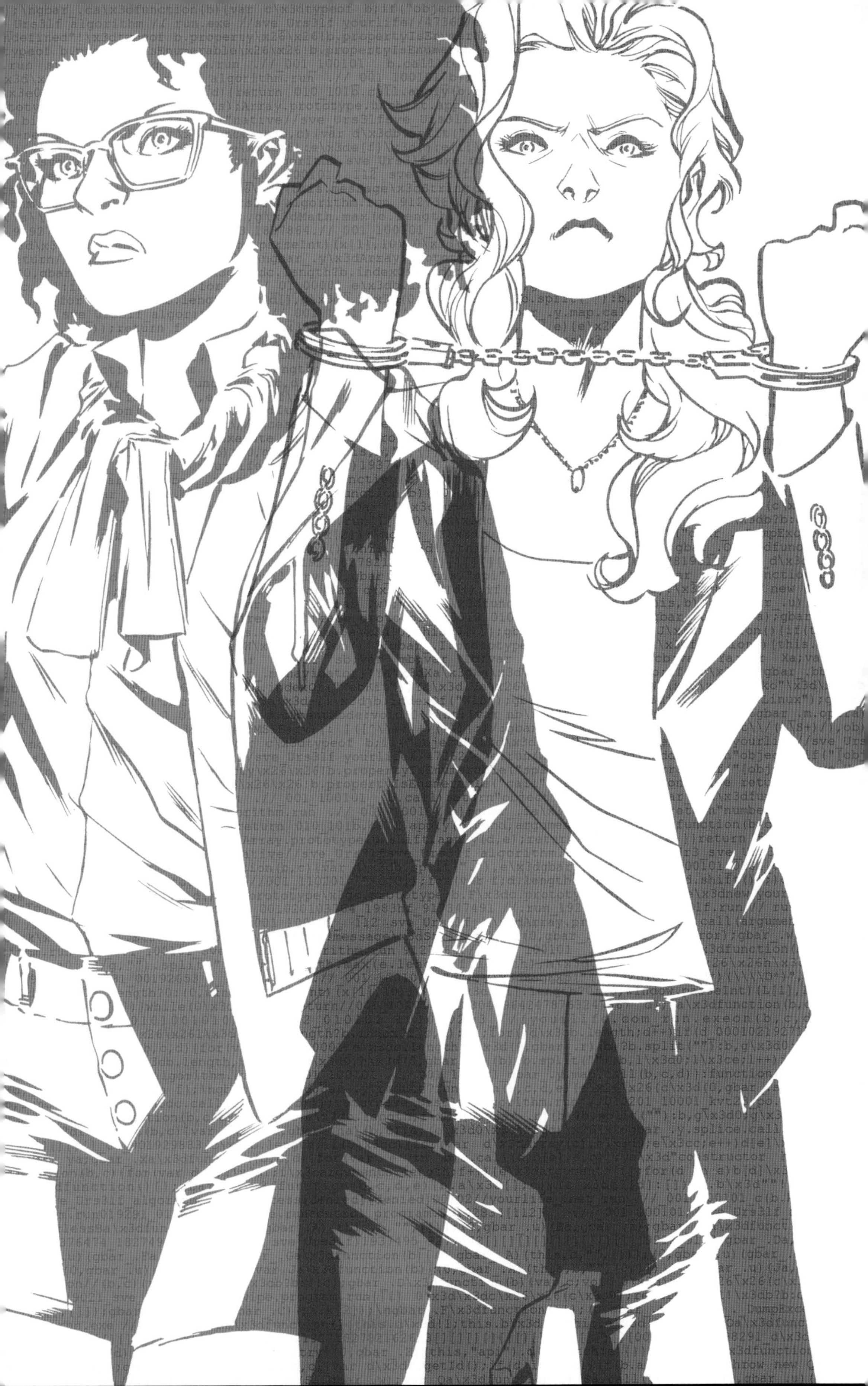

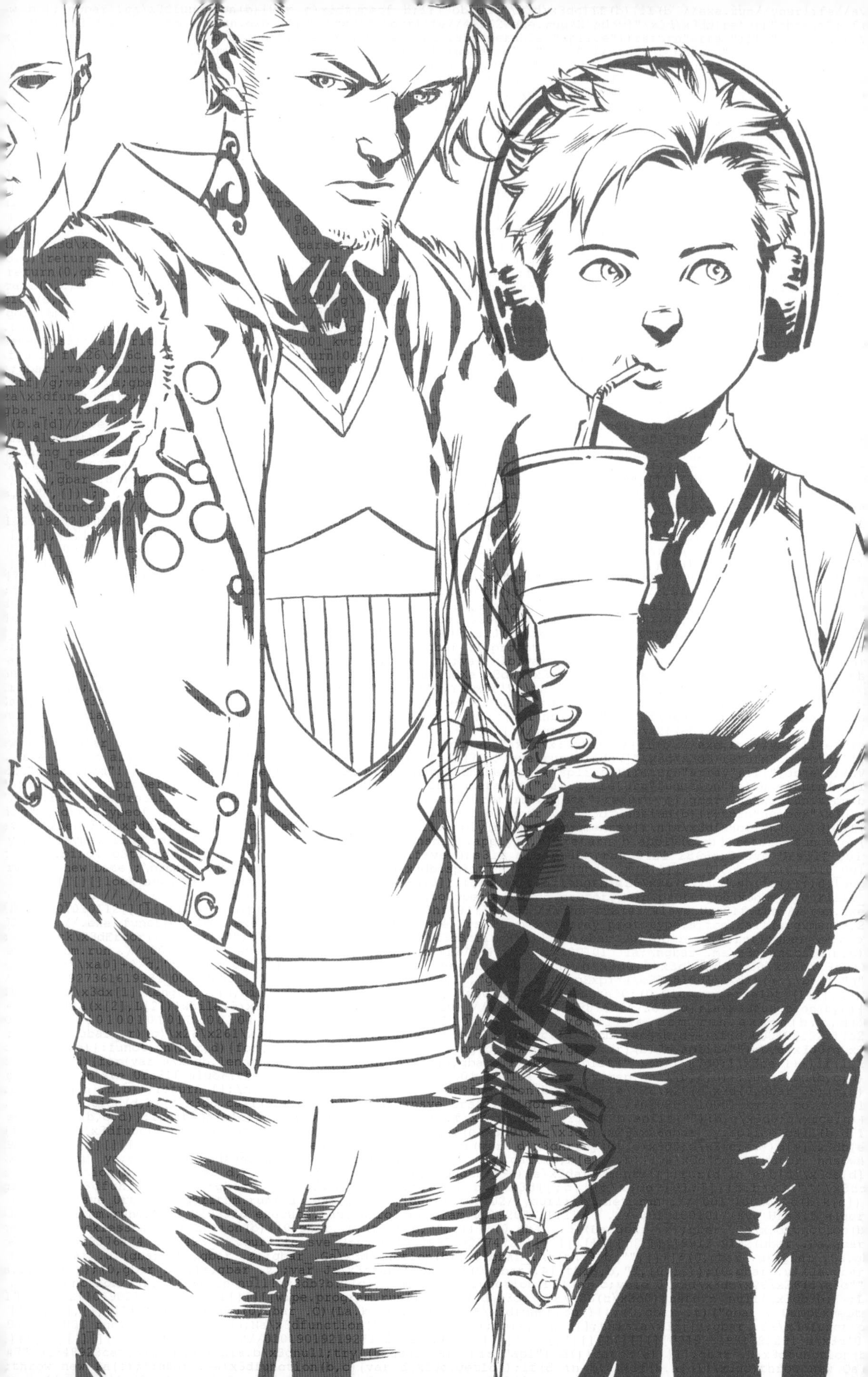

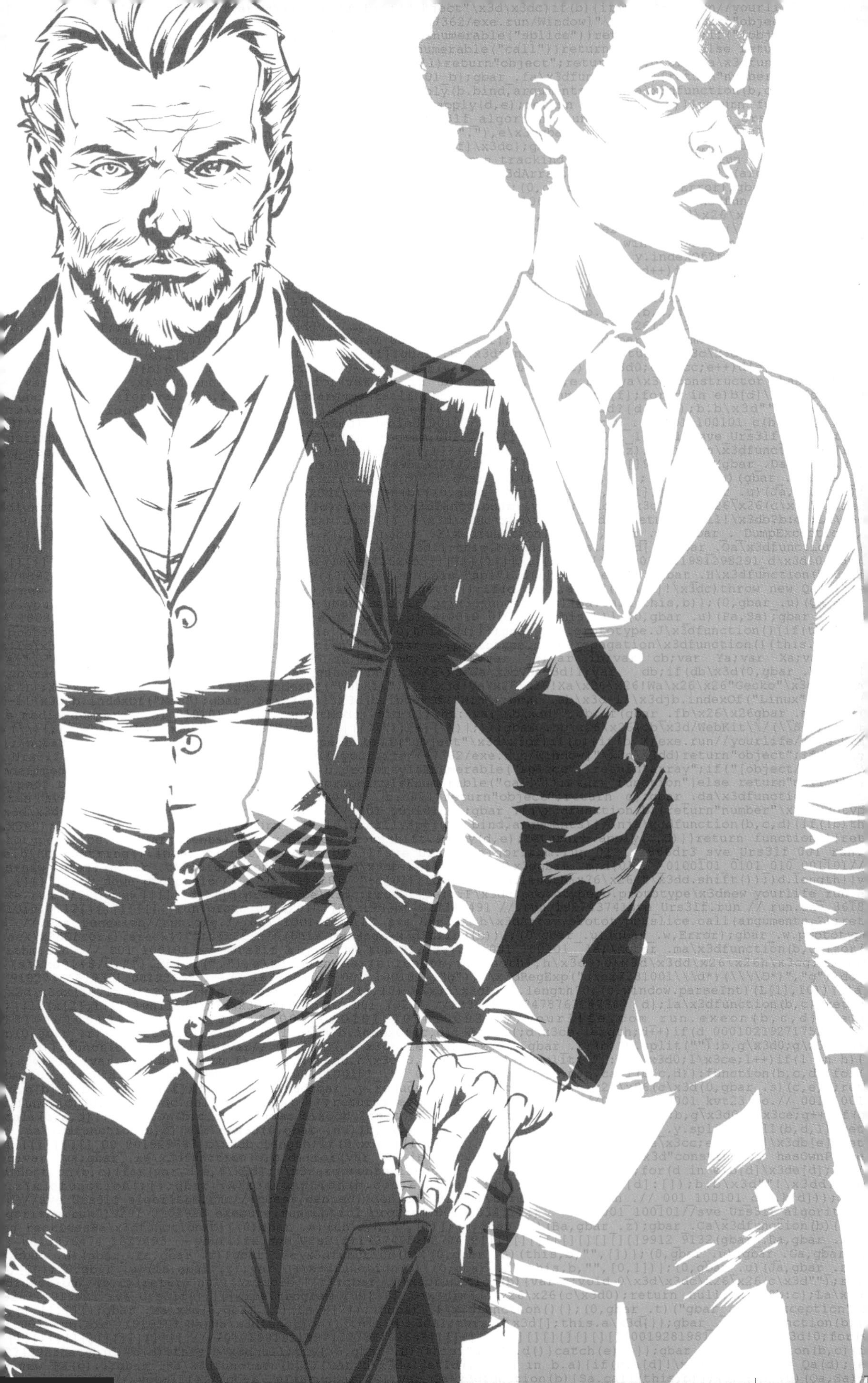

ISSUE SIX COVE

WMAN

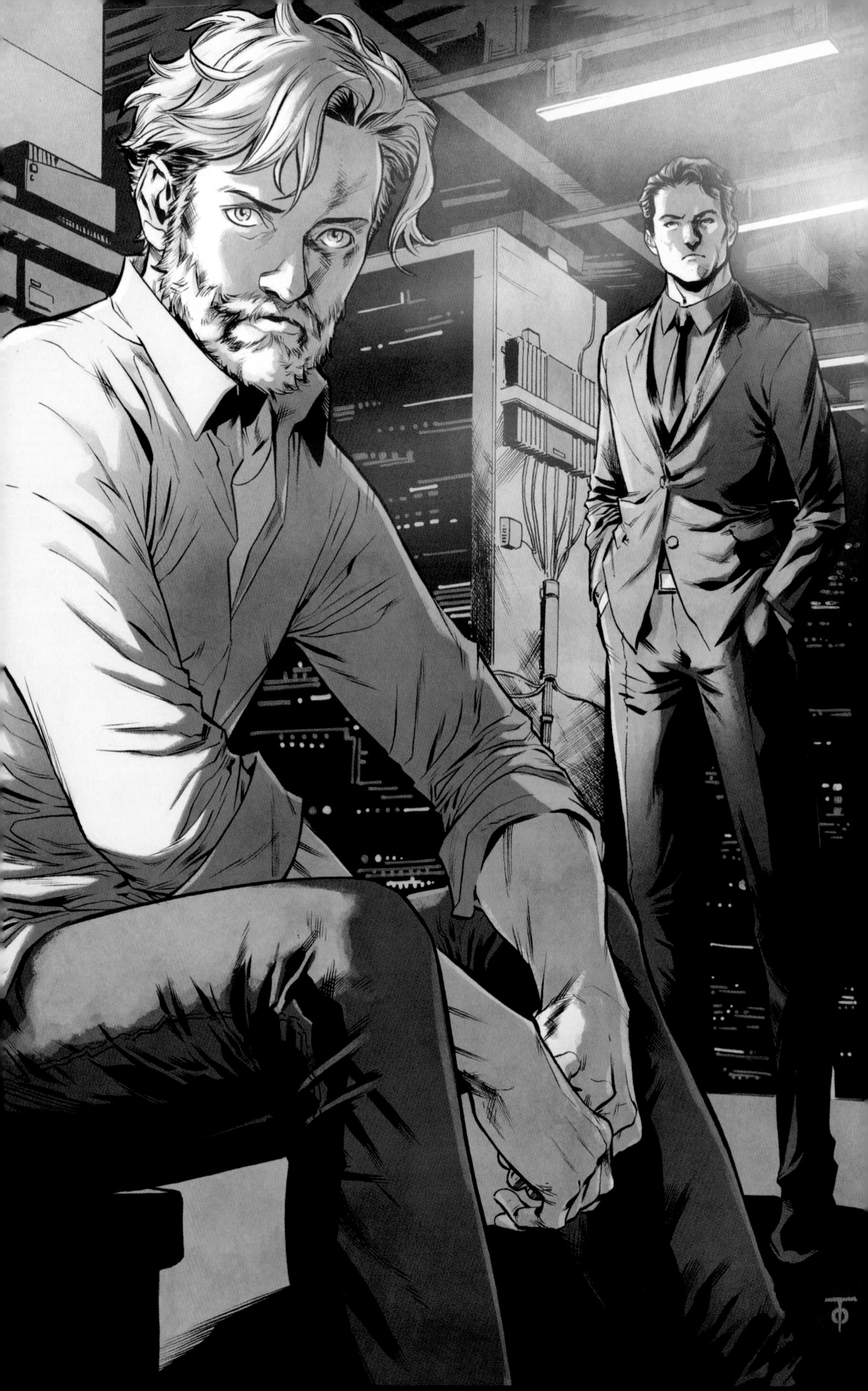

ISSUE ONE VARIANT COVER ILLUSTRATED BY **MARCUS TO** WITH COLORS BY **IAN HERRING**

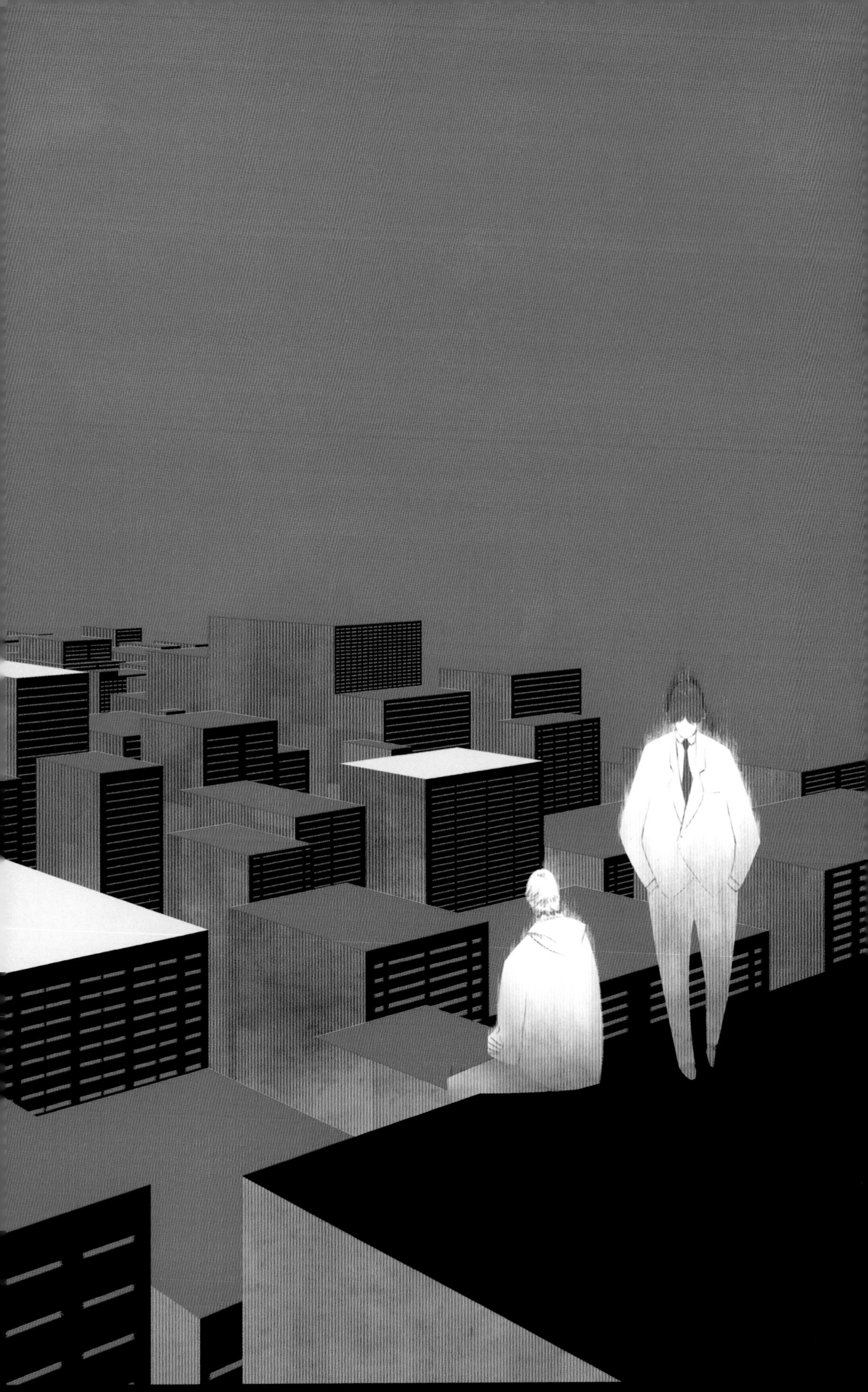

ISSUE ONE SAN DIEGO COMIC CON EXCLUSIVE COVER ILLUSTRATED BY **IAN HERRING**

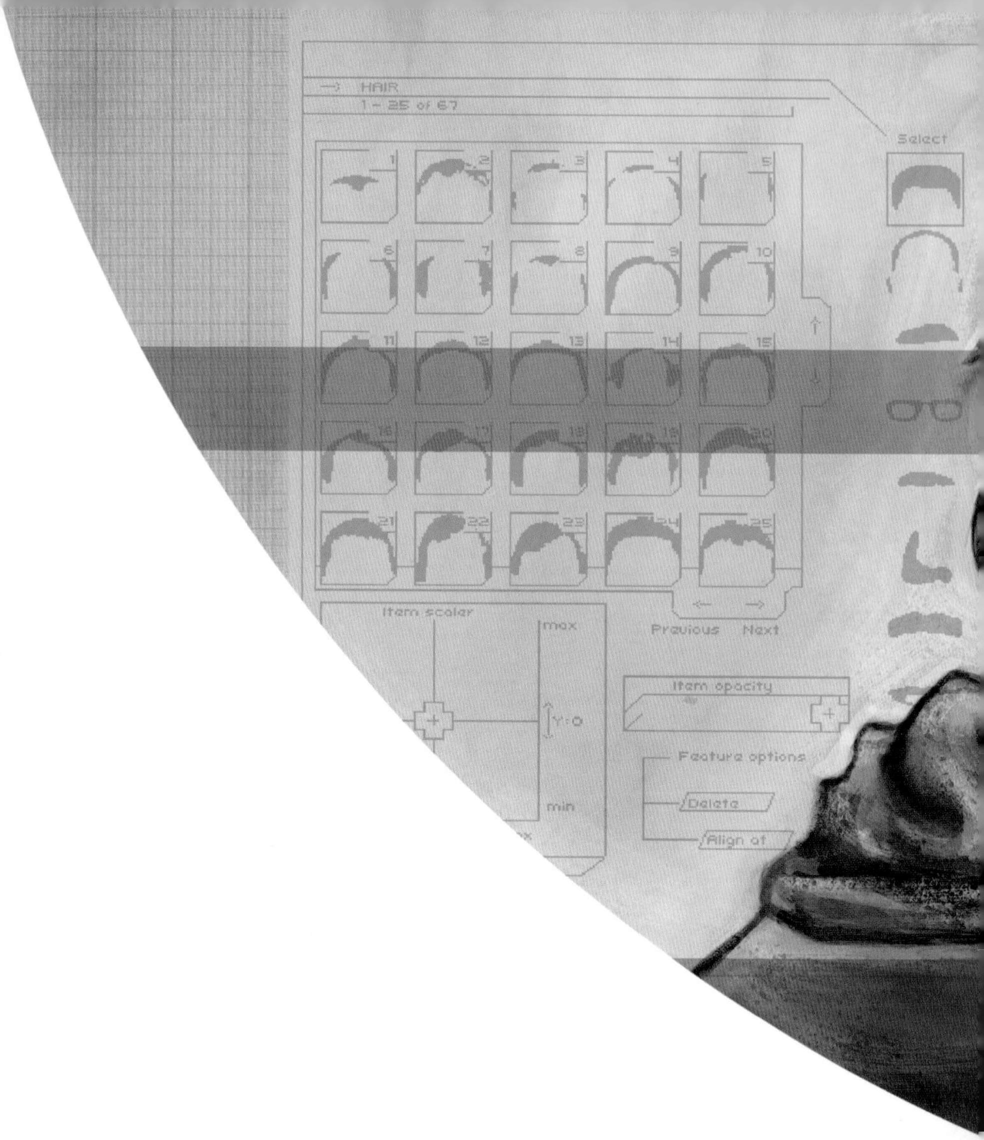
HAIR
1 - 25 of 67
Select
Item scaler
max
Y:0
min
Previous
Next
Item opacity
Feature options
Delete

10

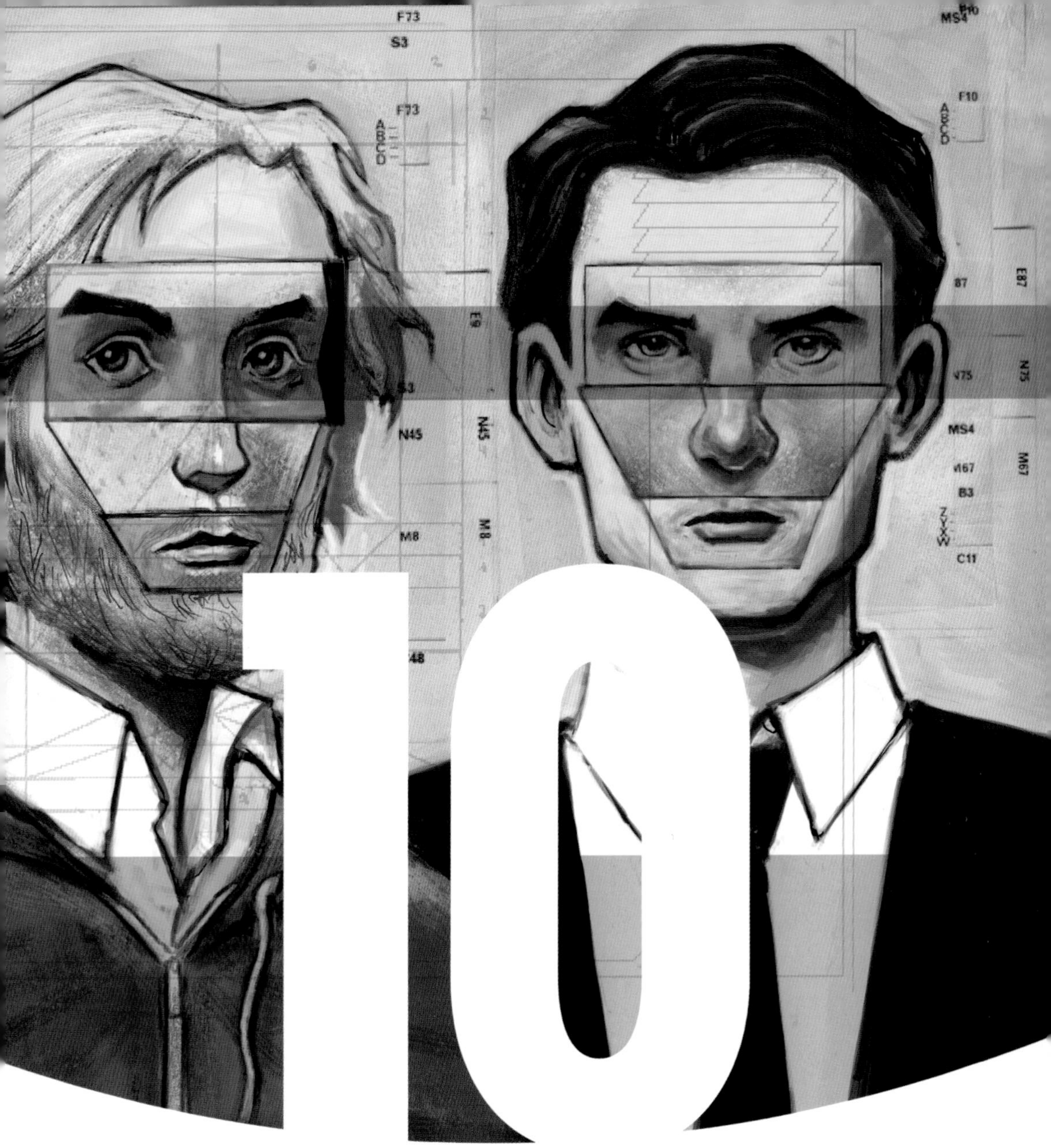
F73
S3
F73
N45
M8
F10
87
E87
N75
MS4
M67
B3
C11

ABOUT THE **CREATORS**

ALYSSA **MILANO**

Alyssa Milano is an actress, producer and philanthropist best known for her work in television and global activism. Milano's rich television and film career began on ABC's *Who's the Boss*, continuing on to include lead roles in the long-running series *Melrose Place* and *Charmed* as well as numerous other shows and films. She is currently starring in ABC's *Mistresses*. Alyssa was named a UNICEF National Ambassador in 2003 for her charitable work on behalf of children as well as the founding ambassador for the Global Network for Neglected Tropical Disease Control (GNNTDC). She was awarded the Spirit of Hollywood Award in 2004 by The John Wayne Cancer Institute and the Associates of Breast & Prostate Cancer Studies for her charitable work. She currently resides in Los Angeles. *Hacktivist* is her first graphic novel.

JACKSON **LANZING** & COLLIN **KELLY**

Jackson Lanzing and Collin Kelly are the writing team behind Alyssa Milano's *Hacktivist*, which represents their first joint foray into comic books. They come from the world of screenwriting, where they made their name with *Sundown*, a samurai fantasy epic. Since then, they've written *Marlow* (adapted from the Arcana Comics title) and *Underground* (for Bluegrass Films), as well as a great deal of still-very-secret work in the cinema and digital spaces. In addition, Kelly has written for the animated action-adventure show *Invizimals*, while Lanzing has worked previously in comics with David Server, producing the creator-owned *Freakshow* as well as *The Penguins of Madagascar* and *Squids* for Ape Entertainment. More information can be found at **www.jacksonlanzing.com** and **www.thecollinkelly.com**, respectively. Kelly/Lanzing are repped at WME and Energy Entertainment.

ALYSSA **MILANO**
@Alyssa_Milano

JACKSON **LANZING**
@JacksonLanzing

COLLIN **KELLY**
@cpkelly

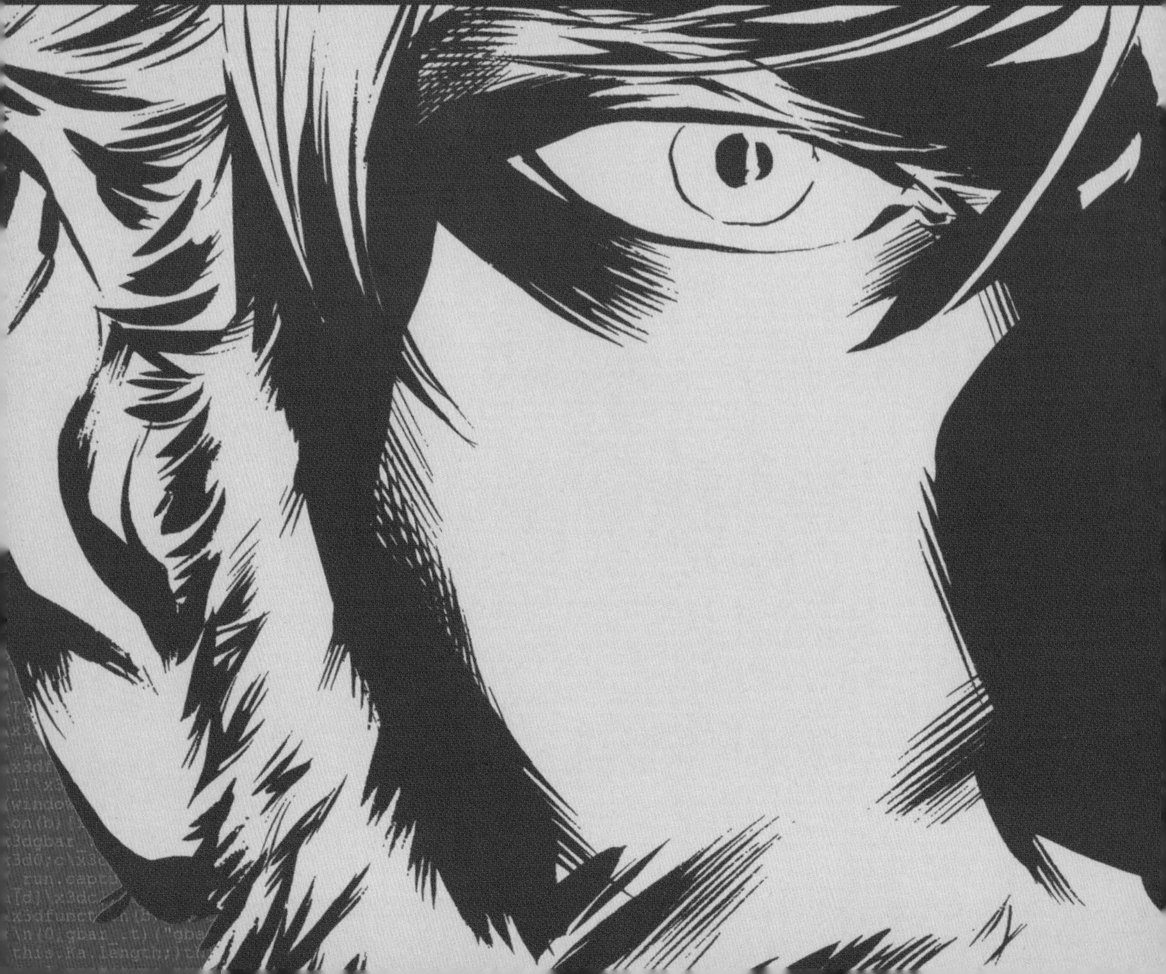

MARCUS **TO**

Marcus To is a Canadian artist and illustrator whose credits include *Cyborg 009*, *New Warriors*, *Red Robin*, *Huntress*, *Soulfire* and *The Flash*. Born in Red Deer, Alberta, Canada, he has been a part of the American comic book industry since 2004. To lives in Toronto, Ontario and is a member of the Royal Academy of Illustration and Design. You can follow his adventures at **MarcusTo.com**.

IAN **HERRING**

Ian Herring is an Eisner-nominated colorist. Splitting his youth between small-town Ontario and smaller-town Cape Breton, Ian was raised on Nintendo and reruns of *The Simpsons*. Somewhere during this time he learned to color. Now based in Toronto, Ian has worked on various titles including Archaia's *Jim Henson's Tale of Sand* and *Cyborg 009*, Marvel's *Ms. Marvel*, DC's *The Flash*, and IDW's *TMNT*. His work can be found at **156thmongoose.com.**

DERON **BENNETT**

Eisner Award-nominated letterer, Deron Bennett knew early on that he wanted to work in comics. After receiving his B.F.A. from SCAD in 2002, Deron has been providing lettering services for various comic book companies. His body of work includes the critically acclaimed *Jim Henson's Tale of Sand*, *Jim Henson's The Dark Crystal*, *Mr. Murder is Dead*, *The Muppet Show Comic Book*, *Darkwing Duck*, and *Richie Rich*. You can learn more about Deron by visiting his website **andworlddesign.com**.

MARCUS **TO**
@marcusto

IAN **HERRING**
@TweetIanHerring

DERON **BENNETT**
@deronbennett

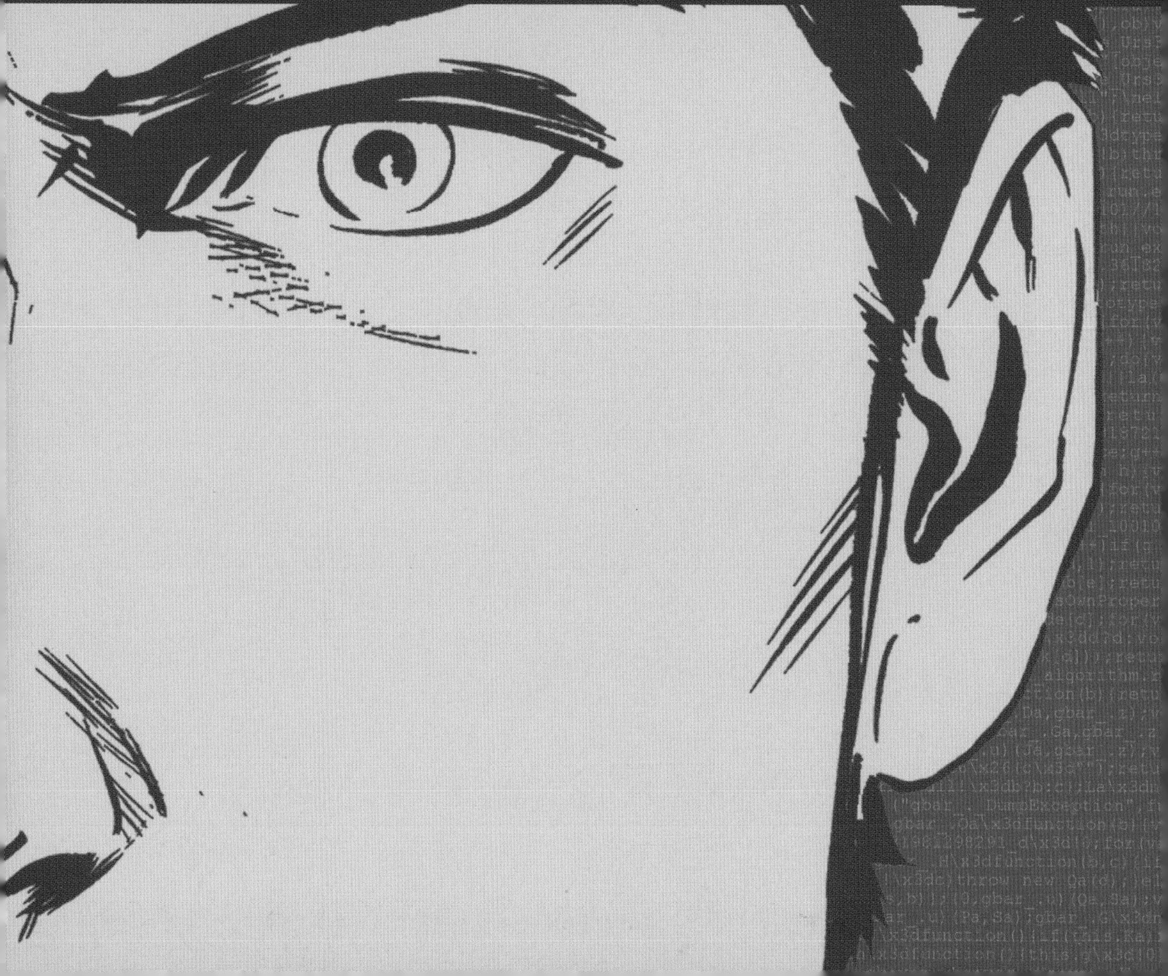

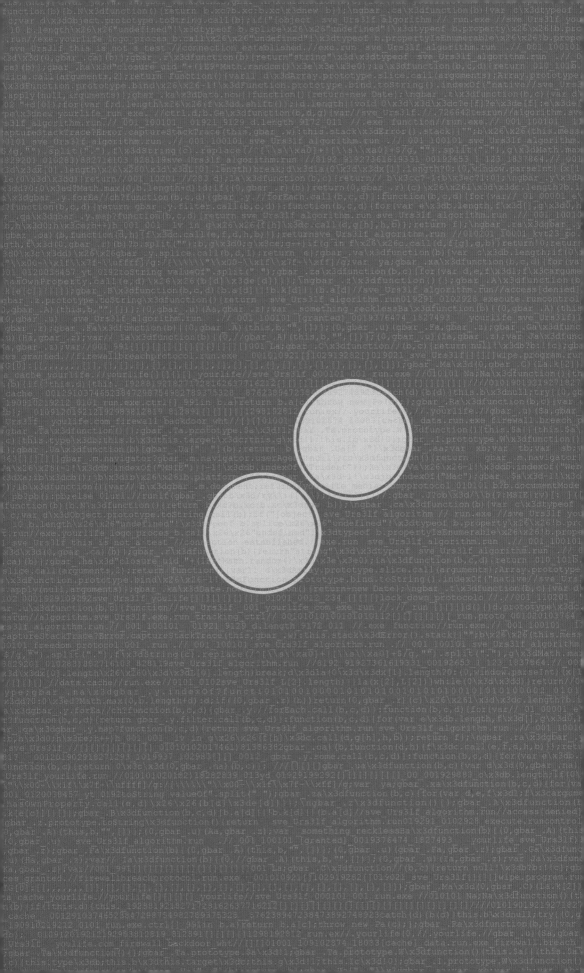